RECREATION PROGRAMMING

Designing Leisure Experiences

SECOND EDITION

J. Robert Rossman
University of Nevada, Las Vegas

SAGAMORE PUBLISHING
Champaign, IL

Production Manager: Susan M. McKinney
Cover Design: Michelle R.Dressen
Cover Illustration: Lori Walls, Fineline Graphics, Denton, Texas
Proofreader: Phyllis L. Bannon

Library of Congress Catalog Card Number : 94-67272
ISBN: 0-915611-95-3

Printed in the United States

For Linda

_____

કશ

Contents

Acknowledgments

Five years ago, when the first edition of this book was released, a few risk takers adopted it. It has been gratifying that the number of adoptions have increased each year since then. I have received much constructive feedback from colleagues and their students about how to improve the book and many of these suggestions have been incorporated into this edition. During Spring semester 1994, the number of requests for the book exceeded the number of books available and some loyal customers could not get books for their classes. Sagamore Publishing and I apologize for this and hope it will not happen again but the demand for the text simply exceeded our most optimistic projections.

The profession and its knowledge base has advanced considerably during the past five years and I have tried to incorporate the latest knowledge about experiencing leisure and managing program services into this second edition. As stated in the first edition, experiencing and participating in leisure is a complex interaction form. Facilitating these experiences through designed recreation programs is equally complex. I remain a student of the subject and am grateful to the many practitioners, students, and colleagues who, over the years, have helped me better understand leisure, recreation, and programming.

I am especially grateful to the following colleagues who have given me feedback about the book that has been useful to me in preparing the second edition.

Dale Adkins, Western Illinois University
Bob Anastasio, U.S. Army Recreational Services
Thersa Beck, Baylor University
Jim Busser, University of Nevada, Las Vegas
Marcia Carter, Baylor University
Robin Cockburn, Joint Leisure Training, Auckland New
    Zealand

Nick DiGrino, Western Illinois University
Ron Dodd, Joliet Park District, Joliet, Illinois
Julie Dunn, Florida State University
Chris Edginton, University of Northern Iowa
Dovie Gamble, University of Florida
Pat Harden, U.S. Navy Recreation Services
Julia Hamilton, Texas A & M University
Dave Holmes, University of Nevada, Las Vegas
Chris Howe, SUNY Brockport
Bob Humke, Madison, Wisconsin
Jean Keller, University of North Texas
Gene Lamke, San Diego State University
Sandra Little, Illinois State University
Rob Lynch, University of Technology, Sydney, Australia
Clare Mitchell, Southern Illinois University
Carol Peterson, University of Nevada, Las Vegas
Janna Rankin, San Diego State University
Mike Wise, Virginia Commonwealth University

Students from the University of North Texas, Southern Illinois University, Virginia Commonwealth University, and the University of Nevada, Las Vegas have also provided valuable feedback about the book.

The help given by the staff at Sagamore Publishing must also be acknowledged. Joe Bannon, President of Sagamore, has continued to provide valuable support for this book. In addition, I am grateful to Susan McKinney for her excellent layout and editing and Michelle Dressen for her help with the cover design of the book.

J. Robert Rossman
Las Vegas, Nevada
June, 1994

Introduction

On Liberty Island, New York, a National Park Service ranger leads a guided tour of the Statue of Liberty. Seven hundred miles away, another N.P.S. ranger is several hundred feet underground leading a tour of Mammoth Cave in Kentucky. Thirteen hundred miles to the west, a different ranger retells the story of Old Faithful in Yellowstone National Park. Although it is the eighth time the ranger has told the story today–and the one hundredth time it has been told this season–these patrons are hearing it now for the first time ever.

In Chicago, a recreation leader guides a group of children in song at a city recreation center. Elsewhere across the country, in cities large and small, municipal recreation workers lead children, adults, senior citizens, and other groups in various recreation activities, and lifeguards diligently watch the swimmers under their care at pools, lakes, and beaches. Camp leaders care for and lead numerous children in activities at hundreds of resident camps operated by churches, youth agencies, and private owners. In northern New Mexico, a leader hired by a commercial outfitter steers a raft through the Rio Grande River on a white-water rafting trip. In hospitals, rehabilitation centers, and nursing homes, therapeutic recreation specialists are implementing individual programs and enabling clients to participate successfully in a multitude of leisure services. At a rehabilitation hospital, a therapeutic recreation specialist is registering contestants for a wheelchair basketball league. In a nursing home, an activity director organizes a drama presentation "starring" several residents. At Disneyland, workers load seemingly endless lines of guests into and on attractions. In health and fitness centers across the country, recreation workers lead aerobics, jazzercise, and other fitness activities. At a local cinema, a recreation worker takes a ticket, seats a patron, and starts today's feature film.

Recreation workers deliver a myriad of different recreation services at hundreds of commercial and public recreation agencies across the country. They range from the Disney operations on the East and West coasts to tiny "mom and pop" pool halls and other recreation establishments located in small and medium-sized cities nationwide. All of these individuals are engaged in the design or delivery of recreation and leisure services. Designing and delivering recreation and leisure services is programming. Programming is a major responsibility in all leisure service organizations: Edginton and Neal (1983) empirically confirmed that producing quality programs was one of the most highly rated organizational goals of municipal park and recreation executives. LaPage (1983) has also suggested that "Providing the environment for a 'high-quality outdoor recreation experience' is a goal of most recreation resource managers–public and private" (p.37). Programming, then, is regarded as a central concern of managers in all leisure service agencies, and it is usually an identified part of a leisure service agency's mission.

Programming: the Focus of the Profession

Designing and delivering recreation and leisure services is the major function of the leisure service profession. Professional practice is based on the recreation and leisure discipline which seeks to understand the antecedents to leisure, the phenomenology of experiencing leisure, and the results of participating in leisure. Programming is not an interim activity to be pursued until one becomes an administrator or assumes some other function in a leisure service organization. It is the reason for the existence of the profession and for the existence of leisure service organizations. Programmers, better than any other professional group, should understand the phenomena of leisure, how humans engage in and experience leisure, the results of this experience, and how to facilitate an individual's experience of leisure. Our professional responsibility is to manipulate environments to facilitate the leisure experience for patrons. Albert Tillman (1973, p. ix) characterized the centrality of programming to the profession when he declared "Crown program. Long live the king!"

x

Most literature about programming has been published in books on the subject (Edginton, Hanson, & Edginton, 1992; Farrell & Lundegren, 1991; Carpenter & Howe, 1985; Russell, 1982), and many of the programming practices recommended have not been logically derived from current knowledge about experiencing leisure. Consequently, practice has not been tied to theory, and techniques for successful programming have been somewhat nebulous. How programmers actually develop programs has not been documented, so programming techniques remain somewhat mysterious. Nonetheless, numerous techniques have been proposed for developing successful programs: planning, brainstorming, needs analysis, community surveys, evaluation, systems analysis, and the latest entry: marketing. All of these techniques can certainly be used in developing successful programs. But none addresses leisure program development directly, comprehensively, and uniquely. They are all only piecemeal techniques that fail to provide the comprehensive insights into programming that are necessary to develop successful programs. I am convinced that information and techniques based on current information about experiencing leisure is needed to develop successful programs. Thus, we need to reframe our concepts about the role and function of programmers and programming.

In order to program, one must understand a number of programming concepts, the theory of how recreation and leisure program services are developed, and how leisure is experienced. More explicit, theory-based information about programming has begun to appear in several journals (Edginton & Rossman, 1988; Cushman & D'Amours, 1989; Busser, 1993). The programmer's knowledge base must enable him/her to operate on two levels. First, the programmer must manage the production and delivery of leisure services within a specific agency context. Second he/she must do this in a manner that facilitates the occurrence of the leisure experience at the behavioral level; i.e. within interactions in social occasions. In *Recreation Programming: Designing Leisure Experiences, 2nd. edition*, the programmer is taught to develop program services by learning both the theory and technique of recreation programming including: 1) basic leisure theory that explains how leisure is experienced; 2) the generic structure of social occasions in which social interaction produces leisure experiences; and 3) procedures and techniques used by programmers to manage recreation programs.

References, Introduction

Busser, J. A. (Ed.). 1993, October. Leisure Today. *Journal of Physical Education, Recreation & Dance, 64*:(8), 25-56.

Carpenter, G. M., & Howe, C.Z. 1985. *Programming leisure experiences: A cyclical approach.* Englewood Cliffs, NJ: Prentice-Hall.

Cushman, G., & D'Amours, M. 1989. Modern leisure management. [Special Issue]. *Society and Leisure, 12* (1).

Edginton, C. R., Hanson, C. J., & Edginton, S. R. 1992. *Leisure programming: Concepts, trends, and professional practice* (2nd ed.). Dubuque, IA: WCB Brown & Benchmark.

Edginton, C. R., & Rossman, J. R. (Eds.). 1988. *Journal of Park and Recreation Administration, 6* (4).

Farrell, P., & Lundegren, H. M. 1991. *The process of recreation programming: Theory and technique* (3rd ed.). State College, PA: Venture Publishing, Inc.

Russell, R. 1982. *Planning programs in recreation.* St. Louis, MO: C. V. Mosby.

Part I: Foundations For Programming

This book is predicated on the notion that programmers facilitate individuals' engagements in leisure experiences. To accomplish this, programmers must understand how leisure is experienced in social occasions, how to structure programs to facilitate leisure experiences, and how leisure service organizations manage the development of recreation program services.

In Part I, a foundation for successful programming is developed. In the first of the five chapters in this part, basic concepts of programming and operational concepts of leisure are defined. Chapter Two discusses the theory of how leisure is experienced through social interaction. Chapter Three covers operational implications for program development based on the theory discussed in Chapter Two. Chapter Four discusses how goals and objectives are used to manage program services in leisure service organizations. And Chapter Five presents an overview of the program development process within the Program Development Cycle.

Photo courtesy of Austin Parks and Recreation, Austin, TX. Photo by Valerie Jewett.

1

Basic Programming Concepts

The ultimate goal of programming is to facilitate leisure experiences for program patrons. To accomplish this requires that the programmer learn the concepts that tie together the definition of a program, the act of programming, and the management activities that must be implemented in an agency to produce programs (Rossman and Edginton 1989).

Programming Concepts Defined

A program is a designed opportunity for a leisure experience to occur. Program is an elastic concept used to describe a variety of different operations including activities, events, or services conducted by leisure service organizations. "Program" can refer to a single event, such as a one-day softball skills workshop; or it can refer to a collection of activities, such as all of the cultural arts classes operated by an organization; or a single service provided, such as a drop-in auto hobby shop; or the entire set of operations offered by an agency, including all of its activities, events, and services. Each of these different operations can be called a program.

This definition is broad and is intended to include much more than typical organized programs with a face-to-face leader. The key point is the notion of design in which the programmer conceptualizes a leisure experience and intervenes in some way to facilitate it for the patron. In some instances this intervention may be minimal, but in others it may be near total. However, design always involves planned intervention, regardless of its magnitude.

There are two assumptions in this definition that need further explanation. First, the notion of designing assumes that we know how leisure experiences are constructed and experienced by individuals and that we can intervene in and facilitate their occurrence. Second, it is assumed that we know the content of leisure experiences, i.e. we know why individuals label some experiences as leisure, but not others. To program requires a thorough knowledge of both how individuals experience leisure, and the content of this experience. This knowledge will be introduced in the appropriate sections throughout the book.

Although programs seem to be the actual activities, events, or services themselves, the properties that make them leisure occasions are not inherent in them. Rather, leisure occasions are determined by how individuals structure their participation and interpretation of what occurs (Csikszentmihalyi 1991; Kelly 1987). Leisure is not a set of identifiable activities, events, or services. Nor is leisure service provision simply a search for the most popular activity that can be offered. Modern practitioners must understand that leisure is a state of mind most likely to be experienced when participants enter freely chosen programs that enable them to achieve realistic personal goals by consciously directing interaction in a social occasion. Samdahl (1988, p. 29) said, "Leisure can be viewed as a distinctive pattern of perceiving and relating to ongoing interaction. That is to say, leisure is a particular definition of a situation." Thus, a program provides an opportunity for leisure to occur, but cannot ensure that it does, since this ultimately depends on the patron's interpretation.

Programming is designing leisure opportunities by intervening in social interaction i.e. manipulating and creating environments in a manner that maximizes the probability that those who enter them will have the leisure experience they seek. Individuals achieve satisfaction from a leisure experience according to how they structure and interpret their participation in the leisure occasion. Because the programmer understands what patrons must experience to conclude an experience is leisure for them and how this experience is produced through social interaction, a program that facilitates, i.e. increases the probability of a leisure experience occurring, can be designed. This is a key notion. The practice of all professions, including a leisure service provision, is predicated on information developed through the scientific method and the application of it to practical problems. The use of database information increases the probability of the desired outcome occurring but does not guarantee it.

Planning the social interactions that will facilitate the leisure experience must be based on knowledge about the content of leisure and how it is produced in social occasions. In many cases, how a program is operated is more important to facilitating a leisure experience than the specific activity itself. For example, there can be softball tournaments that are leisure occasions for players and there can be some that are not dependent on how they are operated. Furthermore, modern programmers must understand and plan for the total leisure experience including the three phases of human experience—anticipation, participation, and reflection (Little 1993; Busser 1993). Good programming, then, is designed intervention based on knowledge about social interaction and the social psychology of experiencing leisure.

Program development is the overall management process in which the programmer designs, manages, and delivers program services within the context of a specific agency. It includes developing and/or understanding an agency's mission, assessing needs, designing program services, delivering them, and finally evaluating them to determine their future. All programs are delivered by some type of an organization and the programmer must successfully manage program services within an organizational context. Successful program development results in programs that meet the needs of the agency, patron, and community. Programming is one key function in program development. The overall process of program development is explained further in Chapter Five. Now complete Exercise 1-1.

Exercise 1-1.
Comparing Programming Concepts

Discuss and compare the definitions of *program*, *programming*, and *program development*. How do the three concepts differ? What is the role of the programmer in each of them?

Definitions of Related Concepts

Concepts we use influence how we act. The linguistic labels attached to various forms of human behavior shape our attitudes and actions. The lack of precise definitions in the recreation and leisure field is often a cause of concern to new students. This area of study seems to expose its inadequacies at the outset, and new students immediately observe that the major concepts in the field lack precise definitions. In other fields of study, new students are simply given definitions of major concepts that suffice for the first few years of study and sometimes longer. But students of recreation and leisure are encouraged to formulate their own definitions for complex concepts such as play, leisure, recreation, games, and so forth.

This book offers a set of concepts and ideas that can be used for successful design and delivery of program services, and this section defines the major concepts necessary to understand and accomplish programming: *leisure, play, recreation,* and *games*. Each concept refers to a different type of leisure experience, and each must therefore be programmed somewhat differently. For our purposes, the definitions should be empirically based, they should sufficiently indicate the concept being defined and distinguish it from other concepts, and they should indicate both what is included and not included by the concept. They should be supported by current research evidence and be commonly used when referring to the phenomena.

In addition to defining leisure, play, recreation, and games, this section will also discuss the concepts in relationship to each other in order to help clarify their meaning. This relationship is illustrated in Figure 1-1 on page 7, in which leisure is shown as the generic, all-encompassing concept, a major part of human endeavor.

Kelly (1983) contends that leisure is central to today's society. He states that leisure is "crucial life space for the expression and development of selfhood, for the working out of identities that are important to the individual. [It is] ... central to the maintenance of the society itself as a social space for the development of intimacy" (Kelly 1983, p. 23). Driver, Brown, and Peterson (1991) take the position that there are multiple behaviors included under the concept of leisure. Leisure, then, is the broadest concept (Neulinger 1981), encompassing play, recreation, and

Figure 1-1.
The Relationship of Leisure, Play, Recreation, and Games

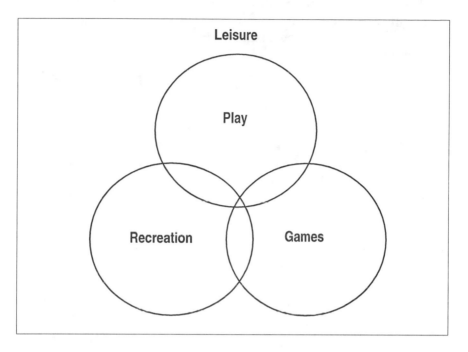

games, each of which can be viewed as forms of leisure that can be distinguished by more specific characteristics.

Leisure

Leisure has been defined in several different ways. Six types were identified by Murphy (1974): classical leisure, leisure as discretionary time, leisure as a function of social class, leisure as a form of activity, antiutilitarian leisure, and a holistic concept of leisure. Neulinger (1974) suggested that all definitions of leisure are either quantitative or qualitative and concluded that leisure is a state of mind characterized primarily by freedom of choice and motivation.

Although participation in leisure has psychological benefits (Mannell and Stynes 1991) the perspective used throughout this book is that leisure is a social event constructed through interaction in social occasions (Samdahl 1988). Iso-Ahola emphasized this point by stating that "leisure studies are a human service field in which social interaction is the main ingredient" (1980, p. 7). Hamilton-Smith (1991) has also assumed leisure is best understood as a social construct that can be defined in a variety of ways including leisure as time, leisure as action, leisure as action within time/space, and leisure as experience.

Leisure is an experience that is most likely to occur during an engagement that is freely chosen for the intrinsic satisfaction inherent in participating in it. After a first reading, this definition of leisure may seem relatively simple, but it incorporates three complex concepts: freedom, intrinsic satisfaction, and experience.

Freedom has been a central element of leisure since man first contemplated the meaning of leisure. Freedom from something and freedom to have or do something have been primary themes of leisure definitions (Sylvester 1987). In our society, the obligations of work, family, friends, civic duties, and so forth can obscure the meaning of "freely chosen" or "free choice," or at least make it more difficult to sort them out. The evidence suggests that individuals must believe that they could have chosen not to do an activity before it meets the test of being freely chosen (Kelly 1982). Leisure occasions can also be determined by the degree to which they free individuals from social role constraints (Samdahl 1988). Finally, they provide ". . . a freedom to become, some space within the rigidities of life to make consequential decisions" (Kelly 1987, p. 17). Therefore, it is best to view leisure as situated freedom in which one is freed from some social role constraints to explore and accomplish something new—not the complete absence of constraint or social structure.

The notion of freely choosing something can only be determined from the perspective of the individual making the choice. Thus, the notion of freedom is a matter of individual perception (Neulinger 1981). Programmers should remember that leisure must be freely chosen from the perspective of the individual making the choice, and that individuals must perceive that they have options and choices in a program in order to explore, move forward in their own personal stream of experience, and to "become" something new by participating in a novel experience, i.e. one that is experienced in this way for the first time. Freedom experienced in this manner creates a unique condition for an optimal, self-actualizing experience to occur (Csikszentmihalyi and Kleiber 1991).

Thus, freedom plays a functional role in operationalizing the leisure experience. Although optimal experiences may occur in other spheres of life; they are more likely to do so when the conditions of freedom just explained occur. Over-programming by providing too much structure will leave the participant few or no choices, and this may destroy the very experience a programmer is trying to facilitate.

Intrinsic satisfaction is the second major dimension of leisure. Psychologists have used several different terms to describe participating in this experience including autotelic activities, arousal-seeking behavior, and optimal experience. "The key element of an optimal experience is that it is an end in itself" (Csikszentmihalyi 1991, p. 67)—it is intrinsically satisfying. The behavior associated with pursuing intrinsically satisfying activities has also been called "arousal-seeking behavior," based on the need to maintain optimal arousal. The theory was proposed by Ellis (1973) and assumes that people are not normally quiescent, but rather that they seek and act to increase stimulation.

Intrinsically satisfying activities provide satisfaction through the interactive engagement itself, and that satisfaction provides sufficient motivation for the individual to continue participating. Thus, no external reward is necessary. The feedback received from such participation indicates that what is occurring is congruent with one's goals, thereby strengthening and validating the self (Csikszentmihalyi 1991). This affords a freedom from concern with oneself that frees one to focus psychic energy more intensely on the demands of the current interactive engagement. These engagements both demand and consume one's complete, focused attention. The motivation to participate in such interaction to seek this experience is powerful and real (Neulinger 1981).

Programmers should understand how this occurs. Unfortunately, intrinsic satisfaction is not wholly contained within activities themselves. In fact, people similarly describe their optimal experiences in different activities, and their descriptions are consistent across sociological and cultural variables (Csikszentmihalyi 1991). So, it is not a matter of prescribing a list of intrinsically satisfying activities and expecting individuals to find intrinsic satisfaction in them.

Intrinsic satisfaction is a personally interpreted perception of a specific situation that is constructed through interaction in a social occasion (Unger 1984; Shaw 1985; Samdahl 1988; Csikszentmihalyi 1991). Individuals' past experiences and current expectations help them determine whether or not an activity is intrinsically satisfying. What arouses an individual today is part of a stream of interactions between the individual's natural abilities and previous experiences. Different individuals find different activities intrinsically satisfying because of factors such as their own skill levels in an activity, their socialization into it, and the previous opportunities and experiences they have had with it. Although these factors influence their likelihood of initially participating, their interpretation of the interactions in an activity on a given day will determine whether or not it is a leisure experience for them.

Thus, how an activity is operated and how an individual interprets his/her participation in it are more important in determining whether or not an individual will have a leisure experience than the activity type, e.g. softball, oil painting, etc. Programmers need to devote more attention to how activities are operated than to continually searching for the perfect activity that will provide a leisure experience.

Finally, to experience an event requires, at a minimum, that one participate in and interpret it. An experience can be enhanced by providing patrons an opportunity to organize and self-direct outcome. Experiencing is more than a passive state of mind; it denotes processing and ordering information in one's consciousness (Kelly 1990; Csikszentmihalyi 1991). Leisure is most likely to occur when individuals play an active role in organizing and self-directing their experience, i.e. they have the opportunity for positive affect (Kleiber, Larson, and Csikszentmihalyi 1986; Kleiber, Caldwell, and Shaw 1992). Ajzen and Driver (1992) reported that "perceived behavioral control" improved their ability to predict leisure behavior; again verifying the importance of having control over outcome to the leisure experience. Thus, leisure experiences are those that are both interpreted in a specific way and self-directed. People experience leisure by active engagement and interaction with various combinations of elements in an environment, and thereby have the perception that they are directing the outcome of the event, and are thus the cause of an act.

This engagement can be as simple as reading a book and interpreting its meaning. In this case, the organization of the interpretation is being self-directed by the reader. It can also include participating in a lively social discussion with friends or family. Participating in rule-bounded games and sports also provides a significant number of opportunities for self-directed social interaction and self-directed outcome.

Overall, then, to experience leisure, an individual must freely choose to engage an environment and perceive that the engagement provides intrinsic satisfaction that will both reward and sustain the engagement. Intrinsic satisfaction partly results from experiences that provide opportunities for positive affect; i.e. self-directing the outcome of engagement. Experiencing leisure is something that individuals do—not something programmers do to individuals. Neulinger (1981) has insisted that leisure is not a noun, but rather a verb that implies action, process, and experience. Leisure is something to be consciously processed and experienced,not something that is acquired and possessed. Programmers can facilitate the processing of this experience by how they organize and operate programs and thus help bring about the leisure experience for patrons.

Games

Games are leisure experiences with formal rules that define the interactional content, attempt to equalize the players, and define the role that skills and chance will play in determining the outcome. Formal rules create an unknown or problematic outcome, the resolution of which can only be achieved by playing the game. This applies to table games, athletic contests, and other gaming situations.

Games are rule bounded, and the rules delineate the arena of focused reality that will be addressed during the gaming occasion (Goffman 1961). Games are popular leisure experiences because the rules of a well-constructed game create an area of focus with a high probability for leisure experience. To create this focus, rules must clearly define the gaming encounter and the role that skill and chance will play in determining the outcome.

Game rules must define the focus of the contest and exactly what is being contested. A game winner should have exhibited more of the particular skill being contested in the game than did other participants. In some games, the rules minimize the role of chance and maximize the effect of skill on the gaming outcome.

On the other hand, chance is solely responsible for the outcome of some games. For example, the winner of "Chutes and Ladders," a popular children's game, is determined entirely by chance. Thus, it is often played by parents with young children who are not able to play a game of strategy or skill. In a game whose outcome is determined entirely by chance, the players are immediately made equal—each is equally dependent on chance.

Some games require a mixture of skill and chance. This mixture is characteristic of many table games that call for sustained interest and comparable skill levels among players. "Trivial Pursuit" is a good example. No matter how many questions are answered, a lucky roll of the dice is still necessary to land a token in the final winning position. A more highly skilled player can answer many more questions than other players and still lose the game because of unlucky rolls of the dice.

The element of chance in a game is usually implemented with the toss of a coin, the roll of the dice, or the use of some type of spinning device. More extensive contests may begin with a coin toss or some other mechanism for determining the order of play or an initial position. In football, for example, the winner of a coin toss may choose which end of the field to defend or to receive or kick the ball to start the game. Depending on weather conditions, this choice can affect the outcome of the game. Nonetheless, it is a matter of chance, unrelated to any of the skills that football is supposed to test. The use of chance, then, as a major determinant of the gaming outcome is often used to make unequal players equal, or to determine initial advantage totally unrelated to any game skill. Game rules define the skills that will be contested and the role that skill and chance will play in determining the outcome.

Denzin (1975) has offered a typology of gaming that includes playing at play, playing at a game, and playing a game. The latter two types of play are distinguished in that one is based on the actual gaming skill of the players, and one is not. In playing at a game, the players do not possess the actual skills required to play, so they simply play at the game by wearing the appropriate attire, acquiring the appropriate equipment, playing in the correct type of facility, and so forth. Because they lack the full skills really needed to play the game, they must modify the rules to play at the game. Leisure service professionals must understand the function of rules in games because much game programming involves modifying rules or facilities to allow those with insufficient skills to participate. Programmers can make players equal and facilitate experiences for underskilled players by using league rules, handicaps, flights, and other mechanisms.

Recreation

Recreation is leisure that is engaged in for the attainment of personal and social benefits. Recreation has always been characterized as socially purposeful and moral; that is, it incorporates a rightness and a wrongness. Hutchinson (1951, p.2) stated that "Recreation is a worthwhile, socially accepted leisure experience that provides immediate and inherent satisfaction to the individual who voluntarily participates . . ." Jensen (1979, p. 8) also commented on the inherent morality of recreation when he said that "In order to qualify as recreation, an activity must do something desirable to a participant." Recreation is considered to have a specific moral purpose in society.

Recreation has always been viewed as restoration from the toil of work. De Grazia assumed this view when he wrote, "Recreation is activity that rests men from work, often by giving them a change (distraction, diversion), and restores (re-creates) them for work" (1964, p. 233). He credited recreation with social significance by functionally relating it to work: recreation is instrumental to work because it enables individuals to recuperate and restore themselves in order to accomplish more work.

Recreation is not only good for individuals—it is also good for society. Recreation has been used as a diversion from government repression, war, economic depression, congested urban conditions, and so forth.

Recreation always has a morality associated with it, and there are good and bad forms of recreation. For example, drug use is considered morally degenerative. Therefore, to a recreation professional, the notion of "recreational drug use" is not possible.

Moreover, organizations that provide recreation services are viewed as social institutions that espouse the positive aspects inherent in the recreation activities they offer. Specific moral ends or purposes are usually attributed to providers such as municipal recreation agencies, churches, the Boy Scouts and Girl Scouts, the armed services, and other similar organizations.

Thus, recreation is a specific form of leisure behavior that is characterized by a pervasive morality. It is an institutionalized form of leisure that is manipulated to accomplish socially desirable goals and objectives that are often defined by the sponsoring agency. It is the form of leisure behavior that programmers most often try to facilitate. In developing recreation programs, the programmer is often expected to go beyond providing a leisure experience and to also intervene to accomplish some additional socially purposeful goal.

Play

Play is leisure with the childlike characteristics of spontaneity, self-expression, and the creation of a nonserious realm of meaning. As a specific form of leisure, play also has further defining characteristics.

Play incorporates a dualism by which it is distinguished from the real world. It involves a lack of seriousness in which interaction is free flowing, and it progresses from place to place and takes on new forms as focus, needs, and demands shift (Denzin 1975). Play is an expansive interactional form that is not guided by conventional rules of interaction. Hunnicutt has suggested that "Play may well be one of those things that we do to understand other things and to create a truth" (1986, p.10).

Play is the most spontaneous form of leisure behavior, and its occurrence depends totally on the consent and conscious participation of the players. Lynch (1979,1980) has shown that players recognize and signal each other when interactions shift into a play mode. The inconsequential nature of play establishes for the player a sense of self and reality that cannot otherwise be attained in daily life. To "play with" an object, a person, or an idea is to experience the meaning of the object, person, or idea in a fundamentally new way. Because of this, play is one of the most difficult forms of leisure to develop programmatically.

Programming Implications

Leisure is considered the most general and encompassing concept, and recreation, play, and games are viewed as specific forms of leisure. The central defining concepts of each term and their relationship to each other are illustrated in Figure 1-2. The boundaries of each concept overlap each other and illustrate the nebulous character of each concept. For example, game rules are often structured to allow players to play in a spontaneous, free-flowing, and creative manner. Nonetheless, when game players serendipitously discover a new move or game strategy that gives them an advantage, rules are modified to quash it or to accommo-date it within the rule structure of the game.

When recreation activities are programmed, they are often made to appear as much like leisure as possible: they allow freedom of choice and build in intrinsic rewards. However, the programmatic goals of the agency sponsoring and operating a program may foster an activity structure that does not permit

Figure 1-2.
Relationship of Central Definitions of Leisure, Recreation, Play and Games

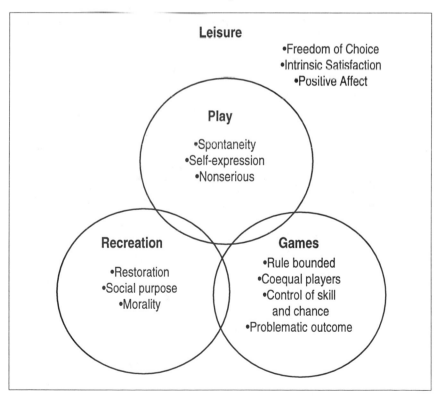

ongoing freedom of choice in the activity. Programmers should realize the central dimensions of each of these human experiences and design and operate programs that are least obstructive to participants' desired experiences. Programmers often confront the situation in which the best programmatic manipulation is simply to avoid destroying the experience desired. In this case, the programmer must understand the experience and make sure that the design or operation of a program does not have built-in blocks to the leisure experience desired by the participant or intended by the agency. Now complete Exercise 1-2.

Exercise 1-2.
Programming Leisure Experiences

In class, discuss the differences in programming play, games, and recreation.
*   How do the differences between these three forms of leisure demand different programming approaches?
*   Which of these three forms of leisure is the most difficult to program? Why?

Conclusion

Programming is the central focus of the leisure service profession and the primary mission of leisure service organizations. Programmers provide opportunities for leisure to occur. Leisure is the primary social space in modern society for the development of self and the expression of intimacy. Leisure occurs through interactions in social occasions that are characterized by perceived freedom, intrinsic satisfaction, and opportunities for positive affect. Recreation, games, and play are all specific forms of leisure with additional defining characteristics.

References, Chapter One

Ajzen, I., and B. Driver. 1992. Planned Behavior and Leisure Choice. *Journal of Leisure Research, 24,* 207-224.

Busser, J.A. 1993. Leisure Programming: The State of the Art (Introduction). *Journal of Physical Education, Recreation and Dance, 64* (8) 25, 33.

Csikszentmihalyi, M. 1991. *Flow: The Psychology of Optimal Experience.* New York: Harper Perennial.

Csikszentmihalyi, M., and D. Kleiber. 1991. Leisure and Self-Actualization. In Driver, B. L., P.J. Brown, and G.L. Peterson, (Eds.), *Benefits of Leisure* (91-102). State College, PA: Venture.

De Grazia, S. 1964. *Of Time, Work, and Leisure.* Garden City, NJ: Doubleday-Anchor.

Denzin, N.K. 1975. Play, Games, and Interaction: The Contexts of Childhood Socialization. *The Sociological Quarterly 16*: 458-478.

Driver, B. L., P.J. Brown, and G.L. Peterson. 1991. *Benefits of Leisure.* State College, PA: Venture.

Ellis, M.J. 1973. *Why People Play.* Englewood Cliffs, NJ: Prentice-Hall.

Goffman, E. 1961. *Encounters.* Indianapolis: Bobbs-Merrill.

Hamilton-Smith, E. 1991. The Construction of Leisure. In Driver, B. L., P.J. Brown, and G.L. Peterson. 1991. *Benefits of Leisure.* State College, PA: Venture.

Hunnicutt, B.K. 1986. Problems Raised by the Empirical Study of Play and Some Humanistic Alternatives. *Abstracts from the 1986 Symposium on Leisure Research,* 8-10.

Hutchison, J. 1951. *Principles of Recreation.* New York: Roland.

Iso-Ahola, S.E. 1980. *The Social Psychology of Leisure and Recreation.* Dubuque, IA: Wm. C. Brown.

Jensen, C.R. 1979. *Outdoor Recreation in America.* Minneapolis: Burgess.

Kelly, J.R. 1982. *Leisure.* Englewood Cliffs, NJ: Prentice-Hall.

Kelly, J.R. 1983. *Leisure Identities and Interactions.* Boston: George Allen & Unwin.

Kelly, J. R. 1987. *Freedom To Be: A New Sociology of Leisure.* New York: Macmillan.

Kelly, J. R. 1990. *Leisure* (2nd ed.). Englewood Cliffs, NJ: Prentice-Hall.

Kleiber, D., L. Caldwell, and S. Shaw. 1992, October. *Leisure Meaning in Adolescence*. Paper presented at the 1992 Symposium On Leisure Research, Cincinnati, OH.

Kleiber, D., R. Larson, and M. Csikszentmihalyi. 1986. The Experience of Leisure in Adolescence. *Journal of Leisure Research, 18*, 169-176.

Little, S. L. 1993. Leisure Program Design and Evaluation. *Journal of Physical Education, Recreation and Dance, 64* (8), 26-29, 33.

Lynch, R.L. 1980. Social Play: An Interactional Analysis of Play in Face-to-Face Social Interaction, (Doctoral dissertation, University of Illinois at Urbana-Champaign, 1979). *Dissertation Abstracts International, 41*, 804A.

Mannell, R., and J. Stynes. 1991. A Retrospective: The Benefits of Leisure. In Driver, B. L., P.J. Brown, and G.L. Peterson.(Eds.), *Benefits of Leisure* (461-473). State College, PA: Venture.

Murphy, J.F. 1974. *Concepts of Leisure, Philosophical Implications*. Englewood Cliffs, NJ: Prentice-Hall.

Neulinger, J. 1974. *The Psychology of Leisure*. Springfield, IL: Charles C. Thomas.

Neulinger, J. 1981. *To Leisure: An Introduction*. Boston: Allyn and Bacon.

Rossman, J. R., and C.R. Edginton. 1989. Managing Leisure Programs: Toward a Theoretical Model. *Society and Leisure, 12* (1), 157-170.

Samdahl, D.M. 1988. A Symbolic Interactionist Model of Leisure: Theory and Empirical Support. *Leisure Sciences* 1: 27-39.

Shaw, S.M. 1985. The Meaning of Leisure in Everyday Life. *Leisure Sciences* 7: 1-24.

Sylvester, C.D. 1987. The Politics of Leisure, Freedom, and Poverty. *Parks and Recreation* (January): 59-62.

Unger, L.S. 1984. The Effect of Situational Variables on the Subjective Leisure Experience. *Leisure Sciences* 6: 291-312.

Photo courtesy of Joliet Park District, Joliet, IL. Photo by Ann Miller.

2

How Individuals Experience Leisure

The practice of a profession is based on a body of knowledge the practitioner is responsible for applying to the everyday affairs of his/her patrons. The body of knowledge programmers use to accomplish this is the theory and knowledge of leisure behavior, which has increased dramatically over the past 15 years. However, we have just recently begun to integrate this knowledge into practice (Rossman 1988, 1989, 1993; Rossman and Edginton 1989; Busser 1993).

To develop program services, programmers must understand how leisure is experienced and produced in occasions of social interaction. This requires an understanding of leisure behavior, the phenomenology of experiencing leisure, and an understanding of the structure of social occasions. These unique bodies of information provide the knowledge base that enables programmers to develop successful recreation programs that facilitate leisure experiences.

A Social Science Theory of Programming

The theory of leisure programming presented in this book is based on a social science theory that views leisure as an interactional episode, consistent with the symbolic interactionist perspective of H. Blumer and N.K. Denzin. Sociological theory has three major approaches: the structure-functionalist, conflict, and symbolic interactionist approaches. Each is useful in different ways for investigating the nature of human social order. The structure-functionalist approach examines the basic structure of society, the roles and functions of its institutions, and how roles and institutions affect individual and collective action in society. Conflict sociology examines the role of conflict in a society and how power struggles affect the order of a society. Symbolic interactionism examines the ". . . different dimensions of the construction of social reality through the seemingly autonomous activities of individuals." Eisenstadt and Curelaru continue:

> Their major contribution [referring to symbolic interactionists] was in the exploration of different levels and types of "informal" and "sub-terranean" situations of human interaction which cut across formal arrangements and institutional settings, of the less fully organized dimension of everyday life: their phenomenology and nature; the structure and rules of interaction that take place within them, as distinct from the formal institutional definition of goals; the mechanisms of interaction through which such situations are constructed and their perception by the participants in them; their impact on different levels of formal social organization (1977, pp. 46-47).

As an approach to understanding leisure behavior, symbolic interactionism has been receiving increasing attention (Kelly 1987; Kuentzel 1990; Lee 1990; and Samdahl 1992). It is a relevant approach because it examines the social process of human behavior in the face-to-face interactions that constitute the bulk of leisure, play, recreation, and game participation. Iso-Ahola (1980) has pointed out that to understand leisure participation, one must understand the dialectic nature of leisure participation. That is, leisure participation includes both a changing individual and a changing social environment in which individuals interact. The sole joy of leisure may be in participating in its construction (Kuentzel 1990; Podilchak 1991). The symbolic interactionist approach is important to understanding how individuals structure their participation in leisure occasions and how they experience these occasions (Samdahl 1988, 1992). Thus, it will be used as the theoretical base of recreation programming presented in this book.

Symbolic Interaction Theory

Symbolic interactionism rests on three premises (Blumer 1969; Denzin 1978). Denzin provides a capsule explanation of the symbolic interactionist's theoretical perspective:

Symbolic interactionism rests on three basic assumptions. First, social reality as it is sensed, known, and understood is a social production. Interacting individuals produce and define their own definitions of situations. Second, humans are assumed to be capable of engaging in "minded," self-reflexive behavior. They are capable of shaping and guiding their own behavior and that of others. Third, in the course of taking their own standpoint and fitting that standpoint to the behaviors of others, humans interact with one another. Interaction is seen as an emergent, negotiated, often unpredictable concern. Interaction is symbolic because it involves the manipulation of symbols, words, meanings, and languages.

Integral to this perspective is the view that the social world of human beings is not made up of objects that have intrinsic meaning. The meaning of objects lies in the actions that human beings take toward them. Human experience is such that the process of defining objects is ever-changing, subject to redefinitions, relocations, and realignments. The interactionist assumes that humans learn their basic symbols, their conceptions of self, and the definitions they attach to social objects through interactions with others. Each person simultaneously carries on conversations with himself or herself and with significant others. Behavior is observable at the symbolic and the behavioral levels (Denzin 1978, p. 7).

Blumer distinguishes three slightly different assumptions of symbolic interactionism. When considered together with Denzin's assumptions, they present a comprehensive picture of symbolic interactionism:

"Symbolic interactionism rests in the last analysis on three simple premises. The first premise is that human beings act toward things on the basis of the meanings that the things have for them. Such things include everything that the human being may note in the world—physical objects, such as trees or chairs; other human beings, such as friends or enemies; institutions, as a school or a government; guiding ideals, such as individual independence or honesty; activities of others, such as their commands or requests; and such situations as an individual encounters in his daily life. The second premise is that the meaning of such things is derived from, or arises out of, the social interaction that one has with one's fellows. The third premise is that these meanings are handled in, and modified through, an interpretive process used by the person in dealing with the things he encounters (Blumer 1969, p. 2).

Implications of Symbolic Interaction for Leisure Programming

A theory that provides a basis for recreation programming should focus the programmer's attention and effort on the factors relevant to facilitating a leisure experience and thus provide direction to one's programming efforts. The symbolic interactionist perspective suggests that *leisure is a special meaning attributed to specific social occasions that are created by the individuals involved through interaction with objects in the occasions* (Unger 1984; Shaw 1985; Samdahl 1988, 1992; Kuentzel 1990; and Csikszentmihalyi 1991). Five points need to be developed for a full explanation and understanding of the implications of the theory for recreation programming—the three phases of the leisure experience, the nature of objects acted on during interaction, how meaning is derived through interaction, how interaction is produced, and the phenomenology of experiencing leisure.

Three Phases of the Leisure Experience

It is useful to conceptualize the leisure experience as occurring in three distinct phases—anticipation, participation, and reflection. These are derived from Mead's (1934) concept of the "specious present"—the moment of participation. It is preceded by mental images of anticipation and succeeded by imaged reflections. Often, programmers deal only with the participation phase and thus do not consider nor plan interventions for the total experience. This may cause the programmer to miss important opportunities for intervention and facilitation of the outcomes desired. Since satisfaction with a program is a function of fulfilling a participant's expectations, during the anticipation phase we must either discover them or try to manipulate them. For example, Skipper (1992) has demonstrated that the wording of advertising flyers can influence the number of participants who register and attend an event. Similarly, a patron's expectations are influenced by how they are dealt with during phone inquiries about a program, registration procedures, etc. (McCarville 1993), all of which occur during the anticipation phase.

Post-program interventions influence reflection on a program. The distribution and solicitation of evaluation information is both an important customer satisfaction activity and a source of information to use in documenting program outcomes and improving future operations of the program (Little 1993; Howe 1993). Publishing photographs, staging reunions, and selling souvenirs are all interventions designed to influence the recollection phase of a leisure experience.

Thus, symbolic interaction theory suggests a need to expand the programmer's responsibility for intervention from exclusively dealing with the participation phase of an experience to also include the anticipation and reflection phases.

The Nature of Leisure Objects

Objects are anything than can be indicated, pointed out, or referred to (Blumer 1969). Objects receive our focused attention and are consciously dealt with during interaction. Human beings act toward objects on the basis of the meanings that the objects have for them and their meaning is derived through interaction.

There are only three categories of objects—physical, social, and abstract. Physical objects are those that may be used in the leisure occasion, such as balls, bats, craft supplies, and so forth. Social objects are other people, including leaders, friends, mothers, and other participants in a program. Most leisure occasions are participated in with family or friends (Cheek, Field, and Burdge 1976). People are the ultimate interactive objects because another person offers more social interaction possibilities than any other type of object. Abstract objects include ideas, philosophies, or doctrines, and they too present possibilities for interaction. That is, individuals can form a line of behavior based on them. Notions about moral or immoral recreation influence the leisure behavior of many individuals. Concepts about cooperation and competition also influence interactions in leisure occasions. Programmers often program in order to reify abstract concepts like those associated with Valentine's Day, such as love, Cupid, hearts, and other symbolic objects.

These three types encompass all possible objects that can be indicated, pointed out, or referred to in social occasions. They are the objects of all interaction. *Programmers need to learn which objects make essential contributions to the leisure experience and which are superfluous so that decisions can be made about which of them must be included in a given program.* In Chapter Three we will focus further on the objects of leisure occasions.

Deriving Meaning from Interaction in Leisure Occasions

The meaning of objects arises out of the interaction one has with them. Meaning is not inherent in an object. "Creating meaning involves bringing order to the contents of the mind by integrating one's actions into a unified flow experience" (Csikszentmihalyi 1991, p. 216). Thus, meaning is derived through interaction with social objects. Blumer (1969) states that:

> [Symbolic interactionism] sees meaning as arising in the process of interaction between people. The meaning of a thing for a person grows out of the ways in which other persons act toward the person with regard to the thing. Their actions operate to define the thing for the person. Thus, symbolic interactionism sees meanings as social products, as creations that are formed in and through the defining activities of people as they interact (pp. 4-5).

Meaning is produced socially through interaction with physical, social and abstract objects. It is therefore situationally specific, and the meaning of an object can change from occasion to occasion. Lee (1990) documented that leisure is situationally interpreted by individuals based on the social context in which they have the experience. Furthermore, the meaning of objects in leisure occasions often differs from the meaning these same objects have in other occasions not defined as leisure. For example, Mann (1973, pp. 42-61) points out that queues for leisure events have a different meaning than queues for other functions. Hunnicutt (1986) suggested that to "play" with an object is to experience it in a totally different way than through any other mode of interaction.

Meaning, then, arises out of the interaction one has with objects. Interaction in leisure occasions has a different meaning than interactions in other occasions because of the perceived freedom of participants, the intrinsic satisfaction of participation, and finally because of the satisfaction of being the cause of an act, that is, being an active participant in creating and sustaining the interaction. Since the meaning of leisure arises from interaction, the occurrence of leisure is situational rather than merely situated (Goffman 1983); that is, it occurs within and as a result of interaction. *Thus, programmers must be concerned with the process of how an activity is experienced by participants—the interactions within the event. Their interventions must facilitate the perceptions necessary for participants to conclude they have experienced leisure, and how an occasion of leisure is conducted, then, is as important as the content of the event.* How this concern is dealt with in programming will be discussed further in Chapter Nine.

How Interaction is Produced in Social Occasions

Meanings are developed and modified through a process of interpretation during occasions of interaction. Individuals interpret the meaning of objects encountered. Face-to-face interaction is defined by Goffman (1959) ". . . as the reciprocal influence of individuals upon one another's actions when in one another's immediate physical presence" (p.15). Goffman later describes how individuals organize their behavior in social occasions that arise from ". . . the co-mingling of persons and the temporary interactional enterprises that can arise therefrom" and characterizes the co-mingling of individuals as "a shifting entity necessarily evanescent, created by arrivals and killed by departures" (1967, p.2).

Social gatherings are constructed by the interactions of minded, self-reflexive individuals who are aligning their actions based on their interpretations of the meaning they attribute to the actions of others in the occasion. It is important to note here that symbolic interactionism has as one of its root assumptions the notion that human beings are capable of minded, self-reflexive behavior (Denzin 1978). That is, they are capable of guiding their own behavior and developing a joint line of behavior with others through interaction with them. This notion is crucial to one of the defining dimensions of leisure experiences: individuals must be actively engaged in the joint construction of the occasion, and this occurrence is a necessary condition for perceptions of competence and consequent intrinsic satisfaction with participation.

In Goffman's view, the social order created by such activity is fragile and can be sustained only by the focused attention of each participant. Leisure is experienced in social occasions where interaction occurs among individuals. The interaction requires the individuals to take account of each other's actions, interpret the meaning of each object in the occasion, and form a line of behavior based on this interpretation. This basic interaction ritual continues through repeated cycles of this same basic scenario. During instances of interaction, the meaning of objects is built up through interaction with them. During interaction, an individual engages in a process of interpretation by carrying on an internal conversation in order to identify the meaning of objects based on the immediate situation and on the direction to be taken. Meanings are thus situational productions constructed by individuals based on internalized conversations with themselves while interacting with physical, social, or abstract objects. The meaning attributed to objects in this manner shapes individual lines of behavior in social occasions, and that is how social occasions are created.

The programmer must be concerned with the order and occurrence of interactions in a leisure event. Assuring the occurrence of key, meaning-deriving interactions, and sequencing them to cumulate in a meaningful experience must be planned. This topic will also be dealt with further in Chapter Nine.

The Phenomenology Of Experiencing Leisure

How, then, do individuals experience leisure? This is the subject of phenomenology—describing how events are experienced and interpreted. "Experience is going through an episode or event as well as processing the perceptions of that time period" (Kelly 1987, p. 20). An episode is interaction in a social occasion that is sensed, interpreted, and directed. It is directed through the conscious control of one's responses. At each point in interaction we have a decision, and the pleasure in an event emanates from making the correct decision, i.e. one that gives order to our participation in the event. Order is perceived when we make decisions that enable us to reach our goals within the context of a given instance of interaction. There are four implications from this theory that directly affect the programmer's efforts.

1. Occasions of interaction are emergent productions. Interaction is constructed in real time in which self-reflexive individuals choose the line of behavior they will follow. Despite staff efforts to plan and predict how behavior will play out in a given program, individuals who enter activities will interpret the meaning of the objects differently, and their respondent actions will differ accordingly. Programmers must understand how humans shape meaning and how that meaning shapes action. Each occasion of interaction is constructed anew each time it is experienced, and a past success is no guarantee that the same combination of circumstances will again lead to the same outcome.

2. Occasions of interaction are fragile. Providing the experience desired in an occasion is sometimes difficult because of the fragility of social occasions. Programmers should avoid imposing structures that are so rigid that they will interfere with an individual participant's perceived freedom and the focused experience they need to achieve intrinsic satisfaction. Programmers can actually destroy the experience they are trying to facilitate by forcing programmatic controls and manipulations to operate a program.

3. People always play a role in constructing leisure occasions. According to symbolic interactionist theory, individuals always play a part in shaping the direction of an interactional episode and the meaning of interaction for them. Csikszentmihalyi (1991) emphasizes this point—"It (happiness) does not depend on outside events, but rather on how we interpret them" (p. 2). Thus optimal experience is something individuals make happen through their conscious interpretation and volitional direction of interaction. The autonomy of the individual must be respected in program development. If the programmer provides too much direction, the patron may not have a sufficient opportunity for involvement.

4. *The programmer must provide some order and direction to events.* It is crucial to understand the concept of order and how it enables those present in an occasion to be set free so leisure may be operationalized. Goffman (1983) points out that all occasions of interaction are directed by a series of enabling conventions, i.e. the rules of interaction, that may range from the very formal through tacitly agreed to conventions. Participating in interaction, then, requires participants to pay the small price of agreeing to abide by the conventions so they may obtain the large convenience of participating in the interaction facilitated by the conventions without having to continually renegotiate the rules.

The conventions necessary to provide order for leisure events come from two sources—the relational history of participants, and the rules of interaction. Many leisure experiences occur in informal interaction with family and friends where an individual's true self is an already known and accepted entity. Thus, there is no need to continually renegotiate who one is (Samdahl 1992), and the true self can interact with a degree of freedom not possible in interaction where the self must be continually renegotiated. In a similar manner, the rules of interaction create or define a social order and the acceptable roles a person is to assume in this defined occasion of interaction. For example, in an occasion with very formalized rules such as a game of racquetball, two players previously unknown to each other may play and know the roles and expectations each is to perform to sustain the occasion of interaction. This is possible because they both know and accept the rules of interaction in racquetball and are thus freed to attend to the defined requirements of the game. In this way, conventions of interaction create the freedom to present a known self and to freely interact. This is a uniqueness of occasions defined as leisure.

Knowledge about the phenomenology of experiencing leisure, then, gives the following direction to programmers. *To facilitate leisure experiences, the programmer must orchestrate a delicate interplay and manipulate the conventions of an occasion to create interactive social space that will permit patrons to be active participants in the construction of the occasion in a manner that results in perceived freedom and intrinsic satisfaction for them, plus provides them fun, enjoyment, or relaxation.* Now complete Exercise 2-1.

Exercise 2-1.
Programming as Symbolic Interaction

Discuss the different roles a programmer would take if he or she were to design a program intended to provide a leisure experience as opposed to a program intended simply to be an opportunity for the leisure experience to occur.

- **What is the role of the programmer if one assumes that interacting individuals play a major role in defining the leisure experience?**
- **What are the three essential perceptual results if individuals are to define programs as leisure? How can programmers ensure that they occur?**

Conclusion

Professional programmers rely on the theory of leisure behavior to guide the development of program services. Symbolic interaction is a theory that attempts to understand behavior at the level of face-to-face interaction and assumes individuals participate in the construction of occasions of interaction and the meaning of them. The theory suggests that programmers must give increased attention to how they operate programs and how they are experienced by the patrons. Understanding how to intervene to facilitate leisure is a crucial programming concept that includes understanding how meaning is produced through interaction and what meanings must result for an occasion to be labeled as leisure.

References, Chapter Two

Blumer, H. 1969. *Symbolic Interactionism.* Englewood Cliffs, NJ: Prentice-Hall.

Busser, J.A. (Ed.). 1993, October. Leisure Programming: The State of the Art in Leisure Today. In *Journal of Physical Education Recreation and Dance, 64* (8), 25-26.

Cheek, N.H., D.R. Field, and R.J. Burdge. 1976. *Leisure and Recreation Places.* Ann Arbor, MI: Ann Arbor Science Publishers.

Csikszentmihalyi, M. 1991. *Flow: The Psychology of Optimal Experience.* New York: Harper Perennial.

Denzin, N.K. 1978. *The Research Act* (2nd ed.) New York: McGraw-Hill.

Eisenstadt, S.N., and M. Curelaru. 1977. Macrosociology Theory, Analysis, and Comparative Studies. *Current Sociology 25* (2): 44-47.

Goffman, E. 1959. *The Presentation of Self in Everyday Life.* Garden City, NY: Doubleday & Co.

Goffman, E. 1962. *Interaction Ritual.* Garden City, NY: Doubleday & Co.

Goffman, E. 1983. The Interaction Order. *American Sociological Review, 458* (2), 1-17.

Howe, C. Z. 1993. The Evaluation of Leisure Programs. *Journal of Physical Education, Recreation and Dance, 64* (8), 43-46.

Hunnicutt, B.K. 1986. Problems Raised by the Empirical Study of Play and Some Humanistic Alternatives. *Abstracts from the 1986 Symposium on Leisure Research:*8-10.

Iso-Ahola, S.E. 1980. *The Social Psychology of Leisure and Recreation.* Dubuque, IA: Wm. C. Brown.

Kelly, J. R. 1987. *Freedom To Be: A New Sociology of Leisure.* New York: Macmillan.

Kuentzel, W. F. 1990, October. Motive Uniformity Across Recreational Activities and Settings: A Synthesis of Research, Paper presented at the National Recreation and Parks Association Research Symposium, Phoenix, AZ.

Lee, Y. 1990, October. Immediate Leisure Experiences: A Phenomenological Approach, Paper presented at the 1990 National Recreation and Park Association Leisure Research Symposium, Phoenix, AZ.

Little, S. L. 1993. Leisure Program Design and Evaluation. *Journal of Physical Education, Recreation and Dance, 64* (8), 26-29, 33.

Mann, L. 1973. Learning to Live with Lines. In *Urbanman: The Psychology of Urban Survival*. J. Helmer and N.A. Eddington, Editors. New York: Macmillan.

McCarville, R.E. 1993. Keys to Quality Programming. *Journal of Physical Education, Recreation & Dance, 64* (8), 34-36, 46,47.

Mead, G. H. 1934. *Mind, Self, and Society*. University of Chicago Press.

Podilchak, W. 1991. Distinctions of Fun, Enjoyment, and Leisure. *Leisure Studies, 10*, 133-148.

Rossman, J. R. 1988. Development of a Leisure Programming Theory. *Journal of Park and Recreation Administration, 6* (4), 1-13.

Rossman, J. R. 1989. *Recreation Programming: Designing Leisure Experiences*. Champaign, IL: Sagamore Publishing.

Rossman, J. R. 1993. Integrating Theory and Practice into Leisure Program Design. In A.J. Veal, P. Jonson, and G. Cushman (Eds.), Leisure and Tourism: Social and Environmental Change: Papers from the World Leisure and Recreation Association Congress, Sydney, Australia, 16-19 July 1991 (485-489). Sydney, Australia: Centre for Leisure and Tourism Studies, University of Technology.

Rossman, J. R. and C.R. Edginton. 1989. Managing Leisure Programs: Toward a Theoretical Model. *Society and Leisure, 12* 157-170.

Samdahl, D.M. 1988. A Symbolic Interactionist Model of Leisure: Theory and Empirical Support. *Leisure Sciences* 1: 27-39.

Samdahl, D.M. 1992. The Common Leisure Occasion. *Journal of Leisure Research,24* , 19-32.

Shaw, S. M. 1985. The Meaning of Leisure in Everyday Life. *Leisure Sciences, 7*, 1-24.

Skipper, B. A. 1992. The Relationship Between Desired Results and the Marketing Tools Used in Recreation Programming (Doctoral dissertation, University of North Texas, 1992). Dissertation Abstracts International, 53, 3364A.

Unger, L.S. 1984. The Effect of Situational Variables on the Subjective Leisure Experience. *Leisure Sciences 6*, 291-312.

Photo courtesy of Austin Parks and Recreation, Austin, TX. Photo by Jim Halbrook.

3

Six Key Elements of Program Production

Leisure is experienced in social occasions that are constructed by interacting individuals. All instances of leisure involve the interactions of one or more persons who are orienting their behavior toward themselves and other physical, social, or symbolic objects (Denzin 1975). This co-orientation of selves occurs in place; that is, it occurs in a social occasion that has an identifiable structure. Erving Goffman dedicated his career to investigating and identifying the dynamics of face-to-face interaction in social occasions in an effort to develop a generic structure of these occasions. From Goffman's work, Denzin (1975) has identified the generic elements that structure all social occasions.

The social interaction that occurs in place (Goffman 1971, cited in Denzin 1975) is made up of six interrelated elements that include:

> differentially self-reflexive actors; place or setting itself (e.g. the physical territory); social objects which fill the setting and are acted on by the actors in question; a set of rules of a civil-legal, polite-ceremonial and relationally specific nature which explicitly or tacitly guide and shape interaction; a set of relationships which bind interactants to one another; and a shifting set of definitions reflective of each actor's co-orientation to self and others during the interaction sequence. (Denzin 1975, p. 462)

These six elements of place are the generic set of variables that structure social occasions. In order to develop program services, a programmer must take account of or manage these six key elements of program production. Their effect on a program is of such fundamental importance that a change in any one element changes the character of the program. That is, if the programmer changes any one element of place, the program has been changed. Collectively the six elements of place situate an instance of interaction and thus an instance of leisure.

Murphy, et al. (1973) state that "The basic method used by agencies to structure opportunities which encourage different kinds of recreation behaviors is the creation and/or manipulation of physical and human environments" (p. 77). The literature on leisure programming has never elaborated on the generic elements to be created and/or manipulated. An assumption of this text is that each leisure program is an interactional episode that occurs in place with a unique configuration of these six elements of place. These six are the key elements of program production, because they are all that a programmer can manipulate or needs to manipulate in developing a leisure program.

Interaction occurs as a linear sequence of actions, with only one action being attended to at any given moment by the individuals in the social occasion. Any one element of place can be the most important element in any single action. The importance of any single element can shift with the transition from one action to another. Interaction is made up of a series of actions that occur in sequential order. Within an individual program, each element of place assumes a shifting role of importance as the interactions of the program unfold.

The task of the leisure programmer is to identify the unique configuration of these six elements of place that compose a program, to anticipate how the series of actions that make up the program will unfold, and to determine how the face-to-face interactions of a program can be manipulated to move participants through the program. The programmer anticipates and plans how the action sequences will unfold and then puts in place the mechanisms needed to guide the occurrence of the intended interactions. The programmer does this vicariously by experiencing the program before its actual occurrence. In this process, the programmer tries to anticipate and predict the outcomes of interactions within a program and the order in which events during the interaction will unfold. The process is analogous to writing the script of a play, except that in leisure programs, the interactants are not bound by the script, but actually play a role in shaping the event. How this is accomplished in designing programs will be explained in greater detail in Chapter Nine.

Adopting this viewpoint makes clear the problematic nature of program design, planning, and operation. Interacting individuals are one of the six elements of place. But once the individuals enter an occasion, they are not bound to follow the action scenarios designed by the programmer. The overall outcome of any one program is dependent on the interactions of individuals with the other five elements of place, the interactions of individuals with each other, and the interaction of all six elements of place with each other. Pfeffer and Salancik (1978) make clear the problematic nature of interdependent events: "Interdependence is the reason why nothing comes out quite the way one wants it to. Any event that depends on more than a single causal agent is an outcome based on interdependent agents" (p. 40). This is the case when designing and operating leisure programs.

A familiarity with social interaction theory will help programmers understand how humans experience and construct their participation in leisure programs. Research on social interaction has led to the development of a generic structure of a social occasion—the six elements of place. These are the elements that programmers can create and manipulate in order to program leisure experiences. Even so, because of the interactional nature of leisure occasions, any program plan is simply a probability estimate of what the programmer believes will happen in an occasion of constructed interaction.

Although the elements that constitute place can be reduced to six generic categories, one would be deceived in believing that only six variables need to be manipulated. The number of possibilities within each element of place is large. Furthermore, the number of possible combinations of elements is even larger. The six elements do, however, provide a compact conceptual framework from which programmers can organize their efforts. Programmers create this situated production by understanding the existence of these elements and controlling or manipulating them. Some elements of place may be unalterable in some programs and therefore not subject to manipulation. In developing a program design, the programmer must anticipate the implications that an unalterable element of place has on the remaining elements that can be manipulated.

Six Program Elements

The six elements of place identified by Goffman and Denzin have been renamed to conceptually clarify their role in program design. The new names are the following: interacting people, physical setting, leisure objects, rules, relationships, and animation. An explanation of the role and effect that each of these elements has in a program is presented in the sections that follow.

Interacting People

Leisure is a human experience created by differentially self-reflexive individuals interacting in social occasions. As discussed earlier, social occasions are constructed by interacting individuals who build a line of behavior after taking account of their own behavior and that of others in the occasion. Effective programming requires the programmer either to anticipate who the specific individuals will be and to design the program for them, or to design the program for a specific type of individual and then recruit this type of individual into the program.

When different individuals come into a program, it changes. A perfect illustration of this point is the operation of programs for youth. Often the same program can be operated successfully year after year. The configuration of the other five elements of place do not change—only the individuals in the program change. For example, in a typical program for youth there may be a different cohort of six-year-old children who participate in the same program each year. Even though the basic program has not changed, it continues to be successful. What has changed are the individuals in the program. Since one of the program elements has changed, the program itself has in fact changed.

Many programmers have had similar experiences. Having operated a program that originally failed, they offer the same program a second time with no change other than the individuals; with this one change, the program succeeds. One possible reason for program failure, then, is that individuals are recruited into a program that is inappropriate for them. If a different group of individuals is recruited, the program may succeed with no other change.

Because people are one of the major elements of program design, programmers must take great care in investigating or anticipating who these individuals are and what benefits they seek from participation. To do so, it is necessary to understand the physical, social, and psychological development of individuals; to understand their gender, age, skill level, and other pertinent information about them; and to understand the benefits they are seeking from participation.

Marketing literature has pointed out the need to design programs for specific individuals through market segmentation (Howard and Crompton 1980, p. 338) and to develop services for a well-defined target market. Although agency goal statements often suggest that programs are for all people regardless of race, age, sex, ethnic origin, and so forth, we know that every program, to be successful, must be targeted for a specific group of individuals whom we can define with some precision. The programmer deals with this issue in one of two ways—either through macro or micro market segmentation (Crompton 1983, pp. 10-19).

Macro segmentation involves developing services for a cohort of individuals who are seeking similar benefits from participation in recreation programs. The notion of a benefit package comes from the personal meaning of leisure that was discussed in Chapter One. Crompton (1983) pointed out that the desires of each potential client are likely to be unique, but agency resources cannot afford to develop services for each client. Because of resource limitations, the programmer is then forced to compromise and to group together individuals who desire similar benefits from participating in specific leisure occasions. These benefits may include any number of psychological outcomes such as achievement, autonomy, socialization, and risk. Driver and Brown (1975) have identified a number of possible psychological outcomes of leisure participation. In macro segmentation, the programmer develops a service to satisfy a projected benefit package that has been identified, and then individuals who want this projected benefit package are recruited into the program.

When macro segmentation is used, programmers project a set of benefits they have determined that a group of individuals in the community wants. But the programmers have no assurance that such a group indeed exists for the service identified. For example, through market research one could produce evidence that a group of individuals desire physical fitness and social interaction. This is a benefit package that is sought. Further investigation identifies an actual group of mothers, 23 to 30 years of age with preschool children, who would like an aerobics fitness program in their neighborhood between 9:30 and 11:30 in the morning with nursery service provided. The programmer then develops this service for the specific individuals identified. Sometimes, however, it is impossible to further identify the specific cohort of individuals who desire this service, so it is developed solely on the basis of data suggesting that there is a group of unidentified individuals who seek this benefit package. In these cases, programs are developed slowly through trial and error until the individuals who desire the benefits of the program can be identified.

When micro segmentation is used, cohorts of specific individuals are identified by using various traditional segmentation variables from one of three categories: geographic location descriptors (neighborhood, city, distance from program location), sociodemographic descriptors (age, income, sex, education), or behavioral descriptors (usage rates, level of specialization, psychological benefits sought) (Crompton 1983, p. 14). Once target groups are identified, the programmer develops specific services that fill the benefit package desired by people in the group.

The difference between these two techniques is in the timing of when one begins dealing with actual individuals. In macro segmentation, a benefit or a package of benefits is first identified, and then the programmer tries to identify the characteristics of the individuals who want the benefits. Sometimes, though, it is impossible to initially identify actual individuals. In this case, the programmer has only a projected benefit package that is desired by a group of individuals whose identity is unknown. In micro segmentation, individuals are identified first, and then the benefits they seek are identified.

The individuals who participate are thus a key element in the design of a program. All programs are either consciously or inadvertently designed to meet the needs of a specific cohort of individuals. Effective programming involves matching the right group of individuals with the correct service so that the benefits sought can be obtained. One possible reason that a program fails is that the programmer did not match the correct group of individuals with the correct service and its benefits. Another possible reason that a program fails is that the programmer did not match the correct group of individuals with a program design that provides the benefits desired by the participants. A principle of program design implied by this element of place can be stated as follows: *When the individuals in a program change, the program changes. Changing the individuals in a program may be the only change needed to make an unsuccessful program successful. Further, it is essential to plan programs for the identified needs of specific individuals or the projected needs of a group believed to exist in the service community. The more information a programmer can obtain about the individuals who will actually be in a program, the better chance the programmer has of designing and operating a program that will meet the needs of the participants.*

The Physical Setting

The physical setting for a program is the second element to be discussed. The physical setting includes one or more of the following sensory components: visual, aural, olfactory, tactile, and taste. Each component will affect a program if it is consciously or unconsciously included in the program design or if it is inadvertently omitted from the design. The physical setting is an expansive concept, so not all possible settings can be discussed here. However, it is important to recognize that the physical setting is also one of the major program elements. If the setting changes, the program itself will change. Three considerations about the physical setting for a program are especially important.

First, programmers must understand the uniqueness of a setting. Too often they try to duplicate a program that was successful elsewhere, only to fail because they do not understand that a unique setting was the key element contributing to the program's success. For example, one military installation started a successful program in which the patrons would bring their lunch every Friday and listen to a small musical combo while eating. Several other installations tried unsuccessfully to duplicate the program. They served the same type of food, had the same type of music, and used the same promotional materials and strategy. Eventually the success of the original program was attributed to its unique setting—an oceanside area where the combos played on a hill with beautiful waves breaking in the background. This unique setting simply could not be duplicated at other installations.

Programmers must be able to analyze what elements contribute to the success of their programs for several reasons. Knowing if a unique physical setting is the major element contributing to a program's success and whether the setting can be duplicated is a critical piece of information needed before attempting to duplicate a program that was successful elsewhere. Sometimes if the setting cannot be duplicated, the program itself cannot be successfully duplicated.

Second, programmers must understand the limits of a setting. Too often the setting is not adequate for a program. For example, the author once was asked to operate a program with active games for elementary school children in a neighborhood recreation center that had not been designed for active play. In fact, to create an open setting, the architect had put glass walls on almost two full walls of the room to be used for active games. After replacing several panes of glass, the administration suspended playing active games "because the building was not designed for active play"! Some settings are simply not suitable for some programs. An inappropriate setting may even detract from an event.

Third, settings can be manipulated with decorations, lighting, and other physical alterations. Programmers should therefore realize when a unique physical setting is necessary for the success of a program. Once it is determined that a unique setting is needed, the programmer can begin trying to find or to create such a setting for the program. If programmers do not understand how a unique setting contributes to the success of a program, they cannot hope to duplicate the program elsewhere.

The more a physical environment is altered, the more expensive the alteration becomes. For example, an artificial ice rink can be kept frozen during the summer, although the high energy consumption that is needed is expensive. Making an inadequate setting adequate is almost always possible if enough resources are available. But the cost of doing so may far exceed any potential benefit. It is therefore very important to understand how essential a unique physical setting is to the success of a program before beginning expensive alterations of the physical environment.

The physical setting is the second program element a programmer must evaluate. Although there is much to consider, it is important to ascertain whether the program to be produced requires a unique setting for success. Knowing the limits of a setting and the many ways to alter it to make it adequate are also important pieces of information.

Leisure Objects

As discussed in Chapter Two, there are three types of objects—physical, social, and abstract. In programming, one must be able to identify the key objects that fill a leisure setting and are acted on when people interact during a program. Not every object needs to be identified, but only the key objects that must be there for a program to occur and be successful. The question to answer that brings focus to this inquiry is: What objects are needed to support the interactions designed into the program?

For example, in Oak Park, Illinois, the author, along with other staff, was attempting to develop a different program design for an annual children's Easter Egg Hunt. Several objects were identified that were considered critical for such an event. The list included enough Easter eggs for all children to have a good probability of finding at least one egg; a beautiful park with grass, trees, and bushes for hiding the eggs; and a costumed Easter Bunny for children to visit in a surrealistic forest created with painted panels. The park itself was obviously the concern of the previous section on physical setting. However, the eggs and the Easter Bunny were important objects that would contribute to this event. They were assumed to be so critical that they could not be excluded; if these objects were not available, the event should not occur.

Too often programmers are willing to continue with an event even though they do not have enough objects or they do not have the objects that are essential to the successful operation of a program. Appropriate objects, whether they are physical, social, or abstract, are sometimes the critical program element. Programmers need to be able to determine which objects are essential, which are optional, and which actually detract from the event being planned and should be excluded. For the Easter Egg Hunt to be successful, it was assumed to be essential that each child find an Easter egg. If there were not enough eggs to make this possible, the event was not going to occur. Easter eggs are an essential object for an Easter Egg Hunt—there is no substitute for them. Special prize eggs were also provided which, if found, entitled the bearer to a large chocolate rabbit. These prizes were considered optional and were to be included as long as the budget allowed their purchase. In previous years, the beginning of the hunt was signaled with a starting gun. During the redesign of this program, the gun was considered detrimental to the event, so the hunt was begun with an air horn.

Programmers must identify the key objects that are essential to supporting the interactions intended in a program. Objects can be either essential to the success of a program, optional to its success, or detrimental to a program.

Rules

Rules guide interactions in a program. They guide how interactions may or may not unfold, and in this sense they make certain interactions possible and constrict others. Here, the term *rules* is being used in a generic sense to include civil-legal, polite-ceremonial, and relational rules. With this conception, all of the rules including laws, administrative regulations imposed by the agency, the codified rules of a game, the ceremonial rules of a game, and the relational rules of everyday discourse need to be considered. How each or all of these rules will affect the interactions in a program must be anticipated and planned into the program design. At the same time, programmers need to make certain there are enough rules to direct interactions in a manner desired, but not so many rules that the perceived freedom needed for the leisure experience fails to emerge from the interactional episode being planned.

The regulating effects that rules impose on a program cannot be underestimated. Their cumulative effect determines how interactions may or may not occur in a program. It is known that the leisure experience is in large part determined by the perceived freedom a participant achieves as a result of his or her interactions in a program. Because of this, too many rules or inappropriate ones can destroy the experience we are trying to facilitate. A Ziggy cartoon that appeared many years ago illustrated this point very well. In the cartoon, Ziggy is shown entering a park, where he is confronted with a series of signs that say: "Keep off the grass," "No picnicking in this area," "No swimming," "No bicycle riding," and so forth. The last sign says:

"This is your park, enjoy it! Your Park Commission." It is not being suggested that leisure settings should have no regulation. However, programmers need to understand how regulation impinges on perceived freedom, and they must make certain that programs are not overregulated to the point that there is no freedom perceived by participants.

Well-written rules can foster perceived freedom. Rules that guide interactions create a known arena for interaction that fosters a perception of freedom for participants. For perceived freedom to emerge, a known structure for interaction to occur must be present. Game rules create a known interactive structure in which specific interaction may and may not occur. Within the permitted range of interactions, game players have total freedom to act. By allowing some actions to be restricted by game rules, players are given total freedom to engage in other actions.

When rule structures are unclear or constantly changing, anxiety is introduced and perceived freedom is quashed. This point was made clear in an article the author was asked to referee. The author of the article had been a participant observer in a river float trip operated by a commercial outfitter. There were several rafts in the group, and each raft was handled by a staff boatman. Members of the group were required to change rafts daily; consequently they also changed boatmen each day. Each boatman had his own rules about how passengers were to sit in the raft when it was going over rapids, where passengers were to sit, how trash was to be disposed of, and so on. The net effect of this constant change was that the boatmen, who were supposed to be providing patrons with a pleasant experience, were constantly at odds with them and badgering them about the proper way of doing things on "their" boat. The pleasure that should have been possible on the trip never fully emerged because of the constant badgering of patrons by the staff. In this case, requiring patrons to deal with rule changes daily interfered with their enjoyment of the event. The stable rule structure necessary for perceived freedom to emerge was never allowed to develop.

The structure that is used to organize and operate a program is also one of its regulatory mechanisms. The programmer can use several structures to operate a program. For example, softball can be offered as an instructional workshop, a league, a tournament, or a special event. Farrell and Lundegren (1978) have termed this organizing structure a *program format* and state that program format is the "basic structure through which an activity is presented" (p. 82). They identified five formats, including (1) clinics, workshops, and classes, (2) tournaments, (3) clubs, (4) special events, and (5) open facilities (Farrell and Lundegren 1978). In their second edition (1983) they retitled these five formats as (1) education, (2) competition, (3) activity club, (4) performance or special event, and (5) open facility (p. 82). The U.S. Navy has identified five similar formats, including open house, special events, skill development, competition, and clubs and groups. They also add to this list a sixth format: self-directed noncompetitive, which includes many of their rental and check-out services through which the Navy Recreational Services unit simply provides equipment of various types to sailors.

Program formats are organizational rules that structure program services. When programmers select a format they are determining to some degree the satisfaction a program patron will have while limiting the probability that other satisfactions will be realized (Rossman 1984). When a format is selected, then, it influences to some degree the experience the patron will have in the program. Program format is one of many rules that will determine the final structure of a program and the satisfaction the patron will experience.

Rules define a social structure in which interaction can occur. Programmers must provide enough structure so that a program takes the form intended and the desired interactions that make up the content of the program can occur. However, overregulation with rules or rules that are unclear will impinge on the perceived freedom necessary for a true leisure experience to occur and will interfere with the experience desired by the patrons or intended by the program designer.

Relationships

Participants in a program may have a preexisting relationship that binds them to each other. People most frequently participate in leisure with family and friends. To properly design a program, the programmer needs to determine whether the participants have a relational history with each other. If indeed they do, it is necessary to determine the nature of this history and to assess its potential impact on the program being designed. If the interactants do not have a relational history, the programmer must determine whether it is necessary to construct a relationship during the operation of a program. Mechanisms for accomplishing this include icebreakers, first-comer activities, and other social recreation activities that can be planned into a program's design.

It may be unnecessary to create a relational history, however. Not all events require that all who attend them know each other and have a friendship relationship with other participants. Recreation personnel tend to force friendliness even when it is unnecessary. Forcing this issue often adds nothing to an event and can even detract from it. Individuals unknown to each other can co-experience many events without knowing the rest of the individuals who are participating. Bus trips to one-day events are an example. Often preexisting small groups of two to five people will attend such an event. But it is not necessary to implement a program mechanism that forces all thirty participants to get to know each other. In fact, doing so may keep individuals from valued interaction time with their own small group and lead to dissatisfaction with the event.

It is also important not to structure events in a way that could destroy relational histories that might otherwise contribute to a participant's satisfaction with an event. For example, at one university, demand for tickets to basketball games increased dramatically because of the team's excellent record. In order to promote open access to games, athletic department officials decreed that henceforth no one would be permitted to purchase more than ten tickets at any one time. There was an unexpected outcry of protest against this policy. What the athletic department had inadvertently done was to destroy the opportunity for friendship groups to attend ball games together. Many preexisting groups from fraternities, sororities, and dorms were larger than ten individuals. Although the demand for tickets in this instance was so great that the policy could stand, clearly the interactants' relational history, which contributed to their satisfaction with an event, was not taken into account in the operational policies. This decision worked to the overall detriment of participant satisfaction with the event.

Understanding the role that relationships play in the interactions of a program and anticipating how they may contribute to or detract from client satisfaction is an important element of place. Programmers cannot simply assume that the best course of action is always to foster or create a relationship between individuals who attend an event.

Animation

Animation deals with how a program is set into motion and how the action is sustained throughout the program. To animate a program, the programmer must structure it in such a way that apparently spontaneous, lifelike movement is affected. This can be accomplished in a number of different ways. Obviously providing a leader is one solution and a possible source of action to move a program through time. How to plan and anticipate the scenario of action that will occur in a program is covered in more detail in Chapters Nine and Eleven. The process, however, is analogous to action planning in other fields.

In theater, planning animation is known as "blocking." A play is blocked by describing and rehearsing where each actor will be situated at each moment, how the actors are to move through each scene, and how and where their attention is to be focused at each moment. In dance, determining the content and sequence of each movement is known as "choreographing." In sport it is known as developing a "play."

In a similar way, to animate a program the designer needs to anticipate how individuals will move through a program and how they will learn about the process and the timing of when they are to move. In addition, programmers need to predict how the sequence of interactions that make up a program will unfold. The program designer must then provide sufficient structure and direction in animating the program so that participants will have the intended experience.

Providing a recreation leader who personally leads and thereby animates a program is one method for dealing with animation. It is important to understand the role that a unique leader can play in a program. Programmers will be unable to duplicate a program whose success depends on a uniquely skilled leader unless they, too, have a similarly skilled leader. The author has observed this phenomenon in the production of a variety show. One agency sponsored an annual variety show modeled after the popular television program "The Gong Show." The variety show was tremendously successful, but other agencies could not duplicate it because its success was dependent on a talented amateur comedian who was the emcee each year. The skills used to emcee the show accounted for a good deal of the show's success. Other programmers failed to understand that unless they could duplicate this animation element of the program, they would be unable to successfully duplicate the program itself, despite successfully duplicating the other five elements. The variety show's success was primarily accounted for by a single individual who animated the program in a unique manner.

Understanding this notion of being an animator can clarify the role that individuals in drop-in types of operations can play. Too often people employed to operate a facility see their role as one of simply opening the facility, regulating its use, and closing it at the appropriate time. They never understand that they are one of the six critical elements that will determine the success or failure of a leisure locale.

Programs can often be animated without a leader. For example, in most of the attractions at Disneyland the program is animated with mechanical and electrical devices. The program moves forward through time whether the patron is ready or not! Self-guided tours are also animated without a leader by using signs with instructions and arrows, recorded messages, and similar devices.

How much direction to provide in animating a program is somewhat problematic. Providing too much direction can interfere with an individual's perception of freedom and of being the cause of an act that is essential to intrinsic reward. However, a lack of enough direction can be anxiety provoking and thereby produce dissatisfaction.

Animation, then, not only involves the use of a leader, but is a higher-level concept that deals with how the participant is going to be moved through a program. Providing a face-to-face leader is one way, but not the only way, of accomplishing this movement. The program designer must anticipate how the patron is to be moved through a program and make certain that the devices necessary to implement this movement are in place and can be understood by the patron. The programmer cannot simply expect that the program will animate itself.

Programming Place

The act of programming involves developing opportunities for leisure by manipulating or creating one or more of these six elements of place. In developing programs, programmers must either control these elements by manipulating them or be aware of the circumstance involving any element they cannot control. They must then take into account the circumstance of the uncontrolled element in their manipulations of the remaining elements. These six elements, however, are the basic organizing framework around which all program services are developed. All programs are simply variations of these elements. Now complete Exercise 3-1 on page 51.

The Service Continuum

How much of a service is actually arranged and provided by the programmer can vary from program to program. Some participants enjoy and want to provide some of the elements of a program themselves. It is theoretically possible for the programmer to completely provide a program so that the participants need do nothing except attend the activity, event, or service. At Disneyland, for example, participants simply pay their admission fee and get on a ride. The provider does everything else. It is also possible that individuals do not need the programmer at all and can completely provide a service without any assistance from a programmer. We know that the majority of leisure occurs at home in self-organized activities. Although the theoretical extremes of this continuum involve unlikely circumstances (see Chapter Three Addendum on page 54 for an explanation of this point), the middle part of the continuum has some very practical implications for program development. Specifically, how much of a program must a programmer provide, and how much may one reasonably expect the participant to provide?

The service continuum is illustrated in Figure 3-1 on page 52. On the left end of the continuum are those services that are totally provided by individuals in a program. When offering services in this mode, the agency is said to be operating in a

Exercise 3-1.
Manipulating the Six Elements of Place

In the left column of the matrix below are listed the six elements of place. Select a recreation program familiar to you and describe each element of the program. Be certain to identify the key contributors in each element, that is, those without which the program could not operate.

Next, redesign the program six times by changing each element in turn. When you are finished, discuss the following questions with other members of the class:

- How did each redesign change the program?
- Did you develop a new or a different program in this process?
- Which modification had the most impact on the original program?

Six elements of place	Describe the elements of a program	Modify progam by changing one element in turn.					
		1	2	3	4	5	6
Interacting people							
Physical setting							
Objects							
Rules							
Relationships							
Animation							

facilitator role. On the right end of the continuum are those program services that are totally provided by the agency. When offering services in this mode, the agency is said to be operating in a direct provider role. Where an individual program is located on the service continuum is a function of the ratio of agency-versus participant-provided program elements.

Figure 3-1.
The Service Continuum

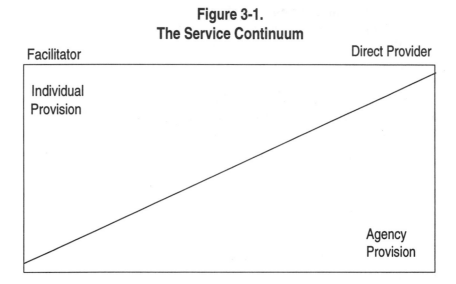

Two major issues affect whether an agency will operate in a facilitator or direct provider role. One is cost. It is assumed that, as one moves from being a facilitator to a direct provider, costs increase. Although this is not true in every case, it is generally true. To be a direct provider of all leisure services in a community would be prohibitively expensive. Allowing the participants to provide part or all of the elements of program service is less expensive for the agency.

The second major issue is how important it is for the participant to play a role in the development and provision of the leisure service. Some individuals want a completely packaged service, while others want to play a major role in designing, planning, and operating a leisure experience. For example, out-door recreation outfitters successfully market two kinds of ser-vices—trips complete with a guide plus an itinerary or simply outfitting groups with equipment for a specified period of time.

In the latter case, the participants are responsible for designing the entire program except for supplying the equipment.

Between the extremes of allowing the participant to do everything and allowing the agency to do everything, there are many organizational formats that require varying degrees of effort from both the individual and the agency. The six organizational formats discussed earlier are placed on the service continuum in Figure 3-2. This figure illustrates that any activity may be operated in a variety of program formats that require varying degrees of agency and individual input into the program. As one moves from left to right on the continuum, the agency assumes an increasing role in developing and operating the program, while the individual assumes a lesser role.

Figure 3-2.
The Service Continuum With Programming Formats

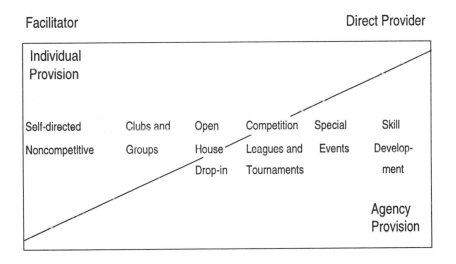

Which type of service an agency will develop depends on the type of agency one is in and the agency's philosophy, role, and mission. Some agencies offer only one type of service. Most comprehensive agencies offer multiple types of program formats to give patrons flexibility in choosing a program style that meets their preferences. Now complete Exercise 3-2 on page 54.

Exercise 3-2.
Experimenting with Programming Formats

Select any activity such as volleyball, oil painting, or guitar playing and identify and discuss how this single activity could be operated as six different programs, using each of the six programming formats included in Figure 3-2. Discuss the different roles of the programmer, agency, and patron in each of the different formats.

Conclusion

Leisure occasions occur in a place that is made up of six interrelated elements. The act of programming is anticipating the circumstance of each of the six elements of place, accommodating or manipulating this circumstance, anticipating the scenario of actions that will make up the program, and anticipating the shifting importance that each element will assume as the program moves through time. Since these six elements of place situate a program, they are all that one needs to control, or can control, in designing a program. The six elements of place are of such fundamental importance that if one of them is changed, the program is also changed. Programmers need to develop the ability to analyze their programs using these elements of place and to determine which element or combination of elements is central to the success of an individual program. To create, manipulate, or duplicate a program requires this level of understanding. Programmers can develop program services that require varying degrees of design input and operational effort from the agency and the individual participant.

Addendum

The two extremes of the service continuum are theoretical points. On the left side, where individuals entirely provide the program for themselves, there is no need for the programmer at all. This point is on the continuum only as a point of reference to illustrate program formats that require the participant to be involved in the design and delivery of the program.

The right end of the continuum, which illustrates programs where the participant has no role, is also a theoretical point. As discussed earlier, the leisure experience always requires the active participation of the participant in constructing the experience. At a minimum, the participant must take in and interpret the meaning of the sensory stimuli provided. So it is never possible to totally provide a leisure experience. Leisure is not something that is done to individuals, but rather something they play a role in constructing. What is being illustrated on the right end of the service continuum, then, are those programs that are designed and operated wholly by a programmer.

References, Chapter Three

Crompton, J.L. 1983. Selecting Target Markets—A Key to Effective Marketing. *Journal of Park and Recreation Administration* 1(1): 7-26.

Denzin, N.K. 1975. Play, Games and Interaction: The Contexts of Childhood Socialization. *The Sociological Quarterly 16*: 458-478.

Driver, B.L., and P.J. Brown. 1975. A Socio-Psychological Definition of Recreation Demand, with Implications for Recreation Resource Planning. In *Assessing the Demand for Outdoor Recreation.* Washington, D.C.:U.S.Government Printing Office.

Farrell, P., and H.M. Lundegren. 1978. *The Process of Recreation Programming.* New York: Wiley.

Howard, D.R., and J.L. Crompton. 1980. *Financing, Managing and Marketing Recreation and Park Resources.* Dubuque, IA: Wm. C. Brown.

Murphy, J.F., J.G. Williams, W.E. Niepoth, and P.D. Brown. 1973. *Leisure Service Delivery Systems: A Modern Perspective.* Philadelphia: Lea & Febiger.

Pfeffer, J., and G.R. Salancik. 1978. *The External Control of Organizations: A Resource Dependence Perspective.* New York: Harper & Row.

Rossman, J.R. 1984. Influence of Program Format Choice on Participant Satisfaction. *Journal of Park and Recreation Administration* 2(1): 39-51.

Photo courtesy of Cincinnati Recreation Commission, Cincinnati, OH.

4

Using Goal and Objective Technology in Program Development

Leisure service agencies use goals and objectives for a variety of purposes. Staff members are directed to develop planning goals, profit goals, program goals, learning goals, performance goals, evaluation goals, and so forth. With so many different uses of goals, one is often given the impression that many separate goal technologies must be learned. In this section we will approach the use and development of goals and objectives as a single technology and then examine the many uses to which it can be applied in the development of program services.

Goal and Objective Technology Defined

Goal and objective technology is the use of linguistic statements to delimit an area of activity that one intends to accomplish. In implementing goal and objective technology, people use written words to describe what they intend to accomplish. This is done through developing a series of linguistic statements arranged hierarchically, beginning with broad statements and moving successively through more narrow and specific statements. One then concludes with a statement of an objective so specific and clear that its accomplishment is measurable and can thereby be documented.

Unfortunately, program staff members in many agencies have had bad experiences with trying to develop goals and objectives because they have been forced into playing what Patton (1978) has termed the "goals clarification game." This game is typically played with the staff by supervisors or administrators or by a hired consultant. In this game, staff members are directed to develop goals that are clear, specific, and measurable. Staff members almost always lose this game and are made to look fuzzy minded and inept because, according to Patton, "Clarity, specificity, and measurability are not clear, specific, and measurable criteria, so each evaluator (or consultant) can apply a different set of rules in the game" (Patton 1978, p. 99). The usual outcome is that either the staff gives up, or the consultant gives up, or the staff actually stumbles onto what the consultant had in mind in the first place.

In and of itself, an individual goal or objective statement seldom will be specific, clear, and measurable. Any goal or objective statement prepared by staff members can therefore be picked apart by an administrator or consultant and the staff badgered about their ineptness. Goals and objectives are linguistic statements that obtain meaning from their syntactical arrangement within the hierarchical arrangement of goal and objective statements. Syntax refers to the way that words and language are assembled and ordered to achieve meaning. Individual goals and objectives achieve meaning not because a single goal or a single objective is written so that it is clear, specific, and measurable, but because they are part of a series of linguistic statements that have been logically and sequentially developed. Examining a single goal or objective statement out of context cannot convey summative meaning any more than a single sentence taken out of context from a novel can convey the summative meaning of the novel.

The inability of staff members to develop acceptable goals and objectives has more to do with the difficulty of the technology and frequent attempts to use it in an incomplete and piecemeal fashion than it does with staff ineptness. Writing goals and objectives and writing novels both require a considerable degree of writing skill and an ability to clearly express one's thoughts with written language in a well-developed, clear, and logical fashion. This skill can be learned.

How to Write Goals and Objectives

The linguistic structure of goals and objectives can be simple or complicated. Neophytes often err by trying to write a statement that is too complicated. For beginners it is recommended that each linguistic statement, that is, a goal or an objective, be written in the following form:

Infinitive: Each statement should begin with an infinitive, which consists of the infinitive marker "to" and a verb that indicates the action to be taken. Each statement should contain only one infinitive. Measuring accomplishment is easier if there is only one action to measure. For an excellent taxonomy of verbs useful for writing goals and objectives, see the work of Gronlund (1970).

Subject: Each statement must have a subject that conveys what is going to be accomplished. There should be only one subject in each statement.

Measurement Device: Each statement should have some device incorporated into the statement that makes clear how the accomplishment of the goal or objective is going to be measured and documented. Often, this measurement device is a time frame that is specified for accomplishing the goal. However, many other measurement devices can be used.

There are exceptions to this last requirement. Some goals and objectives do not contain specific measurement devices, but are simply declarations of an intention to accomplish something or point the agency in a specific direction. When this is the case, other support goals or objectives that are measurable are developed to measure the original goal.

Consider the following agency program planning goal: *To operate a women's softball league during the summer of 1995*. This goal begins with the infinitive *to operate*, which indicates an intention to accomplish by organizing, publicizing, and running the event. *Operate* is a verb that is a summative, final action that includes all of the other actions necessary to complete the operation of the event. The subject of the goal is *a women's softball league*, which is the entity to be developed and operated. The measurement device is *during the summer of 1995*. In stating this, we have said that we will consider our goal accomplished if the league is operated during the summer of 1995. With a timeline, we have created a terminal behavior that is clear and specific enough to be measured.

What is unclear in this goal? The size of the softball league, where it is going to be held, and other details of operation. These details, however, are unnecessary at this level of goal development. The specific details of league operation will be presented later in an additional series of program design goals. What is important in the current goal is that the agency has committed its resources to a specific project with a targeted completion date.

In writing goal and objective statements, one should keep the thought conveyed in one goal or objective simple. Never use a conjunction in a goal or objective statement. If a conjunction is used, a second thought (either a second verb, subject, or measurement device) is added to the statement that will unnecessarily complicate the goal or objective. If there are two goals or objectives, then write two statements—do not try to join them together in one statement. It is also important to be parsimonious in writing goals and objectives. Try to write a simple, clear, concise statement to convey what is intended to be accomplished.

Hierarchical Arrangement

Earlier it was satirically conveyed that clearly written goals and objectives are not attainable. The case was somewhat overstated to make the point that meaning cannot be totally achieved with a single clearly written goal or objective statement. Clear writing is important, but no writing can be clear enough to convey objective, absolute meaning; that is, meaning that is so clear that anyone could read the goal or objective and immediately know what and how something is going to be accomplished.

The application of goal and objective technology in organizations is a means to an end. It is a method for focusing the organization and giving it direction in accomplishing its mission. The task, then, is to develop goal and objective statements that have *operational clarity*. These statements are operationally clear when they are clear to the staff who must implement them. They provide direction to the organization and its staff, and they can be measured so that the accomplishments of the organization can be documented. Operationally clear goals and objectives have operational meaning and provide a way for the organization to focus, organize, direct, and document its activities, thereby helping it accomplish its mission.

Well-written goal and objective statements are certainly more useful than poorly written ones. Additional operational meaning of these statements, however, is achieved by including them in a hierarchical arrangement of goal and objective statements.

Goal and objective statements are arranged in a hierarchical order that has specificity as its primary variable. Statements move from the general and inclusive to the more narrow and specific. This hierarchical transition is illustrated in Figure 4-1. The process begins with the organization's mission or vision statement. This statement delimits, in a general way, what the organization is trying to accomplish. The mission statement itself is not measurable. Its accomplishment is measured by writing a series of linguistic goal and objective statements that are increasingly more specific, until an objective is developed that is operationally clear, specific, and measurable. There can be many succeeding levels of goals and objectives between the mission statement and the final, measurable objectives. How many levels of statements there will be depends on the complexity of the organization and the complexity of the content area for which goals and objectives are being written.

Figure 4-1.
Hierarchy of Goals and Objectives

Linguistic mode	Type of statement
General, unspecific, not measurable	Mission or vision statement
	Goal
Clear, specific, and measurable	Objective

Figure 4-2 on page 63 provides a diagrammatic representation of this hierarchy with some examples. Note that the
mission statement defines the purpose of the agency and provides direction about what the agency will accomplish in the
larger community—but, it is not necessarily measurable. The
short-range planning goals are not measurable either, but outline
an area of program development and begin to state what it is
from the entire universe of possible activities that the agency will
try to accomplish. They are given further definition, and their
accomplishment is measured with the management by objective
statements that usually accompany budget preparation. At this
point, resources are allocated to the accomplishment of a specific
task that is measurable. Finally, program design goals are developed
at two levels. One defines the experience that the programmer
will attempt to facilitate. Each of these statements have some
implication for program design and/or operation, and thus they
must be consciously dealt with in the design or operation of the
program to ensure that they will occur. A second level of development defines what patrons will be able to do after completing
the program; i.e. their terminal performance. Additional examples of these are provided in Chapters Six, Seven, and Nine.

Framing the Mission Statement

"A mission statement is a statement of the organization's
purpose—what it wants to accomplish in the larger environment" (Kotler and Anderson 1993, p. 27). It provides the direction
needed so that the efforts of many independent work groups are
focused toward the accomplishment of the organization's reason
for existing. In a mission statement, it is as important to define
what the agency will not accomplish as well as what it will
accomplish. This notion is illustrated in Figure 4-3 on page 64.
For example, mission statements include the provision of recreation services and facilities. Concomitantly, they exclude other
possible tasks that the agency could undertake, but chooses not
to for a variety of reasons.

Figure 4-2.
Goal and Objective Hierarchy with Examples

Hierarchy	Examples

ORGANIZATIONAL MISSION

Not measurable, defines
purpose of agency

•To ensure that all citizens of
Anytown USA have access to
comprehensive leisure services
including activities, events, and
facilities by serving as a provider, referral agency, or catalyst for their development.

3-5 YEAR SHORT-RANGE
PLANNING GOALS

Defines basic areas of
programming effort; identifies
the types of activities, events,
services, or facilities that
will be provided.

•To develop a comprehensive
sports program for children.

1-YEAR MANAGEMENT
BY OBJECTIVE GOALS

Specific programs to
accomplish, usually tied to a
budget element or
work program.

•To develop a summer softball
league for girls 12-16 years of
age by May 1, 1995 with at least
10 teams.

PROGRAM DESIGN GOALS

Statements of leisure
experiences desired and/or
terminal performance outcomes
to be demonstrated by
participants.

•Each team will have regulation uniforms.
•Each game will have at least
two certified umpires.
•At the end of the league, each
player on a roster will have
played in at least one half of the
innings played.
•At the end of the league, each
participant will score 75% or
more correct answers on a test
about the rules of softball.

Figure 4-3.
Limits Defined by the Mission Statement

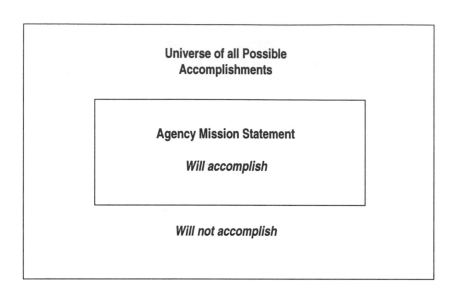

It is also important to recognize that mission statements are somewhat elastic in what they include. They are nebulous in order to provide maximum flexibility for the agency in the future. Mission statements are considered long-term commitments of the agency and are not usually altered in the short run. A very narrow, specific mission statement would commit the agency to providing a narrow range of services to its patron group. A nebulous statement gives the agency maximum leeway to respond to changing demands and needs without continually rewriting the mission statement. Developing a mission statement, then, requires one to define some area for accomplishment without being so restrictive that the agency has no latitude for flexibility in accomplishing the mission. Additional detail about how to write a mission statement is provided in Chapter Six.

Goals and Objectives—How Are They Different?

There is a great deal of confusion about the difference between goals and objectives. Practitioners who have shared stories with the author about hiring consultants to help them develop goals and objectives spent the whole time trying to specify the difference between a goal and an objective. In this book, we will take a pragmatic approach to this problem and assume there is no practical difference between a goal and an objective. *It can thus be deduced that the relationship between goals and objectives is a syntactical one that can only be determined by the position each statement occupies in a hierarchy of goal and objective statements. Furthermore, objectives for some levels in an organization are goals for employees occupying the next lower level.*

However, the relationship between the goals and objectives is important. First, objectives are the measurement points for a goal. Therefore, it is accepted that if all of the objectives identified for a goal are accomplished, the goal is considered accomplished. Secondly, one must consider the location in the organizational structure for which the goal or objective is being developed. Very often objectives for one level become the goals to be accomplished in the next descending level of the organization. In this way, goals and objectives network the activities of the organization and allow work activity to be unified from the highest statement in the organization (mission statement) through the activities of a part-time recreation leader; that is, an objective that states what the leader intends for participants to accomplish in a program.

Two assumptions govern goal and objective theory and the development of goal and objective statements:

1. The accomplishment of a set of goals that support the mission statement or a set of objectives that support an individual goal will be accepted as proof of mission or goal accomplishment.
2. Any list of goals and objectives that we use operationally to document mission or goal accomplishment is only a partial list of the many goals and objectives that could have been developed. Selection of any goal or objective is normative; one must realize that any goal or objective selected is just a sample from a larger list of all possible goals or objectives that could have been selected. This latter point is illustrated in Figure 4-4 on page 67.

Representative Nature of Selected Goals and Objectives

Figure 4-4 on the following page is a further elaboration of Figure 4-3 on page 64. In Figure 4-4, there are three types of boxes: A, B, and C. Box A illustrates the entire universe of all possible accomplishments that the agency could undertake. Box B illustrates the space from the entire universe of possible accomplishments that the agency has delimited with its mission statement and thereby indicated its intent to accomplish. Box C represents the space occupied by any goal the agency has indicated it intends to accomplish.

Figure 4-4 graphically illustrates that any goal or objective is only a representative sample from the entire universe of goals and objectives that could be drawn from the universe defined by the mission statement.

All of the space outside box B but within box A represents possible accomplishments that have been excluded from the agency's mission statement. The space within boxes C1 and C2 illustrates the accomplishments that could be achieved within the space of possible accomplishments defined by these two goals. The space outside boxes C1 and C2 but within box B includes all other possible goals that could be accomplished within the parameters defined by the agency's mission statement. Any set of goals, then, represents only a small portion of all possible goals that could be selected. The Xs within boxes C1 and C2 represent objectives for accomplishing each goal. Again, there is room for many more Xs in each box. This illustrates that any list of objectives identified for a goal is only a partial list of all possible objectives that could be developed to document goal accomplishment.

Selecting goals and objectives should be taken seriously. As illustrated in Figure 4-4, in using goal and objective technology to demonstrate agency accomplishments, one is allowing the agency to be evaluated on only a small portion of the data that could be used. Because of this, it is important that the goals and objectives selected be representative of the agency's total mission and typical undertakings.

Figure 4-4.
Limits Defined by Goals and Objectives

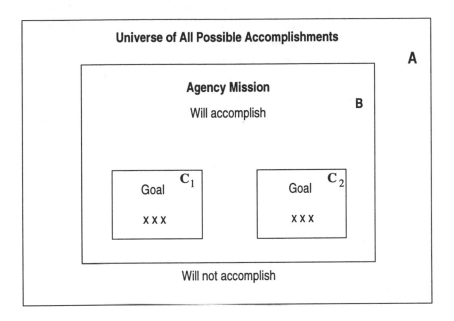

Staff Participation in Developing Goals and Objectives

The process through which goals and objectives are developed and implemented in an organization is extremely important to the success of their use in the organization. It is important to answer the question: Where should goals and objectives originate in the organization? Should they originate at the top and be passed down through succeeding levels to the bottommost employees? Or should goals and objectives originate at the bottom and be passed through each hierarchical stratum until they are all accumulated at the top?

In the former case, employees have very little commitment to goals imposed from above. In the latter case, employees find it difficult to develop goals when isolated from any type of organizational direction. Using this latter method often results in a collection of widely diversified goals, with little of the focus needed for effective organizational action.

The most reasonable procedure is for the goals to originate from the top of the organization and for each managerial level to pass them to the employees below. Through a process of iterative negotiation, the employees will need to develop a set of objectives they intend to achieve in order to accomplish the goal. Although several iterations may be required before a final list of objectives acceptable to both employee and supervisor is developed, this process does allow for employee action that is consistent with the organizational mission and employee input into the final work to be accomplished. In this way, the activities of employees are networked and integrated in an effective manner.

Conclusion

Goals and objectives are linguistic statements that delimit some area of activity to be accomplished. It is important to understand the relationship of goals to objectives and how they are to be written for effective action. By using goal and objective technology, an agency defines what it will accomplish from the large number of possible activities it could undertake. In this way, the collective resources of the agency are focused on accomplishing tasks that demonstrate fulfillment of the agency's mission. It is important to select goals and objectives that are comprehensive and diverse enough to be representative of the agency's breadth of service responsibilities. Additional information and examples of how these concepts are used in programming are included in Chapters Six, Seven, and Nine.

References, Chapter Four

Gronlund, N.D. 1970. *Stating Behavioral Objectives for Classroom Instruction*. New York: Macmillan.

Kotler, P., and G. Armstrong. 1993. *Marketing: An Introduction* (3rd ed.). Englewood Cliffs, NJ: Prentice-Hall.

Patton, M. 1978. *Utilization-focused Evaluation*. Beverly Hills, CA: Sage.

Photo courtesy of Joliet Park District, Joliet, IL. Photo by Michael Curran.

5

The Program Development Cycle

Programs are developed in a methodical and cyclical manner. A conceptualization of the steps included in program development and the order in which they occur are included in Figure 5-1, page 72: the Program Development Cycle.The cycle includes four major stages and nine specific steps. In this chapter, the overall concept of the Program Development Cycle and the function of each step will be briefly explained. In subsequent chapters, the methods and techniques used in each step will be developed further.

Before explaining the cycle, however, we need to comment on the actual nature of program development. Although the diagrammatic representation of the cycle gives the illusion that planning a program is a linear, sequential process, in reality it is an iterative, interactive process requiring continued recycling of these steps until an operational program plan is completed.

Programs are developed through trial and error methods of implementation that continue until a suitable program design is developed. A perfect program is not planned and then implemented. The notion that perfect planning must occur before implementing a program is a myth that is perpetuated in the literature. Peters and Waterman (1982) clearly point out that one of the distinguishing characteristics of successful organizations in America today is that they act on their environment. Successful organizations do not allow new ideas to be "planned" into oblivion. They act on an idea as soon as possible, evaluate their actions, rework the idea, and implement it again. Operating in this manner allows organizations to have a number of experiments under way at all times. Successful ideas are nurtured and developed further. Unsuccessful ideas are dropped. Successful organizations, then, have a number of ongoing experiments at any one time to observe and possibly nurture and expand.

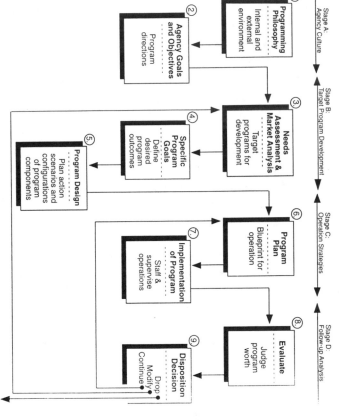

Figure 5-1.
The Program Development Cycle
©1994 J. Robert Rossman

Stage A:
Agency Culture

① Programming Philosophy — Internal and external environment

② Agency Goals and Objectives — Program directions

Stage B:
Target Program Development

③ Needs Assessment & Market Analysis — Target programs for development

④ Specific Program Goals — Define desired program outcomes

⑤ Program Design — Plan action scenarios and configurations of program components

Stage C:
Operation Strategies

⑥ Program Plan — Blueprint for operation

⑦ Implementation of Program — Staff & supervise operations

Stage D:
Follow-up Analysis

⑧ Evaluate — Judge program worth

⑨ Disposition Decision — Drop / Modify / Continue

Terminate

Successful products and programs are the result of ongoing, incremental expansion and improvement over a period of time.

In programming, this same principle needs to be followed. The Program Development Cycle provides a path to follow, and it contains a number of recycling loops that illustrate the need to retrace certain steps in the ongoing development of a program. Because of the way this illustration is drawn, it appears that following the recycling loops is done only because of a failure to implement the system properly in the first place. This is not the case! It is very likely that a successful program will have been through several iterations of the cycle during its development. Having to rework a program through several trial and error operations of the program is the normal course for program development—not an indication of failure.

The Four Major Stages

There are four major stages in the program development cycle. In each stage, the major goal to be accomplished makes a unique contribution to the final program that will be developed.

Stage A: Agency Culture

In Stage A, agency culture, the programmer develops an understanding of the agency's programming philosophy and the overall programmatic goals of the agency. These goals provide a general direction for program development and specify the area of programming that an agency will develop. Most often the document that outlines this direction is the agency's mission statement or statement of philosophy, accompanied by a five-year strategic plan for implementing the agency's philosophy. A programmer often cannot have any short-term influence over the direction outlined by the mission statement because it is a policy-level decision that the programmer is not in a position to influence or because the time frame covered by the document is longer than the more short-range task of program development.

This stage is relatively static because of the stability of an agency's mission and direction. It is usually unnecessary to complete the work outlined in this stage for each program developed. Programmers must make certain, however, to demonstrate that the programs they are developing are contained within the activities defined as the mission and purpose of the agency and that their programs contribute to fulfilling the agency's mission.

Stage B: Target Program Development

In Stage B, target program development, the programmer begins focusing on the unique programming needs of specifically targeted client groups. In this stage, the programmer combines the data from patron needs analyses with the resource limits of the agency and its mission and goals. The programmer then designs and develops programs for specific groups of clients that the agency has indicated it wishes to serve. It is in this stage that programs are designed for specific groups of people who can be identified and described with some precision. Programs are designed to create programmed leisure experiences that will meet client needs within the framework of the agency's policy, resource limits, and mission. To accomplish this requires an understanding of the experience one is trying to create and an understanding of how to organize and coordinate the efforts of a work group to produce leisure services.

Stage C: Operation Strategies

In Stage C, operation strategies, a written program that is a "blueprint for operation" is developed, and the program is implemented. Patrons actually engage the environment created by the programmer and interact with the environment—patrons experience the program. During operation of a program, the programmer oversees the implementation of all details, including program promotion, registering participants, staffing, supervising operations, and perhaps engaging in face-to-face interactions with clients. Patrons who participate in a properly implemented, programmed experience will have the experience envisioned and intended by the programmer during the design step of program development.

Stage D: Follow-up Analysis

In Stage D, follow-up analysis, the program is evaluated and a disposition decision made on the basis of evaluation data about what management action to take with the program. The worth of a program should be determined from many perspectives. With these evaluation data, a decision about whether to continue, drop, or modify a program is made. Evaluation data need to be sufficiently detailed and comprehensive so that appropriate program modifications can be made if warranted. In this book, emphasis is placed on using evaluation data that have been systematically collected from many sources so that disposition decisions can be made from a broad-based analysis of the evidence.

Stage A

Step 1: Programming Philosophy

In step one, the programmer either learns the agency's programming philosophy or helps develop the philosophy. Each recreation organization delivers a different type of service. Differences in these services are partly accounted for by different missions and philosophies of various organizations. For example, the Girl Scouts deliver different services than the Y.M.C.A. The Y.M.C.A. delivers different services than municipal recreation agencies. Municipal recreation agencies deliver different services than church recreation agencies. Church recreation agencies deliver different services than commercial recreation agencies. And so on.

An agency's programming philosophy is formally articulated in the mission statement and is the result of several years of development. According to Pfeffer and Salancik (1978), a mission statement most often reflects an agency's formal declaration of its intended clientele in order to seek the resources it needs to function and ensure its survival. An agency's mission is developed through an analysis of both the internal and external environments of the agency. Accomplishing this requires completing an organizational and community needs assessment.

The mission of the agency is developed from the joint implications of the needs of the community in which it is located; the identified needs of patrons, and the needs, resources, and abilities of the organization itself.

Step 2: Agency Goals and Objectives

In step two, general planning directions for the development of program services are outlined. The long-range philosophy or mission of the agency is further defined with the development of agency goals and objectives. These goals and objectives delineate in a hierarchical, systematic manner what the agency intends to accomplish. Usually these are developed with three- to five-year goal statements that are defined further with one-year management by objective statements.

It is important to recognize that a programmer will often be responding with one-year objectives to three- or five-year goals that have been developed by higher level administrators or by a board. The policy-making body of an organization will establish the agency's mission statement. Staff members, however, are often responsible for developing specific goals and objectives for implementing program services that will fulfill the agency's mission. Upper-level administrators usually develop the three- to five-year planning goals and then ask lower-level staff members to develop specific one-year programming goals to implement the longer-range goals. The programmer, then, is often responding to a three- to five-year goal with a recommendation about annual program services that will be developed to implement the longer-range goals.

Stage B

Step 3: Needs Assessment and Analysis

In the needs assessment step, the programmer tries to identify program services and benefit packages that cohorts of targeted clients may want. The goal in this step is to identify patron desires so that program services can be developed to meet identified client desires. According to Carpenter and Howe (1985), needs assessment is defined as "a process of identifying and discovering constituents' leisure needs, attitudes, values, and behaviors, as well as areas in which clarification, improvement, or reinforcement of leisure functioning is desired" (p. 78).

Needs assessment is a misunderstood step of the program development cycle. The objective in this step is to systematically assess the needs and desires of the organization's client groups so that one can prioritize the allocation of limited resources among competing interests. Too often, programmers simply look at needs assessment as a process that is supposed to identify for them a completed program they can implement. This is hardly ever the case. Needs assessment provides partial information about clients, their needs, possible services for implementation, available resources, and other types of information. The information developed in a needs assessment must be analyzed and interpreted by a well-trained programmer before recommendations for program services can be made from the data generated.

Interpreting needs assessment data and developing program recommendations from them are unique abilities of the leisure service profession. Accomplishing this task requires an understanding of leisure behavior and the factors that contribute to and block the occurrence of the leisure experience. Too much of the literature about leisure needs assessment assumes that the problem with needs assessment is that programmers are not collecting the data properly. The recommended solution is better training in the techniques of collecting social science data. What is needed, however, is better training of programmers in understanding leisure behavior and how leisure experiences are constructed by the individuals in them. This understanding will provide a better framework for interpreting the data. Once programmers understand how to use data in moving from needs assessment to program designs, improving data collection will improve the whole process. But until there is a better understanding of how to use data in the programming process, focusing on acquiring better data is of marginal value. In the assessment step, then, the programmer attempts to systematically collect information about clients that will be useful in developing and revising program services so that agency resources can be allocated to serving identified client wants.

Step 4: Developing Specific Program Goals

Once needs assessment data are collected and analyzed, it should be possible to begin identifying some specific programmatic goals that the data have indicated. These goals will be partial descriptors of the program to be developed. For example, from the data collected one may be able to indicate that there is a need for a program in a specific geographical area of a community, for specific age groups, during a certain time period, with specific outcomes from participation. On a military base, for instance, one may discover a need for a program off base, for servicemen under 21, on weekend evenings, that will offer the opportunity for socialization with members of the opposite sex.

A key point here is that in this step one begins to integrate needs assessment data with the two previous steps, which have already provided some direction regarding program development. Those steps gave some normative policy direction about what programs the agency will develop. Needs assessment represents the first instance in the cycle where the needs of individual clients enter the program development cycle. In step four, the implications of these two are integrated, and a data-based description of a needed service consistent with the agency's mission is developed.

Step 5: Program Design

The purpose of program design is to conceptualize and plan the action scenarios and configurations of program components needed to operate a program. Program design is the major transitional step between needs assessment and operation. During this step, programmers develop leisure experiences for patrons by vicariously experiencing the program before it occurs through projective imagery and other design techniques. During the design process, programs are designed that are within the limits determined by the agency's mission statement, that meet identified client needs determined during the needs assessment, and that are feasible with agency resource limits and operationally possible for the agency in the community where it is located. In the program design phase, needs assessment data are interpreted and analyzed in a manner that results in the design of an actual program.

Stage C

Step 6: Program Plan

In step six, the programmer prepares a written plan that details all of the arrangements and scenarios needed to actually operate the experience conceptualized in step five. The program plan is similar to a musical score for an orchestra or a blueprint for a building. The musical score communicates to each musician his or her role in performing the piece written by the composer. A blueprint coordinates the activities of many different tradespeople so that their collective efforts result in the building intended by the architect. Similarly, a program plan communicates the program concept to all who will be involved in the program's operation and what each person must accomplish so that participants can have the experience intended by the designer. The written program plan is also used to guide future operations of the program.

Step 7: Implementation

In step seven, the program is actually implemented and operated. There is much to be attended to in this step, including obtaining and arranging the physical space for the program, promoting the program, registering patrons, staffing the program, supervising the operation, and other matters. This step occupies the majority of the programmer's time. A myriad of details must be attended to in operating a large number of programs simultaneously. In reality, the programmer usually has a number of programs in various stages of operation going on at the same time. Too many programmers are overwhelmed by the need to attend to all of the implementation details of program operation. As a result, they overlook or circumvent the other steps of the Program Development Cycle. This often leads to unsuccessful programs.

Pressured by implementation details, many programmers focus too heavily on the importance of implementation and often cite inadequate implementation as the primary cause of a failed program. In analyzing and evaluating program failure, the programmer should recycle completely through the Program Development Cycle, as illustrated in Figure 5-1, page 72. Inadequate interpretation of needs assessment information and improper program design are also possible causes of program failure. It is even possible that one has developed a program that does not fit in with the agency's mission or strategic plan outlined in steps one and two.

All that is involved in this step is detailed in subsequent chapters. For now it is sufficient to indicate that at this point patrons actually come into the program, interact in the social occasion designed by the programmer, and have an experience—hopefully a leisure experience.

Stage D

Step 8: Evaluation

In step eight, a post-program evaluation is conducted. Evaluation is a procedure designed to help judge the worth of program services. It is an elastic concept that covers many different activities. There are several ways of conducting evaluations, and an agency will have many different evaluation activities occurring simultaneously. The emphasis in this text will be on developing evaluations that provide value judgments from many value perspectives. Conducting systematic program evaluation assures ongoing managerial review of all program services.

Step 9: Disposition Decision

In step nine, the evaluation data developed in step eight are used to make one of three decisions about the future of a program. The programmer will select one of three alternatives: to continue the program without modification, to continue it with modifications, or to end it. Each of these decisions leads the programmer to different recycling locations of the Program Development Cycle. When programmers end a program, as the arrow in Figure 5-1 illustrates, they leave the Program Development Cycle. However, it is always necessary to predict the implications of program termination before actually ending a service.

The decision to modify a program contains a larger number of possibilities than do the other two decisions. A program may be modified many different ways. Before modifying it, the programmer should thoroughly recycle the Program Development Cycle and not simply assume that the difficulty was with implementation or some other single step. If a program has failed, small omissions and failures at each step of the cycle are as likely the cause of failure as a single glaring omission in one step. As discussed at the beginning of this chapter, a program will often need to be modified several times before a totally suitable operational procedure is developed.

In deciding to continue a program as currently operated, the programmer recycles to step six—the program plan. In this instance, a written plan is ready for implementation at the next operation of the program. Now complete Exercise 5-1.

Exercise 5-1.
Program Development Assumptions

In class, discuss the difference between assuming that programs are planned perfectly before implementation and assuming that they are developed incrementally over time through many iterations of operation.
- What differences are implied by each of these assumptions for programmers?
- How must programmers operate under each of these assumptions?

Conclusion

The Program Development Cycle illustrates all of the steps necessary for designing and implementing a program. Although there seems to be a large number of steps in the cycle, one does not actually complete all of them during the development of each program. For example, steps one and two involving agency culture are not completed for each program developed. The implications of these two steps are incorporated in each program, but the tasks included in these steps are implemented infrequently. The same is true for step three, needs assessment. An in-depth, systematic collection of needs assessment data may occur only annually or every two to three years. However, the implications of these data are incorporated into all programs developed after the data have been collected. Programmers tend to focus too much on implementation details without giving sufficient attention to the other steps of the Program Development Cycle. Program implementation is important, but it is equally important to develop program goals from needs assessment data, to design programs before writing a program plan, to prepare a written   program plan, to properly implement a program, to evaluate the program, and to make a data-based disposition decision regarding the status of the program service.

References, Chapter Five

Carpenter, G.M., and C.Z. Howe. 1985. *Programming Leisure Experiences: A Cyclical Approach.* Englewood Cliffs, NJ: Prentice-Hall.

Peters, T.J., and R.H. Waterman, Jr. 1982. *In Search of Excellence: Lessons From America's Best Run Companies.* New York: Harper & Row.

Pfeffer, J., and G.R. Salancik. 1978. *The External Control of Organizations: A Resource Dependence Perspective.* New York: Harper & Row.

Part II: Determining Agency Culture

In Part II, the first stage of the Program Development Cycle is discussed. This stage involves assessing the culture in which the programming organization operates, developing a mission statement, and developing program planning goals for the organization. The leisure service programs discussed in this book are always designed and delivered by programmers operating in an organization. The programmer must therefore understand the environment in which the organization operates, and how this environment influences the services that the organization can develop and operate.

There are two chapters in this section. In Chapter Six, how the organization's mission statement is developed through assessing the threats and opportunities in its environment and its own internal strengths and weaknesses is explained. In Chapter Seven, the role and use of goal and objective technology in managing the agency's program services is explained and examples are provided.

Photo courtesy of Parks and Recreation Department, Aurora, Colorado.

6

Developing the Agency's Programming Mission

As stated in Chapter Four, a mission statement defines the agency's purpose and outlines what it intends to accomplish in the larger environment. Knowles (1970) describes this environment as a "pool of needs" including individual, organizational, and community needs. Developing successful services requires that programmers not only develop programs that meet identified needs of individuals, but also that the programs developed meet community needs and contribute to the organization's need to fulfill a purpose and role in the community.

To succeed, programmers must understand how the conflicts and demands created by the issues surrounding these three—individual, organizational, and community needs—influence program development. Collectively, this analysis will lead to the development of a mission that will provide direction to day-to-day operations and help confirm the need to develop some programs and restrict the development of others. Although a mission statement is not developed every year, it will influence every program operated. Thus, the programmer must understand the mission and its implications.

The remainder of this chapter deals with the issues that should be analyzed to develop a mission statement. The discussion is roughly organized around the three types of issues that must be analyzed—individual, organizational, and community. The reader is cautioned that these divisions are somewhat arbitrary and there will be overlap in some cases. Furthermore, at this point, individual needs are not completely investigated. The more detailed analysis that permits the development of specific, custom-tailored program services is covered at a different point in the Program Development Cycle and is discussed in Chapter Eight.

Generally, the analysis to develop a mission statement is conducted to answer the following questions:

Individual: Who are our patrons? What kinds of services do they want? What types of services can we provide them, i.e., what business should we be in?

Organizational: What are the strengths and weaknesses of our organization? What are the activities, events, services, and facilities we can develop a unique ability to offer?

Community: What are the threats and opportunities in our environment? Where can we make a difference that matters?

Figure 6-1 diagrams what is included in each of these three.

Figure 6-1.
Issues That Must Be Analyzed to Develop a Mission

Individual	*Organizational*	*Community*
Macro Trends	Resources	Resources
Effects on	Organizing Authority	Community Needs
local community	Organizational	Public Interest
	strengths and	Assessing
	weaknesses	current
		opportunities
		Relationships
		among
		providers

Individual

Every organization must determine who it intends to serve, and this intention should be articulated in the mission statement. Government agencies are required to serve all who are within their jurisdiction, so their mission statements are usually inclusive. However, a commercial agency may want to serve individuals in one activity, for instance a tennis club, who have higher incomes. Thus, their mission statement would narrowly define their service population. Many not-for-profit organizations may also have a mission statement that reflects a more restricted target population whom they intend to serve.

If there are restrictions on the type of service the agency intends to provide or any other similar restriction, it should also be reflected in the mission statement. For example, Little League organizations have both a restricted age group they serve and a single activity that they provide.

Assessing the Macro Environment

The needs of any population are influenced by social forces that create opportunities and pose challenges for an agency. These forces can be local, regional, or national in origin. Information about them and their potential effects—either positive or negative—on the leisure service agency are gathered by an ongoing scanning and interpreting of information about the agency's environment. Potential sources of information for this analysis include local, regional, and national print and broadcast media; government-issued technical reports; planning reports; political activity; and developments in the entertainment industry.

It is almost impossible to give directions about the reports, information, and so forth that one should take into account. Programmers do need to remain aware of possible threats to program continuation and special opportunities to seize for program development. For example, the larger percentage of working women today threatens mother-tot programs unless they are scheduled around the workday. Unless the programmer alters the scheduling of these types of programs, they are likely to fail because no client group is available to attend them.

Programmers must also remain aware of national trends and media happenings in order to seize on ideas and develop timely programs. Several years ago, Michael Jackson look-alike contests were popular. Today, few programmers operate these programs. There is a timeliness to programming that can only be achieved by scanning the external environment of the organization for emerging trends. In each case, the programmer must answer the question: *What are the specific operational implications of this, if any, for my agency?*

Programmers should prepare themselves to systematically track what is happening in five areas: demographic, social, technological, economic, and political. Developments in each of these areas are certain to have discernible effects on programming. The first three of these will have the greatest effect on individual leisure needs. The latter two could affect any of the three—individual, organizational, or community needs. Each of these trends should be analyzed from a local, regional, and national perspective. It is important to ascertain whether national or regional developments will actually affect the local community. For example, although the nation may be suffering from an economic recession, the local community may not be suffering any of its effects. A brief review of key indicators to observe is outlined below.

Demographic

The average age of the U.S. population has been rising steadily for the past decade. We are becoming a nation of older citizens, and future program services and facilities will need to be developed with this fact in mind. In developing program services, programmers should analyze the age groups of their service community. What is the age of the majority of the citizens? In what age groups are most of the clients? Is the population distributed normally or are there concentrations of patrons in specific age ranges such as senior citizens or young adults? Are there significantly large populations in transitional age cohorts, such as teenagers? If so, are your program services prepared for their demands when they reach their next age range?

Social

Are there emerging life styles, customs, or habits that will affect programs? What effect will single-parent families have? What will be the effect of large numbers of single people of all ages on programming? What effect will women who are working have on programming? What effect will newly immigrated people from Hispanic and Asian cultures have on current programs? What is the educational level and social status of the clientele? What are the local customs and mores of the community?

Unlike organizational and aggregated individual needs, community needs are created by social forces in society. They are also created because people live in communities with a shared value system that binds them together and because people take joint responsibility for preserving those values.

Thus, the reader should understand that the concept of community used here is inclusive and could include religious, corporate, military, or other communities that would have a shared value system that would need to be reflected in the development of a mission statement.

Technological

What emerging technology will have an impact on program services? For example, there were many heated discussions about whether snowmobiles, when they first appeared, should be allowed in park areas because of the environmental damage they caused. Which new technologies should an agency try to use or service? What new technologies are patrons likely to purchase and bring to agency facilities to use? What new technologies will they need instruction to use? Should video games be allowed in community recreation centers, Y.M.C.A.s, or church recreation centers? What impact will newly developed home entertainment devices have on attendance at programs?

Economic

What is the basis of the local economy? Is it diversified and therefore likely to remain stable? Is it an economy based on a single industry? What is the current economic stability of this industry? How much annual income do the majority of patrons have? How much discretionary income do the patrons have? What percentage of the leisure service market share does the agency currently have? Is this likely to increase, resulting in increased income? Are there additional competitors who are likely to cut into the agency's market share? If so, what are the financial implications of this? What is the current tax base and tax rate? Is either of these likely to increase or decrease? If so, what are the programming implications?

Political

What is the political orientation of the local elected officials? Are they supporters of public recreation? How political is the administration of the agency? How many jobs in the agency are patronage jobs? How receptive are local elected officials to using the powers of government to encourage privately developed recreation enterprises? What is the political climate in the state? What is the political climate in the nation? Is it conservative or liberal, and what are either of these attitudes likely to do to funding and program operations?

Organization

Organizations are dynamic entities whose needs must be met to keep them operating. One of the most important needs of an organization is to continue its existence. This is most assured if it fulfills an identifiable role in the larger society that controls its resources. Thus, the development of any mission statement is a search for unique opportunities the agency can fulfill. A unique opportunity is either one that few others are fulfilling or one that the agency has some differential advantage over other agencies to provide. Since no agency will be omnipotent, the analysis will try to identify the agency's strengths and weaknesses (Zikmund and d'Amico 1993) relative to its possible uniquenesses.

Resource Dependency

Programming organizations are resource dependent: their survival depends on successfully acquiring the resources needed to deliver services to their client groups. The level of resources available will determine, to some degree, what the organization's mission may be. Adequate or unique resources will create the differential advantage to provide some unique opportunities, but a lack thereof will be a limitation and thereby restrict what the agency can accomplish. Thus, resources are an issue at both the organization and community levels. Pfeffer and Salancik (1978) have taken the following position:

> Our position is that organizations survive to the extent that they are effective. Their effectiveness derives from the management of demands, particularly the demands of interest groups upon which the organizations depend for resources and support. (p. 2)

The organization's mission must be developed to focus organizational effort toward meeting the needs of its relevant clients and publics. Resource dependency is complicated by the fact that no organization is completely self-contained, and organizations both compete with and depend on other organizations for resources. Pfeffer and Salancik (1978) comment on this dilemma by stating:

> Organizations are embedded in an environment comprised of other organizations. They depend on those other organizations for the many resources they themselves require. (p. 2)

What an organization may accomplish is partly dependent on what other organizations will allow it to accomplish or want it to accomplish. Organizational success, then, is partly determined by the organization's external environment.

Organizing Rationale

Often, leisure service organizations are created to offer specific types of recreation programming and to achieve specific purposes. Kraus (1985) has identified eight different types of organizations that exist to offer recreation service: public recreation and park agencies; voluntary, nonprofit organizations, including sectarian and nonsectarian; commercial recreation enterprises; private-membership organizations; armed forces recreation; campus recreation; corporate recreation; and therapeutic recreation.

Each of these organizations has specific social ends that they are attempting to promote through participation in recreation activities. An overriding need of such organizations is the need to accomplish the social ends identified as part of the rationale for creating the organization in the first place. As Tillman (1973) has observed, "Agencies use [a] recreation program as a tool for obtaining their objectives" (p.19). Different agencies offer different leisure services because of the social ends they are organized to promote. For example, the Boy Scouts of America offers different programming than Y.M.C.A.s. Although they may serve similar youth, their program services differ because their perceived social missions differ.

Marketing literature suggests that individual needs should be the central driving force in organizations. This is a desirable goal to strive for in all leisure service organizations. However, organizational social ends will narrow the range of programs that may be provided and thereby have an overriding influence on the organization's mission in the short run. For example, the organizational mission of campus recreation organizations limits their concern to students, faculty, and alumni from a specific university. Once this parameter is accepted, the organization becomes concerned with what targeted client groups want, and marketing concepts and ideas about how to determine individual wants become useful. Similarly, armed forces recreation providers are solely concerned with active duty military personnel, their dependents, and retirees. All of the programming efforts in the armed services are directed towards helping one or more of these three groups of individuals. The organization's mission will influence the program services it delivers. Examine this concept further by completing Exercise 6-1.

Exercise 6-1.

Identify and discuss how the same program service, such as a Fourth of July Day Special Event, would differ if organized by each of the agencies paired below.
- How does the organization's mission influence the way this program would be developed?

Air Force Recreation Services .... Y.M.C.A.
Public recreation agency .... Private country club
University campus recreation .... Corporate recreation
Easter Seal (community based) .... An institutional therapeutic recreation setting for physically disabled children

---

Assessing the Organization

Assessing the strengths and limitations of the organization is done by examining a number of factors. A checklist approach for self-evaluation of public leisure service organizations has been outlined by van der Smissen (1972). The list includes six categories of organizational performance: philosophy and goals; administration; programming; personnel; areas, facilities, and equipment; and evaluation. An outline of the major organizational categories and the standards of performance identified for assessment by the van der Smissen model are contained in Exhibit 6-1 on page 94. Each standard has an accompanying written description and supporting performance measures that can be used to determine the degree of compliance exhibited in an agency. As van der Smissen (1972, p.9) recommends, an organization should be rated on how well it meets each of these criteria, using the following scale:

> "Yes" : total compliance
> "Almost" : almost full compliance
> "To Some Degree" : compliance to a limited extent
> "No" : complete lack of compliance
> "Does Not Apply"

As van der Smissen (1972) emphasizes, the manual is not intended to be a quick checklist, but rather a study guide that can identify organizational weaknesses and thereby point out areas in need of strengthening. She states:

> This guide has been developed to help recreation and park professional personnel and the lay citizenry evaluate their overall program. It is meant to be a study manual, not a quick-check, self-evaluation questionnaire.

> The standard and evaluative criteria apply to *all* public recreation and park departments inasmuch as they are considered to be fundamental aspects of an effective operation. But it is recognized that communities differ and must adapt the standards to the conditions of their situations. The term "program" includes all activities and services of the department in all aspects—

administration, financing, areas and facilities, staffing, activity selection, et cetera. (p. 5)

Although the van der Smissen model is designed for public recreation organizations, many of the factors in it are also important for commercial and not-for-profit leisure service organizations. The model can be adapted and used in these two types of organizations.

Exhibit 6-1.
Organizational Assessment Criteria

Philosophy and Goals
1. Philosophy
2. Goals

Administration
3. Organizational structure
4. Administrative manual
5. Cooperative community planning
6. Cooperative operations agreements
7. Financial administration
8. Public relations
9. Service statistics

Programming
10. Objectives
11. Actionable experiences
12. Types of opportunities
13. Varied participant requirements
14. Scope of opportunities
15. Total community programming
16. Education for leisure
17. Demonstration projects and research
18. Selection of program content
19. Participant involvement

Personnel
20. Professional staff
21. Job analyses
22. Personnel practices
23. Supporting services
24. Recruitment
25. Orientation program
26. Staff development
27. Supervision
28. Professional organizations
29. Consultants
30. Volunteers

Areas, Facilities, Equipment
31. Physical planning
32. Management of areas and facilities
33. Mobile equipment
34. Administrative space and equipment

Evaluation
35. General evaluation

(From van der Smissen, 1972)

In assessing an organization's strengths and limitations it is essential to obtain the perceptions of the organization's relevant publics. Kotler (1982, p. 88) recommends that an image study of how the organization is perceived by its key publics be used in addition to a self-appraisal. This approach will yield a more comprehensive view of the organization. He defines image as "the sum of beliefs, ideas, and impressions that a person has of an object" (p. 57). In the public sector, this is accomplished by surveying the entire population of a jurisdiction. For a Y.M.C.A. or other similar not-for-profit organization, one would need to thoroughly examine the beliefs of its members and also sample nonmembers to investigate whether they hold views substantially different from members. In a commercial agency, it is necessary to examine a sample of the total market, that is, all actual and potential buyers. Below is a method for accomplishing this.

A Marketing Approach to Organizational Assessment

Marketing literature has also provided a list of key organizational resources and components that may be examined (Kotler, 1982, p. 89). A modification of the items to be included in such a list is presented in Exhibit 6-2 on page 96. Included in this list are the board, management, staff, finances, facilities, management systems, and marketing practices of an organization. These items are key indicators of organizational performance that, when present, usually result in a well-organized and well-run organization.

In conducting the assessment, one should use the two-dimensional scale illustrated in Exhibit 6-2. This scale provides a measure of both strengths and limitations (Kotler 1982, p. 89; Crompton and Lamb 1986, p. 83). The scale measures respondent opinion about each organizational criterion with scale anchors ranging through the following: high, medium, or low strength; neutral; low, medium, or high limitation. With this scale, it is possible to determine a respondent's opinion about whether an item is a strength or a limitation of an agency, how serious a limitation or beneficial a strength the item is perceived to be, and the magnitude of the respondent's opinion about the limitation or strength of an item.

From these data, a picture of the organization's current strengths and limitations will emerge. These will influence the

Exhibit 6-2.
Organizational Assessment Criteria

	Strength				Limitation		
	H	M	L	N	L	M	H
Board							
Authority?	H	M	L	N	L	M	H
Leadership?	H	M	L	N	L	M	H
Responsiveness?	H	M	L	N	L	M	H
Management							
Skilled?	H	M	L	N	L	M	H
Leadership?	H	M	L	N	L	M	H
Staff							
Adequate?	H	M	L	N	L	M	H
Skilled?	H	M	L	N	L	M	H
Enthusiastic?	H	M	L	N	L	M	H
Loyal?	H	M	L	N	L	M	H
Service-minded?	H	M	L	N	L	M	H
Knowledgeable?	H	M	L	N	L	M	H
Finance							
Adequate?	H	M	L	N	L	M	H
Flexible?	H	M	L	N	L	M	H
Equitable?	H	M	L	N	L	M	H
Facilities							
Adequate (size, number, and quality)?	H	M	L	N	L	M	H
Flexible?	H	M	L	N	L	M	H
Accessibility?	H	M	L	N	L	M	H
Management Systems							
Management information systems?	H	M	L	N	L	M	H
Planning system quality?	H	M	L	N	L	M	H
Evaluation system quality?	H	M	L	N	L	M	H
Marketing							
Marketing intelligence?	H	M	L	N	L	M	H
Patron base?	H	M	L	N	L	M	H
Networking base?	H	M	L	N	L	M	H
General reputation?	H	M	L	N	L	M	H

(Adapted from Kotler, 1982, p.89)

organization's mission in a variety of ways, depending on the results of the investigation. For example, in a large suburb of a major midwestern city, it was discovered that a unique strength of the recreation operation was in its lakefront parks. Programs operated in these parks were almost sure to succeed and further enhance the residents' image of living in a unique community.

In a medium-sized Southern city, it was discovered that a major limitation for the recreation organization was the image of its staff, facilities, and programs. In this instance, the organization needed a major overhaul to successfully operate programs that would attract any target market in sufficient numbers. There were too many serious limitations in essential areas of operation. It was therefore recommended that new personnel policies be implemented, that the structure of the agency's financial base and practices be reorganized, that the organizational structure be changed, and that the powers and duties of the board be changed. In this case, the organization itself needed radical change to begin meeting the leisure needs of the community and its individuals.

No organization has enough resources to operate from a position of strength in all areas; that is, to operate all programs for which need could be demonstrated. The idea of assessment is to document organizational strengths and limitations in order to develop a mission that will direct organizational effort toward its strengths and to avoid operation in areas where the organization has limitations. A more long-term alternative is to strengthen the organization in areas where it has limitations. The notion of strategic planning and marketing is to match clients' expressed desires with organizational strengths and resources so that targeted markets are well served. To be significant contributors to overall organizational effort, programmers need to understand the role and process of organizational assessment and how it relates to the development of the organization's mission.

Once a mission is written, programmers are expected to develop program services that contribute to that mission within existing organizational strengths and limitations. Successful programming is measured in part by how well the services developed contribute to the identified organizational mission and operate within the resource limitations of the agency. "Recreation In the Streets" (Rossman 1973) is an example of a program whose success was partly attributable to its contribution to overall agency mission and identified community needs. An analysis of the program is included as Case Study 6-1. The "Warrior Games" developed by the U.S. Navy is another example of a program that meets individual, organizational, and community needs. It is presented in Case Study 6-2 on page 99.

Case Study 6-1.
Recreation in the Streets

"Recreation in the Streets" was developed in 1973 in Oak Park, Illinois. The community is the first suburb west of Chicago's corporate boundary. During the late 1960s and early 1970s, the population in the Chicago neighborhoods east of Oak Park had changed from all white to all black. The typical pattern of racial turnover in segregated, white Chicago neighborhoods was one of increasing distrust of new neighbors (black or white) and increasing isolation of existing residents in their own homes. This isolation intensified until each resident, at his or her own breaking point, moved and the neighborhood once again became totally segregated, this time with all black residents. Oak Park developed a community goal of establishing and maintaining racially integrated neighborhoods. To accomplish this, it was necessary to find both white and black buyers for homes offered for sale and to create open neighborhoods where residents know and trust each other.

All city departments were asked to foster and facilitate an open dialogue among residents. The goal was to encourage them to interact with each other and in doing so create a safe, stable neighborhood (Jacobs 1961). To contribute to this policy, the Oak Park Recreation Department developed the "Recreation in the Streets" program with the following goals:

1.   To place leaders from local, neighborhood playgrounds into neighborhoods one day per week in order to create visibility for the leaders and their program and to foster trust in the leadership provided at the neighborhood recreation centers.
2.   To create interaction among neighbors on city blocks and to create a visible program service that would enable residents to come out of their homes and meet each other.
3.   To temporarily create additional play space in an urban environment by making the street into a playground.

The program consisted of having three leaders from a neighborhood recreation center visit a residential block one morning per week from 9:00 a.m. until 12:00 noon. Traffic was blocked off from the street, and a trailer filled with recreation equipment was delivered to the block at about 8:30 a.m. When leaders arrived, they set up a volleyball net, a puppet stage, and other equipment in the street. The leaders then conducted an

(continued)

organized program consisting of events such as parachute games, bicycle and tricycle races, street hockey, volleyball games, chalk drawing on the street, and craft projects. The morning concluded with a luncheon cookout, and the street was reopened at noon. Each of the seven neighborhood recreation centers visited a different block each week for the seven weeks of the summer program.

In addition to facilitating interaction during the event, "Recreation in the Streets" was designed to require the interaction of neighbors in requesting and operating the event. To be selected for a visit, a block resident had to obtain the signatures of at least fifty percent of the block residents on a petition for service to be provided by the Recreation Department. Blocks to be visited were selected on the basis of their existing service (blocks farthest from existing services received highest priority) and their previous history of receiving visits. Once a block was selected for a visit, the individual who initiated the petition was responsible for designating a home on the block where the trailer could be parked, for circulating notices that the street would be closed the next day for the event, and for obtaining a charcoal grill for the cookout. Residents clearly had to interact before the event; otherwise, it could not occur.

"Recreation in the Streets" is an example of a program that was designed to build on an existing strength of the Oak Park Recreation Department, that is, its well-distributed neighborhood recreation centers. In addition, it met an identified community need to foster interaction among residents. In this program, individual, community, and organizational needs, as well as organizational mission, were all met within the resource limits of the agency.

Case Study 6-2.
Warrior Games
(This program was created by John "Pat" Harden, Chief Trainer, U.S. Navy.)

In 1985 a ship commander requested that Navy recreation personnel create a program for sailors who were given twenty-four-hour duty leave from extended training missions operating out of Guantanamo Bay, Cuba. Ships operating out of the bay are sent on training missions that simulate actual combat situations for fourteen to twenty-one days at a time. They return infrequently to base for a twenty-four hour leave. It was important that some type of recreation be available to provide release from the continual strain of simulated combat conditions. It was equally important that the training mission of creating esprit de corps, teamwork, and leadership not be broken during these short leaves. The recreation program, then, needed to provide opportunities for fun, teamwork, and leadership.

A series of "Warrior Games" were developed and were operated as competitions among units. These games presented the sailors with a problem that needed to be solved. The solution did not require superior strength or skill. To successfully solve

(continued)

the problem and win the competition, someone in the unit had to exercise leadership and get the unit to operate as a team. For example, in one game a unit had to submerge a large inflated ball in a swimming pool by organizing unit members to lock hands and legs to form a "human cargo net" to drape over the ball. This could be done only with the organized cooperation of the entire unit. Similarly, in each "Warrior Game" a different problem had to be solved quickly through the cooperation of the entire unit.

In this program, organizational needs (the Morale, Welfare, and Recreation unit's need to contribute to combat readiness), community needs (command needs to continue the themes of the training mission), and individual needs (for a playful diversion) were all met with a single program operating within the resource limits of the organization. Excellence in organized recreation programming requires that the needs of all three entities be met simultaneously.

Community

A notion of community implies a set of common ideas or shared beliefs that serve as a binding force for a group of people. Obviously there are many ideas and beliefs that compete for attention and resources in any larger community. The community analysis, then, focuses on identifying threats and opportunities (Zikmund and d'Amico 1993) in the environment that will affect the agency's delivery of leisure services.

Community Needs

A marketing approach to assessing community needs suggests that one should examine the organization's external environment, including its market environment, public environment, competitive environment, and macro environment (Kotler 1982). The results of this assessment will establish the organization's functional role in a community by determining the following: what organizations and interest groups the organization must deal with in the community; the various publics and special interest groups who may influence the organization's functioning in the community; who the organization will need to compete with directly in delivering services; and the larger social forces that will influence program services and client wants.

Kraus (1985) has expressed concern about the use of marketing concepts as a major philosophical orientation for the delivery of leisure services. He states:

At the same time, unquestioning acceptance of the marketing point of view raises a number of important issues in terms of the role that recreation and park agencies have traditionally had. When recreation is viewed primarily as a product to be sold, the issue of social value or achieving positive personal outcomes through leisure involvement becomes secondary. (pp. 70-71)

Kraus reflects the viewpoint of many recreation professionals regarding marketing as a strategy for developing park and recreation services. Their concern is that the role of recreation as a basic community service, which is made available through public financing to meet identified community needs, is being altered to one of service for a fee. These services are delivered to meet only the needs of individuals who can afford to pay to participate.

The community-need orientation of community recreation has been part of the movement since its origins at the beginning of this century and is part of the social-welfare, social-reform movement of the period. The traditional viewpoint assumes that recreation is provided to meet a greater community need, as well as individual needs. During the past ten years, the prevalence of marketing concepts and the concern with pricing services to raise revenue have obscured some of the original notions of recreation as a public good that contributes to the public interest.

Recreation and the Public Interest

The notion of public interest implies a certain relationship of people to society. Friedmann (1973) describes the public interest as follows:

The public interest is a republican idea whose origins reach back to the golden age of Greece. It has not always gone by its present designation. At other times, it has been called the commonweal, the general welfare, or the public good. All these terms express the notion of something shared or held in common. To the extent that something is held in common, that which is shared binds men to one another: the good that is shared creates a moral community whose members agree to be jointly responsible for that which is precious to them. The idea of a public good therefore implies the existence of such a community and the commitment of its members to it (p. 2).

For many years recreation was considered one of several public services (such as education, libraries, police protection, and fire protection) to be provided in the public interest. A rationale for its provision by government is presented by Peterson and Schroth (undated):

Leisure, used in a constructive manner, is basic to the self-fulfillment and life enrichment of the individual and therefore helps to strengthen the stability of the family, the community and the nation.

How people use their leisure time is an important social question. By providing recreation resources, a community is contributing to the physical, mental and social health of its residents.

Leisure and recreation are recognized as effective ways to enhance life in a community by developing leadership potential and stimulating popular participation for community betterment.

It is only through public recreation services that a large portion of the population will have access to many recreational facilities, such as pools, tennis courts, picnic areas, and golf courses.

Recreation and leisure services consume space. Local government is best suited to acquire, develop and maintain that space in the best interest of the entire community.

Government sponsorship of recreation services assumes equal participation by all ages, races and creeds, all seasons of the year; it is democratic and inclusive.

By providing a park and recreation agency, the combined wisdom of citizen participation on park and recreation boards can be assembled and a community can focus attention on protecting public lands and developing facilities and programs. Concentration on long-range plans will help assure proper growth of the system as the community expands.

It is only through government that equitable fair-share financing is available for the acquisition, development, and maintenance of park facilities and programs.

A park and recreation board can, through cooperative agreements with school boards, library boards, and other governmental agencies, energize and maximize the leisure and recreation potential of a community (pp. 2-3).

Recreation is still a service to be provided by government in the public interest. What is the public interest in a specific community and what is to be included in local government's provision of recreation services vary widely from community to community, depending on each community's identified needs and resources.

The notion of community needs also extends beyond the public interest notion of community recreation. Other organizations that sponsor recreation programs do so to serve a larger sense of community and community need. They too have a parallel notion of community need that should be met. For example, in armed forces recreation operations the notion of organizational needs focuses on the recreation organization contained in the Morale Welfare Recreation unit. The notion of community needs would be the overriding needs of the armed service community of which the recreation organization is a part. Similarly, in a corporate recreation operation, organizational needs would refer to the needs of the recreation unit within the larger organization; community needs would refer to the needs of the larger entity—the sponsoring corporation. The notion of community need, then, is of concern not just to community recreators, but also to recreators in all organizations.

Assessing Leisure Opportunities

Assessing the needs of a community requires an assessment of the existing range of leisure options in a community, an understanding of the leisure service system and the role of each provider in the community, and an understanding of the macro environment affecting the community. Remember, the notion of community need is not simply the aggregation of identified individual needs, but rather the needs created by a sense of community and the moral contract between individuals who are part of the community and jointly responsible for the overall good of the community.

Each community has a leisure delivery system made up of public, private, voluntary or quasi-public, and commercial subsystems (Sessoms 1980). A comprehensive assessment of community needs begins with an inventory of existing service options offered by the complete leisure service delivery system. It is important to determine the scope and depth of service already available in the community (Bannon 1976) and the individuals served and not served by the current system.

The public recreation organization has the responsibility in every community to ensure that the leisure needs of the entire population are met. This does not mean they must provide all leisure service. It does mean they are ultimately responsible for assessing community recreation needs, maintaining an inventory of the complete community recreation system, conducting individual needs assessments, interpreting needs assessment data, being the catalyst for implementing needed services, and coordinating the entire system. To accomplish this, the public system may encourage the establishment of a commercial recreation enterprise to meet an identified need or encourage the development of a Y.M.C.A. The public recreation organization is the provider of last resort. One of their unique functions is that they are ultimately responsible for meeting the overall leisure needs of the community. To do this, they must coordinate the entire leisure delivery system. As Sessoms (1980) indicates:

> Efforts are made sometimes to coordinate each subsystem without much concern for overall integration. More and more municipal leisure service agencies are beginning attempts to bring the resources of the public, voluntary, private, and commercial interests into play, but in the past these efforts were the exception, not the rule. (p. 126).

The public recreation organization, then, has the unique role of assessing and coordinating the development of the community leisure service system, including all of its subsystems. A community assessment should include the items displayed in Exhibit 6-3.

Exhibit 6-3.
Community Needs Assessment Agenda

Open Space Inventory

- Total amount of public park acreage in the community
- Total amount of acreage devoted to recreational use owned by other providers and an estimate of the percentage of population served by the provider
- A map indicating the location of all recreation spaces
- Knowledge about the size of each recreation space

Facility Inventory

- A list of all public recreation facilities, including type, location and who is serviced by the facility
- A list of all other recreation facilities including type, location, and who is serviced

Program Services

- A list of all program services offered by public, private, commercial, and quasi-public recreation agencies in the community, including the types of services offered and who is serviced by the programs

---

Once these data have been gathered, they must be analyzed to place the information into a meaningful pattern and permit insights into met and unmet needs. Farrell and Lundegren (1991) have proposed one method for analyzing such data—the programmer's evaluation cube. The cube is diagrammed in Exhibit 6-4 on page 106.

Exhibit 6-4.
The Programmer's Evaluation Cube

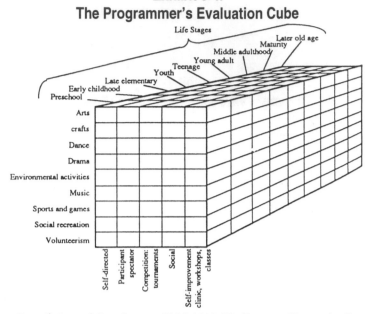

From: Farrell, P., and Lundegren, H.M. 1991. *The Process of Recreation Program-
     ming: Theory and Technique* (3rd ed.). State College, PA:Venture Publishing,
     Inc.

The evaluation cube is a three-dimensional matrix, with life stages on one axis, program activity types on a second axis, and programming formats on a third axis. In conducting this analysis, the programmer is examining current service to see if it is comprehensive and complete on a number of dimensions deemed important. The basic idea of using a cube for this analysis can be expanded by changing the variables on the cube to further analyze the comprehensiveness of services. For example, program distribution by gender, geographic neighborhoods, and family income would be just as legitimate a set of variables to analyze. It is axiomatic that the overall leisure service delivery system should make sure that its comprehensive services include the following:

1.   A wide variety of activity types, including sports, individual activities, fitness activities, hobbies, art, drama, music, and social recreation, are available in the community.

2.   A variety of programming organizational formats are available.

3.   Service opportunities are available for all age groups.
4.   Service is available, through some provider in the system, to all residents in the community regardless of age, sex, religion, socioeconomic class, geographical location, or other factors.

In examining these data to determine community need, the programmer is searching for gaps in existing service. These gaps may be due to resource limitations or to a lack of interest and resources, or may simply be inadvertent because the gap was previously unknown. In any case, some analysis of existing gaps should be conducted to determine whether they need to be filled with additional service.

Relationships Among Providers

The adequacy of cooperation and coordination among providers in a community should also be assessed. This is accomplished by examining all documents of cooperation among agencies. Indicators of a coordinated community leisure service system include the number of joint ventures among leisure service providers; the number of joint programs, evidence of sharing resources, facilities, and staff; evidence of coordinated scheduling; and other similar types of evidence.

Focusing on the Individual?

It is interesting to consider which of these three entities—individual, organizational, or community needs—is the driving force that determines agency direction and consequently, the content and focus of program services. This dilemma has been conceptualized and discussed elsewhere as a problem of determining whether the organization will have a selling or a marketing orientation (Howard and Crompton 1980; Crompton and Lamb 1986). A sales orientation places community or organizational needs first and assumes that the organization will convince patrons to consume what they have produced. In contrast, a marketing orientation places consumer needs and wants first. In this case, the organization will first discover what patrons want, then focus on producing it.

Kotler's (1980) societal marketing concept further explains the relationship of these three need packages to each other. He states:

> The societal marketing concept is a management orienta-
> tion that holds that the key task of the organization is to
> determine the needs and wants of target markets and to
> adapt the organization to deliver the desired satisfactions
> more effectively and efficiently than its competitors in a
> way that preserves or enhances the consumers' and
> society's well being (p. 35).

With this concept, the driving force is the identified wants and needs of target markets, that is, groups of individuals the agency intends to serve. The responsibility of the program manager in this case is to *restructure the organization as needed* to respond to identified client wants and needs. However, program services to be offered are still limited by community needs or desires because anything offered must "preserve or enhance" both the "consumers' and society's well being." Because of this latter requirement, developing a philosophy and mission for a not-for-profit organization is somewhat more problematic than developing a philosophy and mission for a commercial recreation operation.

Relationship of the Three Entities to Mission

Figure 6-2 on page 109 illustrates the relationship of each of these entities to the other. Agency mission is represented as the outermost ring in a series of concentric rings. As this figure illustrates, agency mission must encompass individual needs, community needs, and organizational strengths and limits. However, since no agency has unlimited resources, not all iden-tified needs can be met, so priorities for the distribution of scarce resources must be established. Individual needs are seen as the centermost priority. They influence community needs, organi-zational needs, and agency mission. The identified needs of

Figure 6-2.
Relationship of Mission to Indvidual, Community, and Organizational Needs

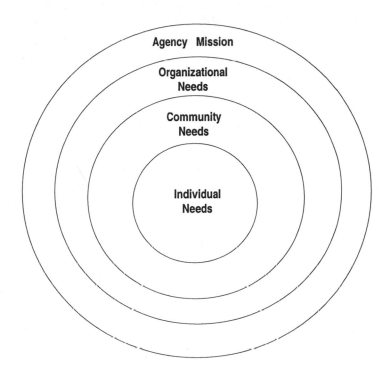

individuals are tempered and influenced by community needs and organizational strengths and limits before they become part of the agency's mission. Kotler (1982) recognized this when he stated that the agency mission should be "feasible, motivating, and distinctive" (p. 36).

An agency's mission should be feasible within the limitations imposed on the agency by its own resource limits, by community needs, and by individual wants. Staff members should not be asked to accomplish results that they lack the skills or resources to achieve. The mission should motivate staff members by giving them clear direction about what they are to accomplish. Finally, the mission should be distinctive in order to separate the mission of the organization from other organizations providing similar services.

To be successful, organizations must meet organizational needs and the needs of the environment in which they operate. Determining organizational and environmental needs is antecedent to developing an agency philosophy or mission statement. One may eventually try to change the organization or community perceptions of its needs to better accommodate identified individual needs. But one must first take inventory of the current state of affairs to have a starting point.

Writing the Mission Statement

The use of goal and objective technology in an organization begins with the development of a mission statement. An overview of the role of an agency's mission statement was provided in Chapter Four. Thus far, in this chapter, we have reviewed the issues that need to be analyzed in order to prepare to write the agency's mission statement. The analysis portion of this task is complex, but the actual mission statement must be clear and as simple as possible. There are no step-by-step guidelines to direct its preparation. The reader is reminded that its purpose is to announce to external parties the unique role and function of the agency to the community and to provide direction to employees within the agency to ensure their activities contribute to accomplishing the agency's mission. Four examples of mission statements from different agencies are presented in Exhibit 6-5. Please read and compare these and then proceed with the copy on page 113.

Exhibit 6-5
Mission Statements

Leisure Resource Center, Peoria, Illinois

To provide a comprehensive system of leisure service delivery in the greater Peoria area which assists people with disabilities in the development of leisure skills, attitudes and awareness and promotes their personal and community leisure participation. (Leisure Resource Center, undated)

(continued)

U.S. Air Force MWR Division

We are dedicated to providing professionally managed and diversified morale, welfare, and recreation programs based on the needs and desires of those we serve. We shall reflect the highest ideas of integrity and pride in job accomplishment. Let our success be the personal knowledge that we have increased the mission effectiveness through improved quality of life for all Air Force people. (Directorate of Morale, Welfare, and Recreation, undated)

Knoxville Bureau of Recreation, Knoxville, Tennessee

To provide comprehensive year-round opportunities for recreation and use of physical resources which are accessible to and respond to the articulated needs and desires of all residents of the city of Knoxville with an emphasis on educating citizens on the value of learning and practicing lifetime leisure skills and appreciations and serving as a catalyst and facilitator for the provision of recreation programs by other organizations in the community.

Discussion
The mission statement for the Bureau makes clear its responsibility in the community of serving as one of the primary providers of recreation. The Bureau has a responsibility to initiate services in areas currently being underserved and to serve as a community catalyst to get other agencies to initiate services to meet identified needs. However, the Bureau will not be able to meet all needs identified in the community so its operational mission will, by necessity, be more strategic and selective. Currently, program operations are heavily team sports oriented. In order to meet the mission objective of offering a comprehensive program, development of recreation opportunities in other program areas will need to occur.
While the Bureau's mission statement addresses only opportunities for recreation and leisure services, in actual operation the mission will include all of the resources needed to make these opportunities available including facilities, land acquisition, land development, adequate financing, and other resources needed to produce recreation and leisure opportunities (Management Learning Laboratories, 1985).

School-Community Recreation Department
Madison Metropolitan School District, Madison, Wisconsin

Philosophical Basis for Recreation
All people struggle for self-realization and personal fulfillment in life. The goal of reaching full potential as human beings requires that each person exercise rights and freedoms in ways that are personally meaningful without usurping the rights of others. Important among these is the way each person chooses to exercise the right to find fulfillment through education and intellectual achievement, through work, through

(continued)

worship, and increasingly through a positive approach to the use of free or unobligated time. While it is true that free time may be utilized simply as diversion or respite from life's responsibilities, it is important to recognize that many of life's most creative and meaningful achievements come not only during periods devoted to study and work, but during those times and activities often referred to as leisure, recreation, or play. Moreover, it is during these times and through these activities that people often make the greatest gains toward essential elements of self-realization; psychological, social and physical well-being.

Definitions

Recreation can be defined as those free time experiences which bring true pleasure and personal satisfaction. Such experiences typically come through participation in activities which emphasize physical movement and coordination, social integration and psychological safety, cultural and aesthetic appreciation, learning and intellectual stimulation or combinations of these. While many people directly equate leisure with self-realization or self-actualization, leisure is generally considered to be free or unobligated time, the time which presents the most opportunities for engaging in recreational activities.

Recreation is first and foremost a personal matter. What is recreation for one person—bringing pleasure and satisfaction—may not be for another person. There is a tremendous range in people's recreational interests. This range is further dramatized when consideration is given to the diversity of ages, ability levels, ethnic backgrounds and economic well-being of people in society. However, individual benefits can accrue when people have opportunities to come together in recreational groups: groups with similar ages, interests, backgrounds, or abilities. When these opportunities are varied, when they occur often, when they are local and when they are affordable—these are the circumstances under which the greatest number of people can benefit from recreation participation.

Reasons for Government Involvement

The provision of local, public recreation enables local governments to provide at least some services for all people of the community through an equitable tax and fee system. By definition, public recreation services are democratic and inclusive, encompassing citizen participation in decision making and access to all taxpayers. Public recreation has other related benefits:

- It is comparatively inexpensive, providing equality of opportunity for persons with low as well as higher incomes.
- It makes the most efficient use of public facilities and other community resources.
- It gives a sense of continuity and permanence to a vital area of human service.
- It helps bring renewed freshness and vitality to the community, literally increasing its attractiveness and life quality, raising its value to both present and prospective residents.

(continued)

Recreation in the Schools

The State of Wisconsin, through forward-looking legislation passed in the early part of the 20th century, is the national leader in provision of community recreation services through local school districts. Madison's decision to provide these services as a function of public education, made in 1926 and strongly supported ever since, implies some additional directions and obligations for community recreation:

- Recreation programs should directly reach children in the schools.
- Recreation programs should take full advantage of school resources: people, facilities and funds for initiating, implementing and evaluating services.
- Recreation programs should help all community people, especially those not directly reached by daytime school offerings, receive a direct return on the investment in the school system by providing opportunities responsive to their interests.
- Recreation programs should exemplify educational ideals; high quality teaching, prefaced by careful preparation and based on solid learning principles; provision of physical, social and psychological environments conducive to desired out-comes; and sound administrative and policy-making practices which ensure continuing support for services vital to full human development.

Department Purposes

With these understandings as a base, the staff of the Madison School Community Recreation Department summarizes the department's purposes as follows:

1. To provide year-round recreation opportunities which are accessible to all residents of the Madison Metropolitan School District, responding to expressed interests and making maximum use of available resources in the School District.
2. To educate community citizens, with emphasis on children and youth of school age, on the value of learning and practicing lifetime leisure skills and appreciations.
3. To serve as a community resource and catalyst for recreation services: providing referral information, organizational expertise and planning with other agencies, organizations and citizen groups in order to more fully meet the recreational needs of all community residents. (Madison Metropolitan School District School-Community Recreation Department 1982)

Each of these mission statements is very different. Yet they each use linguistic statements to define or "frame" an area of reality that the agency will attempt to accomplish. None of these statements is clear, specific, or measurable. They do, however, begin the process of specifying what the agency will accomplish. From the entire universe of all that the agency could do, the mission statement begins limiting what the agency will actually do. The mission statement draws a linguistic frame around an area of reality to delimit it from the entire universe of possible actions.

The mission statement from the Madison Metropolitan School District School-Community Recreation Department differs from the other statements because it explicates the philosophy underlying its mission. It is important to recognize that all mission statements have an underlying philosophy that serves as the foundation for action in the agency. Often this philosophy is not explicated; it is made apparent only through ongoing actions taken by the organization. Whether explicated or not, an underlying philosophy guides the actions taken by an agency. Now complete Exercise 6-2.

Exercise 6-2.
Mission Statements

Discuss the following:

- **What operational philosophies are implied by the mission statements for the Leisure Resource Center, the U.S. Air Force, and the Knoxville Bureau of Recreation?**
- **Discuss how a mission statement both excludes and includes possible agency activities. Cite examples from the mission statements included in this book.**
- **Discuss why it is important to write a mission statement that will allow for flexibility.**

Conclusion

The agency's mission statement emerges from an analysis of individual, organizational, and community needs. The issues to consider and methods for analyzing them were discussed and sample mission statements from four agencies were provided. The mission statement should state the purpose of the agency and identify the population it will serve. It should be based on an analysis of the organization's strengths and weaknesses and an analysis of the threats and opportunities for the agency in the larger community environment. For programmers to achieve ongoing success requires that their programs meet individual, organizational, and community needs, and case studies of two such programs were provided.

References, Chapter Six

Bannon, J.J. 1976. *Leisure Resources: Its Comprehensive Planning.* Englewood Cliffs, NJ: Prentice-Hall.

Carpenter, G.M., and C.Z. Howe. 1985. *Programming Leisure Experiences.* Englewood Cliffs, NJ: Prentice-Hall.

Crompton, J.L., and C.W. Lamb, Jr. 1986. *Marketing Government and Social Services.* New York: Wiley.

Directorate of Morale, Welfare, and Recreation. Undated. Air Force Morale, Welfare, and Recreation Student Work Experience Program. Randolph AFB, TX: Air Force Manpower and Personnel Center.

Farrell, P., and H.M. Lundegren. 1991. *The Process of Recreation Programming: Theory and Technique* (3rd ed.). State College, PA: Venture.

Friedmann, J. 1973. The Public Interest and Community Participation: Toward a Reconstruction of Public Philosophy. *Journal of American Institute of Planners* 39(1), 2-12.

Howard, D.R., and J.L. Crompton. 1980. *Financing, Managing and Marketing Recreation & Park Programs.* Dubuque, IA: Wm. C. Brown.

Jacobs, J. 1961. *The Death and Life of Great American Cities.* New York: Vintage Books.

Knowles, M.S. 1970. *The Modern Practice of Adult Education.* New York: The Association Press.

Kotler, P. 1980. *Marketing Management* (4th ed.). Englewood Cliffs, NJ: Prentice-Hall.

Kotler, P. 1982. *Marketing for Nonprofit Organizations* (2nd ed.). Englewood Cliffs, NJ: Prentice-Hall.

Kraus, R.G. 1985. *Recreation Program Planning Today.* Glenview, IL: Scott Foresman.

Leisure Resource Center. Undated. *Student Field Placement Manual.* Peoria, IL: Leisure Resource Center.

Madison Metropolitan School District School-Community Recreation Department. 1982. *Action Plan for the 1980s: Perspectives on Programs—Projections For Progress.* Madision, WI: Madison Metropolitan School District.

Management Learning Laboratories. 1985. *Assessment of the Management Function of the Knoxville Bureau of Recreation Knoxville, Tennessee: Report 1, Review of Existing Organizational Structure.* Champaign, IL: Management Learning Laboratories.

Peterson, J.A., and R.J. Schroth. Undated. *Guidelines for Evaluating Public Parks and Recreation.* West Lafayette, IN: Cooperative Extension Service, Purdue University.

Pfeffer, J., and G.R. Salancik. 1978. *The External Control of Organizations; a Resource Dependence Perspective.* New York: Harper & Row.

Rossman, J.R. 1973, March/April. *Recreation in the Streets.* Des Plaines, IL: Illinois Parks and Recreation, 4-5.

Sessoms, D.H. 1980. Community Development and Social Planning. In S.G. Lutzin (Ed.), *Managing Municipal Leisure Services* (pp. 120-139). Washington, D.C.: International City Management Association.

Tillman, A. 1973. *The Program Book for Recreation Professionals.* Palo Alto, CA: Mayfield Publishing.

van der Smissen, B. 1972. *Evaluation and Self-study of Public Recreation and Park Agencies: A Guide With Standards and Evaluative Criteria.* Arlington, VA: National Recreation and Park Association.

Zikmund, W.G., and M. d'Amico. 1993. *Marketing* (4th ed.). Minneapolis/St. Paul, MN: West Publishing Co.

Photo courtesy of Parks and Recreation Department, Aurora, Colorado.

7

Writing Program Management Goals

Additional direction and focus are given to an agency's programming efforts by the development of program management planning goals. As indicated in Chapter Four, an organization's mission statement is not measurable. The sample mission statements included in Chapter Six are not measurable. Therefore, a series of goals and objectives must be developed to provide a means for operationalizing and measuring an organization's mission statement. This is accomplished in Step 2 of the Program Development Cycle. The next level of goal development is a series of three- to five-year planning goals that are often followed with one-year "management by objective" type goals. These goals delimit some specific programmatic directions the agency will try to take.

Short-Range Planning Goals

An example of statements of three- to five-year short-range planning goals is provided in a planning document for the Knoxville Bureau of Recreation, Knoxville, Tennessee (Management Learning Laboratories 1985). The bureau's mission statement, which was presented in Chapter Six, is developed below with eight short-range planning goals:

1.   To enhance the quality of life for all citizens of Knoxville through the provision of public recreation services.
2.   To employ a professionally trained staff and to provide staff an environment fostering personal and professional growth.
3.   To improve the efficiency and effectiveness of maintenance operations.

4.   To increase revenue production and to implement a budget process at the operational level in the Bureau.
5.   To be future oriented, planned and prepared to meet the changing needs and wants of citizens regarding recreation services.
6.   To maximize citizen involvement in the planning and development of recreation programs and services.
7.   To more effectively market the Bureau's services to the citizens of Knoxville.
8.   To act as a facilitator or catalyst for the provision of recreation programs by other public or private organizations.

These eight goals are examples of statements that have no measurement devices included in them. Goals of this type must be further specified and given meaning by the development of more specific statements that will be used to measure them. To further illustrate this process, the first goal identified—To enhance the quality of life for all citizens of Knoxville through the provision of public recreation services—will be developed further. A series of objectives for accomplishing this specific goal could include the following objectives:

1.   To establish a senior citizens program.
2.   To establish an athletic facility reservation system.
3.   To establish a cultural arts division.

These three objectives are still short-term planning statements, that is, for three to five years. They are, however, objectives for the goal previously specified. For purposes of illustration, only three objectives have been developed, but they are by no means exhaustive of all that the agency could do to enhance the quality of life for all Knoxville citizens. They do, however, represent what could be done. (See Figure 4-4, page 67, and its accompanying explanation for a review of this concept.)

To continue with the Knoxville example: It is possible to illustrate how an objective for one level of the organization becomes a goal for the next stratum in the organizational hierarchy. For example, the chief executive officer of the organization may have the goal of "enhancing the quality of life for all citizens of Knoxville through the provision of public recreation services." This same individual may have developed the three short-range planning objectives outlined above in order to accomplish the goal.

Next, this individual passes his or her objective of "establishing a cultural arts division" down the organizational hierarchy to the director of recreation for whom it becomes a goal to be accomplished. The director of recreation then must develop objectives for demonstrating its accomplishment. Although it is not mandatory that the director develop objectives with a one-year time frame, for purposes of illustration we will use one-year objectives.

An example of how to develop the goal "to establish a cultural arts division" includes the following one-year objectives:

1. To hire a cultural arts supervisor within the first two months of FY 95.
2. To budget $30,000 for cultural arts programs during FY 95.
3. To develop fifteen cultural arts programs during FY 95.

Several important dimensions of using goal and objective technology are made apparent here. First, it is clearer now that goals and objectives are not definitive categories and that a goal can often later become an objective and vice versa in the actual implementation of a goal and objective hierarchy in an organization. Second, the objectives just presented do have measurement devices in them. Since they were developed by the director of recreation, we know who is to be held accountable for their accomplishment. And since they include measurement devices, we will know if they have been accomplished. For example, the director of recreation is responsible for hiring a cultural arts supervisor within the first two months of fiscal year 1995. Third, these objectives all have a one-year time line. The time frame for accomplishment is getting more specific. In this case, the fiscal year is the time frame being used.

These examples are illustrative of the objectives typically used in a management by objectives system. They are action oriented, specifying what managerial action is going to be taken to accomplish a task and what criteria will be used to judge its success. It is also important to note that this is where program planning activities are integrated with budgeting. The development of a specific program service has become a budget element with resources committed to its implementation.

It is assumed here that the chief executive officer and the director of recreation jointly agree that the successful accomplishment of these three objectives will be accepted as proof that the goal has been accomplished. This is the implicit assumption of the technology. We accept this, knowing that the three objectives identified are just a partial list of all that one could do to establish a cultural arts division. In this case, the three objectives are representative of what the director of recreation must accomplish in one year to establish a cultural arts division.

Networking Goals and Objectives Further Into the Organization

Continuing with the Knoxville example will help to further illustrate how goals and objectives are networked through the organization and used to provide further direction and focus to program management. Once the director of recreation hires the cultural arts supervisor and budgets the funds for the year, the director will give the objective of "developing fifteen cultural arts programs for FY 95" to the new cultural arts supervisor as a goal. The director will ask for a list of objectives outlining how the cultural arts supervisor intends to accomplish this goal. The supervisor could then develop the following list of objectives:

1.   To operate a cultural arts fair during the spring of 1995.
2.   To operate a summer cultural arts workshop for children with three different media during the summer of 1995.
3.   To operate a concert in the park series during September 1995.
4.   To offer an arts instructional program for adults with at least five different media during fall (October and November) 1995.

These statements could be made more specific still with additional measurement devices. For example, the second objective could be rewritten to read, "To operate a summer cultural arts workshop for children with three different media and an enrollment of at least seventy-five students during the summer of 1995." The addition of this new measurement device further defines the successful accomplishment of the objective and the goal which it measures. How detailed one must be is a matter of professional practice in a specific organization. Remember, using goal and objective technology is a means to the end of developing useful programs and services and of measuring and documenting the organization's accomplishments. Goals and objectives should be developed to the point that they provide operational clarity and help the organization achieve and document its accomplishments.

It is certainly possible to develop these objectives further. For example, to accomplish the objective of offering "a summer cultural arts workshop with three different media during the summer of 1995," this objective can be treated as a goal. The following objectives to document its accomplishment can then be prepared.

1.   To offer a children's drama class during the summer of 1995 with at least fifteen enrollments.
2.   To offer an oil painting class during the summer of 1995.
3.   To offer guitar for beginners during the summer of 1995.

Preparing concise program management goals is an important skill that programmers must develop to effectively provide direction to the development and management of program services. Remember, however, that we have not yet developed program design goals; this will be discussed in Chapter Nine. Practice developing program management goals by completing Exericse 7-1.

Exercise 7-1.
Writing Goals and Objectives

Develop a hierarchy of goals for the following goal:

To establish a senior citizens' program (or some other appropriate goal) and develop a hierarchical set of goals and objectives for at least three organizational levels in a recreation programming agency.

Trade the goals and objectives and critique each other's work. When finished, discuss the following questions:

- Do the statements have operational meaning?
- Does each program management objective have a completion date?
- Does each objective have an appropriate measurement device?
- Are the statements clear and concise?
- Is each statement written so that it is clear who is to accomplish the objective?
- Is there a clear hierarchical order to the development of the goals and objectives?

Using Goals and Objectives to Establish Programming Standards

Program management goals and objectives can also be used to establish operational standards. McCarville (1993) indicates that "Standards provide precise standards that staff members may use to monitor their own success in providing programs and services" (p.36). Exhibit 7-1 includes program management goals for the operation of recreation centers for the Army V Corps in Germany. Using goals and objectives in this manner helps direct the program that will be developed at each recreation center.

Exhibit 7-1.
Recreation Center Programming Goals
V Corp Recreation Center
A Morale Support Activity
"Your Link to Leisure"

These are recommended MINIMUM programming standards for community recreation centers in V Corp, based on minimum staffing as it exists in some communities. If there is one full time professional and at least two recreation aides, the following variety of programs can and should be offered in each recreation center. When there is more staff (a full time program director) the number and variety of programs should be increased, reflecting the needs and interests of the constituency as well as modern

(continued)

trends of American life-styles. Naturally, the use of other MSA core programs and community agency staff as well as volunteers is urged.

DIRECTED PROGRAMS: Minimum of three nights per week.

FILLER PROGRAMS: Maximum of two nights per week.

SPECIAL INTEREST GROUP MEETINGS: Maximum of one night per week.

CLASSES: Maximum of two nights per week.

THEME PROGRAMS: Minimum of one day/night/weekend.

COMMUNITY-WIDE PROGRAM: Minimum of one per quarter.

SPECIAL ENTERTAINMENT PROGRAM: Minimum of twice per quarter.

The following definitions are offered:

DIRECTED PROGRAM: A program which requires professional staff (GS/UA 5 or above) to lead patrons (regardless of whether one, ten or 100 show up) in an active activity, i. e. open forum discussion group with guest speaker, new games, quiz show-type games. This means the director conducts the program, and participates actively, it does not mean the director passes out pieces of paper or serves refreshments only. A directed program may require props, audio-visual equipment, some decorations and gimmicks, but not to the extent that a theme program does.

FILLER PROGRAM: A program which can be executed by trained professionals GS/PS 2-4 which usually involves passive activity such as video movies, but can also be active such as bingo, challenge-the-staff, pub night, small games, card tournaments, kitchen activities.

SPECIAL INTEREST GROUP MEETINGS: Six or more individuals who share an interest in the same activities, be it chess or mountain-climbing, constitute a "special interest group." There are no dues, no elected officers and no constitution and by-laws. These groups usually develop around one or two highly enthusiastic individuals who attract followers—they are loosely organized but need recreation center support in order to exist. This kind of program can usually take place in another room of the recreation center while something else is going on. However, if the group grows very large, such as a computer interest group, that meeting or activity may become a valid program on its own in the main area of the recreation center, but not more than once a week.

CLASSES: Program involving six or more individuals who are being instructed by a contracted individual not on the recreation center staff. Also a program which can be conducted in another area of the recreation center in addition to other programs being conducted simultaneously.

THEME PROGRAMS: A program conducted within the recreation center or other facility which contains at least six of the ten elements of a theme program. The ten elements of a theme program are:

(continued)

1. Activities (active games)
2. Refreshments (food, beverages)
3. Decorations/props
4. Entertainment (live)
5. Audio-visuals (films/slides/video tapes)
6. Costumes
7. Lighting (special room arrangement)
8. Prizes
9. Music (canned, for atmosphere)
10. Gimmick (giveaways, mystery or special guests, special effects, etc.)

All ten elements are geared toward one overall concept or idea, the most natural being the holidays that occur throughout the year. There is at least one theme to celebrate each month and these are the most basic:

January: Ice, snow, winter
February: Valentine's Day, Presidents Day
March: Mardi Gras, Fasching
April: Easter
May: Spring, Memorial Day
June: National Recreation and Park Month
July: July 4th
August: Summer
September: Native Americans
October: Halloween
November: Thanksgiving
December: Christmas, New Years

COMMUNITY-WIDE PROGRAM: A program which contains the elements of a theme program, but is coordinated with other MSA core programs and community agencies. The program can and should take place outside the recreation center facility at other locations, i. e. Renaissance Fair, Winter Ski and Travel Expo, Auto Flea Market, etc.

SPECIAL ENTERTAINMENT PROGRAM: Organic variety shows and revues, coffee-house-style in-house informal shows, talent and "no" talent shows, rock concerts, dinner theater, drama club skits, DOD touring shows, celebrity nights, improvisations, and commercial entertainment.

NOT ACCEPTABLE to stand alone as programs titled on a publicized program calendar are "food" program nights such as "Make Your Own Sundae," "Make a Pizza," "Taco Night," or "Steak Night." These foods and the sale of these foods should be incorporated into a directed or theme program and should not appear as the sole activity for an evening.

(continued)

Tour departures listed on a program calendar are misleading. Tours are not programs for patrons in the recreation center. Although the calendar square for that date is filled, there is, in reality, nothing happening in the recreation center facility.

Recommend departure from the calendar style of program promotion. If every square is not filled with definitive, exciting activity, do not use that format. Empty calendar squares indicate no activity and do not motivate patrons to use facilities or attend programs.

Program titles appearing on printed publicity should have fresh, new and interesting approaches.

(H. Rice, Director, V Corp Recreation Centers 1986)

Program management goals such as the above ensure that program operations at a recreation center are organized and controlled so that a minimum level of programming is provided. They establish customer service standards. Similar types of program management goals are used to direct the management of day camps, swimming pools, craft centers, and the like. In service industries, these types of goals are analogous to production goals used in manufacturing organizations. Program management goals are used as quality assurance guidelines to direct program production at a number of similar facilities or programming entities. Now complete Exercise 7-2.

Exercise 7-2.
Program Management Goals

Develop program management goals for the operation of a chain of commercial recreation facilities. Each facility has a nursery, a weight room, an exercise machine room, an indoor swimming pool, a running track, a concession and lounge area, twelve racquetball courts, and separate shower and locker facilities for men and women. Each facility is family oriented; 85 percent of the membership in each facility is made up of families.

After developing program management goals, discuss the following questions:

•Are the goals comprehensive and explicit enough to guide less capable staff members? That is, if the goals are met will a facility have an acceptable program?

•Is there enough flexibility to allow creative staff members leeway to develop a program further?
•Are the goals written to recognize differences among facilities with regard to the number of members, the number of staff, and the size of the budget?

A Systems Approach

Peterson (1976) has explained how goal and objective technology can be combined with systems theory to develop a comprehensive, networked set of agency goals and objectives. The process offered by Peterson shows how to operationalize the concepts illustrated in Figure 4-4, page 67. In this system, one assigns numbers to each succeeding level of goal and objective development. The entire program of the Leisure Resource Center in Peoria, Illinois, was developed in this manner. Their program will be used to illustrate this point.

The first statement in the Leisure Resource Center's manual (undated) is their statement of purpose:

To provide a comprehensive system of leisure service delivery in the greater Peoria area that assists people with disabilities in the development of leisure skills, attitudes, and awareness and promotes their personal and community leisure participation.

This statement of purpose is operationalized with the following nine goals:

1. To provide services that assist in the development of leisure skills.

2. To provide services that assist in the development of leisure awareness, responsibility, and potential for involvement.

3. To provide opportunities for ongoing leisure involvement and utilization of existing and newly acquired leisure skills.

4. To provide services that enable the acquisition of leisure resource information.

5. To promote physical and architectural accessibility of leisure-related facilities and programs.

6. To provide training, consultation, and other resources to assist other agencies in the provision of recreation and leisure opportunities for people with disabilities.

7. To promote community awareness of the leisure needs, abilities, and rights of people with disabilities.

8. To provide development and educational services for professionals and students related to the leisurability of people with disabilities.

9. To advocate for the leisure rights of people with disabilities.

These goals define how the Leisure Resource Center will accomplish its mission. The governing board and the community accept the center's accomplishment of these goals as proof that it has accomplished its mission. Other goals could have been selected, but these were chosen for a variety of reasons, including staff skills, agency resource limits, unique opportunities available to the agency, and client needs. These goals do not have measurement devices or time limits on them. They are typical of planning goals that are developed to provide programmatic direction to an agency for a three- to five-year period. Some of these same goals may continue as part of the agency mission for a number of years if periodic review and evaluation determine that they are still desirable for the agency to pursue.

In Figure 7-1, the nine goals are placed in a figure and each is given a code number from one through nine. These goals thereby become the nine components of the Leisure Resource

Figure 7-1.
Easter Seal Leisure Resource Center Goals

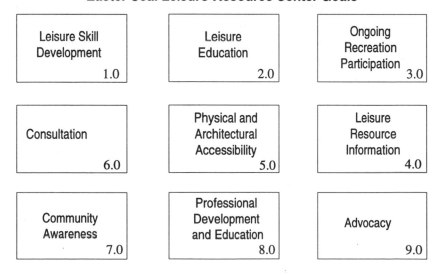

Center's program. For each of the nine components, additional goals can be developed that further define what is to be included in each component. In Figure 7-2, the support goals for component 3.0, Ongoing Recreation Participation, are placed in a figure.

Figure 7-2.
Ongoing Recreation Participation Goals

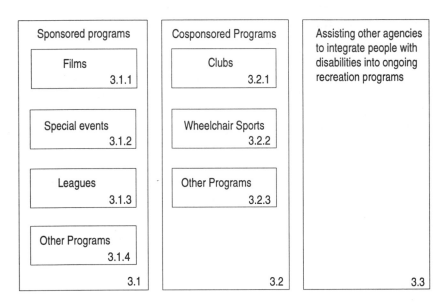

From the goals in Figure 7-2, one can begin to develop annual goals for programming purposes. For example, for Films (3.1.1) it would be possible to develop the following goals:

To offer a film each Saturday night during October 1995 with 50 or more clients in attendance at each screening (3.1.1.1).

To offer a Holiday Film Festival by showing a Christmas film on each of the four Saturdays preceding Christmas 1995 (3.1.1.2).

To instruct a film-making class during the summer programming season 1995 with 12 or more enrollments (3.1.1.3).

Thus each of the goals included for the Leisure Resource Center is further defined and developed in the hierarchical manner discussed earlier. When a numeric coding system is added, the purpose of each activity, program, or other undertaking of the organization can be traced through the hierarchical structure of the goals and objectives that have been developed.

Using this hierarchical arrangement helps the organization in three ways. First, development of the goals and objectives helps translate and interpret the organization's purpose or mission into operating ends, that is, desired programs for development or activities to undertake. Second, the uncertainty surrounding the management of programs is thereby given direction and focus through a sequential, logical, and orderly process of goal and objective development. So much of what is done in a leisure service organization is normatively determined on the basis of any number of factors, including resource limitations, client interests, staff skills, abilities and interests, and unique opportunities available to the agency. The use of goals and objectives to develop program directions helps the agency interpret to its public why it exists and what it will accomplish. Third, employee effort is networked throughout the organization. Through the information and networking provided by a hierarchical arrangement of goals and objectives, employees at all levels understand their role in helping the organization achieve its mission.

It can be confusing to develop a hierarchical arrangement of goals and objectives that is logical, that is constructed in the correct order from general to specific, and that has measurable statements. The systems approach offered by Peterson (1976) can bring structure and clarity to the process by using a numerical coding system that allows one to quickly identify the place of a goal or objective statement and its relationship in the overall hierarchical structure. Now complete Exercise 7-3.

Exercise 7-3.
A Systems Approach to Writing Goals and Objectives

Use the list of goals and objectives prepared in Exercise 7-2 and place them in the codified system explained in the section on a systems approach.
- Does the use of this system help keep the process organized?
- Discuss how this system might help provide direction to the agencyand help account for the services it produces.

Conclusion

Goal and objective technology is used to provide further direction to program development within a program agency. Three- to five-year program planning goals are developed to provide short-range planning direction for the agency. Each of these goals is further defined through the development of one-year, management by objective goals statements. Additional development of goals with supporting objectives continues until operational clarity and direction are achieved. How program management goals can be used to establish customer service standards was discussed. Incorporating goal and objective technology with systems theory results in a numerical coding system for tracking the management of the agency's programs.

References, Chapter Seven

Leisure Resource Center. Undated. *Student Field Placement Manual.* Peoria, IL: Leisure Resource Center.

Management Learning Laboratories. 1985. *Assessment of the Management Function of the Knoxville Bureau of Recreation, Knoxville, Tennessee: Report 1, Review of Existing Organizational Structure.* Champaign, IL: Management Learning Laboratories.

McCarville, R.E. 1993. Keys to Quality Programming. *Journal of Physical Education, Recreation and Dance, 64* (8) 34-36, 46-47.

Peterson, C.A. 1976. *A Systems Approach to Therapeutic Recreation Program Planning.* Champaign, IL: Stipes.

Rice, H. 1986. *Come On . . . Let's Get With the Program-ing!* Baumholder, Germany: U.S. Army V Corps D.C.A. Recreation Center Training Workshop. (Mimeographed workshop handout.)

Part III: Targeted Program Development

In Part III, the second stage of the Program Development Cycle is discussed.

This stage involves assessing the needs of individual clients, aggregating these needs into target markets, developing operational program goals and objectives, and using the data generated in the first parts of the cycle to creatively design programmed experiences for patrons. The programmer's responsibility is to design creative programs based on demonstrated patron needs and wants.

Part III contains three chapters. In Chapter Eight, the concept of need and techniques for assessing leisure needs are discussed. In Chapter Nine, a technique for designing programs is discussed as well as how to use needs assessment data to develop program goals and objectives. In Chapter Ten, the use of creative techniques in designing programs is discussed and demonstrated.

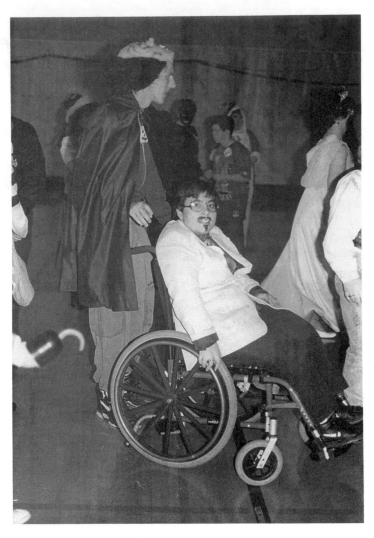

Photo courtesy of the Joliet Park District, Joliet, Illinois. Photo by Ann Miller.

8

Assessing Patrons' Needs

In this step, patrons' needs are assessed for eventual use as program design objectives in the development of program services. Carpenter and Howe (1985) state that "In leisure programming, needs assessment performs two major functions: the generation of program ideas and the facilitation of input from constituents and responsiveness to constituents by service providers" (p. 77).

Embodied in this definition are two major objectives of needs assessment—(1) helping the agency determine the direction it will take in developing program services and (2) incorporating citizen input in the decision-making process. These two objectives arise from two bodies of literature that contribute to needs assessment. The first is social policy literature, which has sought to justify the services provided to citizens by suggesting that the services fulfill indentifiable needs. The concept of *needs* as used by McKillip (1987) exemplifies this point of view: "Needs are value judgments that a target group has problems that can be solved" (p.7). McKillip makes very clear his view that needs and therefore decisions about them are value laden—not objective.

The second body of literature, which is exemplified by the work of Summers (1987), stems from political science. He states:

> Citizen participation in decision making is the essence of needs assessment. It concerns grass roots democracy and the importance of people being free and able to express their views on matters that affect their lives, families, and communities. Needs assessment is a social institution that integrates ideas from political theories of democracy with practices flowing from the mainstream of social science research (p. 3).

Summers (1987) goes on to say that needs assessment "is a special case of citizen participation, and participation issues are essentially questions of value" (p. 3). The second objective of needs assessment, then, is how to best incorporate citizen input into making value judgments about what needs actually exist and which needs to serve.

Often, programmers feel unsure about the needs assessment step of the Program Development Cycle. They are uncertain about the appropriateness and adequacy of their needs assessment methods. Programmers have an especially difficult problem with needs assessment because of the multiplicity of leisure needs and the very personal nature of leisure participation preferences. Developing a better understanding of needs and assessment methods will help reduce some of the uncertainty about the process.

The literature has made clear several operational principles about needs assessment that will help programmers understand its limitations and its role.

First, the literature suggests that needs are not objective entities—they are value judgments. What programs are to be developed is always a matter of choice, not fact.

Second, any needs assessment will identify more needs than an agency can fulfill. Any needs assessment method must eventually lead to a decision about which competing needs will be met. These decisions are also value laden. McKillip (1987) suggests that decisions to choose among competing needs should be based on an analysis of the cost, impact, and feasibility of alternatives.

Third, because of the multiplicity of needs, needs analysis is not a maximizing strategy. That is, it will not lead to a final, objective determination about the one, clear course of action that programmers should follow. At best it will help clear up some of the uncertainty about which programs should be developed.

Fourth, in actual practice, needs assessment is an iterative process. Programmers must constantly assess needs and develop programs based on current information.

Fifth, needs assessments can fulfill three roles: (1) they can provide data that enable the agency to better understand the individuals who will be affected by the agency's actions; (2) they can assess patron response to new program proposals; and (3) they can help establish priorities among alternative courses of action (Summers 1987).

Ultimately, the goal of needs assessment is to use client input in identifying and documenting recreational needs that can be successfully met with leisure services developed by the agency. To systematically assess needs, programmers should understand both definitional and methodological issues of needs assessment. The remainder of this chapter involves examining the concept of leisure needs and current methods used to assess them.

Need Concepts

Recreational need is one of several terms used to provide a rationale for the provision of leisure services. In discussing leisure interest "finders," Witt and Groom (1979) point out that the literature often fails to distinguish between needs, wants, interests, demand, and other similar terms. Recreation professionals tend to use these terms interchangeably with little explanation of their meaning. Marketing literature (Kotler 1980) has provided a pragmatic approach to defining *need* and related concepts that will be used to give insight into leisure needs assessment.

Need

A need is a state of deprivation arising out of the basic innate biological characteristics of humans. A need is not created by society but exists apart from and prior to society. There is considerable evidence that humans have a need to participate in activities that are intrinsically rewarding, that stimulate arousal, and that are intrinsically motivating (see for example, Ellis 1973; Csikszentmihalyi 1975; Neulinger 1974; Iso-Ahola 1980, 1982). The need for experiences provided in leisure and recreation is innate; it does not have to be created by programmers through marketing, advertising, program design, or any other technique.

Interest

An interest is an awareness or feeling about what one would like to do or acquire. Interests are learned and are influenced by social forces. An individual's self-concept can also precipitate an interest in a specific activity.

Want

A want is a culturally learned behavior pattern for satisfying specific needs. Individuals need food, but learn to want a Big Mac, a steak, a taco, or a dish of sushi. Individuals need intrinsically rewarding and stimulating behavior, but learn to want to participate in tennis, bowling, oil painting, or reading to satisfy the higher order, innate needs identified earlier. People have few needs, but many wants. Wants are constantly being altered by social forces, including family, friends, and social institutions such as churches, schools, and the business community. Furthermore, satisfying a want often leads to the creation of additional wants (Witt and Groom 1979). Programmers can influence, manipulate, and satisfy wants.

Intention

Intention is the commitment to acquire specific satisfiers of wants under given market conditions. When someone intends to participate in a specific activity, he or she intends to do so at a given time, location, and price. Many people are interested in or want to scuba dive on a Caribbean island; considerably fewer intend to commit the necessary time and money to do so. For recreation program planning, it is essential to understand the number of individuals who actually intend to participate in a program under a defined market condition.

Leisure needs assessment is actually an attempt to determine the interests, wants, or intentions of potential clients. It is important when interpreting data from a needs assessment to know if one actually has data that reveal interests, wants, or intentions. These three concepts imply varying strengths of intention to participate. Because each of these three concepts implies different degrees of intention to participate, each level of intention will also require varying degrees of promotional effort to actually get patrons into a program.

An individual with an interest in an activity has the lowest level of motivation to participate. An individual who wants a program has a stronger motivation and is therefore more likely to participate. An individual who intends to participate has made a strong commitment to actually participate in an activity and is likely to do so if given market conditions are met.

Practitioners have often been disappointed with the reliability of needs assessment data since there has not been a significant correlation between what individuals indicate they intend to do and what they actually do. In many cases this lack of reliability is caused by poor framing of the data collection questions, i.e. they are not specific enough. Fishbein and Manfredo (1992) point out that although intention is a good predictor of specific behaviors, it is less accurate for predicting intention to reach goals or classes of behavior. For example, an individual's intention to participate in a company sponsored, adult softball league, that would be offered the next summer on Tuesday and Thursday evenings from 6:30-7:30 p.m. at a price of $100 per player could be predicted with a much greater degree of accuracy than one's intention to get more physically active (a general leisure participation goal) or to play in an adult sports league (a general class of behavior).

Unfortunately, many needs assessment instruments have simply tried to identify general interests or wants rather than framing questions with specific market conditions about specific activities. Exhibit 8-1 on page 140 presents examples of needs assessment questions that contrast the difference in examining wants and intentions. The questions that examine intentions point out the additional detail needed if one is to accurately assess an individual's intention to participate and to gather sufficient data to actually develop a program that can be offered under a given set of market conditions.

Complete Exercise 8-1 on page 143 and develop some needs assessment questions.

Exhibit 8-1.
Contrasting Want and Intention Questions

WANTS

Listed below are many recreational activities. Some are activities that are currently offered by the [agency] and others are new activities that may be offered in the future. For each activity listed, indicate by checking the appropriate response whether you would participate in the activity if it were offered by the [agency] next year, and if so, would you pay for the cost of the activity program?

	Definitely No	Probably No	Unsure	Probably Yes	Definitely Yes
Baseball	( )	( )	( )	( )	( )
Cooking	( )	( )	( )	( )	( )
Cross-country skiing	( )	( )	( )	( )	( )
Scuba Diving Lessons	( )	( )	( )	( )	( )
Tennis Instructions	( )	( )	( )	( )	( )
Volleyball League	( )	( )	( )	( )	( )

INTENTIONS

Following is a list of leisure activities that you may enjoy. For each activity, please tell us:

1.   If you *participated* in the activity in this past year and/or
2.   If you *intend to participate* in it this coming year.

For those activities in which you intend to participate next year, please tell us:

3.   The *frequency* with which you intend to participate in a typical month (if seasonal, when the activity is in season);
4.   The *primary participants* in the activity, that is yourself alone, or with family, or with friends;
5.   The *location* where you usually participate, (agency owned facility or other supplier);
6.   The *time(s)* of the day or week you prefer to participate;
7.   The *price* at which you no longer can afford to participate; and
8.   Potential *barriers*; if any to your participation.

(continued)

[Note: below are the items to be included on an instrument. Although they are laid out vertically in this exhibit, they should be displayed horizontally for each activity for which information is sought.]

Baseball

1. Experienced last year?   Yes ( )   No ( )

2. Intend to participate this year?   Yes ( ) (Go on to 3)
                                                                     No ( ) (Go on to next activity)

3. Expected frequency (in season)   Daily   ( )
                                                                     Several times per week   ( )
                                                                     Several times per month   ( )
                                                                     Once per month   ( )
                                                                     Less often than once
                                                                          per month   ( )

4. Primary participants (Select one)   Alone   ( )
                                                                     With family   ( )
                                                                     With friends   ( )

5. Location (Select one primary location)

                                                                     [Name of agency
                                                                          facility]   ( )
                                                                     Competing facility
                                                                          or facilities if
                                                                          appropriate   ( )

6. Preferred activity times (Select all that apply)

	Early Morning	Mid-Morning	Lunch time	Early afternoon	Mid-afternoon	Night
Monday	x	x	x	x	x	x
Tuesday	x	x	x	x	x	x
Wednesday	x	x	x	x	x	x
Thursday	x	x	x	x	x	x
Friday	x	x	x	x	x	x
Saturday	x	x	x	x	x	x
Sunday	x	x	x	x	x	x

(continued)

7. Circle the dollar amount at which you would no longer be able to afford to participate in this activity. Please use only one section depending on whether this activity is paid for on a per-participation basis or per-session basis.

7. a. Activities Paid For on a Per-Participation Basis

Could not afford to participate if there were a fee 1
$1.00 per participation 2
Over $1.00 but under $3.00 per participation 3
Over $3.00 but under $5.00 per participation 4
Over $5.00 but under $7.50 per participation 5
Over $7.50 but under $10.00 per participation 6
Over $10.00 but under $15.00 per participation 7
Over $15.00 but under $25.00 per participation 8
Over $25.00 but under $40.00 per participation 9
Over $40.00 per participation 10

7.b. Activities Paid For on a Per- Session Basis

Could not afford to participate if there were a fee 1
$5.00 per session 2
Over $5.00 but under $10.00 per session 3
Over $10.00 but under $15.00 per session 4
Over $15.00 but under $20.00 per session 5
Over $20.00 but under $25.00 per session 6
Over $25.00 but under $30.00 per session 7
Over $30.00 but under $50.00 per session 8
Over $50.00 but under $74.00 per session 9
Over $75.00 per session 10

8. Potential Barriers. Please indicate the barriers listed below that are most likely to keep you from participating in the activity. (Select no more than three)

Activity unavailable near my home .... ( )
Lack of child care .... ( )
Lack of transportation .... ( )
Poor facility .... ( )
Inconvenient hours of operation .... ( )
Poor management of facility or program .... ( )
Lack of program information .... ( )
I am not skilled enough .... ( )
I am uncomfortable with other users .... ( )

(Adapted from the Leisure Needs Survey Instrument, U.S. Navy Recreational Services Program)

Exercise 8-1.
Developing Needs Assessment Questions

In class, discuss the different kinds of information you would have with the two types of responses to the needs assessment questions included in Exhibit 8.1. Which of these instruments would provide the most complete information for developing and designing a program? Which would be the most expensive to administer?

After the discussion, write needs assessment questions for the following three activities to be held at a public swimming pool:

Swimming lessons
Scuba lessons
Public swimming

Now exchange questions with a class member and critique each other's questions. Remember to try to determine a patron's intention to participate. The more specific you can be about the activity, time, place, and price, the more likely you are to obtain reliable information.

Needs From a Social Policy Viewpoint

Mercer (1973) has pointed out that, from a social policy standpoint, some types of needs are more debilitating than others. Therefore, resources are more urgently needed to alleviate these needs. Mercer has identified four types of needs—normative, felt, expressed, and comparative.

Normative needs are more or less objective standards defined by various organizations and groups that are qualified to do so because of their training or position. The *Recreation, Park, and Open Space Standards and Guidelines* (Lancaster 1983), published by the National Recreation and Park Association, is an example of such standards. Many communities develop their own park and open space standards in developing a park master plan.

When using normative standards, the need documented is the difference between what a community or neighborhood may have and what the normative standard suggests they should have. How much need exists in a community can obviously be manipulated by supplying more so that the gap between what is provided and what should be provided is narrowed or by raising the standard so that the gap between what is and what should be is widened.

Felt needs are perceptions about what an individual believes he or she would like to do. They are analogous to the wants, interests, and intentions identified earlier. Felt needs may be thought of as latent demand. That is, they are demands that could be turned into actual consumption. Felt needs are shaped by social forces leading individuals to conclude that they have a need for specific services or facilities.

Expressed needs are needs fulfilled through actual participation. They are included as a need because, if the supply currently fulfilling the need were terminated, they would immediately become a felt need again, demanding attention and resources.

Comparative needs are actual variations in service provided or variations in access to leisure opportunities experienced by different groups. Variation in leisure facilities and services provided to different neighborhoods is often a major point of contention in the delivery of community recreation services. It is also a concern in many other types of leisure service organizations. Two examples of comparative need problems in various agency settings are (1) variations in the opportunities provided to different work shifts in corporate recreation settings and (2) variations in service access by different personnel ranks in the military. Mercer (1973) suggests that, although one may be able to document one of these four types of need for various individuals, from a social policy standpoint those most in need of additional service have a combination of needs. This conceptualization of a rank order of urgency to fulfill needs is especially useful when demand is too great for the limited resources or in retrenchment situations.

Approaches to Needs Assessment

Programmers are often overly concerned about whether they are correctly conducting needs assessments. Because of their possibly ineffective needs assessment methods, they are concerned about overlooking a tremendous pool of unfulfilled needs. The inadequacy that many programmers feel stems from their not conducting a systematic random survey of the population on a routine basis. Often this is not done for a variety of reasons, including a lack of skill or resources. In addition to surveys, however, several methods can be used to assess needs.

The National Park Service (undated) has defined needs assessment as gathering information directly from the public and analyzing it. Analysis involves placing that information into meaningful patterns that will lead to the development of leisure services that meet unfulfilled needs.

Many approaches can be used to conduct community needs assessments. Approaches can generally be placed into one of two general assessment methods: group approaches or surveys. Miller and Hustedde (1987) have identified nine methods of group approaches, including town meetings, public hearings, charrettes, futures conferences, the Delphi approach, nominal groups, jury, workshops, and consciousness-raising efforts. The reader interested in additional approaches should see Miller and Hustedde (1987).

The National Park Service (undated) has identified four approaches that are frequently used in conducting leisure needs assessments: citizen advisory committees, public meetings and workshops, unstructured inputs and structured exploratory interviews, and surveys (p. 64). These four approaches will be explained below.

Citizen Advisory Committees

Citizen advisory committees are composed of community residents who are either appointed or elected to a committee whose responsibility is to advise the agency staff or board. Advisory groups can be very valuable in providing a communication link between the agency and its constituency.

Summers (1987) has pointed out that citizen advisory groups can be misused by both agencies and citizens. Agencies can mobilize citizen groups to support their own already-formulated policies under the guise of citizen input. People often form citizen advisory groups to lobby for very narrow interests rather than to represent the general public interest. In this latter role, advisory groups can become formidable political forces that lobby to have scarce resources directed to their own activity interest. However, the most positive approach to the use of citizen advisory groups assumes that because of their knowledge and interest they will consider all dimensions of an issue. These groups can provide programmers with valuable insight into the program needs of patrons.

Public Meetings and Workshops

A public meeting is frequently used to solicit citizen input on policy development, planning issues, budget allocations, or leisure needs and preferences. In some instances, agencies are required to conduct such meetings to satisfy a grant or legislative requirement. In conducting a public meeting, the agency establishes two-way communication with its clientele and facilitates an outlet for expressing emotion about an issue. Often during a public meeting, a programmer can sense the strength of emotion accompanying an issue.

A workshop is a more organized public meeting during which people participate in small discussion groups with a focused agenda. Facilitating citizen input with an organized agenda will often lead to more productive meetings.

With either method, citizens self-select who will attend, and it is likely that those who do attend will have the strongest opinion either for or against an issue. Determining how closely the opinions expressed at public meetings and workshops represent the view of the general population is problematic.

Interviews

An interview is a meeting in which information is obtained. Programmers can acquire needs assessment information from both unscheduled and scheduled interviews.

Unscheduled interviews

While programmers are fulfilling their responsibilities, they will have many opportunities to obtain information from current and prospective patrons. Unscheduled interviews include the face-to-face unsolicited comments and telephone calls made by constituents to programmers. Being a programmer in an agency places one in a position of access to the public. The public will come to you with information including complaints, compliments, and suggestions.

These are valuable pieces of information, but they often require that the programmer be prepared to probe client comments immediately in order to discover all information that may be useful. In order to provide structure to these interviews and thereby obtain the most information possible, it is important to have a basic interview schedule prepared so the most critical pieces of information may be obtained. Exhibit 8-2 includes a list of questions that may be used to provide structure to unstructured interviews.

Exhibit 8-2.
Unscheduled Interview Agenda

1.   Obtain the name and address of the patron.
2.   Identify the specific program, facility, policy or staff member the patron is commenting about.
3.   Ascertain if the patron is making a complaint, giving a compliment, or making a suggestion.
4.   Make certain the patron identifies the specific issue they are concerned about.
5.   Try to discover what resolution or outcome the patron would like to have.
6.   Make note of all follow-up actions taken.

As with all unsolicited comments from self-selected individuals, it is important to ascertain how widespread the viewpoint is throughout the population.

Structured interviews

Structured interviews are arranged and scheduled. They are conducted with an interview schedule and are given some direction by the interviewer. Several types of group interview techniques may be used, including nominal group interviews and focus group interviews. What follows is a general description of how to conduct a focus group interview for needs assessment purposes.

Focus group interviews can be used for one or more of the following:

- To develop hypotheses for further testing
- To provide information for structuring questionnaires
- To provide overall background information on programs
- To solicit patron impressions about new program concepts
- To stimulate new ideas about older programs
- To generate ideas for new programs
- To interpret previously obtained quantitative results

The focus group technique involves three distinct phases: preparing for the interview, conducting the interview, and analyzing the results.

Preparing for the interview

Although it seems obvious, it is extremely important to prepare well before the actual face-to-face interview begins. Before good interview questions can be developed, one must have a thorough understanding of the problem being examined. Thorough preparation requires identifying a focused problem statement, developing questions logically deduced from the problem, and preparing topical areas that will be used to introduce the questions. Topical areas help the interviewer keep the interview moving smoothly in a logical fashion, thus providing coherence to the whole process.

The reader is cautioned against trying to develop a problem statement and questions that are too broad. The focus group interviewing technique is useful because it facilitates an in-depth examination of a problem and can lead to new insights into the problem. Covering too many topics in one session often precludes the in-depth examination of a problem or concept. Exhibit 8-3 on page 149 includes a focus group problem and an agenda.

Exhibit 8-3.
Focus Group Interview Problem Statement and Agenda

Problem Statement:

To determine how single-parent families with children from six to twelve years of age make decisions about their children's participation in summer recreation programs.

Opening Narrative:

Welcome. Today we are going to discuss a topic I think you will find interesting and you know a lot about—your children's summer recreation activities. We are interested in learning when and how decisions about summer recreation participation are made, who makes them, and what is important to you and your children about the activities selected.

Before we start, I have a couple of requests: first, that only one person speak at a time so that we can truly interact with each other; second, that you feel free to say exactly what you think—we want both positive and negative comments. Give us your true feelings.

Now, to get started, let's go around the table one at a time and have you tell us a little bit about yourself and your family. All of you are single parents—we would like to know how many children you have, their ages, their gender, and a little bit about them and each of you.

Focus Questions:

1. How would your children answer the following comment: I have to participate in this program because _____. (Probe:What reason do they most frequently give about why they must be in a program?)

2. Who do your children most like to participate with in recreation activities? (Probe:Friends, siblings, schoolmates?)

3. How would you answer the following comment: I want my children in summer recreation programs because_____ . (Probe:What reasons do you give your friends, neighbors, or former spouses about why your children must be in a specific recreation program?)

4. In my home_____ decides which recreation activities my children will select to participate in. (Probe:Is the decision made mostly by the children, the parent, jointly, or between the resident and nonresident parent?)

5. When do you normally make decisions about which summer recreation activities your children will be in? (Probe:How far in advance of summer do parents want to know what their children's schedules will be?)

6. How would your children answer this question: I wish I could _____ this summer. (Probe: Identify programs that children may want or programs that parents may want for them.)

7. I will not let my children be in a recreation program unless I am sure _____ . (Probe:What must a program do or be before parents will allow their children to participate?: Keep the discussion going on this until all fruitful information is obtained.)

The second part of preparing for the interview is to select the people to be interviewed. Because only a few individuals will be included in the interview, they must be selected carefully. The following points should be considered when selecting group members:

• It is important to keep the group small enough to facilitate open communication. Between six and ten group members would be appropriate.

• The group should have both homogeneity and contrast (Wells 1979). It is especially important to maintain homogeneity on factors that might otherwise inhibit open communication. For example, well-educated, middle-class individuals may inhibit the full participation of lower-class, less-educated individuals in a focus group. In this case, it would be best to interview two groups, each made up of people with similar backgrounds. But some spark should also be provided through contrasts in the composition of the group. For example, in a focus group interview designed to examine the operation of an indoor tennis facility, it would be desirable to include both users of the agency's tennis facility and some users of a competitor's tennis facility. Groups, then, must be carefully constituted to ensure that there will be an open exchange of ideas and that the group is made up of members who can contribute to a thorough discussion of the idea, including its pros and cons.

• A decision about where to conduct the interview must be made. There are generally three choices—the agency's facilities, a neutral site, or the client's facilities, such as someone's home.

Conducting the interview

How the interview is conducted is critical to obtaining the information desired by the agency. The interview can be conducted in a directive or a nondirective style. In the nondirective style, the interviewer acts as a facilitator whose role is to introduce prearranged questions, get the group discussing them, and intervene only to keep the discussion within fruitful bounds. Ideally, the interviewer does not participate in the discussion, although this cannot always be avoided.

In the directive style, the interviewer provides much more structure and controls the flow of discussion. The interviewer generally introduces a topic and keeps the discussion going until the topic has been covered to the interviewer's satisfaction; a new topic is then introduced. With either style, the interviewer should elicit responses that are the true beliefs and feelings of the group members. The choice of style is influenced by the purpose of the interview, the content of the questions to be asked, and the members of the group.

Analyzing the results

Analysis can range in detail and thoroughness from a brief impressionistic summary of the principal findings through a very detailed content analysis of tape recordings from the interview. In either case, results from an interview should be organized around the principal questions asked during the interview. Written results should reflect participant views, including the distribution of views, the strength of conviction, and new viewpoints elicited during the interview.

Surveys

Although the use of systematic random surveys is widely recommended in recreation literature, their use as a needs assessment method has been questioned. Heberlein (1976) suggests that public involvement includes four major functions: informational, interactive, assurance, and ritualistic. The informational function includes getting information from the public. Surveys are excellent for doing this but poor for giving information to the public.

Dillman (1987) has pointed out that the uniqueness of the survey is its ability to "tell the proportion in a population who have a certain attribute and the proportion who do not" (p. 192). This makes it a powerful tool for needs assessment. Dillman has also argued that it is possible to conduct scientifically valid surveys and meet the need for citizen involvement if the survey process is done appropriately. However, what it takes to successfully conduct a needs assessment survey has changed dramatically over the past decade because new survey methods and techniques have been developed.

A properly conducted survey is the method of choice to ensure the most representative view of all citizens. Technical information about how to conduct surveys is contained in the chapter on evaluation (Chapter Twelve). Implementing a needs assessment survey requires simultaneously coordinating many tasks; many errors can therefore be made. Readers interested in conducting a needs assessment survey are encouraged to read Dillman (1987, pp. 192-208) for a succinct briefing on how to avoid problems with nine tasks essential to implementing a survey.

There is some confusion among practicing programmers because survey methods are used for both needs assessment and for evaluation. Although the technology is the same, the focus of the questions is not. Program evaluation deals with the past and judges the worth of what was done. Needs analysis deals with the future and asks what should be done (McKillip 1987, p. 29).

Integrating the Four Approaches

Each of these four approaches has strengths and weaknesses. No single approach can give a completely accurate picture of the needs in a community and provide the social action often needed to implement solutions. Although surveys are the method of choice, they are expensive and are usually not conducted annually in every organization. If possible, however, an agency should conduct one annually. Certainly a needs assessment survey should be conducted no less often than every three years.

The other three approaches are used to supplement the survey data and to provide focus to a survey when it is conducted. Survey data often do not provide sufficiently detailed information to make programmatic decisions, so one of the other approaches such as a focus group may be used to gather additional, focused information. In the latter case, exploratory methods may be used to discover issues or needs whose actual distribution in the population can only be assessed through a systematic random sample survey. The four methods identified, then, are used in a complementary manner to form a comprehensive needs assessment program for an agency.

Needs Assessment Questions

One can ask many different questions to determine wants that an agency can satisfy. Part of the uncertainty that programmers have about whether they are conducting an adequate needs analysis has to do with their lack of understanding of what actually constitutes needs assessment questions. The following are questions identified by the National Park Service (undated, pp. 63-64).

- What do its constituencies believe the agency should be doing? (Setting objectives)
- What needs and wants do citizens have? What are the characteristics of those who have a particular need (want)? How many are affected? What makes individuals decide to use or not use existing services? (Identifying target markets)
- How do potential target markets react to various service alternatives that could meet these needs (wants)? (Product development)
- What price should be charged? (Pricing)
- How can its availability be best communicated? (Promotion)
- At what time and locations should it be offered? (Distribution)

A needs analysis is being conducted whenever one seeks answers to these or similar questions in a systematic manner and analyzes the responses. The quality of the effort will depend on how pertinent the questions are, how the data are analyzed, and how representative the data are for the entire population. In conducting leisure service needs assessments, one can almost always identify a program need, develop the service to fulfill the need, have the program populated, and believe that needs are being fulfilled. However, programmers are concerned that an even greater need may not have been discovered. The only solution to this concern is to continue to do needs assessment and to revise program services as indicated by new information.

A Marketing Approach to Meeting Needs

In recent years it has become popular to apply marketing principles to the operation and management of program services in leisure service organizations. One of the first articles to advocate using marketing concepts in analyzing leisure services was written by Crompton (1978). Crompton has continued to promote the usefulness of marketing principles as a major program management strategy for park and recreation services. However, Shultz, McAvoy, and Dustin (1988), have expressed concern about the adoption of business management strategies as the management paradigm for providing leisure services.

The position in this book is that marketing literature contains a number of useful concepts and methods for program development and management that programmers can use. However, programmers are not simply marketers—they are programmers. Although marketing techniques are used in programming, programmers possess the unique ability to design programs that provide maximal opportunities for the leisure experience. Programmers can do this because they have been educated in how humans experience leisure in social occasions and how these occasions can best be structured to maximize the opportunity to experience leisure. This unique professional ability does not stem from training in marketing. How, then, does marketing help programmers accomplish programming? To understand the contribution that marketing can make to leisure program development, one must understand some of the basic concepts.

Marketing and Exchanges

First, what is marketing? The American Marketing Association (cited in Zikmund and d'Amico 1993) states that "Marketing is the process of planning and executing the conception, pricing, promotion, and distribution of ideas, goods, and services to create exchanges that will satisfy individual and organizational objectives" (p. 9). Kotler and Armstrong (1993) define marketing ". . . as a social and managerial process by which individuals and groups obtain what they need and want through creating and exchanging products and value with others" (p. 3).

Crompton and Lamb (1986) state, "Marketing is a set of activities aimed at facilitating and expediting exchanges" (p. 16). Marketing is focused on meeting identified patron needs, including their logical extension through interests, wants, and intentions. In addition, all of marketing is based on the notion that needs are met through exchange processes. Understanding the notion of exchange is critical to understanding marketing.

An exchange occurs when two or more parties satisfy their needs and wants through the interchange of something of value. In many cases, one of the items of value is money, although good will, satisfaction, and other intangibles are also valuable items that may be exchanged. Kotler and Andreasen (1987, p.70) identify four conditions that an exchange condition assumes:

1.   There are at least two parties.
2.   Each can offer something that the other perceives to be a benefit or benefits.
3.   Each is capable of communication and delivery.
4.   Each is free to accept or reject the offer.

This latter point is the one that creates both a concern and a justification for using marketing concepts in administering municipal recreation and not-for-profit leisure services. Since municipal and not-for-profit providers have third-party funding sources to subsidize and keep the price of leisure services artificially low, how they incorporate patron desires into their programs becomes a major issue. These agencies have a monopoly in offering low-cost leisure opportunities, so patrons are less free to accept or reject them. Given this situation, these agencies can adopt one of three orientations (Kotler and Andreasen 1987) or operating philosophies. They can adopt a product orientation and offer what they believe is good for the public. They can adopt a sales orientation and try to stimulate interest in the agency's existing services. Or they can adopt a customer orientation and try to develop services that meet identified patron needs and wants. This third one is a marketing orientation. The justification for using marketing techniques in agencies that have the financial resources to offer subsidized recreation is to incorporate, at the front end, patron input into the development of services. In addition, marketers are also admonished to practice "societal marketing," which advises them to not only consider individual needs and wants, but also the collective needs of society (Zikmund and d'Amico 1993). Marketing provides a number of useful concepts and techniques for helping to accomplish this end.

A Market Defined

Kotler and Armstrong (1993) state "A market is the set of actual and potential buyers of a product" (p.7). Thus, they believe the programmer should be concerned with both current and potential buyers of a product. On the other hand, Zikmund and d'Amico (1993) state that, "A market is a group of potential customers for a particular product who are willing and able to spend money or exchange other resources to obtain the product" (p. 9). They believe one should focus on those who are ready and willing to purchase. All individuals in a market desire to obtain a similar product or service that can fulfill a specific need or want. An ongoing problem, however, is how much must occur to move those who may be interested to actually become consumers.

Segmenting Markets

Any market may be large or small, but it will usually be made up of identifiable subgroups called market segments. For example, fishermen make up a recreation market. This market can be segmented by subdividing all fishermen into two groups: saltwater or freshwater fishermen. The market could be further segmented into groups that include shore or boat fishermen. Further segmentation along any number of variables is possible. O'Sullivan (1991) has identified five classes of descriptor variables that may be used to segment leisure markets: leisure needs/interests, geographic, sociodemographics, behavioral, and synchrographics. An adaptation of these, including examples of some descriptors is displayed in Exhibit 8-4 on page 157.

Exhibit 8-4.
Common Descriptor Classes with Example Variables

Leisure Needs
Physical Activity
Achievement
Social Interaction

Geographic
Urban/rural location
Location of residence
Location of employment
Access to leisure locales

Sociodemographics
Education
Age/life cycle stage
Gender
Income
Employed/unemployed
Family/marital status
Ethnicity

Leisure Interests
Socialization into
a specific leisure
activity
Sports & Games
Outdoor Recreation
Arts
Exercise Activities
Travel, etc.

Synchrographics
Studying time as a
variable that may
define specific markets
Time of day
Day of week
Duration of program
Season of the year

Behavioral
Activity skill level
Usage rate
Loyalty to activity
Specialization in activity
Benefits sought

(Adapted from O'Sullivan, 1991)

Markets are segmented to further refine and identify the group of individuals with whom an agency may want to develop exchanges. Weinstein (1987) defines segmentation as "the process of partitioning markets into segments of potential customers with similar characteristics who are likely to exhibit similar purchase behavior" (p. 4). If the many variables identified in Exhibit 8-4 are used, markets can be segmented almost infinitely.

How much segmentation is enough? This is a difficult question to answer. In actual practice, segmentation must be managed to be effective. Weinstein (1987) identifies three reasons that this is true: (1) not everyone is a potential customer for every service the agency may develop; (2) an agency's service mix must be limited because of limited resources and economic efficiency; and (3) since the number of potential customers and the number of services available are limited, it is most efficient to match services with potential customers. No agency has the resources to meet all identified market segments; therefore, strategic choices about which markets to serve must be made. Market segmentation, then, helps agencies be more efficient in matching customers with services.

Differences in segments must have a practical difference that warrants separate marketing attention. Kotler and Armstrong (1993) suggest that four criteria must be met before segmentation is justified. First, the segment must be measurable. One must be able to determine its size, the ability of the population to purchase service, and other differences in market behavior that are unique to the market segment. This is why some recreation programmers reject marketing. Often it is cheaper to simply offer a program and see if it succeeds than it is to confirm the existence of the market segment before offering the program.

For example, the author was once asked how to determine the market for weekend rentals of recreation equipment kits for picnics. Conducting a marketing survey for a community of 10,000 to determine the demand for the kits was more expensive than simply buying the equipment for five kits, publicizing the program, and adjusting from observed use. Because measuring many recreation markets is expensive, marketing is not the answer to every program development problem.

Second, the market must be accessible. It is possible to identify markets that need services but simply cannot be reached efficiently. In a city as large as Los Angeles, there may be a market of individuals who want to play Scottish bagpipes. Because the people are widely scattered, however, the critical number needed to make up a program may never materialize. The market simply cannot be readily accessed.

Third, a market segment must be substantial enough to warrant separate marketing attention. In commercial agencies, the test is whether or not a segment is large enough to be profitable. In not-for-profit operations justifying serving identified market segments is more complicated. Two common tests are whether or not the segment is large enough to be served efficiently or whether it has a unique, demonstrable need that is part of the agency's service mission.

Fourth, the market segment must be actionable. Does the agency have the resources to treat the segment separately? Is the segment likely to respond to separate marketing attention and is their unique characteristic likely to remain stable over time? In recreation there are often many different market segments that can be identified for a single facility. For example, in a public swimming pool there are children who want to play in the water, people who want to practice springboard diving, those who simply want to swim laps for an aerobic workout, those who want to snorkel or scuba dive, and so on. Some of these segments will be too small to justify separate treatment. In addition, some of these uses interfere with each other and therefore the agency may not be able to take action on all segments.

Target Marketing

Once the total market is segmented, the agency may adopt different strategies for trying to complete exchanges with the various segments identified. Some segments, for reasons outlined previously, will not be served. Market segments with whom the agency desires to have exchanges are termed target markets. Crompton and Lamb (1986) have defined a target market as follows: "A target market is a relatively homogeneous group of people or organizations that have relatively similar service preferences with whom the agency seeks to exchange" (p. 112).

The major reason for segmenting markets is to determine whether the market should be targeted as a whole, or whether specific segments should be handled differently. Marketers influence the target market through the marketing mix— ". . . the set of controllable marketing variables that the firm blends to produce the response desired in the target market" (Kotler and Armstrong 1993, pp. 40-41). The four variables most frequently cited as being controllable by marketers are product, price, promotion, and place.

A different market mix is developed for each target market identified. One or more of the four market mix variables is altered for each target market identified. *Product* is a generic term used to describe the service, product, or facility the agency is developing, making, or constructing for the client. Many products could be developed. Changes in the product itself, i.e. changes in the six key elements of program production, will obviously have a tremendous impact on the market mix. The *price* at which a product is sold, including a zero price, will affect consumption. Pricing recreation services is dealt with in detail in Chapter Fifteen.

Promotional campaigns for the same leisure product can be designed differently for different target markets. For example, one could simply alter the promotion campaign to emphasize different benefits from the same service and distribute the different publicity campaigns to the different target markets. This could be done to promote a fitness facility to two different markets, one of which is most interested in opportunities to meet new friends and the other in keeping physically fit. The two groups could use the facility at the same time but would be attracted to it for different reasons. These differences would need to be incorporated into two different promotional campaigns. *Place* involves distribution of services, including the day, time, and location of service. Changing the place of a service will often change the market that the product will appeal to. Additional information about developing promotional campaigns is included in Chapter Twelve and additional information about scheduling leisure products is included in Chapter Eleven.

It is important to realize that developing different market mixes for each target market is more expensive than developing a single market mix for the entire market. For this reason, one should be sure that there are enough differences between market segments to justify developing separate market mixes.

Target Marketing Strategies

Kotler and Andreasen (1987) have identified three target marketing strategies: undifferentiated, differentiated, and concentrated. These three are illustrated in Figure 8-1 on page 161.

The undifferentiated strategy assumes that the entire market will be handled as a single entity. Any existing market segments are not recognized, and a single market mix is developed. Or perhaps there are not enough differences between the market segments to warrant developing different market mixes. In this case, the undifferentiated strategy is justified. Often, however, this strategy is used for the wrong reason—the agency simply does not want to develop additional market mixes.

Figure 8-1.
Alternate Target Marketing Strategies
(adapted from Kotler and Andreasen, 1987, p. 151).

Undifferentiated Strategy

Single marketing mix	→	Market

Differentiated Strategy

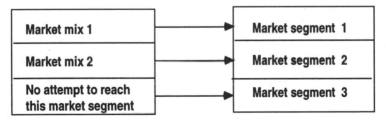

Market mix 1	→	Market segment 1
Market mix 2	→	Market segment 2
No attempt to reach this market segment	→	Market segment 3

Concentrated

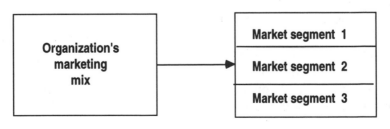

Organization's marketing mix	→	Market segment 1
		Market segment 2
		Market segment 3

Using the differentiated strategy means that the agency will operate in two or more segments of the market and will design different mixes for each segment. It is assumed that better service will result from developing a unique mix for each target market. When using this strategy, it is important that each service have a unique position in the market. Kotler and Armstrong explain: "Market positioning is arranging for a product to occupy a clear, distinctive, and desirable place relative to competing products in the minds of target consumers" (1993, p. 39). The service must possess this quality and the promotional campaign must communicate it to the target market for this strategy to fulfill its potential benefit. Generally this method of operation will be more expensive, but it will result in deeper market penetration and more clients.

The concentrated target marketing strategy recognizes the existence of two or more market segments, but devotes the agency's major marketing effort to only one. With this strategy, the agency simultaneously ignores some market segments while developing a market mix for one targeted segment. This strategy may be adopted when the agency does not have sufficient resources to service all identified markets or when the agency wants to service market segments not currently being served by other providers. An example of the latter instance would be the development of a public golf course with inexpensive green fees in a community that has private country clubs with limited memberships and a commercial golf course with high green fees. The public sector would thus be target marketing golf to middle and lower income players who could not afford to play at the other two courses.

Public agencies and some not-for-profit agencies often have an ethical problem in applying the concentrated target marketing strategy. Which market segments may they ignore? Which should they try to serve? Often the temptation is to serve easily accessible markets, when in reality the public system should serve the most vulnerable clients. For example, Spigner and Havitz, discussing recreation opportunities for the unemployed, point out "... that the unemployed are rarely singled out as a target market" (1993, p. 52). The individuals who constitute these types of markets are often the most difficult to reach and therefore the most costly to serve.

Comparing Marketing and Programming

Marketing contributes to program development in several ways. The market mix is made up of price, promotion, place, and product. Changing any of these four variables alters the market that may be served. Of the four variables included in the market mix, product is the one for which programmers have unique expertise. They understand the leisure experience and how to structure leisure occasions. Techniques and skills for accomplishing this have been discussed elsewhere in this text.

The major contribution of marketing to recreation programming is in providing methods for identifying needs to be developed into programs and knowledge about how to successfully exchange the services developed with target markets. Understanding the role of promotion, pricing, and place (distribution) in the consumption of leisure services is the primary contribution of marketing techniques to recreation programming.

Some cautions about the misuse of marketing concepts are in order. Marketing technology provides excellent techniques for isolating market segments that are truly in need of social services. Although these techniques have been in use in recreation and leisure service agencies for over fifteen years, they have generally been used to develop services for the average, middle-class constituent who can function in a market-driven, fee-for-service economy. Programs are rarely targeted for anyone other than the average person (Spigner and Havitz 1993). Marketing technology has not been used to help public and not-for-profit agencies focus their efforts on markets that are specifically targeted by their mission statements—the implementation of societal marketing. The need to accomplish this makes marketing in public and not-for-profit agencies more complicated than in commercial and private agencies. Furthermore, as target marketing techniques become more sophisticated, their summary effect is to provide the agency the ability to manipulate the patron. Smith (1992) has stated "Privacy in the 1990s includes not only the right to control personal information about oneself and how it is used but also the right to be free of manipulation, whether in the marketplace or by the government" (p 19). Thus, agencies whose missions include contributing to the public good must make certain that they are ethically using these techniques to further the legitimate interests of their patrons and community rather than the sole interest of the agency.

Conclusion

Needs assessments are undertaken to identify program components desired by constituents to be eventually used in the design of programs. A need for leisure participation is assumed; therefore, needs assessments are used most often to identify patrons' wants and intentions so that the most salient wants can be identified for program development. Several methods for implementing needs assessments complement each other. Marketing concepts are used to help an agency obtain ideas to incorporate into program design and develop services for specific markets, so that services may be successfully exchanged with identified markets.

References, Chapter Eight

Carpenter, G.M., and C.Z. Howe. 1985. *Programming Leisure Experiences.* New York: Prentice-Hall.

Csikszentmihalyi, M. 1975. *Beyond Boredom and Anxiety.* San Francisco: Jossey-Bass.

Crompton, J.L. 1978. Development of a Taxonomy of a Leisure Services Delivery System. *Journal of Leisure Research* 10(3), 214-218.

Crompton, J.L. 1983. Selecting Target Markets—a Key to Effective Marketing. *Journal of Park and Recreation Administration* 1(1), 7-26.

Crompton, J.L., and C.W. Lamb, Jr. 1986. *Marketing Government and Social Services.* New York: Wiley.

Dillman, D. 1987. Elements of Success. In D.E. Johnson, L.R. Meiller, L.C. Miller, and G.F. Summers (Eds.), *Needs Assessment, Theory and Methods* (pp. 188-209). Ames, IA: Iowa State University Press.

Ellis, M.J. 1973. *Why People Play.* Englewood Cliffs, NJ: Prentice-Hall.

Fishbein, M., and M.J. Manfredo. 1992. A Theory of Behavior Change. In M. J. Manfredo (Ed.), *Influencing Human Behavior: Theory and Applications in Recreation, Tourism, and Natural Resources Management* (29-50). Champaign, IL: Sagamore Publishing Co., Inc.

Herberlien T.A. 1976. *Principles of Public Involvement.* Department of Rural Sociology Staff Paper Series in Rural and Community Development, University of Wisconsin—Madison. Cited in D.E. Johnson, and L.R. Meiller, 1987, Community Level Surveys. In D.E. Johnson, L.R. Meiller, L.C. Miller, and G.F. Summers (Eds.), *Needs Assessment, Theory and Methods* (126-141). Ames, IA: Iowa State University Press.

Higginbotham, J.B., and K.K. Cox. 1979. *Focus Group Interviews.* Chicago: American Marketing Association.

Iso-Ahola, S.E. 1980. *The Social Psychology of Leisure and Recreation.* Dubuque, IA: Wm. C. Brown.

Iso-Ahola, S.E. 1982, February. Intrinsic Motivation: An Overlooked Basis for Evaluation. *Parks & Recreation,* 32, 33, 58.

Kotler, P., 1980. *Marketing Management* (4th ed.). Englewood Cliffs, NJ: Prentice-Hall.

Kotler, P., and A.R. Andreasen. 1987. *Strategic Marketing For Nonprofit Organizations* (3rd ed.). Englewood Cliffs, NJ: Prentice-Hall.

Kotler, P., and G. Armstrong. 1990. *Marketing: An Introduction* (3rd ed.). Englewood Cliffs, NJ: Prentice Hall.

Lancaster, R.A. (Ed). 1983. *Recreation, Park and Open Space Standards and Guidelines.* Alexandria, VA: National Recreation and Park Association.

McKillip, J. 1987. *Need Analysis: Tools For the Human Services and Education.* Beverly Hills, CA: Sage.

Mercer, D. 1973. The Concept of Recreational Need. *Journal of Leisure Research,* 5 (1), 37-50.

Miller, L.C., and R.J. Hustedde. 1987. Group Approaches. In D.E. Johnson, L.R. Meiller, L.C. Miller, & G.F. Summers (Eds.), *Needs Assessment, Theory and Methods* (3-19). Ames, IA: Iowa State University Press.

National Park Service. undated. *Marketing Parks and Recreation.* State College, PA: Venture.

Neulinger, J. 1974. *The Psychology of Leisure.* Springfield, IL: Charles C.Thomas.

O'Sullivan, E. L. 1991. *Marketing for Parks, Recreation, and Leisure.* State College, PA: Venture Publishing, Inc.

Schultz, J.H., L.H. McAvoy, and D.L. Dustin. 1988, January. What Are We in Business For? *Parks & Recreation*, 52-54.

Smith, R. E. 1992. Target Marketing: Turning Birds of a Feather into sitting ducks. *National Forum*, 72 (1), 18-21.

Spigner, C., and M. E. Havitz. 1993, November. Societal Marketing or Social Justice: A Dialogue on Access to Recreation for the Unemployed. *Parks & Recreation*, 51-57.

Summers, G.F. 1987. Democratic Governance. In D.E. Johnson, L.R. Meiller, L.C. Miller, and G.F. Summers (Eds.), *Needs Assessment, Theory and Methods* (3-19). Ames, IA: Iowa State University Press.

Weinstein, A. 1987. *Market Segmentation: Using Demographics, Psychographics and Other Segmentation Techniques to Uncover and Exploit New Markets.* Chicago: Probus.

Wells, W.D. 1979. Group Interviewing. In J.B. Higginbotham, and K.K. Cox (Eds.), Focus Group Interviews (2-12). Chicago: American Marketing Association. (Reprinted from R. Ferber 1974, *Handbook of Marketing Research.* New York: McGraw-Hill.)

Witt, P.A., and R. Groom. 1979. Dangers and Problems Associated with Current Approaches to Developing Leisure Interest Finders. *Therapeutic Recreation Journal* 8(1), 19-30.

Zikmund, W. G., and d'Amico, M. 1993. *Marketing* (4th ed.). St. Paul, MN: West Publishing Co.

Photo courtesy of Metro-Dade County Parks and Recreation, Miami, Florida.
Photo by Helene J. Layne.

9

Program Design

Program design is a transitional step that specifies the details of how a program will actually be operated to facilitate a leisure experience for participants. It is implemented as the final step in Stage 2 of the Program Development Cycle. In this step, the programmer uses data collected in Stages 1 and 2, including the agency's philosophy and goals, marketing and needs assessment information, and other background data that would indicate the need to develop a specific program plus data about the proposed program's content, e.g. a Spring Arts Festival. This data is combined and a program design is prepared.

The programmer must develop a plan that will animate a program to move it through time and orchestrate its flow (Edginton, Hanson, and Edginton 1992) by altering the pattern of attention demanded by the program so there is variety in the content and intensity of consciousness demanded. This results in a managed experience pattern. Evidence for this phenomenon is provided by Hull, Stewart, and Yi (1992), who, while discussing a hiking experience, indicated that ". . . a recreation experience is dynamic: it fluctuates over the course of the engagement. Moods change. Scenic beauty varies. The degree of absorption in one's activity fluctuates" (p. 249). Furthermore, they document that these experience patterns not only vary over the duration of the experience, but that there are subsets of participants that have different experiences. Thus, the same program can provide different individuals with a different experience. They speculate that recreation experience patterns may be influenced by the management of the recreation site. Program design, then, is a process that attempts to anticipate and facilitate this notion of an experience pattern.

Program Design Defined

Program design is *planning the step-by-step action scenarios and configurations of the six program elements that will guide participants through the social interactions necessary to facilitate the leisure experience intended by the designer.* It requires a technique that enables the programmer to anticipate and predict social interaction and to vicariously experience a model of the program. The technique should also facilitate easy iterations for redesign.

How this is accomplished by progra.nmers is not specified nor discussed in the literature. My own experiences as a programmer and my interviews of numerous programmers have convinced me that imaging is a primary technique that is used, and a systematic method for using it in the design of program services is explained in the following pages.

A Program Design Model

Figure 9-1, page 171, is a diagram of the program design model. There are three major components to the model, including design goals, design components, and design tactics. In the first component, the programmer must specify the design goals, i.e. the program outcomes that will result from participation in the program. At a minimum, a program is to provide a leisure experience for participants. Remember from Chapter Two that this requires the program be designed to provide perceptions of freedom, to allow it to be intrinsically satisfying, and to provide opportunities for positive affect, plus be relaxing, fun, and/or enjoyable (Kleiber, Caldwell, and Shaw 1992; Kleiber, Larson, and Csikszentmihalyi 1986).

There can be two additional sources of goals—the agency and participants. The agency may have specified social goals that it attempts to achieve through leisure programming. These are derived from the three- to five-year program management goals and/or the one-year MBO goals [see Chapter Seven].

For example, a corporate recreation operation may try to build esprit de corps among its employees in all programs offered. In addition, the outcomes desired by patrons that are deduced from needs assessment data [see Chapter Eight] are a third possible source of program design goals. These can only be incorporated as a design goal if the patrons' desires are known and there is sufficient consensus about them. In the first component, then, program design goals need to be specified using goal and objective technology [see Chapter Four] and their realization becomes the aim of the design. [*Additional material about how to write program design goals is included at the end of this chapter.*]

Figure 9-1.
Program Design Model

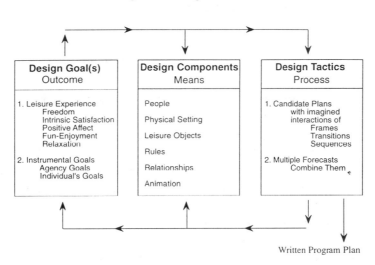

The second design component includes the six key elements of program production that were discussed in Chapter Three. They are the major elements that may be manipulated to affect the outcomes of occasions of social interaction. They are the process of program delivery and participation and the means through which the design will be achieved. The final element of these six, animation, involves determining how the program will move through time and how changes in the other five elements will occur as a program progresses through time. In this component, these five elements are altered through planned animation of social interaction to facilitate the leisure experience.

Finally, the third component requires one to use a technique to develop the design intended. Since leisure programs occur in real time, a major problem in leisure program design is finding a technique that can simulate the passage of time in the design process and thus permit the programmer to experiment with and model various operations of a program. Practitioners in many fields can use techniques that permit real-time rehearsals. For example, musicians practice their musical scores, actors rehearse their scripts, and athletes practice their plays. However, leisure services are often operated and delivered simultaneously, and thus cannot be rehearsed in real time. Using projective imagery can simulate this time dimension in the design process and provide a technique that facilitates experimentation with different models of a program at the speed of thought and at almost no cost.

Techniques for Implementing Program Design

There are several concepts and techniques that need to be mastered to implement the design process that is illustrated in Figure 9-1. The goal of the process is to determine the specific actions that need to be implemented to reach the design goals specified. These actions are termed *design tactics,* the actions that must be implemented to animate a program, i.e. to actually operate it. "Tactics are specific actions that are intended to facilitate implementation of a plan and to produce progress toward their goal" (Beach 1990, p. 8). One may actually prepare a script of a program's operation, but in many cases this is not necessary, and the goal is to identify the key configurations of the six program elements and the key transitions needed to meet the design goals.

Design tactics are developed through *imagined interactions* ". . . a type of instrumental thought process as well as a type of simulation heuristic" (Honeycutt 1991, p. 122). The notion of imagined interactions stems from symbolic interaction theory discussed earlier in the book [Chapter Two].

Mead (1934) identifies the ability of humans to carry on an internalized conversation with oneself as a distinguishing feature of human intelligence. The notion that we are self-reflexive indicates we are capable of becoming an object in our own mind and thereby take the role of others in an effort to understand how they see us. This internal dialogue can be focused on imagined interactions with others. Edwards, Honeycutt, and Zagacki (1988) indicate "This type of mental activity is important, because one may consciously take the role of others, imagining how they might respond to one's messages within particular situations, and thus one can imagine and test the consequences of alternative messages prior to communication" (p. 24). They conclude that ". . . imagined interactions are one mechanism allowing individuals to plan and to measure social action. Imagined interactions allow for the rehearsal, and perhaps discovery, of situational dependent behaviors. Individuals may use imagined interactions to search for or practice behaviors relevant to anticipated conversations" (Edwards, Honeycutt, and Zagacki 1988, p. 41).

Using projective imagery, the programmer simulates the possible social interactions of a program in his/her mind and experiments with various configurations of the key elements of program production. With these images the programmer rehearses and models the program's operation, thereby simulating and projecting different outcomes with different configurations.

Analogy with a previous sequence of events or with imagined future events is the major underlying representational system that should be used. This is supported by Kaufmann's work on the use of mental imagery in problem solving. He states ". . . that in imagery we try to imagine what will happen under actual or hypothetical perceptual conditions (rather than inferring it through logical transformations)" (1988, p. 234). Although the images are heuristic and thus created to experiment with "what if" questions about various configurations that could be attempted, they are also volitional and therefore use directed consciousness to select different combinations of program elements for experimentation.

With this technique, the programmer develops *candidate plans;* alternative design tactics that could be used for program implementation. Each candidate plan should receive conscious attention and be developed until it is a feasible solution to the design problem. To achieve this, one must imagine *multiple forecasts* of candidate plans so that several solutions to the design problem may be developed and considered. Techniques for pushing the formulation of multiple forecasts are discussed in Chapter Ten on creativity and innovation.

Once several candidate plans are developed, they must compete with each other for adoption as the final solution. In addition, they may be altered and various parts of individual candidate plans combined into a final plan.

Projective Imaging Techniques

Forecasting and modeling candidate plans is accomplished through *visualization* of imagined interactions. In your mind's eye, the actual operation of the program, i.e. the interaction scenarios of a program, are visualized. However, this involves more than sight and can include all of the senses (Green 1976). It may also produce emotional feelings (Penfield 1961, cited in Green 1976). Thus, one vicariously experiences the sense of a program including being there, going through the program step by step, and feeling the emotion of participating in the program.

A variety of skills must be learned to successfully use visualization. The first is to discover how you personally organize your visual images. We tend to routinize this behavior and organize them in only one way. Therefore, we must consciously force ourselves to visualize a program differently. Following are several techniques for accomplishing this.

Any visualization will occur from one of two perspectives—external or internal (Weinberg 1988). During *external* visualization you become an object to yourself. For example, you may observe yourself participating as the leader of an event. It is analogous to watching a videotape of yourself leading the event. The goal is to experiment with various leadership styles and strategies in order to forecast the optimal style for the event. During *internal* visualization you attempt to actually be at a program and to vicariously experience it from beginning to end. The goal is to understand how the program will affect a patron, i.e. what is it like to participate in this program? One normally assumes one of these two perspectives when imaging and must consciously convert to the other to thoroughly use visualization to design a program.

You may also force yourself to change your physical *viewpoint* of the program. What will it look like from an aerial view? What if you reversed the sequential order of the program? Take a side view of it or an under the ground view. What will it look like to a child who is 36 inches tall? Attempt to see the program from a different geographical location or physical position.

It is also useful to change the *social role* you are using to visualize the interactions of the program. Changing from leader to participant is one such change. But you must also internally visualize the program from the roles of other program partici- pants such as parents, spectators, the program manager, referees, and other similar roles. It is important to be thorough in this, so all possible difficulties and problems can be predicted and dealt with in the design of the program rather than during its opera- tion.

Using Projective Imaging to Animate the Program Design

A useful icon to image while experimenting with candidate plans is the *vignette* (Ableson 1976) of a cartoon strip. Visualize, as illustrated in Figure 9-2, that your program is a series of frames and transitions between frames that occur in a temporal se- quence. Each *frame* (Goffman 1974) is a single configuration of the six key elements of program production. The length of time that a frame will exist is the amount of time the elements in the frame will occupy the conscious attention of program participants. Each frame, then, represents a single experience, and a program is composed of numerous experiences that occur in temporal order.

Figure 9-2.
Planning Frames

SEQUENCE: temporal order					

Frame 1	T^1	Frame 2	T^2	Frame 3	T^3
People		People		People	
Physical setting		Physical Setting		Physical Setting	
Leisure Objects		Leisure Objects		Leisure Objects	
Rules		Rules		Rules	
Relationships		Relationships		Relationships	
Animation		Animation		Animation	

Frame: a single configuration of the six program elements
T = Transitions: a reconfiguration of the six program elements

The spaces between frames are *transitions* from one frame to another when the six key elements of program design are being reconfigured and the conscious attention of participants is shifting from one element in a frame to another. An additional design consideration is identifying the intervention(s) that must occur to move participants from one frame to the next.

For example, how does one move patrons from one exhibit to the next in a museum? This can be accomplished with arrow signs, through instructions included on an audio tape tour, with an employee guiding the tour, or through a physical layout that creates a natural progression through the exhibit.

The icon of the cartoon strip, then, is a useful one that graphically depicts a temporal sequence of experience frames. The programmer, using this technique, may rewrite the experience in each frame or change their temporal order at will. Each candidate plan that is visualized is a rewritten vignette. Animation of the overall experience is created, because there are designed changes in the following:

- the configuration of key program elements in each frame is changed,
- the temporal order of frames is rearranged, and
- interventions for key transitions are directed.

This succession of changes and the need for patrons to give conscious attention and interpretation to them produces interaction and thereby animates a program.

For an example of how changes of focus on the elements from frame to frame create animation, visualize the three frames in Figure 9-2 (page 175) . Let us assume we are going to program the dedication of a new recreation facility complete with a tour and buffet dinner. Participation is by invitation only. Imagine that in the first frame the primary focus is on the interactions between the people as they arrive. Renewing acquaintances and meeting new people is the first experiential sequence of this program. The interactions in this frame could be facilitated with "ice breaker" social recreation activities or it could be allowed to occur without intervention. The relational history of the group, an additional program design element, would certainly need to be considered in determining the type and extent of intervention to use.

In frame two, the focus of attention is on the new facility. Thus, the physical place is the key element in frame two. The place could be decorated, illuminated, or treated in some other special manner to highlight it during this frame to further focus attention on it. How individuals will be moved from the opening frame to the facility tour is a design problem to solve as well as how they will be moved through the tour itself. For example, will they be placed in small groups and be given a guided tour? Or will they be allowed to do a self-guided walk through?

In the third frame, food, a social object, will be the main focus with a secondary focus on social interaction as the meal is consumed. Moving the participants to the meal location after the tour, queuing them in the buffet line, and seating them at an appropriate table are transition design problems that also must be resolved. In this example, a different program element was the focus in each frame—interacting people, the physical facility, and finally leisure objects. This program would probably have additional frames of dedication speeches, ribbon cutting, etc.

A second method of creating animation is to change the temporal order of the frames. In the current example, the frames could be reordered by allowing the second frame to be the meal and the third frame the facility tour. In any program, attention must be given to the temporal order of panels so the overall flow of the event, i.e. its impact on attention and emotion, are carefully orchestrated to achieve the desired effect. In this program, one could assert that the facility tour should be the final frame used to showcase the new facility rather than ending the event with the meal. Reordering frames in this manner changes the flow of a program and the overall experience.

The third method involves orchestrating the transitions between frames in a variety of ways. These need to be designed so that they contribute to the overall experience desired. For example, at Disneyland, queues for rides, which are a transition, are orchestrated to place the patron in a mood that contributes to the overall theme of the ride itself. In the dedication program being used as an example, how participants are to be moved either to or from the building tour is a key transition design problem.

Summary

Participation in a program, then, can be thought of as a sequence of experiences. These experiences consist of interactions in frames in which conscious attention is given to various configurations of the six key elements of program production. Program design must be conducted from this knowledge base— programming involves understanding and intervening in social interaction by using the six program elements to create and manipulate each frame, to reorder frames, and to design key transitions between frames. Visualization techniques provide a method for the programmer to simulate the interactions of a program. These are used in the design process to develop and experiment with a variety of candidate plans that are eventually combined into a single set of design tactics that solve the design problem.

Five Preplanned Forecasts

The number of visualizations that are possible can be overwhelming. However, experience with program operations can provide us with a useful guide for getting started. Below are five preplanned visualization forecasts to use in formulating candidate plans for each program.

1. Use external imaging to visualize the entire operation of a program.

2. Use internal imaging to experience the program from the participant's perspective.

3. Use internal imaging to experience the program from the perspective of each of the other participants who may be in the program, e.g. spectators, parents, referees, etc.

4. Use external imaging and again visualize the entire operation of the reconfigured program from the program manager's perspective.

5.   Use external and internal imaging to visualize the final program with imagined interactions, changing roles from observer to participant and give special attention to evaluating how the currently configured program operation addresses the design goals developed earlier.

Criteria for Evaluating Candidate Plans

How does one determine which candidate plan to adopt or which to alter and combine into the design tactics to be implemented? How well a candidate plan solves the design problem (as specified by the design goals) prepared in the first component of the design process is the primary criteria. How well the candidate plan facilitates a leisure experience for the participant is the first consideration. Thus, the candidate plan that facilitates perceived freedom by creating choices, that facilitates intrinsic satisfaction, that provides opportunities for positive affect, and that makes the program fun, relaxing, and/or entertaining will be adopted. Second, the candidate plans that contribute to accomplishing specific agency and/or patron goals will also be adopted.

Writing Program Design Goals

Program design goals are the final stratum of goals in the hierarchy of goals and objectives. They evolve from planning and management goals that were developed earlier in the cycle and explained in Chapters Six and Seven. For an example of the entire hierarchy, see Figure 9-3, page 180. In this figure, the mission is included in Box A. It establishes the overall direction of the agency and was discussed in Chapter Six. Three- to five-year planning goals are included in Box B. They were discussed in Chapter Seven and are used to further define the programmatic direction of the agency. One-year, MBO-type objectives are included in Box C. These were also discussed in Chapter Seven. It is at this point that program planning and budget development are integrated and resources are actually committed to the development of a specific program. Program design goals are included in Box D. Their function is to provide direction and definition to a program and they are discussed in the following pages.

Figure 9-3.
An Example of Networked Goals and Objectives

BOX A

MISSION: To provide comprehensive year-round opportunities for recreation and use of physical resources which are accessible and respond to the articulated needs and desires of all residents of the city of Knoxville with an emphasis on educating citizens on the value of learning and practicing lifetime leisure skills and appreciations and serving as a catalyst and facilitator for the provision of recreation programs by other organizations in the community.

BOX B

1 of 8 Goals. To enhance the quality of life for all citizens of Knoxville through the provision of public recreation services.
1. To establish a senior citizens program.
2. To establish an athletic facility reservation system.
3. To establish a cultural arts division.

BOX C

1. To operate a cultural arts fair during the spring of 1994.
2. To offer an arts instructional program for adults with at least five different media during fall (October and November) 1994.
3. To operate a concert in the park series during September 1994.
4. To operate a summer cultural arts workshop for children with three different media during summer of 1994.
    1. To offer a children's drama class during the summer of 1994 with at least fifteen enrollments.
    2. To offer an oil painting class during the summer of 1994.
    3. To offer guitar for beginnners during the summer of 1994.

BOX D

1. By the end of the class, students will be able to play at least three songs with different chords.
2. By the end of the class, students will be able to tune their guitars.
3. At the end of the program, 90% of the students will be able to correctly identify the parts of the guitar.
    1. When requested, paticipants can identify the following parts of the guitar:
        1. Neck
        2. Body
        3. Sound Hole
        4. Strings
        5. Tuning Keys
        6. Frets.

Program design goals must describe the service in detail by articulating what is supposed to happen to people as a result of their participation, so design tactics to facilitate occurrence can be imaged. Writing them requires a shift in the focus of goal development from "what staff will do" to "what will happen to individuals in the leisure experience." The more precise and descriptive one can be, the better the chance of designing and providing the service intended.

Program design goals are developed with varying levels of specificity. They should define the program design problem; that is, a program needs to be designed that will facilitate the experiences outlined in the design goals. Exhibit 9-1 includes a series of program design goals for a concert in the park series, which was a one-year objective for the goal of establishing a cultural arts division included in Box B of Figure 9-3. Design goals, in this case, serve as a framework around which the program is designed. Decisions about what to include or exclude from a program are guided by the goals specified.

Exhibit 9-1.
Program Design Goals: Concert in the Park Series

- To provide a free, live music concert series
- To locate the concerts in a single, easily accessible downtown area with a natural, park-like setting
- To feature a band that will play a variety of musical styles
- To create a festive, picnic atmosphere at each concert

These goals are not exhaustive; complete details will be provided in the program design and the program plan. These goals do, however, provide form and direction to the program. They provide a basic outline of the experience that will result from participation in the program. In this case, it is assumed that patron needs assessment data were incorporated into the goals. Patrons may have expressed a desire for quality, live entertainment and to have events in their downtown area. Now complete Exercise 9-1 on page 182.

Exercise 9-1.
Goal Networking

The program design goals included in Exhibit 9-1 are the final set in a complete network of goals and objectives. Return to Chapters Six and Seven and trace these goals to their origin in the agency's mission statement. After doing this, consider the following questions:

- Can you identify the three- to five-year, short-range planning goals and the one-year, management by objective-type goals associated with this program?
- Can you see how this series of goals is networked through the agency's organizational structure?
- Do you understand how a goal for one level of the organization can become an objective for another level of the organization?
- Do you understand how the program design goals provide direction in deciding about program components and processes?

Programmers are cautioned that frequently the patron needs assessments will only provide information for a partial list of design goals. Programmers must often complete the design goals with additional data from their organizational environment, clientele, and previous professional experience. For example, an assessment may make apparent the need for a program that will serve mothers with preschool children during the morning hours in a noncompetitive activity allowing the mothers to socialize. This need is obviously not a program, but it could serve as a partial list of program design goals. The programmer would need to add more goals and then design a leisure program to solve the original design problem. Another example of design goals is provided in Exhibit 9-2.

Exhibit 9-2.
Program Design Goals: Easter Egg Hunt

- To permit each child to find an Easter egg
- To provide opportunities for children to visit the Easter Bunny
- To keep parents from hunting eggs
- To help parents enjoy seeing their children hunt Easter eggs

Basically, these goals outline an Easter egg hunt designed so that each child can find an egg and search without competition from parents or other children, but in a way that will permit parents to observe their own children. Opportunities to visit the Easter Bunny will also be provided. The critical attributes of the experience to be created are outlined with goals that define the design problem.

Design problems frequently involve developing programs for a specific facility. For example, unused time at a bowling alley, recreation center, swimming pool, or ice rink may need to be filled with a program service. In these instances, it is an organizational need to fill a facility that is the primary impetus for the development of a program. Patron input from a needs assessment is then added to the design problem, and a program is developed to meet articulated client needs and fulfill the organizational need of facility utilization. Now complete Exercise 9-2.

Exercise 9-2.
Program Design Goals

Prepare design goals for a Fourth of July theme party at a nursing home. Be sure to list the experiences you want to create. When finished, discuss the following questions:

- How might patron input be solicited and incorporated as design goals?
- Are the essential experiential elements of this program apparent from the list?
- Is the list explicit enough to guide the design of the program?
- Does the list make apparent the unique experience that will be offered in this program?

Participant Goals

The most specific type of program design statement is the terminal performance objective, which states an observable behavior to be performed by the participant in terms that are measurable. A program is then designed to facilitate the behaviors specified. Exhibit 9-3 presents an example of participant performance objectives for a baseball clinic.

Exhibit 9-3.
Participant Objectives: Baseball Clinic

At the end of the clinic:

- Participants will be able to correctly answer 70 percent or more of written questions on baseball rules.
- Participants will be able to correctly answer 70 percent or more of written questions on baseball strategy.
- Participants' batting averages will increase by .050 or more.
- Seventy percent or more of the participants will indicate that their skill at playing the position they chose increased significantly.

It is important to recognize that the subject in this list of goals is different from the subject in many of the previous lists. In this list, the subject is the participant in the program. Instead of implying that the staff will accomplish them, this series of goals clearly indicates what the participants will accomplish.

Presumably, these demonstrated abilities will result from their participation in the program designed and operated by the programmer. Another example of this is provided by the goals and objectives included in Box D of Figure 9-3. Specifically, program design goal #3, "At the end of the program, 90% of the students will be able to correctly identify the parts of the guitar" is operationalized with the sample program design objective #1 under it—"When requested, participants can identify the following parts of the guitar: neck, body, sound hole, strings, tuning keys, and frets." Each of the other program design goals would also have program design objectives developed for them that would provide additional direction to the design of a program. Furthermore, they would be written so they can be measured and their attainment thereby verified.

Comprehensive refinement of terminal performance objectives for use in program design should always be completed for programs providing instruction and therapy. Their use can also improve professional practice in other types of programs.

Program Design Standards

Program design is often dictated by the program standards used in an agency. In this case, an agency develops a list of goals and objectives for a specific type of program, and the standards provide a generic design. An example of program standards for "Theme Programs" used by the U.S. Army V Corps is presented in Exhibit 9-4.

Exhibit 9-4.
Ten Elements of a Theme Program

Theme Program: A program conducted within the recreation center or other facility which contains at least six of the ten elements of a theme program. The ten elements of a theme program are:

1. Activities (active games)
2. Refreshments (food beverages)
3. Decorations/props
4. Entertainment (live)
5. Audio-visuals (films/slides/video tapes)
6. Costumes
7. Lighting (special room arrangement)
8. Prizes
9. Music (canned, for atmosphere)
10. Gimmick (giveaways, mystery or special guests, special effects, animals, etc.)

(From H. Rice, Director V Corps Recreation Centers 1986)

Theme programs are a specific form of program service that military recreation employees who work in the Army V Corps Recreation Centers are required to develop. A theme program is one that includes at least six of the ten elements of a theme program. Obviously, each program element is to be developed around a single theme.

The goal in this instance is to develop a theme program. The ten elements serve as predesignated design objectives. If six of the ten elements are incorporated into the program's design, a theme program will have been produced. The design of a theme program in this agency is thus guided by program standards.

Incorporating patron desires into the final design will increase the probability of developing a successful program. Exhibit 9-5 includes an example of program design goals developed with this concept.

Exhibit 9-5.
A Caribbean Christmas Theme Program

(Note: research at the library how Christmas is celebrated in the Caribbean Islands and incorporate those elements.)

Program Element #1: Activities
        a. Limbo contest
        b. Seashell hunt
        c. Straw hat decorating
        d. Salsa/Caribbean dancing

Program Element #2: Refreshments
        a. Fresh fruits(tropical)
        b. Fruit cocktail bowl with shredded coconut
        c. Other recipes researched in library or from family
           members of Caribbean origin.

Program Element #3: Decorations/Props
        a. Hanging suns (large colorful swatches of fabric stapled to
           walls in interesting patterns)
        b. Palm trees, banana trees (potted)
        c. Large seashells made of paper-mache

Program Element #4: Entertainment
        a. Steel band
        b. Caribbean music group

Program Element #5: Audiovisuals
        a. Movies (travelogues) of the Caribbean Islands
        b. Slides of scenes from the Caribbean Islands
        c. Records of Caribbean drums playing

Program Element #6: Costumes
        a. White shirts open to the navel for men with colorful cummerbunds
        b. Colorful sundresses for women
        c. Someone wears an authentic medicine man costume

Program Element #7: Lighting
        a. Colored spotlights with bright colors: red, orange, yellow, etc.
           illuminating the room.

Program Element #9: Music (canned)
        a. Steel drum music
        b. Have a limbo expert perform

(Adapted from an original program concept by Darmstadt Recreation Center Staff)

Now complete Exercise 9-3.

Exercise 9-3.
Developing Program Standards

Develop programming standards for one-day workshops in an agency. When finished, discuss the following questions:

- How will patron input be solicited and incorporated into the final program design?
- Does the description make the workshop a unique programming format in the agency?
- Do your workshop programming goals give enough guidance and direction to programmers who wish to develop workshops?

Conclusion

To design a program, the programmer must specify the actual interventions that will be used to operate the program and create the leisure experience intended. Imagery provides a technique for animating a program and modeling a variety of candidate plans that eventually compete for adoption. The final design should specify the content of the experience frames and their sequences. Developing clear, specific, and measurable program design goals that describe the experience to be created or specify what the patron will be able to do as a result of his/her participation will expedite the program design process.

References, Chapter Nine

Ableson, R. P. 1976. Script Processing in Attitude Formations and Decision Making. In *Cognition and Social Behavior*, J.S. Carrol and J. W. Payne (Eds.). Hillsdale, NJ: Erlbaum.

Beach, L. R. 1990. *Image Theory: Decision Making in Personal and Organizational Contexts*. New York: John Wiley & Sons.

Edginton, C. R., C.J. Hanson, and S.R. Edginton. 1992. *Leisure Programming: Concepts, Trends, and Professional Practice* (2nd ed.). Dubuque, IA: Wm. C. Brown Communications.

Edwards, R., J.M. Honeycutt, and K.S. Zagacki. 1988. Imagined Interaction as an Element of Social Cognition. *Western Journal of Speech Communication, 52* (Winter 1988), 23-45.

Goffman, E. 1974. *Frame Analysis: An Essay on the Organization of Experience.* New York: Harper Colophon Books.

Green, H. 1976. *Mind and Image: An Essay on Art and Architecture.* Lexington, KY: University of Kentucky Press.

Honeycutt, J. M. 1991. Imagined Interactions, Imagery, and Mindfulness/Mindlessness. In R. G. Kuzendorf (Ed.), *Mental imagery* (121-128). New York: Plenum Press.

Hull, R. B. IV., W.P. Stewart, and Y.K. Yi. 1992. Experience Patterns: Capturing the Dynamic Nature of a Leisure Experience. *Journal of Leisure Research, 24,* 240-252.

Kaufmann, G. 1988. Mental Imagery and Problem Solving. In M. Denis, J. Engelkamp, and J. T. E. Richardson (Eds.), *Cognitive and Neuropsychological Approaches to Mental Imagery* (231-239). Dordrecht, Netherlands: Martinus Nijhoff.

Kleiber, D., L. Caldwell, and S. Shaw. 1992, October. *Leisure Meaning in Adolescence.* Paper presented at the 1992 Symposium On Leisure Research, Cincinnati, OH.

Kleiber, D., R. Larson, and M. Csikszentmihalyi. 1986. The Experience of Leisure in Adolescence. *Journal of Leisure Research, 18,* 169-176.

Mead, G. H. 1934. *Mind, Self, and Society.* Chicago: University of Chicago Press.

Weinberg, R. S. 1988. *The Mental Advantage: Developing Your Psychological Skills in Tennis.* Champaign, IL: Leisure Press.

Additional Readings

Gronlund, N.E. 1970. *Stating Behavioral Objectives For Classroom Instruction.* New York: Macmillan.

Rossman, J.R. 1993. Program Design Through Imagery. *Journal of Physical Education, Recreation, and Dance, 64* (8), 30-33.

Photo courtesy of Joliet Park District, Joliet, IL. Photo by Ann Miller.

10

Creative Programming

Throughout industry, the search for creative products and services and innovative methods for implementing them is underway. We are constantly barraged with new problems that cannot be solved with current approaches. Many organizations have responded by creating "idea centers" where employees from throughout the organization are sent to create and innovate (Ward 1985). Programmers, too, must create new program services and develop innovative ways of operating them.

Creative programming is different from program planning. In the latter, the programmer examines existing alternate solutions to a problem and then selects the best solution. This methodology stems from problem-solving literature that identifies the following steps: problem definition, identification of alternatives, evaluation of alternatives, implementation of the alternative selected, and finally, evaluation of the solution implemented. Creative programmers not only synthesize the facts available and identify existing alternate solutions, they also consciously create possible programmatic solutions to the identified design problem. Furthermore, they may also develop innovative procedures for their implementation. Thus, creativity may be applied both during program design and in developing the implementation plan.

Understanding Applied Creativity

Are you a creative person? Can you find creative solutions to programming problems? Can you develop innovative implementation procedures? In all likelihood you can, if you put forth enough effort with the techniques outlined in this chapter.

What is creativity? Although there are many definitions of it, there is little consensus about its definition. On the one hand, it refers to that rare gift of genius and insight that enables one to unlock great mysteries of the universe. This cannot be taught. On the other hand, creativity also refers to the ability to overcome problems by approaching them in novel ways and by systematically developing innovative solutions to them. According to Tudor Richard (cited in Howard 1985), the opposite of this type of creativity is "stuckness"; habitual thinking that generates the same solutions to problems. Creativity training will not produce a Michelangelo, but it does help one escape from "stuckness" and develop more novel solutions to programming problems.

von Oech (1990) suggests that to be creative one must first have a broad base of knowledge about a subject. This knowledge base does not guarantee creativity, but is a prerequisite to it. Secondly, by using techniques that manipulate this knowledge and experience, one is opened to new ideas and thoughts about the subject. He calls getting unstuck opening our "mental locks" that keep us from seeing things differently.

Finke, Ward, and Smith (1992) have developed a model of creativity based on their research. It is called the Geneplore Model and is illustrated in Figure 10-1 on page 193. Creativity is modeled as an iteration between generating preinventive structures with special properties that promote creativity and an exploration of these by reinterpreting their meaning in a new context. This iterative process occurs within the constraints of the program being developed. They conclude that creativity is the result of not one, but several mental processes that lead to creative insight and discovery (Finke, Ward, and Smith 1992). Applied creativity, then, requires the development of a kit-bag of techniques.

Although the search for the origins of creativity and the mental processes that give rise to it continues, programmers operate in the present and thus must develop innovative programs for people to enjoy tomorrow. A pragmatic definition of creativity for use in organizations that can direct our efforts is offered by Ackoff and Vergara (1988). "We have defined creativity in problem solving and planning as the ability of a subject in a choice situation to modify self-imposed constraints so as to enable him or her to select courses of action or produce outcomes that he or she would not otherwise select or produce and that are more efficient or valuable than any he or she would otherwise have chosen" (Ackoff and Vergara 1988, p. 87).

Figure 10-1.
The Geneplore Model

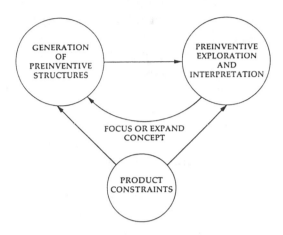

From: Finke, R. A., T.B. Ward, and S.M. Smith. (1992). *Creative Cognition: Theory, Research, and Applications*. Cambridge, MA: The MIT Press (p. 18).

The processes and techniques used to develop creative programs, then, must provide the means to first unlearn and second to see things in a new way. Specifically, they must prevent the imposition of our default responses to identified problems— the blocks to innovation. These are a result of our training and/ or our routinized responses to the same or similar problems. Once we have removed our default blocks, we need techniques to facilitate the generation of novel ideas. In this case, novel means an idea we would not normally have developed given our previous assumptions and methods of operation. These may seem like modest goals, but in many cases, our thinking and methods of operating have become so routinized that we do not realize how stuck we actually are!

Creativity in Developing Programs

There are several unique factors of recreation programs that are relevant to the use of creativity. First is the unique problem-solving mode faced by recreation programmers. There

are few widely recognized and accepted protocols for the operation of leisure programs. Step-by-step implementation procedures for specific programs are not included in the literature of
the field. Thus, the creative problem-solving situation faced by
the programmer is one in which there are few established procedures that would allow for computational transformations based
on rule governed interferences such as deductive or inductive
reasoning (Kaufmann, 1988). Engineering is a discipline in which
computational transformations would likely be used, but recreation programming is not one of them.

The programming problem to be solved, then, is most
likely a novel, complex, and ambiguous one because of the many
different approaches that may work if placed in the correct
context. Solving the kinds of problems faced by recreation programmers is more likely to be accomplished by using analogy to
simulate mental models of what might happen, rather than
inferring what will happen through computational transformations. The mental imagery techniques outlined in the previous
chapter are an example of an analogical technique.

Second, you will remember from Chapter Three that there
are six fundamental elements of program design, and that a
change in any one of them will result in a different program. The
effort to create a new program does not necessarily require a
completely new program. A change in any one element will
result in a new program, and thus our goal in being creative is to
change at least one element in a way that will make a difference.

Finally, a program is new if it has not been previously
experienced by its patron group. So "new" does not necessarily
mean it is new to you or your staff, but rather that it is new to its
patron group.

Creative Program Design Process

Is there a method to creativity? How does one organize
efforts to systematically approach creativity? Wallas (1926) identified four stages of the creative process including (1) preparation, (2) incubation, (3) illumination, and (4) verification. In the
first edition of this book, these stages were presented as a linear
model of creativity. Based on the work of Finke, Ward, and Smith
(1992) the model has been revised, and the work of these authors

plus the work of Wallas were used to develop the model presented in Figure 10-2.

Figure 10-2.
Creative Program Design Process

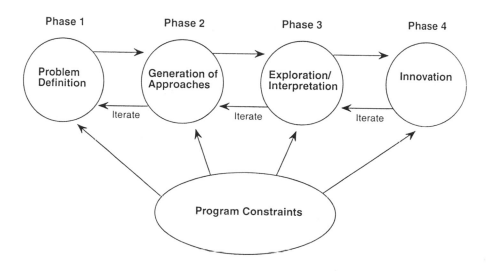

Adapted from Wallas (1926) and Finke, Ward, and Smith (1992).

The model is not linear, but rather assumes that creativity and innovation occur as the cumulative result of activity conducted in four phases including Problem Definition, Generation of Approaches, Exploration and Interpretation, and Innovation. Individuals iterate between the phases as insights become apparent. A good definition of the problem or well-developed program design goals facilitate the creative process. Thus, prior to implementing techniques to facilitate the generation of novel approaches, one must frame the problem appropriately and thereby prepare to solve the right problem. What is commonly called creativity is the iterative process that occurs between the generation of approaches phase and an exploration and/or interpretation of their applicability phase. The cumulative effort between these two phases produces novel approaches for solving the program design problem.

The first three phases of problem definition, idea generation, and interpretation of the ideas should lead to creative, novel ideas. However, these must be transformed into something that is tangible and useful. This is innovation—verification of the applicability of the novel ideas generated to solve the program design problem and the development of methods to implement them.

The entire process is constrained by the known limitations of the program. These could include constraints or predefinition of any of the six program elements (Chapter Three). For example, the programmer may be attempting to develop an innovative program for the use of an existing, older recreation center. Hopefully, in this case, there will be total creative freedom beyond the constraining fact that an existing facility must be used.

Four Phases of the Creative Process

Phase 1. Problem Definition

The major goal during this phase is to develop a statement of the problem, i.e., the difference between the way things are and the way we believe they ought to be or desire them to be. The initial effort is to make certain the real problem is understood by asking a series of focusing questions. What is known? What is unknown? What are the assumptions underlying the problem? What if we make different assumptions? These and other similar questions should be asked. Additional focus will result from data about the program that is gathered from a variety of sources. These could include a completed needs assessment, a market study, observed incongruities in current operations, observations of successful or unsuccessful program operations, or other similar sources.

Once the data is gathered, it must be analyzed. To completely analyze the problem, it is necessary to explicate the complete problem by breaking it down into its parts and determining the relationship among parts and all parts to the whole. Time spent in this step is well invested, for it is unlikely that the programmer will develop a good solution to a problem that is not well understood.

There are many techniques that can be used to further one's understanding of a problem. One of the key efforts is to "unlearn" what we already "know"—to remove those mental blocks (von Oech 1990) that keep us from seeing things in a new way. Pablo Picasso once said "Every act of creation is first of all an act of destruction."

To facilitate this we must use techniques that force us to look at things in a different way by changing the question, using different words to ask the same question, or denying there is a problem in the first place. Use the following two techniques and see if they give you insight into the problem.

Try questioning the basic assumptions of your organization by playing "Fools and the Rules" (von Oech 1990). "You take your holiest sacred cow and sacrifice it on the altar of foolishness" (von Oech, 1990, p. 148). The idea is to use humor to make fun of agency products, rules, or policies and to expose their basic assumptions and possible flaws. Here is an example of this technique given to me by Julia Dunn (1991).

Rule: We will have state-of-the-art programs.

Fool: Who needs state-of-the-art programs? They create state-of-the-art problems. Why not let someone else be the innovator and we'll copy what they've done? It would be cheaper.

Redefining the problem can often trigger a solution.

Consider the following example. The author was once involved in deciding what was to be done with a piece of playground equipment at a park-school site. A rather large number of children had fallen from the two slides on a large, integrated wooden play unit. The local school principal and a P.T.A. committee had decided that the slides were the problem and thus needed to be removed. I was asked to meet with them to discuss the problem. Before the meeting, however, I observed children actually using the equipment.

From my observations, it was apparent that the problem was the placement of the two slides and the large number of children who wanted to play on them. The slides were placed so that the children could slide down one and immediately get in line to slide down the second one. Going down the second slide put the children in a position to get in line to use the first slide again. Thus, the two slides were actually being used as one, and there were simply too many children to be accommodated by this arrangement.

After the analysis, the problem was redefined as insufficient slides and incorrect slide placement. A two-fold solution was proposed: (1) move one slide so that the two could not be used in a circular manner, and (2) add a third slide, thereby increasing the number of opportunities to slide. The solution was innovative compared with removing the slides, and it was developed primarily by analyzing and restating the problem. I might add that the solution has worked for over 15 years.

The final effort in this phase is to develop a statement of the problem. How detailed this statement will be depends on the known constraints of the program being developed. The best problem statements are those that have emergent properties (Finke, Ward, and Smith 1992). They are written with the fewest restrictions possible and thus enhance rather than inhibit the generation of novel approaches. The problem statement should have clear implications for the key needs to be addressed and the key program elements to be manipulated. Consider the following two problem statements.

To develop a one-week special event to serve as the finale of a summer sports camp for boys and girls 8-12 years old.

To develop a program for working mothers with children 1-3 years of age to provide them with quality interaction time with their children.

The second example leaves the most room for creative discovery because there is less specified in the problem statement. The constraints imposed by a specific program will partly determine how restrictive a problem statement must be. Too often however, more is included than is necessary and creativity is thereby inhibited.

Phase 2. Generate Approaches

The major goal during this phase is to generate novel approaches. Some of the key creative efforts are to be impractical and irrational, to be playful, to suspend judgment to facilitate a free flow of imagination, and to relax and spend time (von Oech 1990). There is some disagreement about how one's time is best spent in this phase. There is a dilemma between using techniques whose purpose is to force the generation of many ideas and those that focus effort on producing a few good ideas. One theory suggests that if you generate enough ideas, you will surely include one good enough to solve your problem! However, a second school of thought suggests that one should be more contemplative, mull over ideas, and use critical judgment in order to generate a few good ideas. Buffington (1987) suggests that the best problem solvers "creatively worry and carry a problem around with them even while doing other tasks" (p. 121). Their effort is to produce quality over quantity. After all, you only need the one good idea that will solve your problem! You must develop the style that works for you.

Miller (1988) has identified two methods of thinking, either of which may lead to the generation of good approaches: linear and intuitive. Linear thinking helps us "... organize information in ways that give us new 'entry points' for solving problems" (p.116). Through the use of logical, incremental, sequential thinking, one is led to where to look for novel solutions. In contrast to this, intuitive techniques provide the means to make inferential insights that facilitate a conceptual leap to a whole solution.

Each programmer needs to develop a variety of techniques that will facilitate the discovery of approaches one would normally not have considered. I will provide you with some techniques that have worked for me. However, you need to go to the sources referenced at the end of this chapter and identify techniques that work for you since the correct technique is a matter of personal style and the type of problem being addressed.

The use of matrix analysis (Miller, 1988) is an excellent example of linear thinking. The Programmer's Evaluation Cube (Exhibit 6-4 on p. 106) is a three-dimensional matrix that can show the programmer, through logical extension, where to look for new program ideas. By cross-tabulating life-cycle stages, program formats, and activity types, one can document existing services and concurrently identify voids to possibly be filled with new services.

Brainstorming is a common technique used in this phase to generate a large number of ideas. It is divergent thinking that is characterized by five distinct skills: (1) fluency: the ability to generate a large number of solutions; (2) flexibility: the ability to use many different approaches or strategies in solving a problem, a willingness to change directions; (3) originality: the ability to produce clever, unique, and unusual solutions; (4) elaboration: the ability to expand, develop, particularize, and embellish ideas; and (5) irrationality: the ability to allow the right side, the irrational, creative side of the brain to dominate one's thinking. All divergent thinking techniques attempt to systematize the ability to accomplish these skills. However, realizing what one is attempting to accomplish enhances one's ability to get the job done.   See Exhibit 10-1 on page 201 for explanations of two divergent thinking techniques.

Rather than employing techniques that force us to innovate, to get unstuck, to get out of our routine, and come up with the next logical extension, some succeed by engaging in the "creative worrying" identified earlier. One consciously sets aside a period of time for the mind to wander completely and to be free of the conceptual discipline imposed by analytical and linear thinking techniques.

Paul MacCready, who developed the Gossamer Albatross, the first human-powered airplane to successfully cross the English Channel, was aware of how others were attempting to solve the problem by building a very small aircraft, barely capable of carrying a pilot. He sat the problem aside and went on vacation. While observing birds in flight, particularly birds soaring, it occurred to him that the solution was to make the plane large rather than small, so there would be enough wing surface to provide the lift needed to get the craft airborne. Super light plastics provided the material needed to build a large, but still lightweight aircraft. Once airborne, the craft was more of a glider than an aircraft. Yet technically it was a man-powered aircraft. Waiting, contemplating, and reinterpreting seemingly incongruent data are also successful strategies for developing novel approaches.

Analogies are an example of intuitive thinking. They require us to find a correspondence between dissimilar things by thinking in a way that makes the familiar strange and the strange familiar. Reconciling these incongruities produces insights into novel associations. For example, von Oech (1990) recommends imagining how others would solve your problem. What analogies might result if Superman rather than you were going to develop the program? How might a surgeon, an airline pilot, or

Exhibit 10-1.
Divergent Thinking Techniques

Brainstorming is one of the most widely known and widely used divergent thinking techniques. It is organized ideation by groups whose goal is to generate as many ideas regarding a design problem as possible within a given time limit. Ideas are generated in an atmosphere of "suspended judgment," that is, the goodness or badness of any idea is suspended during idea generation. Brainstorming sessions are conducted with the belief that generating a large quantity of ideas will produce good ideas for problem solutions.

To conduct a brainstorming session, the leader should clearly define the problem to the group before starting the session. It is best if the individuals making up the group have diverse backgrounds so that idea generation will not be stifled by "groupthink." When the session begins, group members are allowed to say anything that comes to mind as a possible solution to the identified problem. The group leader records all ideas as they are given. Everyone is encouraged to piggyback on a previous idea by adding to it, combining it with others, and so forth. During brainstorming sessions, the following four principles should be followed:

- Suspended judgment. To encourage as many ideas as possible and to encourage "wild" ideas, critical evaluation of their feasibility and worth are temporarily suspended.
- Encourage quantity. The more ideas that are generated, the more likely you are to get the one that will solve the problem.
- Piggy-Back. Encourage individuals to cross-fertilize, add to, innovate from, or combine with the ideas already generated.
- Encourage wild ideas. Encourage people to reveal their wildest ideas and not prejudge their feasibility or acceptability by the group.

Brainwriting is a modification of brainstorming; participants write down their ideas rather than give them orally. Participants do not identify their own papers. After a given time, papers are exchanged and each person is to modify, combine, or in some way build on the work of the previous writer. The exchange of papers continues until all apparent possibilities are exhausted.

This technique works better than brainstorming for some groups. This is especially true for groups that may have some dominant members or groups in which unequals in terms of job position may be working together.

an Army tank commander approach your program? What questions would they ask, what assumptions would they make, what tools, equipment, and places would they use, or what processes would they employ?

An analogy I have successfully used is to ask students to compare (identify the similarities and differences) operating a recreation program with giving a stand-up comedy routine. Some of their answers were:

They both play to an audience.

They have their ups and downs.

They must be novel to sustain interest.

Both depend on a good leader.

Either can fail!

A good plan/script is essential for success in either.

A final effort in this phase is to keep focused on the correct problem. It is recommended that you continually define and redefine the problem based on new insights gained through your efforts in Phase 2. This process helps focus the unconscious thought process on the critical issues needed to successfully solve the problem. By doing this, the unconscious thinking will be sharpened and kept on target. The check may reveal some insight or unifying direction that will provide the adaptations or innovations needed to unify the direction of further thoughts. Often one needs to keep redefining the problem until a more suitable problem statement is developed. Complete Exercise 10-1 to obtain additional insight into how to redefine problem statements.

Exercise 10-1.
Redefining Problem Statements

When confronted with a new problem, we usually attempt to fit it into a familiar problem and then proceed to solve it. Identify a problem statement and then use the series of questions below to aid in moving the problem to a more familiar basis. In attempting to redefine a problem, ask some of the following questions:

• Have you seen the problem before, perhaps in a slightly different form?

- **Have you seen a problem with a similar unknown?**
- **Identify a solution to a similar problem. Can you use its results or its methods?**
- **Can you use different words to describe the problem?**
- **Can you solve any part of the problem?**
- **Try the fit of a solution of a related problem. Although it may be more general, more specific, or analogous to your current problem, see if it will work!**

Phase 3. Exploration/Interpretation.

The primary goal in this phase is to synthesize the approaches generated in Phase 2 into an acceptable solution. This is accomplished by exploring and interpreting the feasibility of the ideas generated in the previous phase for solving the programming problem. This, too, can be difficult. Sometimes we cannot recognize a solution even though it is before us, because we simply have not discovered the cognitive structure that will allow the pieces to come together as a solution. The creative efforts in this stage require rearranging ideas to make seemingly diverse elements converge. Various types of analogies and projective imagery (discussed in Chapter Nine) are useful techniques for completing this phase.

Another method is to use several different analogical positions to shift the context of an experience to test the applicability of approaches. Try each of the following four analogies.

Personal Analogy. Place yourself at the center of the program and identify how each novel approach would contribute to your leisure experience in a program. What are the paradoxes, the problems, or the conflicts? How might they be combined and resolved?

Direct Analogy. Draw a direct comparison to another event. How would the novel approaches you have developed be used in a trip to the moon? How would they be used to stage an arts festival or the Olympics? How would they be used in the NCAA Final Four tournament or the Super Bowl?

Symbolic Analogy. Try to find the symbolic essence of the approaches. For example, when I lived in Texas, the state celebrated its sesquicentennial. Since these events occur so infrequently, it isn't certain what events are appropriate for celebrating a sesquicentennial. The essence of the event, though, seemed to be to celebrate patriotism and political liberty. Most community celebrations included events similar to those normally operated on the Fourth of July. There were symbolic similarities between the two events.

Fantasy Analogy. In this case, you may go beyond objective reality into fantasy. What would the program be like if it were operated for the Flintstone family? What would a Star Wars production of your program be like?

You may also expand the conceptual space used to frame the program problem. For example, instead of conceptualizing a city-wide annual softball tournament, think that you are planning a national or international tournament. If you think of a larger, more encompassing event, will the approaches be useful?

After you have given this your best effort, get dissatisfied with everything. Change it all to see what happens! Osborne's (1953) manipulative verbs can be applied to help accomplish this. Ask the following: What if I adapt, modify, magnify, minify, substitute, rearrange, reverse, or combine the concepts? Applying these verbs will rearrange, combine, and recombine your approaches to help investigate their feasibility.

When do you stop? von Oech (1990) offers important advice about this. One needs to accept that there may be more than one right answer. Much of our education and training is organized around finding the correct answer to a question, as if there is only one! Because of this, he recommends finding the second right answer. Thus, the effort continues until one finds a second solution that is the approximate equivalent of the first right answer. If you find one that is better, you keep going, of course!

Phase 4. Innovation

The primary goal during this phase is to be innovative and shape your proposed solution into a feasible program. You must first verify that your final proposal truly solves your program design problem. Then, you must screen the program to determine its feasibility for implementation. Discoveries during this phase may require some redesign of the program or development of a new method of operation.

Simonds (1961) has designed five preplanned scenarios that can be used to verify the conceptual harmony of the final design. This results from the integration of all working relationships, functions, and elements so that each complements the other and the overall design. During this process, one will often again use projective imagery to vicariously experience the program and to model its operation.

Simonds's five scenarios are (1) outward and inward plan progression, (2) expansion and contraction of plan concept, (3) satellite plan, (4) integral planning, and (5) proving the plan.

In examining the outward and inward progression of a design, one must consider the effect of each design element from the innermost point of its generation to its final outcome. Conversely, one must make certain that each design element included in the final design is a logical conclusion of the outermost components and implications of the overall design. For example, in outward progression, the designer would need to examine the effect on the participant's overall experience of waiting in line for 30 minutes before an event. What effect would this have on the participant's overall leisure experience? It is well documented that standing in line creates anxiety. This type of anxiety would interfere with a leisure experience, so some other method of queuing would need to be developed in order to meet the design goal.

In inward progression, one needs to consider the outermost components of the design and logically progress into the most minute details of the design to make certain that they are consistent. For example, if a programmer had advertised a noncompetitive volleyball tournament, but then staged it in a gym with a center arena, spectator seating surrounding a center court, and a public address system announcing the score after each point, the operational details of the event would be inconsistent with the overall design concept. Although this is an extreme example, failure to verify the details of a plan in this thorough, detailed manner often leads to operations that are inconsistent with original design goals.

In expansion and contraction of the plan, the designer expands the areas of consideration to the farthest extensional aspects of the plan and contracts each part down to its most trivial detail. In doing this, the designer is attempting to develop a worst-case and best-case scenario of actual program operation in order to anticipate and plan for the most probable events. Consider the role of weather in the design of an outdoor program. If the possibility of good weather is extended to rainy weather, how does this affect program design? Will it alter the equipment used, the location, the date, or require that the program be cancelled? What if too many or too few participants show up? Does this need to be known in advance? What are the implications of either of these? If this expansion and contraction technique is applied thoroughly, it should raise many questions that need to be planned for during the design process.

In using the satellite plan verification scenario, one examines the relationship of each part of the plan to the whole plan. Each element of the plan design must be in harmony with the whole design concept. In leisure program design, consideration must be given to the wholeness of a program, including aspects such as the procedure for registration, as well as clean-up procedures, the location and timing of refreshments, and so on. To be thorough, the programmer should examine the choices made for each of the six elements of program production discussed in Chapter Three to make certain that each contributes appropriately and complementarily to solving the identified design problem.

Integral planning puts further order and conceptual harmony into the program design with a final check of the key program frames, the key program production elements that are assumed to be central to each frame, the key transitions planned, and the appropriateness of the sequential order of them. Some frames and transitions and some of the program production elements are more critical to accomplishing the design goals than others. This is the final opportunity to take steps to assure that these key design features are incorporated into the design and the operational plan (which will be discussed in Chapter Eleven) to maximize the probability that the experience intended will occur.

As one example, let us look again at the Easter Egg Hunt discussed previously. Although there were many considerations, two key design frames were an integral part of this event. First, each child needed to find an Easter egg and, secondly, parents needed to be able to watch their children hunt, but be kept from helping them. Once these key design frames were identified, all other design elements considered for inclusion were evaluated by the degree to which they would maximize the probability of these two elements occurring. In integral planning, then, one attempts to make certain that the elements integral to accomplishing the overall design goals are included in the design.

Finally, Simonds (1961) calls for proving the plan to determine if the design created does indeed correspond to the original design concept. The designer must aim to make the final solution an accurate reflection of the original problem statement. An easy mistake to make when manipulating elements is to invent new needs, to inflate the importance of one, or to deemphasize another. Once again, the test for this is to vicariously experience the program step by step as if actually participating in it, seeing it, and touching it. Through projective imagery, programmers must imagine themselves not as designers, but as participants—an older participant, a younger participant, or even a participant of another race or socioeconomic background.

Throughout verification, the programmer must be faithful to the original programming problem. If the design does not solve the original problem, you have not succeeded. Accomplishing the original design goal involves correlating established and prioritized relationships of the major determinants (design elements, goals, objectives and so forth) with the whole. The detailed scenarios just discussed will direct the designer in successfully searching for all relationships and interactions among the six elements of program production.

The final effort in this phase is to screen programs to make certain it is feasible to implement them and that they are truly innovative i.e. sufficiently different from current offerings. Figure 10-3 on page 208 is an instrument for conducting this screening. Each of the components on the instrument are scored and then the scores are summed. Programs that is scored with a total of 28 points or more are considered to be feasible to implement and innovative enough to be worth the effort.

Figure 10-3.
Program Screening Instrument

	Program Characteristic	Score			
		4 Excellent	3 Good	2 Fair	1 Poor
1	Provides Benefits To Target Patrons				
2	Significantly Different From Other Programs				
3	Can Be Produced Economically				
4	Can Be Marketed Economically				
5	Fits In With Rec. Dept. Image				
6	Rec. Dept. Personnel Have The Needed Skills To Produce And Promote It				
7	Rec. Dept. Personnel Have Time Needed To Produce And Promote It				
8	Adequate Facilities Are Available				
9	Contributes to Agency Mission				
10	Material Resources Are Readily Available				
	Sub Totals				

Total Score [ ]   Programs scoring 28 or more points are innovative and feasible.

Adapted from a form used by the U.S. Navy Recreational Services Unit.

Conclusion

Creativity is an iterative process used to identify novel approaches to programs and innovative methods of operating them. It is used to create alternative solutions for programming problems and should be a routine part of the program design and planning steps of the Program Development Cycle.

There are four distinct phases to the creative process with identifiable techniques to facilitate one's efforts in each. Throughout the process, one must continually return to the problem itself to make certain it is correctly defined and that the assumptions made about the constraints imposed by the program are valid. In many cases, which techniques may be used to facilitate one's effort is a matter of personal choice and style. Thus, the programmer must develop a kit-bag of techniques that may be applied until one that works in a given situation is identified.

Creative program design is hard work and requires the application of many diverse skills. However, if the techniques and processes presented in this chapter are thoroughly applied to identified program design problems, programmers will be able to develop innovative programs for their constituents. Good luck!

References, Chapter Ten

Buffington, P. W. February, 1987. *Sky: Delta Airlines Inflight Magazine*. Miami, FL: Halsey Publishing Co.

Dunn, J. 1991. Personal communication.

Finke, R. A., T.B. Ward, and S.M. Smith. 1992. *Creative Cognition: Theory, Research, and Applications*. Cambridge, MA: The MIT Press.

Howard, N.A. 1985, March. How To Generate Bright New Ideas. *Success*, 54.

Kaufmann, G. 1988. Mental Imagery and Problem Solving. In M. Denis, J. Engelkamp, and J. T. E. Richardson (Eds.), *Cognitive and Neuropsychological Approaches to Mental Imagery* (231-239). Dordrecht, Netherlands: Martinus Nijhoff.

Kuhn, R. L. (Ed.). 1988. *Handbook for Creative Innovative Managers*. New York: McGraw-Hill.

Miller, W. C. 1988. Techniques for Stimulating New Ideas: A Matter of Fluency. In R. L. Kuhn *Handbook for Creative Innovative Managers*, New York: McGraw-Hill.

Osborn, A. F. 1963. *Applied Imagination*. New York: Scribner & Sons.

Simonds, J.O. 1961. *Landscape Architecture*. New York: McGraw-Hill.

von Oech, R. 1990. *A Whack on the Side of the Head: How Can You Be More Creative?* New York: Warner Books, Inc.

Wallas, G. 1926. *The Art of Thought*. New York: Harcourt, Brace and Co.

Ward, B. June, 1985. Centers of Imagination. *Sky: Delta Airlines Inflight Magazine*. Miami, FL: Halsey Publishing Co.

Additional Readings

Alexander, C. 1970, March. Changes in Form. *Architectural Design*, 122-125.

Broadbent, G.H. 1966. Creativity. In S.A. Gregory (Ed.), *The Design Method*. London: Butterworths.

Gordon, W.J. 1961. *Synectics: The Development of Creative Capacity*. New York: Harper and Brothers.

Howard, N.A., W. Hoffer, D. Ingber, E. Raudsepp, J. Niemark, and H. Johnson. 1985, March. Creativity: A Special Report. *Success*, 54-61.

Jones, J.C. 1980. *Design Methods: Seeds of Human Futures*. New York: Wiley.

Smith, E.T. 1985, September 30. Are You Creative? *Business Week*, 80-84.

Weisberg, R.W. 1986. *Genius and Other Myths*. New York: W. H. Freeman.

Part IV: Operational Strategies

In Part IV, Operational Strategies, the program design that has been developed for a targeted population is written so that it may be shared with all who will help implement the program. When the plan is prepared, the realities and limitations of agency resources must be dealt with and the program design altered to fit the resources. During this stage, all of the preparations for implementation are completed and the program is actually implemented.

Chapter Eleven explains how to write a program plan. Chapter Twelve includes the techniques normally used in recreation agencies to promote program services. How to queue and register individuals is covered in Chapter Thirteen. Staffing and supervising program services are discussed in Chapter Fourteen. Issues involved in developing an agency's program pricing policy is the subject of Chapter Fifteen. Methods for determining program costs are outlined in Chapter Sixteen, and how to establish a price for a program is developed in Chapter Seventeen.

Photo courtesy of Henderson Parks and Recreation Department, Henderson, Nevada.

11

Preparing the Program Plan

In most instances, programmers will be unable to produce a program single-handedly. To produce a program as the designer intends, one must communicate details of the design to other staff members who will help implement it. Through a written program plan, programmers communicate the role of each person involved in producing a program. Clear communication through the program plan is therefore necessary for successful implementation.

The written program plan is analogous to the architect's blueprint or the project manager's network diagram. Through a blueprint, an architect communicates to various tradespeople their roles and functions in completing a structure as designed by the architect. Project managers in many professional areas, such as construction planning, movie production, and political campaigns, plan the execution of projects with a written plan that outlines all of the activities to be accomplished and the development of a timeline for their completion.

Once the program design is well thought out and clear in the programmer's mind [this is accomplished with the techniques covered in Chapters Nine and Ten], a written program plan is prepared. Although one might believe that the program is well designed and clear, actually writing down the plan in detail often exposes design flaws that must be corrected. One benefit of writing a program plan is that flaws can be discovered and corrected before actual implementation. Even though the planning step is illustrated as separate from the design step, one will often iterate between the two as the plan is written and the need for redesign becomes apparent.

Successful programs are operated or experienced four times. First, they are vicariously experienced by the designer during the design step. Second, in writing the program plan, the designer must again vicariously experience the program and develop the interaction scenarios necessary for animating the program. Third, the program is actually operated. Fourth, in evaluating the program, the designer relives it vicariously through regressive imagery, and the program is modeled with proposed modifications using projective imagery.

The written plan is a working document that is subject to ongoing revision. It is written to serve one or more of the following purposes:

- To provide a record of information about the current status of the program
- To provide a record of the resources used to operate the program
- To provide a reference for use during future operations of the program
  (Adapted from Kliem 1986).

A program plan will contain all of the details of program operation. An outline of a plan is included in Exhibit 11-1 on page 215. Although a plan will contain many details, to be useful it must clearly explicate the following. It must communicate the design goals of a program so that the program will become the leisure experience intended by the designer. By writing a thorough explanation of the methods and techniques that are necessary to produce the program, designers share how they intend to create the program with others who will need to implement and operate the program.

The program plan must also document how resources available for a program will be allocated to the various elements needed to operate it. Although there are many alternate ways to allocate a given amount of resources, allocations in systematic program planning are guided by the design goals developed during the design step.

A program management plan, including a timeline for scheduling and coordinating the program's implementation, must also be included in a program plan.

Exhibit 11-1.
The Program Plan

1. Program title
2. General mission and programming philosophy
3. Need for the program
4. Design goals of the program
5. Operation details:
   a.   Promotion plan
   b.   Budget and pricing information
   c.   Registration plan
   d.   Staffing and staff orientation plan
   e.   Supply and material needs
   f.   Facility plan
   g.   Management plan
   h.   Cancellation plan
   i.   Animation plan
6. Program evaluation plan
7. Disposition decision plan

The management plan should identify all activities necessary for implementing the program, and it should identify the person responsible for implementing each activity. In addition, the management plan should outline the relationship of all activities to each other, as well as the order in which these activities must be completed to produce the program on schedule.

Finally, the program plan should indicate how the actual program will be animated. This requires a written, step-by-step, sequenced scenario of how the interactions necessary for the intended program to occur will play out.

Contents of Program Plan

The following is a brief explanation of what is involved in each of the steps numbered in the program plan outline presented in Exhibit 11-1.

Program Title

This section should include the name of the program, the sponsoring agency, and a brief, introductory, descriptive paragraph indicating the who, what, when, where, why, and how of the program. After reading this paragraph, the reader should have basic familiarity with the leisure experience the program is to create.

General Mission and Programming Philosophy of the Agency

A statement of the agency's mission and its programming philosophy should be included in the plan to make it apparent why the agency is involved in producing this program.

Need for the Program

A statement of the need for this program should be included. It should answer the question: Why is this program needed and how was this need determined?

Design Goal of the Program

Specific statements about what this program is supposed to accomplish should be written. The design goals should specify what leisure experiences the program is supposed to create, and the participant outcomes expected. A rationale for how these goals are consistent with the agency's goals and objectives should also be included.

Operation Details

The operational details included in this section should create a detailed record of instructions about how the program is to be implemented and operated. There is always a question of how detailed the information included in this section must be. Unfortunately, programmers too often provide so little detail that only someone who has previously observed the program being operated could actually use the "details" to reproduce the program. At the very minimum, one must provide enough details so that another professional programmer from a different agency could obtain the plan and reproduce the program. Generally, if there is any doubt about the need to include additional detail or description—include it.

Promotion Plan

In this section the target market for the program and the plan for how the program will be promoted to this market is explicated. Details about the types of promotional materials, their distribution, and the timeline for implementing the promotion plan should be included. How to develop promotional materials is discussed in Chapter Twelve.

Budget and Pricing Information

The budget for the program, including revenues, income projections, expenses, and how the price for participation was determined should be included. How to budget and price programs is discussed in Chapters Fifteen and Sixteen.

Registration Plan

If registration is required, how it will be done should be detailed in this section. When registration will occur, who will conduct it, where it will occur, and how it will be conducted should all be specified. If there are any special registration requirements for this program, they should be specified. For example, only individuals who hold American Camping Association certification as Campcrafters may be permitted to register for a wilderness camping program. How to conduct registration is discussed in detail in Chapter Thirteen.

Staffing and Staff Orientation Plan

The number and qualifications of the staff needed to operate the program should be specified. How the staff is to be hired, oriented, and trained should also be specified. Staffing is discussed in Chapter Fourteen.

Supply and Material Needs

A list of supplies and materials needed to operate the program should be included in the plan. Any special supply or material needs should be noted and their availability and source indicated. Supplies and materials that may need to be acquired through a bidding process or that take some lead time to obtain should be identified.

Facility Plan

A list of the facilities needed to operate a program should be developed. A map indicating the location of facilities and a diagram of the facilities themselves should be included in the plan. Any unique facility attributes needed for the program should be noted. For example, rhythmic gymnastics cannot be conducted properly in a gymnasium with less than a thirty-foot ceiling height.

Management Plan

Implementing programs is rarely accomplished by a single individual. Program operation most often requires the coordinated effort of many individuals. Program implementation is most analogous to project management. According to Moder, Phillips, and Davis (1983), "A project is a set of tasks or activities related to the achievement of some planned objective, normally where the objective is unique or non-repetitive" (p. 3). A project is not repeated in an identical manner as is the case in product production. Project management techniques include critical path and network planning techniques designed to identify the activities needed to complete a project or to specify their interrelationships, and to schedule their completion in an acceptable time span, given a finite set of resources. How this is accomplished in recreation program management will be discussed later in this chapter.

Cancellation Plan

A plan detailing what will happen if the program is cancelled should also be included. Many alternatives could be considered, but contingencies need to be specified. For outdoor events, there could be an alternate indoor location. Often, there is simply an alternate date for outdoor programs cancelled because of unfavorable weather.

If weather conditions are unsettled, the programmer should delay making a decision to cancel a program until the last moment possible. If bad weather clears shortly before the scheduled starting time, patrons will appear and expect service. To avoid bad public relations, the program staff must be ready to operate the event or be at the event location to redirect patrons to an alternate place or date. The major point here is that you must cancel an event and manage its cancellation—events will not cancel themselves.

For events for which a fee was paid, it is best to let patrons know how their fee will be refunded at the time of cancellation. Failure to inform patrons about refunds at the cancellation of an event will lead to many individual inquiries.

Animation Plan

A description of the key animation frames, transitions, and scenarios should be included in the written program plan. How this is dealt with in a recreation program plan is included in a later section of this chapter.

Program Evaluation Plan

The specific instruments and techniques for evaluating the program should be outlined. Techniques and instruments for conducting program evaluations are included in Chapters Eighteen and Nineteen.

Disposition Decision Plan

The basis on which the future of the program will be determined and who will do so should be specified in the plan. How this is accomplished is detailed in Chapter Twenty.

The Management Plan

Once the program has been conceptualized and designed, it is necessary to develop a management plan that outlines how the event will be implemented. Gantt charts and the flow chart method (see endnote) have been discussed in the recreation programming literature as methods for managing the implementation of recreation programs. These are specific techniques for identifying and sequentially ordering and prioritizing the tasks that must be completed to implement a program. When a timeline has been well developed, it should specify what tasks are to be done, when they will be done, who will do them, and how long each task will take.

To implement a management plan, some general steps must be followed:

1. Break down the total job into activities. As Moder et al. (1983) stated, "An activity is any portion of a project which consumes time or resources and has a definable beginning and ending" (p. 23). It is also important to identify all of the activities that must be accomplished and their interrelationships.

2. Place all activities into major function categories: for example, promotion, registration, staffing, supply and material acquisition, and so on.

3. Establish a timeline for the project, including the order in which activities are to occur and the amount of time each is estimated to take.

4. Identify and illustrate the relationship of each activity to all other activities and to the overall project itself.

Charting time frames for program implementation will enable the programmer to anticipate and prevent potential problems. For example, if it will take a printer three weeks to produce a brochure, the programmer must be organized to accommodate this timeline. During the process of identifying all of the activities needed to implement a program and putting them into major function categories, the work of delegating jobs to others and coordinating their efforts is made easier. This process also makes clear to the staff working on the project the scope of the whole project and each person's specific role in it. With a well-developed timeline, the programmer can estimate the impact of proposed or necessary changes on the program. Finally, the timeline chart document makes an excellent record of work accomplished and a good guideline for use in the next operation of the program.

Gantt Charts

Developed during World War I to help plan the war effort, Gantt charts are most useful in putting a time perspective on a project. Especially during the early stages of a project, they enable the programmer to estimate the time needed to complete the project.

Only three steps are involved in constructing a Gantt chart. First, identify all the functions of a project. Second, estimate the amount of time each function will take, and determine the order in which they must occur. Some will need to proceed sequentially, and others may occur simultaneously. Finally, graphically display the data developed in the Gantt chart by representing time on the horizontal axis and project functions on the vertical axis.

Exhibit 11-2 on page 222 contains the development of a Gantt chart for implementing an eight-week summer neighborhood day camp program. As can be seen in the chart, the program will require the programmer's time from January through the end of the program's operation in August.

Programmers rarely manage only one program at a given time. This is one major difference between programmers and other types of project managers who use these management planning devices. Recreation programmers will be working on several programs simultaneously, and each will require differing amounts of attention at various times.

Gantt charts are useful for illustrating the overall time needed for each activity in a project. However, they are not sophisticated enough to illustrate the dynamics of actual effort needed within an activity. For example, although the entire promotion campaign may be completed over a period of eighteen weeks, during some of this time the program manager is not actually working on the project.

The programmer will be heavily involved in planning the promotion campaign, preparing flyers, brochure copy, and news releases; getting the materials to a printer; and distributing the finished materials.

At other times during the eighteen-week period, various individuals will be taking care of promotional tasks. The printer will be printing brochures and flyers. Newspapers will be printing news releases. Patrons will be reading the promotional materials. The programmer, then, does not work continuously for eighteen weeks on the promotional campaign, although the campaign takes eighteen weeks from the time it is begun until it is finished. This can be accounted for on Gantt charts by indicating with a special icon those periods when the programmer must invest time to complete specific activities for the program. How this might be done is illustrated in the Gantt chart included in Exhibit 11-2.

Exhibit 11-2.
Preparation of a Gantt Chart

Step One
Identify Functions

> Supplies and Materials Acquisition
> Program Design
> Staff Recruitment and Selection
> Staff Training
> Site Selection
> Promotion
>
> Registration
> Actual Operation
> Evaluation

Step Two
Estimate Time and Order of Occurrence

> Program Design–2 weeks
> Site Selection–2 weeks

(continued)

Staff Recruitment and Selection–8 weeks
Promotion–18 weeks
Registration–7 weeks
Supplies and Materials Acquisition–10 weeks
Staff Training–2 weeks
Actual Operation–8 weeks
Evaluation–1 week

Step Three
Writing the Gantt Chart

Function

	J	F	M	A	M	J	J	A
Program Design	xx							
Site Selection		xx						
Staff Recruitment and Selection				x **** xxx				
Promotion				x*** xx **************				
Registration					xx ***xx			
Supplies and Materials Acquisition				xx *** * xx * xx				
Staff Training						xx		
Actual Operation							xxxxxxxx	
Evaluation								x *

X indicates when there is actual work to be accomplished for the activity.
*indicates that activity is continuing, and may need occasional attention.

Flow Chart Method

The flow chart method provides an elementary network diagram (Murphy and Howard 1977; Russell 1982). According to Kliem (1986), "A network diagram is a graphic representation of a series of activities and events depicting the various aspects of a project and the order in which these activities and events must occur" (p. 35). The flow chart method has been identified by Russell (1982, p. 244) as the most useful to her as a practicing programmer. It will serve the needs of most recreation programs.

This method uses the data generated in the preparation of the Gantt chart and places it along a single timeline–a critical path. Specific critical tasks within each activity are identified on the timeline so that the temporal order of each task and the interrelationships of tasks and activities to each other are illustrated. Exhibit 11-3 on page 225 is a flow chart for the same program developed in Exhibit 11-2.

The flow chart in Exhibit 11-3 illustrates that the chart must be explicit about what needs to be accomplished, when it needs to be accomplished, and the relationship of the activities of each function to each other and the overall project. Its simplicity and thoroughness make it a very useful technique for managing the implementation of a recreation program. Experiment with Gantt charts and flow charts by completing Exercise 11-1.

Exercise 11-1.
Developing Management Implementation Charts

Select a program and develop a Gantt chart for it. Also develop a flow chart.

Critique other class members' charts and discuss the following points:

- Are all of the functions needed to implement the program identified?
- Are all of the critical activities identified?
- Is enough time allowed to complete the activities?
- Is the chart too detailed?
- Is the additional information contained in a flow chart worth the time it takes to prepare it?
- With the data on the flow chart, develop some "what if" scenarios. For example: What if the printer were delayed two weeks in obtaining the brochure?

Exhibit 11-3.
The Flow Chart Method

Program Design
- 1/15 - Design program

Site Selection
- 1/30 - Select sites

Staffing
- 4/1 - Announce staff positions
- 4/21 - Interview staff
- 5/1 - Hire staff

Promotion
- 2/1 - Plan promo flyer
- 3/1 - Complete flyer
- 3/4 - Flyer to printer
- 3/30 - Flyer mailed
- 4/15 - News release
- 5/15 - News release

JAN	FEB	MAR	APR	MAY	JUN	JUL	AUG

Acquiring Supplies & Materials
- 3/15 - Order supplies & materials
- 4/15 - Monitor supplies & materials (reorder if needed)
- 6/18 - Deliver to sites

Registration
- 5/15 - Registration
- 5/30 - Assign campers

Staff Training
- 6/15 - Staff training

Program Operation
- 6/21 - Program begins

Evaluation
- 8/15 - Evaluation report

Developing a management plan that outlines how a program will be implemented is a very important component of a program plan. Time spent in developing a good plan will help coordinate the great number of activities that are needed to implement a recreation program.

Animation Plan

Through the animation plan, the program designer shares with other staff members the frames of interactions, the transitions and their sequence that will be used to create a specific experience for patrons.The animation plan is analogous to the playwright's script or the sport coach's play diagram. Each of these documents communicates to a number of different individuals their role in producing a scenario of actions called a play. Actors, stage technicians, the director, and others all take direction from the playwright's script in order to produce the play as it was designed and written. The players in different sport positions take direction from a coach's play diagram about the scenario of actions that must occur for a play to be executed.

The animation plan for a leisure program describes step by step, frame by frame, how patrons will move through their program experience. A thorough understanding of the leisure experience intended and how it may be facilitated, which was developed during the design phase, is crucial to explicating the animation plan.

This plan contains many cause-and-effect predictions by the program's designer. The designer assumes that if X happens, patrons will respond in a predictable manner. For example, if there are identifiable places to form lines, the designer assumes patrons will queue in the designated area. All animation plans are predictions based on knowledge of the patrons to be served; this information comes from data acquired through research or previous experiences with similar patrons.

Exhibit 11-4 on the following page contains an animation plan for a Fourth of July Balloon Ascension. The animation plan outlined in the exhibit details what is to happen to patrons and how staff members are to interact with them. How detailed an animation plan must be depends on the complexity and size of the event. The plan should be sufficiently detailed so that staff members understand the total program and their role in facilitating the leisure experience. Complete Exercise 11-2 on page 232 and prepare an animation plan.

Exhibit 11-4
Animation Plan for Balloon Ascension

Program Design Goals

To provide a non-skill based balloon flying contest on the morning of the Fourth of July.

To provide an event that will attract family units and foster parent-child interaction.

Schedule

The Balloon Ascension is scheduled for 11:00 a.m. Staff should report at 6:00 a.m. to begin filling balloons with helium. Gates will open at 10:00 a.m. Most patrons will begin arriving at 10:30 a.m. Taped patriotic music will begin at 10:00. The event will be completed by 11:30 a.m.

Staff Orientation

Patrons who attend the Balloon Ascension will most likely be family units so there will be many parents with small children. There will also be unaccompanied children from about 12 to 15 years of age. Since this is primarily a family event there are usually few discipline problems. Patrons come fully expecting to be able to help their children launch a balloon in a pleasant, enjoyable atmosphere. Your job is to help them in a low-key, courteous manner to obtain a card and a balloon, tie the card to the balloon, and be in the appropriate area to launch their balloon on time.

Because we have a large number of staff members at this event in order to personalize leader-patron contact, we will not use the P.A. system except to help create an upbeat atmosphere with taped patriotic music and to announce the final instructions and countdown to launch. You will give directions and encourage interactions by speaking to small groups of individuals and keeping them informed about what must occur.

The day will probably be very hot. You may become easily irritated with patrons who may not understand instructions or procedures. It is very likely that you will have to explain the same point over and over. Be sure you know how the event will operate and be prepared to answer questions. Patron pleasure at the event will depend on your courteous treatment of them. It will require effort to remain pleasant, but all staff members are expected to do so.

(continued)

Scenario of Frames and Transitions (with key elements)

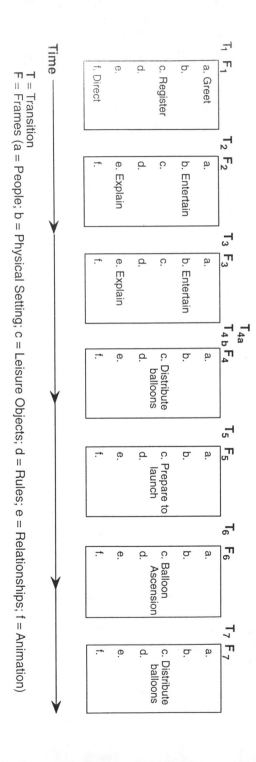

T_1 F_1	T_2 F_2	T_3 F_3	T_{4a} T_{4b} F_4	T_5 F_5	T_6 F_6	T_7 F_7
a. Greet	a.	a.	a.	a.	a.	a.
b.	b. Entertain	b. Entertain	b.	b.	b.	b.
c. Register	c.	c.	c. Distribute balloons	c. Prepare to launch	c. Balloon Ascension	c. Distribute balloons
d.	d.	d.	d.	d.	d.	d.
e.	e. Explain	e. Explain	e.	e.	e.	e.
f. Direct	f.	f.	f.	f.	f.	f.

Time → ↓ ↓ ↓ ↓

T = Transition
F = Frames (a = People; b = Physical Setting; c = Leisure Objects; d = Rules; e = Relationships; f = Animation)

(An explanation of each transition and frame is included on the following pages.)

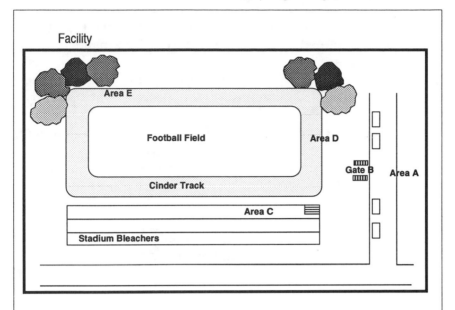

Facility

Area E

Football Field

Area D

Gate B

Area A

Cinder Track

Area C

Stadium Bleachers

Animation of Program Production Elements

T1 Patrons are directed to the tables in Area A by staff assigned to this area.

F1
a. Patrons are greeted at the tables by staff.
b.
c. Post cards are completed for each participant.
d.
e. Staff will make an effort to address family units.
f. People are directed to Gate B.

T2 At Gate B patrons are directed to be seated in Area C.

F2 For those in Area C
a. Families are seated together and are advised by staff in the area that at approximately 10:45 they will proceed to the track and be given their balloon which must be securely tied to the card.

(continued)

b.   The U.S. Flag will be flying from the flag pole and the whole area decorated with red, white, and blue banners and streamers.

c.   Patriotic music will be played and flyers announcing the remainder of the community sponsored Fourth of July events will be distributed.

d.   Emphasize that everyone will launch their balloon at the same time, on signal after a countdown.

e.   Encourage parents to help make certain that balloons are securely tied to cards.

f.

T3   At approximately 10:45, Gate B is closed and patrons arriving from Area A are queued outside Gate B.

F3   For those queued in Area B

a.   Staff will reassure the families in line that they will be admitted and that there are sufficient balloons for all.

b.

c.   Patriotic music will be played and flyers announcing the remainder of the community sponsored Fourth of July events will be distributed.

d.   Emphasize that everyone will launch their balloon at the same time, on signal after a countdown.

e.   Encourage parents to help make certain that balloons are securely tied to cards.

f.

T4[a]. Staff will move patrons seated in Area C, row by row, to Area D.

T4[b]. Once all of the patrons in Area C have been moved through Area D to Area E, Gate B will be opened and those in the queue outside Gate B will be moved through Area D to Area E. This may occur sooner if the queue outside Gate B gets too long and the staff in Area D seem to have the capacity to handle more patrons.

(continued)

F4. At Area D
a.   Staff will greet families when possible. Helium-filled bal-
      loons will be distributed to all participants with cards—
      only one per participant.
b.
c.   Balloons and tying cards to balloons is the focus of atten-
      tion. Patriotic music continues.
d.   Emphasize that everyone will launch their balloon at the
      same time, on signal after a countdown.
e.   Encourage parents to help make certain that balloons are
      securely tied to cards.
f.   Everyone must be moved through Area D and onto Area E.

T5. It is very important that staff effectively and courteously
move the first patrons from Area D to the end of Area E, or there
will not be room for all patrons. This will be accomplished by
individual requests from staff members, not by P.A. announcements.

F5. At Area E
a.   Parents prepare their children to launch their balloon.
b.   Staff should keep patrons on the track and off the grass
      infield.
c.   Balloons to launch is the primary focus of this frame.
d.   Staff should encourage patrons to hold onto the balloon
      until the signal to launch is given.
e.   Encourage parents to help their children with the activity.
f.

T6. After all of the balloons are distributed and people are
assembled in Area E, the P.A. announcer will stop the patriotic
music and give people final instructions about the event. They
will then give a countdown and at the end of the countdown an
air horn will sound. This is the signal to launch.

F6. At Area E—after the launch
a.   Parents and their children will stand and watch the bal-
      loons fly away for about 3-5 minutes after launch.
b.   Staff should keep patrons on the track and off the grass
      infield.
                        (continued)

c.   The balloons ascending is the primary focus of this frame.
d.
e.
f.
T7. As balloons fly out of sight and the patrons get ready to leave, they should be directed to Gate B. Staff should attempt to keep them on the track during this process. At Area D each child will receive a balloon to take home. It is important for staff to assure parents that there are enough balloons for everyone so there is not a rush to Gate B.

F7. At Area D and Gate B
a.   Staff and patron interaction is fostered by giving each child a balloon as they leave. Flyers announcing the rest of the community Fourth of July events are also to be made available.
b.
c.   Patriotic music begins again. Getting a balloon to take home is a key in this frame.
d.
e.
f.

Exercise 11-2
Animation Plan

Get into groups of five students. Each group should prepare an animation plan for a one-hour Valentine party to be held in your classroom for the rest of the class. Discuss the following questions:

- Is the plan sufficiently detailed?
- Do staff members understand from the plan the leisure experience you are trying to create and their role in facilitating it?
- Does the plan explain how patrons will move through each activity and from one activity to the next?

Scheduling Programs

Developing a comprehensive schedule of programs in an agency is an important task. Appropriate scheduling is necessary to maximize attendance and patron satisfaction. Four elements must be considered simultaneously in scheduling program services—balance, impact, location, and timing.

Balance

A program schedule needs to be balanced along two dimensions. First, it is wise to avoid simultaneously scheduling similar activities that may appeal to the same target group of patrons. To avoid overlap, one must be familiar with all of the agency's program services and with programs being offered by other providers in a given service area. Scheduling a balanced variety of activity types at a given time will also maximize the attendance at all activities. At any given time, it is best to have an art, drama, individual sport, team sport, and fitness activity scheduled, rather than five team sport activities.

Impact

In developing a schedule, one should understand how different activities scheduled in close proximity to each other will affect patron enjoyment. For example, scheduling a Valentine dance for teenagers and a Valentine dance for senior citizens at the same time in different rooms of the same facility would not be a good idea. Each group would adversely affect the enjoyment of the other because of incompatible age groups, loud noise, incompatible activity requirements for the same space, and similar problems.

Location

The location of a program will affect attendance. Individuals seek out programs that are accessible either because they are close to home or easy to get to by automobile. Access promotes use; therefore, it is wise to schedule programs at locations that are accessible to the target population.

Timing

When a program is offered will partly account for attendance at the program. When scheduling a time for a program, programmers should know the personal schedules of the typical target patron. Any program is competing for all other available uses of a patron's time, so the programmer needs to know the time use habits of patrons to make wise decisions about when to hold a program.

Information about program balance is developed from acceptable practice in the profession. It is generally recommended to offer a balanced program, although documented local interest and past participation history would justify an unbalanced set of program offerings. Information about how to avoid adverse effects is derived through a thorough understanding of, and previous experience with an event.

In scheduling the location and timing of events, the programmer has two choices. First, market research data or needs analysis data should include questions that will enable the programming staff to determine when individuals are available and where they are located. Obviously, scheduling programs that are available when patrons can participate in them and that are close to their residence is the best option. Second, facilities are not always available at the appropriate time or patrons' schedules are unknown. In these instances, the programmer will need to develop a program schedule based on prevailing practice.

Scheduling Formats

The time frame used to cycle program changes and periods of operation will vary from agency to agency. Community customs and accepted practice will most often determine the formats used. The usual program scheduling formats are explained below.

Annual

The first step in developing an annual schedule is to obtain a calendar with lots of space to make entries for each day. Scan the calendar and make notes on the days of obvious programming events. Christmas, Easter, the Fourth of July, Jewish holidays, Memorial Day, Thanksgiving, and so on are examples of days when special programs will most likely be operated. In addition, identify any special days or seasons for which local custom would dictate the need of a special program. For example, flower festivals during the spring or fall are popular in many communities; Lincoln's birthday (February 12) is celebrated in Illinois; and Juneteenth (June 19) is the day many Texas Afro-Americans celebrate the implementation of the Emancipation Proclamation. Many other examples of local customs can be identified as special programming days.

It is also important to block out programming seasons. Many public park and recreation systems organize their program offerings around winter, spring, summer, and fall. The specific dates on which these seasons start and end need to be specified. There are other time periods around which program seasons can be scheduled, including every two weeks, every four weeks, monthly, every six weeks, bimonthly, and so on. Once operating seasons for the year are identified, specific program services that will fill each season can be specified.

It is equally important to identify dates that must be avoided. Local custom will dictate these dates. For example, in many communities Wednesday night is church night. Because of this, schools and public recreation departments avoid scheduling events on Wednesday nights.

Seasonal Scheduling

As suggested above, some agencies schedule their programs according to the seasons of the year. This arrangement usually makes good sense because many recreational activities are dictated by the weather.

Some recreation operations can operate only seasonally. For example, marinas, ski resorts, outdoor ice-skating rinks, golf courses in many parts of the country, waterparks, and so on are usually seasonal operations. In these cases, the first step in developing a program schedule will be to specify when the operation will open and when it will close.

In some settings, seasonal scheduling will be dictated by other events. In industrial recreation, for example, production schedules will sometimes influence how workers' time is organized and therefore when patrons will be available for programs. On some military training bases, recreation scheduling seasons conform closely to the training schedule. If servicemen are rotated in and out of a base after completing a ten-week training course, then the recreation department's programming seasons will need to be coordinated with this schedule.

In a similar manner, different agencies schedule program services with other time frames, including monthly, weekly, daily, or hourly scheduling. Regardless of the time frame, the general method of scheduling is similar. The programmer simply has time and space that must be filled with leisure program opportunities. Try developing schedules as required in Exercise 11-3.

Exercise 11-3.
Scheduling

Use a calendar for the month of December in the current year. Develop a program schedule for December for two facilities.

The first facility is a private health club with a swimming pool, weight room, running track, sixteen racquetball courts, snack bar, and nursery. The facility is usually open from 6:00 a.m. through 12:00 midnight Monday through Saturday and from 9:00 a.m. through 12:00 midnight on Sunday. Membership in the health club is mostly families with school-age children.

The second facility is a recreation center on a military base. The facility includes a game room with a pool table and table tennis; a hall for banquets, dances, cards, and so forth, complete with a catering kitchen; a snack bar with video games; and a TV lounge. Eighty percent of the base population will be on leave beginning December 20th. Those remaining after that will be mostly young singles. The commander wants the recreation center open and operating every day of the month.

Discuss the following:

- What data do you need to collect first?
- What are the most obvious dates for scheduling special programs?

Facility Scheduling

Scheduling a facility is one of the easiest tasks programmers must complete. However, an ineffective scheduling system leads to double-booking, with much patron displeasure and an adverse image for the agency. To schedule competently requires a good scheduling system and constant attention to implementing the operational details of the system.

The most foolproof system is to create a scheduling matrix appropriate for the facility. Each facility and each hour that it may potentially be scheduled must be included on the matrix. By creating such a matrix, one has created blank spaces that represent the potential hours that each program in a facility may occupy. Exhibit 11-5 on page 238 is such a matrix for a small, neighborhood recreation center with two rooms.

When the specific facility is scheduled, the name of the individual, group, or program that will occupy the space is written onto the schedule in the appropriate place. In this way each space can be scheduled only once. To avoid confusion, there should be only one scheduling matrix. All methods, even computerized scheduling programs, use this simple, basic procedure.

How, then, can scheduling go wrong? Inattention to detail is the most frequent error. Busy staff members may give out a reservation but fail to write it on the master schedule. This error often results in double-booking. It is obviously important to have a system that is designed so that each space available can be scheduled only once. Normally, recreation operations do not overbook facilities for which they take reservations.

The most detailed scheduling matrix that is usually used in recreation operations is a facility schedule. Exhibit 11-6 on page 239 is an example of a scheduling matrix for the courts at a racquetball club. Properly scheduling such a facility requires a schedule for each day of operation, with an hourly schedule for each court in the facility. Other facility schedules can be developed with a similar system.

Exhibit 11-5.
Recreation Center Schedule

Upper-level Room

Time	M	T	W	T	F	SA	SU
8:00							
9:00							
10:00							
11:00							
12:00							
1:00							
2:00							
3:00							
4:00							
5:00							
6:00							
7:00							
8:00							
9:00							
10:00							
11:00							

Lower-level Room

Time	M	T	W	T	F	SA	SU
8:00							
9:00							
10:00							
11:00							
12:00							
1:00							
2:00							
3:00							
4:00							
5:00							
6:00							
7:00							
8:00							
9:00							
10:00							
11:00							

Exhibit 11-6.
Racquetball Court Scheduling Matrix

Day: Date:

Time	1	2	3	Court 4	5	6	7	8
6:00 a.m.								
7:00 a.m.								
8:00 a.m.								
9:00 a.m.								
10:00 a.m.								
11:00 a.m.								
12:00 p.m.								
1:00 p.m.								
2:00 p.m.								
3:00 p.m.								
4:00 p.m.								
5:00 p.m.								
6:00 p.m.								
7:00 p.m.								
8:00 p.m.								
9:00 p.m.								
10:00 p.m.								
11:00 p.m.								

In scheduling a facility, one must not ignore the need for facility maintenance, custodial care, and set-up and tear-down time. An attractive, clean, well-maintained facility contributes to patron satisfaction. However, to accommodate the level of maintenance and custodial care desired, an appropriate amount of time must be included in the schedule for these operations.

Conclusion

The written program plan is used to share the operational details of what must occur so that patrons can have the leisure experience intended by the program designer. Writing the plan requires that the designer clarify design and operational details. A written program plan should contain enough detail so that the program could be duplicated by another programmer.

A management plan provides organizational details to the many activities that must be accomplished to implement a program. Management planning identifies all activities that must be completed to implement a program and places them in the order in which they need to occur. Gantt charts and the flow chart method are most frequently used in managing the implementation of recreation services.

A unique component of a recreation program plan is the animation plan. In this plan, the scenario of interactions, including the contents of each frame, the transitions and their sequence, that must occur for patrons to have the leisure experience intended by the designer are explicated.

To maximize attendance and make efficient use of facilities, there needs to be an overall design in the scheduling of recreation program services. The programmer may use a variety of time frames for scheduling programs. Documented patron preferences are the best data to use in scheduling. Facility scheduling can be done with the development of a scheduling matrix appropriate for the facility being scheduled.

Endnote

Two other methods of network diagramming—the program evaluation and review technique (PERT) and the critical path method (CPM) are also mentioned in the recreation programming literature. There are distinct differences between each of these methods. Generally, PERT can accommodate projects requiring flexibility in timing. It is therefore especially useful in research and development projects where the exact amount of time needed to complete activities is unknown because of the newness of the activities. Farrell and Lundegren (1983) outline how PERT may be used in managing the implementation of a recreation program.

The critical path method is most useful for scheduling activities whose required time for completion is already known and the primary planning objective is one of cost control and adherence to the shortest completion time possible, that is, the critical path. Mittelstaedt and Berger (1972) and Russell (1982) discuss the use of CPM in implementing recreation programs.

PERT and CPM are both designed to manage the implementation of projects that are considerably larger than most recreation programs. In addition, there are several methods of drawing the network diagrams used to illustrate implementation details. Drawing network diagrams is a technical, complicated technique used in implementing large, complex projects. The interested reader should see Moder et al. (1983) for complete information on the subject.

References, Chapter Eleven

Farrell, P., and H.M. Lundegren. 1983. *The Process of Recreation Programming Theory and Technique* (2nd ed.). New York: Wiley.

Kliem, R.L. 1986. *The Secrets of Successful Project Management.* New York:Wiley.

Mittelstaedt, A.H., and H.A. Berger. July, 1972. The Critical Path Method: A Management Tool for Recreation. *Parks & Recreation* 7(7), 14-16.

Moder, J.J., C.R. Phillips, and E.W. Davis. 1983. *Project Management With CPM, PERT, and Precedence Diagramming* (3rd ed.). New York: Van Nostrand Reinhold.

Russell, R.V. 1982. *Planning Programs in Recreation.* St. Louis: C.V. Mosby.

Photo courtesy of Austin Parks and Recreation, Austin, Texas. Photo by Jim Halbrook.

12

Techniques for Program Promotion

The next three chapters deal with implementing programs. Programmers allocate more of their time to implementing program services than to any of the other steps of the program development cycle. Spending time on this step is easy to justify because it involves completing tasks that have an obvious direct relationship with producing program services. Doing a good job in implementing services is an important step in the Program Development Cycle. However, programmers must guard against allowing this step to dominate their time to the exclusion of other steps in the cycle. Often, programmers have the view that the best use of their time is implementing more programs rather than offering fewer programs that are based on a thorough needs analysis, well designed and properly evaluated.

Furthermore, there is a tendency to believe that all program failures are traceable to inadequate implementation. Inadequate implementation could be the cause of failure, but there are also other possible explanations. For example, failure could be traceable to an inadequate analysis of needs and the consequent development of a program service for which there is simply no demand. The programmer, then, is cautioned that spending too much time on program implementation and too little time on the other steps of the Program Development Cycle can create problems for the programming agency.

Program implementation involves promoting the program, registering participants, queuing patrons at registration and in events, staffing programs, and supervising operations. These functions are discussed in the next three chapters.

Program Promotion

Howard and Crompton (1980) define promotion as "basically communication which seeks to inform, persuade, or remind members of a potential client group of an agency's programs and services" (p. 448). To this list, Crompton and Lamb (1986) add "to educate." Kotler and Andreasen (1987) suggest that "any communication process involves a message sender and a message receiver (a target audience)" (p. 506). To truly communicate in promoting program services, the programmer must not only be concerned with the form and content of the message to be sent, but must also understand the educational and cultural background of those who are intended to receive the message.

Promotion will be more successful if it is accompanied by services that have been developed within a marketing framework (Russell and Verrill 1986). A good promotional campaign will not be able to sustain participation in services that are not well designed and based on identified patron wants. Only one of the four primary marketing elements, promotion, must also be supported with a product that is well designed, delivered at the right time and place, and made available at the appropriate price.

An agency's promotional campaign, then, will involve fulfilling one or more of the following functions—to inform, to educate, to persuade, or to remind. There is some disagreement about which of these functions is most appropriate for a leisure service agency to use in attempting to attract patrons. Which strategies will dominate an agency's promotional campaign will depend on the type of leisure service organization that is offering the program.

Persuasion

Persuasion is a different activity than the other three forms of promotion since its articulated goal is to bring about a change in attitude or behavior (Manfredo and Bright 1991). Persuasive communication theory suggests that individuals are persuaded with either the central or peripheral methods (Ajzen 1992). The central method assumes patrons exercise a high degree of information processing through rational behavior involving a thorough examination and evaluation of the ideas and information presented which results in selecting the best alternative from all that are possible.

The peripheral method assumes patrons are not as thorough at processing information because of a lack of interest, ability, or time. In this instance, persuasion is achieved with factors tangential to the content of the message e.g, the credibility of the presenter or the communication channel.

Most practitioners today recommend using advertising strategies that simultaneously account for both methods (Manfredo, Bright, and Haas 1992) since the likely case is that patrons use both methods for processing information about leisure participation. For example, one may carefully decide to begin participating in an exercise program and is persuaded to do so with information provided from several sources, which is high, rational processing. However, once the decision to participate is made, little time may be spent in selecting a health club to join, and in fact the decision may be based on an advertised testimonial from a local professional athlete featured in one health club's advertisement—low information processing.

The persuasiveness of any form of communication will be affected by the following—comprehension of the advertisement, effects of prior knowledge, involvement with the topic, repetition of the message, credibility of the source, and attitudes toward the advertisement (Manfredo, Bright, and Haas 1992). Current information about persuasive communication is too voluminous to reiterate here. However, several myths that persist must be dispelled. First, too much material is written at a reading level above the ability of the intended recipients, and they consequently cannot comprehend it. The programmer must know the target market very well to correct this.

Second, information acquired from direct experience has the most salience and will therefore be the most difficult to alter. Inexperienced or infrequent participants of a given activity will be easier to influence than experienced, frequent users. This is also why it is critical to make certain the agency is ready to effectively and efficiently provide a service prior to launching it. The knowledge and image that accompany a bad experience with an agency's service, acquired from direct experience, is very difficult to alter.

Third, continued repetition of an advertisement does not increase the recipient's favorableness toward the advertisement in a linear fashion. There is usually an initial increase in favorableness followed by a point of diminishing return when it declines. The dynamics of this variation depend on a number of factors including the type of advertisement, the complexity of it, and the attitude of the recipient about the advertisement itself (Manfredo, Bright, and Haas 1992).

Persuasion is usually accomplished through advertising, which is not neutral. It is at least mildly aggressive in attempting to persuade someone to purchase the sponsor's product or service (Russell and Verrill 1986). Commercial recreation operations often use an aggressive advertising campaign to attract customers to use their services instead of the services of another supplier, that is, they try to increase their market share.

Communication Channels

The type of promotion used should be selected to bring the agency's services to the attention of the intended audience, thereby channeling the promotional campaign to its target market. Kotler and Andreasen (1987) explain that "a channel is a conduit for bringing together a marketer and a target customer at some place and time for the purpose of facilitating a transaction" (p. 473). Leisure service agencies normally use at least two channels to promote their program services.

One channel is aimed at the general public. Because of concern about equity of access, municipal leisure service agencies in particular must inform patrons about available services, thus allowing general access to program services. Although commercial recreation operations may conduct a promotional campaign directed at the general public, equal access to program information in these cases is a marketing rather than an equity decision.

A second channel is a more targeted effort directed to the target market for the service. The purpose of this second channel is to inform and remind individuals who are most likely to participate in the program. Targeting a promotional campaign is considered more cost effective since it places information about a program in the hands of individuals most likely to purchase or use the service.

The usual medium for the channel directed to the general public is an agency publication that includes all of the agency's services for a given period. These publications educate the public about the agency, its services, and its facilities. Often this type of publication is mailed to all residents of a community, or it is distributed as an insert in a community newspaper. In addition, news releases may be sent to a local newspaper. The usual medium for the more targeted effort is an in-house-produced, single-page flyer that is distributed at recreation centers, the agency's main office, neighborhood locations, and perhaps mailed to previous participants of the same or similar programs.

To effectively promote program services, programmers need to be proficient at writing copy that describes their programs and services for inclusion in a general agency publication. They must also be proficient at preparing public service news releases for the local press and be able to produce single-page flyers to promote a program. Techniques for producing each of these will be discussed below.

Writing Brochure Copy

Writing copy that will effectively promote a program is challenging. Unfortunately, many agencies do no more than inform patrons about their services because information copy is the easiest to write. Copy written to simply inform patrons does not need to include any more than the basic five Ws and the H used by reporters to ensure the completeness of a story, that is, who, what, when, where, why, and how (Ryan and Tankard 1977, p. 71).

Well-written copy also tries to capture the expectations of the target market and convey how the program will provide benefit by meeting these expectations (Leffel 1983). Contrast the two pieces of copy for a men's weight-training class, contained in Exhibit 12-1, p. 248. One piece of copy was taken from a seasonal brochure published by a municipal recreation department. The other was taken from a publication of a commercial recreation operation. (Both sets of copy have been altered to protect the identities of the agencies.) Can you guess which is from the commercial agency? Which one captures the interest of the reader? Which one communicates the benefits to be derived from participation? Does either of them overstate what one could reasonably expect to accomplish in a few hours of instruction? What else do you notice about the copy?

Exhibit 12-1.
Sample Promotional Copy

Weights for Men
      Learn how to use the Universal weight machines under the guidance of a knowledgeable instructor. No black sole athletic shoes. Instructor: Jim Smith. Class: Z4756. Day: T/TH. Time: 7:30-8:30. Length: 8 wks. Start: 10/09. Fee : $20.

Weight Training for Men
      There is nothing more appealing than a toned body. Weight training is an effective way to achieve the kind of physique you've always wanted—but thought was impossible! In the comfortable setting of Fairmount Gym you will be thoroughly introduced to free weights and machines. An individual program for your specific needs and goals will be designed for you. You will develop a clear understanding of the anatomy of your body and diet and nutrition in relation to weight training.
      Coach and instructor for North Community College, Bill Smith is a physical educator who has coached and taught weight training for 15 years. In 1982 he coached the N.C.C. weight-training team to the state championship. Fairmount Gym, Tues. April 4, 11, 18, 25, 7:30-9:00. Course Fee $40.

Writing creative copy is an art. It is therefore difficult to offer cookbook solutions about how to write good copy. Following are nine guidelines for preparing creative copy that Foster, (1990, pp. 29-31) offers:

1. Clarity—simple, clear sentences and words are preferred
2. Details—providing detail creates familiarity with a program
3. Use The Senses—using references to the senses keeps a reader's interest and humanizes the content of the copy
4. Use Personal Experiences—both your own and those of your satisfied customers to create interest and association with a program and its benefits
5. Use Conversational Speech—reading dialogue creates a sense of "being" there and sharing in an experience
6. Opposition—contrasting long with short sentences, fast and slow pace of reading, etc. creates interest

7.   General versus Detail—anchor detail (usually unknown information) to more general information that is more likely known
8.   Repeat—repeat and repeat words, phrases, and details that are strong and add support to one's point when repeated
9.   Parallel Construction—of sentences and phrases is a more sophisticated form of repetition that can be used for additional emphasis.

Writing concise, informative, and interesting copy for a promotional brochure requires practice. Complete Exercise 12-1 and see how many ways you can write up the same program.

Exercise 12-1.
Writing Brochure Copy

Write at least four different pieces of brochure copy for the following program, a pastry baking class. In one, emphasize the setting in which the program will occur. In the second, emphasize the opportunity for sociability that the program will present. In the third, emphasize the opportunity for personal achievement that the program will present. Write one more with an emphasis of your own choosing.

Program Facts

Who: Program participants and the instructor, Helen Cork, head pastry chef for the Farmint Hotel, Clarksberry bake-off winner for 1990, and state fair bake-off winner for 1991.

What: Holiday pastry baking class, including cookies, fruit cakes, and ethnic breads.

When: One night per week, 6:30-9:30 p.m. for the six weeks before Christmas.

Where: In the test kitchen of the Farmint Hotel.

Why: To become better at baking, to prepare excellent holiday baked goods, to make Christmas presents for family and friends, and others.

How: Sign up by November 1, 1995, at the Recreation Department office; class fee is $45, including all supplies.

Preparing News Releases

Writing news releases requires preparing longer copy than that for promotional brochures or flyers. Space in newspapers for items actually considered news is free to the sponsoring agency. However, when news releases are submitted, the writer is competing for a limited amount of space with other organizations seeking publicity. To increase the probability that a news release will be published, the programmer should know and meet the newspaper's deadlines and prepare well-written copy.

Many newspapers will rewrite a news release submitted by a programmer. Expect your wonderfully written copy to be rewritten. Newspaper editors know that the same news release has probably been submitted to several different outlets, and they do not want the same copy appearing in their own paper. Many smaller papers, however, do not have the staff to rewrite news releases, so the copy prepared will most likely appear verbatim. In fact, well-written copy that requires little or no rewrite will probably be given priority and published because of tight production schedules. News organizations live by the clock. If you do not meet their deadlines, the materials submitted will not be published, no matter how well written or important they are.

Preparing a news release involves writing copy in a specific style and preparing the copy according to standard newswriting conventions. All news stories should be brief but accurate. They should have a good lead and use the inverted pyramid form of writing. The lead is the first paragraph or two of a story that immediately lets the reader know what the story is about. Ryan and Tankard (1977) suggest that "good, straight news leads quickly satisfy a reader's need and desire for information, and attract a reader to the rest of the story" (p. 101).

The inverted pyramid form of writing requires that the most important pieces of information be placed at the beginning of a story. The assumption is that the reader may stop reading at any point. The story should therefore be written so that the reader has the pertinent facts immediately and each succeeding paragraph contains progressively less important information.

Formatting a news story is also important. A newsroom is a busy place, and a lot of copy crosses an editor's desk each day. Each story should therefore have a slug, which is placed in the top left corner of each page of the story. The slug should include the writer's name, address, and phone number; the title of the story; a release date for the story; and the approximate number of words. All news releases should be double-spaced to allow room for the editor's proofing marks and corrections. If the story is longer than one page, the bottom of each page, except for the last page, should end with "more." The end of the story is signified by "end." Exhibit 12-2 contains a sample news release for a balloon flying contest. After reading the news release, complete Exercise 12-2.

Exhibit 12-2.
Sample News Release

NEWS RELEASE
Anytown Park and Recreation Department

Fred Bloom
Recreation Supervisor
(xxx) 565-2651
Twenty-Fifth Annual Fourth of July Balloon Fly
Release any time after June 20, 1995
Approximately 220 words

Twenty-Fifth Annual Fourth of July Balloon Fly

Silver balloons will be used when Anytown Park and Recreation Department conducts its twenty-fifth annual Fourth of July Balloon Flying Contest. The Balloon Fly will take place at Veterans Park, 5th and Locust at 11:00 a.m. Registration will begin at 10:00 a.m. There is no charge, and all children through 16 years of age may participate.

Last year, the winning balloon flew over 300 miles to eastern New Mexico. The farthest any balloon has ever flown over the past twenty-four years is 500 miles. In 1976 a balloon flew the 500 miles to eastern Arizona in about twelve hours.

The silver balloons being used this year to celebrate the 25th anniversary of the event are several mills thicker than the balloons usually used. The extra thickness will allow the balloons to remain airborne longer and thus fly farther. According to Sid Kinder, Assistant Director of the Park and Recreation Department, "We expect to set a new record this year."

Usually about 1,500 balloons are released each year. Mr. Kinder said, "This event is very popular with families. We want everyone to know that all children are welcome and every one of them will get a balloon to release." In case of rain, the event will be held at the same time and place on the following Saturday morning, July 8, 1995.

Exercise 12-2.
Preparing News Releases

In class, critique the news release included in Exhibit 12-2 by answering the following questions:
- Does the news release have a good lead?
- Is the news release written in the inverted pyramid style?
- Does the news release invite participation?
- Rewrite the news release.

It is important to be selective in the types of materials submitted to newspapers. Not everything done in the agency is newsworthy. The programmer is most likely to have material published that meets one or more of the following news values (Ryan and Tankard 1977).

• News events that involve local events with local people. Almost all news releases by not-for-profit recreation agencies meet this requirement.

•News releases that are timely. For example, an announcement of a Turkey Trot race has a high likelihood of being included in a series of articles about Thanksgiving.

•News releases that involve prominent individuals or institutions. When the mayor of a local community joins a fitness program at a local Y.M.C.A., an event that would not normally be newsworthy becomes so. Stories involving a large number of people and that have human interest are newsworthy. Tot swimming programs always generate fascinating copy and excellent pictures for a news story. Stories that involve novel happenings are almost always newsworthy. Agencies that have zoos have an almost unlimited supply of novel, interesting stories.

Successfully obtaining space in newspapers requires that the programmer selectively submit newsworthy items, that they be well written in a journalistic style, and that they be written in the conventional journalistic format. Some newspapers have policies about distributing space to local agencies and organizations. It is therefore important that the programming agency understand what it most needs to do to get published in the local paper. A frank discussion with the news editor about the most essential pieces of information needed to get into the paper is often necessary so that the agency's allocation is wisely used.

Preparing Flyers

Flyer Production

Almost all agencies use individual program, in-house-produced flyers to promote their program services. The quality of these flyers varies among and within agencies. The quality of a program flyer produced to promote a service often depends directly on how much revenue a program produces.

Regardless of the agency, it is highly likely that programmers will need to be skilled in producing single-page promotional flyers. To produce them, the programmer will need to do the design, art work, layout, copywriting, and should understand how the flyer will be reproduced. Furthermore, the programmer may even need to actually reproduce the flyer.

Flyer Design

Nelson (1981) states that "designing means creative action that fulfills its purpose" (p. 112). When designing a flyer, programmers should remember its purpose. In most instances, the purpose will be to inform, educate, remind, or in some cases to persuade individuals to participate in a program. The design should include attractive art work, good layout, well-written copy with complete information, and good quality production. Unfortunately, many flyers produced in-house are often of poor quality and give patrons a bad image of the agency and its programs. Some effort at producing well-designed flyers is a good investment in the agency's overall promotional campaign.

Flyer design results in a pasteup of the flyer. A pasteup is simply a black and white original from which the flyer is actually printed. It is called a pasteup because the final composition is often made up of copy and art work that are pasted to a piece of white cardboard or paper. The pasteup is then either copied in a copying machine or reproduced with any number of printing methods.

All copy, however, begins as black and white copy. To obtain color, one may print on colored paper, print with colored ink on white paper, or print with colored ink on colored paper. A flyer is most often printed on twenty-pound paper, but a heavier paper will produce a more substantial flyer. Obtaining more than one color of printing on a flyer requires a more complicated pasteup and printing process. This usually requires professional help, which increases production costs considerably. Therefore, multiple color printing is seldom done unless one is preparing a flyer for a major program.

Art Work

When a flyer is being prepared, the art work will often be selected or created first. The illustration becomes the central theme around which the remainder of the flyer is developed. In all cases, it is important that the art work contribute to the purpose of the flyer and that it not simply be appended to it to "make it look good." Art work included in a flyer should be a part of the overall message.

Obtaining good-looking art work on in-house-produced flyers can be a problem unless the programmer is artistic or has access to a staff artist. Many agencies use stock art (or clip art), which is a published series of black and white line drawings of many sizes and of many different subjects. There are several publishers of stock art. It can be purchased at most art supply or graphic art stores. The use of stock art produces copy that is far superior to amateur drawings.

Several personal computer programs on the market can simplify the process of developing good art work and flyer copy. Print Master and Gem Draw are two popular programs that are IBM compatible. Microsoft Word, PageMaker, and MacDraw are equally popular for Apple products. With a word-processing system and an art program, a programmer can easily produce attractive flyer copy in a very short time. Exhibit 12-3 on page 255 is an example of a flyer produced by pasting up copy and producing illustrations with a word-processing system and Print Master.

Exhibit 12-3.
Sample Program Flyer

$\mathcal{BALLET}$

You can walk with more grace and have a more poised posture! Shape up those legs and thighs and trim down your tummy!

Learn the basic fundamentals of classical ballet in the Russian tradition. Basic movement and ballet positions will be taught.

Classes are available for adult students (16 years or older) interested in the toning and exercise benefits of ballet and for students interested in the serious study of classical ballet.

REGISTRATIONS are now being accepted by mail or in person at the New Town Recreation Center, 4th and Vine, 383-9304.

MADAM VICKERY, who trained and studied until age 19 in her native Russia, instructs all classes. She has danced in many local productions. Madam Vickery has instructed adults in ballet for over 35 years and believes that participation in ballet offers many physical fitness benefits.

CLASSES ARE SCHEDULED at 7:00, 8:00, and 9:00 p.m. on Monday and Wednesday, or Tuesday and Thursday evenings. Enrollment is $40.00 per month. New Students are welcome anytime.

Layout

The layout gives visual form to the arrangement of graphic illustration and copy. According to Wills (1965), during layout these two elements are arranged and adapted to each other to produce the flyer. Nelson (1981) suggests that illustration and copy need to be laid out with the following in mind: balance, proportion, sequence, unity, and emphasis.

Formal and informal balance

The flyer should be at rest with itself, leaving the reader with an overall pleasing visual image. Balance can be achieved by using formal or informal balance. In formal balance, everything that is done on one half of the flyer is repeated on the other half. Formal balance is achieved with symmetry.

Informal balance is asymmetrical. An asymmetrical layout that is balanced is a more difficult undertaking for someone who is inexperienced at layout. The objective is still an overall pleasing visual image, but it is more difficult to achieve. Informal balance is achieved by rearranging the various design elements in different ways until an overall visual balance is achieved. Neither copy nor illustrations should be pasted in place until the desired balance is obtained.

Proportion of elements

Proportion is the relationship of sizes of the various design elements to each other and to the overall flyer. For example, what is the proportion of illustration to copy? What is the proportion of the title lettering to the rest of the flyer? What is the proportion of "white space" — that is, the ratio of space left blank to the space printed with copy or illustrations? Ideally, the flyer should have enough "white space " to look uncluttered.

To achieve the most pleasing overall look, one should avoid arranging spaces with obvious mathematical relationships. Dividing a flyer into halves or quadrants is less interesting than other ways of dividing space. Unequal division of spaces results in the most interesting flyers.

Sequence of presentation

The layout will determine how the reader progresses through the flyer while reading it. The material should present both the copy and the illustrations in a logical sequence that leads the reader through the flyer to a conclusion or final point. In Western civilization, individuals naturally progress through written material by reading from left to right and from top to bottom. Layout should be arranged to accommodate this habit.

To add interest, however, one can redirect how the eye will move through a flyer by taking advantage of other likely sequences of eye movement. Nelson (1981) has suggested that "the eye moves naturally, too, from big elements to little elements, from black elements to lighter elements, from color to noncolor, from unusual shapes to usual shapes" (p. 119). With either type of sequence, the goal should be to enable the eye to progress smoothly through the contents of the flyer.

Unity of content

The illustrations, copy, and overall look of a flyer should make a harmonious presentation. It should make a single statement to the reader and not create visual or rhetorical dissonance. An example of visual dissonance would be the inclusion of photographs and line drawings on the same flyer. Using two different styles of type—for example, Old English and Western—on the same flyer would create visual dissonance. Undesirable rhetorical dissonance would be created by using different verb tenses in different sections of the copy on a single flyer or by writing in a different person in various sections of the copy.

Emphasis

Something on the flyer should be emphasized: the headline, art work, or copy. If there are several pieces of art work, one of them should dominate. If there are several copy blocks, one of them should receive primary emphasis. When nothing on a flyer is emphasized, everything and nothing stands out! When laying out a flyer, one should take control of what will be emphasized, make certain it is the dominant feature, and make certain nothing else upstages it.

Nelson (1981) suggests that the best test of good layout is to remove one element. The relationship of elements should be so strong that after one is removed, all others need to be repositioned. If this is not the case, the original layout was not properly designed.

Writing copy

Copywriting for flyers is similar to copy produced for the general circulation brochure. But brochure copy will normally be written in paragraph form and therefore clustered together, whereas flyer copy may be split apart and dispersed throughout the flyer. It is therefore important not to simply split apart the sentences of the copy used for the brochure and display it on the flyer. Normally, one needs to expand brochure copy into complete, logical passages that can then be distributed throughout the flyer and intermingled with art work and other illustrations.

Production Methods

Many agencies use copying machines for producing a small number of flyers. Many of these machines can accommodate colored paper. Many agencies also use some type of offset printing. In any case, you will need to produce good, clean, camera-ready copy. This means that the pasteup you present for reproduction will need to have good contrast between the black copy and the white background. There should be no extraneous pencil marks or smudges on the pasteup. What you present for reproduction is what you get! Printing will not cover up sloppy pasteup work, bad layout, or poorly written copy.

Although an agency's promotional campaign may involve more than what has been discussed above, in most cases programmers will be expected to write clear, concise copy describing their programs. This copy will be included in agency brochures, news releases, and flyers. Promoting a program, then, is one of the first processes in implementing a program. The promotional campaign for any program must be started well in advance of registration for the program. Well-written and well-designed promotional materials that are not made available to the target market on a timely basis will be of little benefit in promoting programs.

Conclusion

Implementing program services occupies a large portion of the programmer's time. But one should not allow this step in the Program Development Cycle to occupy a disproportionate amount of time. Carefully completing the other steps of the Program Development Cycle will also contribute to the development of good program services.

Developing the material for a promotional campaign is an early step in program implementation. Usual methods of promotion include an agency brochure, news releases, and individual program flyers. In most agencies, programmers must do much of the copywriting and other promotional work themselves. Promotional materials must be well written and the promotional campaign executed in a timely manner.

References, Chapter Twelve

Arnold, E. 1982. *101 Memos for Reporters*. Lawrence Ragan Communications (no location given).

Ajzen, I. 1992. Persuasive Communication Theory in Social Psychology: A Historical Perspective. In M. J. Manfredo (Ed.), *Influencing Human Behavior: Theory and Application in Recreation, Tourism, and Natural Resource Management* (1-28). Champaign, IL: Sagamore Publishing Co., Inc.

Crompton, J.L., and C.W. Lamb, Jr. 1986. *Marketing Government and Social Services*. New York: Wiley.

Foster, K. 1990. *How to Create Newspaper Ads*. Manhattan, KS: Learning Resources Network.

Howard, D.R., and J.L. Crompton. 1980. *Financing, Managing and Marketing Recreation and Park Resources*. Dubuque, IA: Wm. C. Brown.

Kotler, P., and A.R. Andreasen. 1987. *Strategic Marketing For Nonprofit Organizations* (3rd ed.). Englewood Cliffs, NJ: Prentice-Hall.

Leffel, L. G. 1983. *Designing Brochures for Results*. Manhattan, KS: Learning Resources Network.

Manfredo, M.J., and A.D. Bright. 1991. A Model for Assessing the Effects of Communication on Recreationists. *Journal of Leisure Research, 23,* 1-20.

Nelson, R.P. 1981. *The Design of Advertising* (4th ed). Dubuque, IA: Wm. C. Brown.

Russell, T., and G. Verrill. 1986. *Otto Kleppner's Advertising Procedure* (9th ed.). Englewood Cliffs, NJ: Prentice-Hall.

Ryan, M., and J.W. Tankard, Jr. 1977. *Basic News Reporting.* Palo Alto, CA: Mayfield.

Wills, F.H. 1965. *Fundamentals of Layout for Newspaper and Magazine Advertising, For Page Design of Publications and For Brochures.* New York: Dover.

Photo courtesy of City of Oakland Parks and Recreation Department, Oakland, California.

13

Registration Procedures

Registering individuals involves developing a list of persons qualified to be in a specific program. It is an inconvenient process for both staff and patrons and therefore should not be undertaken unless such a list is necessary. Most frequently, registration is conducted for programs that require a fee for participating but it is also useful for purposes other than documenting who has paid for a service. Registering patrons is necessary in the following four cases:

1. *Patrons must pay a fee to be in the program.* These programs require registration because only those who have paid the fee are qualified to be in the program.

2. *The number of spaces in a program is limited.* If a program has a limited capacity, it is wise to have people register even if a fee is not being charged. Patrons thus secure one of a limited number of spaces by their position in a queue or some other qualifying method.

For example, Oak Park, Illinois, annually operated an Easter Egg Hunt, which was designed to handle 200 children. It was estimated that approximately 2,000 children would want to hunt eggs. To accommodate the estimated demand, ten hunts were operated during the day, with 200 children per hunt. Although each hunt was free, children were required to obtain a ticket to a specific hunt. In this way, queuing for determining who could be admitted to each hunt was arranged beforehand. In this case, being "qualified" simply meant that a person had obtained one of a limited number of tickets for a particular hunt.

Spaces in a program may also be limited because of the carrying capacity of the facility. In outdoor recreation, often the number of participants permitted into some wilderness areas is restricted because of the physical limits of the ecological systems or because the perception of an area as a wilderness would be impaired with too many people in the area. Sometimes, then, it is necessary to limit participation in order to maintain the leisure experience that the agency is trying to offer. Thus individuals need to register to obtain one of the limited spaces available.

3. *Places in the program are expensive to provide.* Because of this, it is necessary to know the number who will participate. In some events it is also necessary to know how many people are going to attend so that proper arrangements can be made. Dances with sit-down seating, parties or events involving a caterer, and so forth are examples of such events. In these programs, some type of invitation with an R.S.V.P. system or other registration system is often used to enable the programmer to have a reasonable estimate of the number who will attend.

4. *Some special qualifying procedure for admission to a program is required.* Some programs are open only to those with special qualifications. In these cases, a list of those qualified must be developed. In sports, for example, tryouts are often necessary to place players into leagues or programs appropriate for their skill levels. In outdoor adventure programming, one often must make certain that individuals have the requisite skills. For example, patrons may be required to demonstrate a level of swimming proficiency before being permitted to participate in a canoe trip.

Sometimes, the special qualification may simply be that the patron has provided the agency with certain information. Some recreation centers require all patrons to register during their first visit to the center. Registration is free, but people must register and provide their name, address, phone, and the name of someone to contact in case of emergency. The City of Santa Clara, California, Parks and Recreation Department uses this system at its Youth Activity Center. Exhibit 13-1 on page 265 displays a copy of the registration card used. After the card is completed, the child is issued a picture identification card. Registration and the first card are free, but there is a charge for replacement cards. Registrations for drop-in day use, which includes paying an admission fee and signing a liability release waiver are also being used more frequently.

Registration, then, is often a necessary part of program implementation. When registration is undertaken, it should be conducted to maximize convenience for patrons rather than for staff. The timing and location of the registration should be convenient for patrons.

Exhibit 13-1
Registration Card

dBASE_____   Residency_____   Picture _____

CITY OF SANTA CLARA
PARKS & RECREATION DEPARTMENT
RESIDENT YOUTH CARD

PARTICIPANT_____

Last Name   First Name

The undersigned, in consideration of participation in this activity, agrees to indemnify and hold the
City of Santa Clara harmless, and release the City of Santa Clara from any and all liability for any
injury which may be suffered by the above named individual arising out of, or in any way
connected with, participation in any activity the above named individual is registered in.

PARENT SIGNATURE_____DATE_____

Day Pass

PARTICIPANT INFORMATION

NAME (Print)_____PHONE_____

ADDRESS_____CITY_____ZIP_____

DATE OF BIRTH_____AGE_____SCHOOL_____

FATHER NAME_____WORK PHONE_____

MOTHER NAME_____WORK PHONE_____

IN CASE OF EMERGENCY, CONTACT:

1._____PHONE_____RELATIONSHIP_____
2._____PHONE_____RELATIONSHIP_____

PREVIOUS INJURIES, ALLERGIES, MEDICAL CONDITIONS:_____

Photo Retake

There are trade-offs between patron convenience and having a manageable, well-organized registration with adequate cash collection procedures. One of the most convenient registration methods is to have patrons register with the program leader at the first class meeting. Although this method may maximize convenience, cash collection occurring in many locations makes it very difficult to have adequate cash control procedures. Following are six registration methods that could be implemented; each is characterized by specific advantages and disadvantages.

Registration Methods

Central Location Method—Walk-in

In the central location method, all registration for many different programs takes place at a central location such as a recreation center, school building, or other facility. Parking should be adequate for the number of people anticipated, queuing should be well organized, and staff members conducting the registration should be well oriented and trained to answer patrons' questions. Registration workers should provide correct information. If a question cannot be answered correctly when first asked, the best solution is to have the employee call the patron once the correct information has been obtained. It can be damaging to the agency if questions are answered incorrectly.

In a very large operation, it is often wise to specialize operations and have a station-to-station method of completing registration. It is especially important to centralize cash collections so that the money collected is accounted for in the proper accounts. Centralized registration has the following advantages and disadvantages:

Advantages:

- All registration is accomplished at one time and in one place.
- Centralized registrations are easiest to advertise and supervise.
- A centrally located staff can serve patrons better by answering questions about all of the agency's programs from one well-publicized location.

- The central location method also makes possible central-ized cash collections and excellent cash control. This mini-mizes the opportunity for embezzlement and makes it easier to supervise the posting of cash received to the proper accounts.

Disadvantages:

- Participants do not see the actual program meeting place or meet the actual program staff. These meetings often raise people's level of anticipation about participating in a pro-gram. These interactions can also lead to additional regis-trations from people who initially may not have been aware of a particular program, did not realize what a program involved, or for some other reason did not initially choose to register for a program.
- Attracting all registrants to one location can mean long lines with accompanying frustrations, if the registration procedures and queues are not well planned and managed.
- Registration fee accounts may be mixed up if good account-ing procedures are not in place.

Program Location Method—Walk-in

In the program location method, registration takes place at the program site, such as a swimming pool, tennis court, or playground. This method has the following advantages and disadvantages:

Advantages:

- Registrants become familiar with the program site.
- Registration affords a good opportunity for patrons to meet and interact with program staff.

These first two advantages are important features when registering young children. This method gives them an opportu-nity to become familiar with the setting and the staff of the program before being left "alone."

- There is no delay in registering while waiting for people who are registering for other programs. These delays often occur in the central location method of registration.

Disadvantages:

- This method requires considerable travel time and standing in more than one queue for patrons who may be registering for several different programs.
- Decentralized registration is more difficult to supervise.
- Problems associated with cash collection and cash control are increased when registration occurs in several locations.

Mail-In Method

In the mail-in method of registration, patrons complete a registration form and mail it, along with any payment required, to the agency. This method is a centralized system that is accessible to people throughout the community. It has the following advantages and disadvantages:

Advantages:

- This method is convenient because it requires very little of a patron's time.
- The mail-in method allows for the greatest flexibility in scheduling staff to process registrations.
- Since the payment accepted with mail-in registration is something other than cash, the need to supervise cash collections is eliminated.

Disadvantages:

- This method allows no interaction between agency staff and patrons.
- To receive answers to questions, patrons must place a phone call to the agency.
- Participants do not see the location of the program until the first session.
- If the agency accepts credit card payments, a return receipt will need to be mailed.

Telephone Method

With this method, registrants simply telephone the agency to register for a program. Usually, all calls are directed to a central location. This method has the following advantages and disadvantages:

Advantages:

- Staff members can keep accurate, up-to-date records of the registration status of each program, that is, the number of spaces filled and open at any given time.
- The agency is relieved of the burden of managing a physical queue. If demand for registration is heavy, however, some method of queuing phone calls needs to be implemented. It is possible to obtain electronic equipment that will mechanically answer and queue phone calls.

Disadvantages:

- There is no face-to-face interaction between patrons and the program staff.
- The participants do not see the program location until the program begins.
- If there is a fee involved in registering for the program, collection is often a problem unless the agency accepts credit card payment for fees.
- If the agency accepts credit card payments, a return receipt will need to be mailed.
- When the fee is not paid at the time of registration, registrants may not appear when the program begins.

FAX-in Method

In the FAX-in method of registration, patrons complete the registration form, the same as in the mail-in method, but must supply their credit card information on the FAX form. The completed registration form is then FAXed to the agency's facsimile machine. This method has the following advantages and disadvantages:

Advantages:

- This is a very convenient method for patrons who may FAX their registration at any time.
- Because the facsimile machine may receive at any time of the day, it expands the time the agency is "open" to receive registrations with no increase in staffing costs.
- The agency does not need to manage a queue and, since the facsimile machine can receive only one transmission at a time, there is an order of receipt of registrations.

Disadvantages:

- There is no interaction between patrons and staff and thus no opportunity to answer questions or give out additional information about the program.
- The program participants do not see the program location until the first class session.
- If there is a fee charged for the program, the agency must use credit cards or bill the patron. In either case, this method usually requires the agency to mail something to the patron—a bill or a credit card receipt.

Combination of Methods

The agency may decide to permit patrons to register using two or more of the methods outlined above. Typically, the central location or program methods are combined with the mail-in, telephone, and/or FAX methods. Sunnyvale Parks and Recreation Department, Sunnyvale, California has created a centralized registration center that accepts walk-in, mail-in, phone-in, and FAX-in registrations in one location thus enabling them to coordinate all registrations from one location. Using a combination of methods offers the following advantages and disadvantages:

Advantages:

- Patrons have the greatest flexibility and opportunity in completing their registration.

- In making registration convenient, the agency maximizes its chances of fully enrolling its programs.

Disadvantages:

- When registration is accepted in several locations, lists can be confused and programs overenrolled without careful coordination. Using remote computer terminals with a centralized database for maintaining program rolls is one solution. The allocation of a given number of spaces in each program to each registration location is another solution. In this case, staff members at any one location may accept only a given number of registrants unless additional spaces are approved by a central coordinator.
- Patrons may be confused about which registration method they are to use when several methods are available.

It is important to indicate how registrations will be queued when a combination of methods is used. For example, does a patron who has phoned to register receive priority over someone who may be standing in a queue in the outer office? How are mail-in registrations queued compared with walk-in and FAXed registrations? What happens with mail-in registrations that are received before or after a deadline?

The Registration Form

Dobmeyer (1986) believes the registration form should be placed inside the last page of the catalog or brochure. This placement allows utilization of the prime space in the front of the publication to promote programs. Patrons reach the form when they are most likely ready to complete it. When this is done, messages should appear throughout the brochure informing patrons about the location of the registration form e.g. FOR REGISTRATION INFORMATION, PLEASE SEE PAGE 25. In addition, using the last page usually means the returned registration form will also include the mailing label which will contain information that can be used for marketing purposes.

However, the City of Kettering, Ohio places their registration form in the center of their brochure. It is included in a center pull-out that is printed on clay-coated paper inserted among the rest of the pages that are printed on recycled newsprint. This seems to be an equally effective placement since the recipient of the brochure is almost forced to open to the center section first because of the stiffness of the paper relative to the remainder of the paper in the brochure.

What to include?

One is often faced with two mutually exclusive objectives in designing the form itself—keeping it simple to complete and obtaining as much information as possible for use in marketing. Current practice is to keep it simple and easy to register for a program. To facilitate this, design registration forms that request only information that is needed and easily supplied by the patron. Exhibit 13-2 on page 273 is a sample registration form that includes the following:

- today's date,
- the registrant's name, address, day and evening phone,
- the program(s) they want to register for,
- the fee for each program,
- to whom the check should be written,
- what to expect after they register (*e.g. will they receive a confirmation or should they consider themselves registered un- less they are notified differently*),
- a liability release form,
- information about the method of payment, and
- instructions about where to send the registration.

Depending on the type of agency involved, some of this information may be omitted or may be handled differently. In a club, such as a YMCA or a commercial club, that has an existing membership list the patron may not need to supply more than the enrollments desired and their name and membership number. In these cases, treating them like members, someone who is well known to the agency and thus voiding the need to again supply information that is already known, enhances the relationship. Club members may not even be required to make payment to register—they are simply billed every thirty days for their club activities.

To maintain the illusion that the form is easy to complete, it should be kept as small as possible. This can be difficult in some situations. For example, in public agencies, the brochure is often mailed to a household and the registration form must be large enough to accommodate a family that is likely to have multiple registrants in multiple programs. The inclusion of credit card information and a release of liability also increases the size and reduces the ease of completing a registration form.

Exhibit 13-2.
Sample Registration Form

Name _____   Date _____

Address (Include Apt # if applicable) _____

City _____   State _____   Zip _____

Day phone _____   Evening phone _____

In case of an emergency, please provide the name and phone number of a local person to contact if there is no answer at the above number.

Name _____Phone (   ) _____

Each adult participant must sign below. In addition, the signature of a parent or legal guardian is required for youth participants (under 18 years of age).

I, the undersigned or parent/guardian of the individual named below do hereby agree to allow the individual named herein to participate in the afore-mentioned activity, and I further agree to indemnify and hold harmless the City of Sunnyvale and its employees, officers, and agents from and against any and all liability, save and except for the sole negligence of the City or its employees, resulting in injury associated with that individual's participation in this activity. I/ we agree to allow use of my/our photograph for program publicity. I/we have read and agree to the registration and program policies.[1]

Check the appropriate box(es) and sign.

(continued)

——— Participant (18 or over)   ____ Parent ____Legal Guardian

Signature/date

Signature/date

Signature/date

Participant's Name	Birth -date (If under 18)	Sex	Class No.	Class Title	Fee
1					
2					
3					
4					
5					
6					
7					

Total Fees____

Make checks payable to: Anytown USA

Participants are automatically enrolled in activity unless notified otherwise by the [agency].

NOTE: NO CONFIRMATION WILL BE MAILED
Send completed registration to: Anytown Recreation Agency, 1621 Main Street, Anytown, USA

FOR OFFICE USE ONLY
Fees accurate   Refund Due   Notes
Clerk   Date Processed

[1.]   *Taken from the Sunnyvale, California Parks and Recreation Department's GUIDE, Fall 1993. This release is used for illustration purposes only. No warranty is given regarding the legal appropriateness of this statement for the reader's use and the reader is cautioned to not copy this statement as any such statement should be developed and approved by the agency's legal counsel.*

Liability Release Form

Since the law regards anyone registered in an agency's program as an invitee (Peterson and Hronek 1992), the agency is held to the highest legal standard of care in operating its programs. Thus, the completion of liability release forms as a part of registration is becoming increasingly common. The release form included in Exhibit 13-3 is on the reverse side of the registration form used by the City of Santa Clara, California and thus it is a physical part of it. The degree of risk a patron is asked to waive in advance of participation will vary between agencies. For example, compare the release in Exhibit 13-3, used by the City of Santa Clara with the one used by the City of Sunnyvale (included in Exhibit 13-2, page 273). Although Sunnyvale excepted negligence in its release, Santa Clara asks participants to release it from negligence.

Exhibit 13-3
Liability Release Form

Release of Liability and
Assumption of Risk Agreement

In CONSIDERATION of the acceptance of the application for entry into the classes or activities listed on the Registration Form on the reverse side of this agreement, I hereby WAIVE, RELEASE and DISCHARGE any and all claims for damages for death, personal injury, or property damage which I may have, or which may hereafter accrue to me as a result of my participation in said classes or activities. This release is intended to discharge in advance the City of Santa Clara, City Council, its officers, agents, and employees, the Santa Clara Unified School District and the School Board, its officers, agents and employees from and against any and all liability arising out of or connected with my participation in said classes or activities, even though that liability may arise out of NEGLIGENCE or CARELESSNESS, on the part of the persons or entities mentioned above.

I HAVE READ THE DESCRIPTION IN THIS CATALOG OF EACH CLASS OR ACTIVITY FOR WHICH I HAVE REGISTERED, AND I AM AWARE THAT THESE CLASSES OR ACTIVITIES SUBJECT ME TO PHYSICAL

(continued)

RISKS AND DANGERS. NEVERTHELESS, I VOLUNTARILY AGREE TO ASSUME ANY AND ALL RISKS OF INJURY OR DEATH, AND TO RELEASE, DISCHARGE, AND HOLD HARMLESS ALL OF THE ENTITIES OR PERSONS MENTIONED ABOVE WHO, THROUGH NEGLIGENCE OR CARELESS-NESS, MIGHT OTHERWISE BE LIABLE TO ME, OR MY HEIRS, PERSONAL REPRESENTATIVES, NEXT OF KIN, SPOUSE, OR ASSIGNS.

It is understood and agreed that this waiver, release, and assumption of risk is to be binding on my HEIRS, PERSONAL REPRESENTATIVES, NEXT OF KIN, SPOUSE and ASSIGNS.

I have carefully READ this Agreement and fully UNDERSTAND its content. All participants in the classes or activities, including minors 13-17 years of age, must sign this Agreement.

Date: _____

ADULT PARTICIPANTS SIGN BELOW
Signature:_____   Print Name: _____
Signature: _____   Print Name: _____

PARTICIPANTS, AGE 13-17, SIGN BELOW
Signature: _____   Print Name: _____
Signature: _____   Print Name: _____

TO BE COMPLETED BY PARENT OR GUARDIAN OF MINORS

I have fully read this Agreement and fully understand its content. Furthermore, the significance of this release of liability and assumption of risk agreement has been EXPLAINED TO THE MINOR.

Signature of parent or guardian: _____Date: _____
Print Name: _____
Address: _____
Please indicate whether you are signing as:
Parent ___ Guardian ___

Note: *Taken from the* <u>Santa Clara Recreation Activities Guide</u>, *Fall 1993, Santa Clara Parks and Recreation Department, Santa Clara, California and used for illustration purposes only. No warranty is given regarding the legal appropriateness of this statement for the reader's use and the reader is cautioned not to copy this statement as any such statement should be developed and approved by the agency's legal counsel.*

Distribution

The obvious key to distributing the advertising brochure is to get it to the market for the program. Depending on the agency involved, this can include different groups of individuals. For example, governmental agencies, because of their responsibility to all citizens in a community, try to distribute the brochure to all citizens. Many will use the bulk mail method utilizing the POSTAL PATRON, LOCAL addressing method. With this method, the agency must pre-sort the brochures and the postman will leave one in each mail box on their route. However, the post office allows between two to five days to deliver this type of mail and therefore citizens in various parts of town will receive them at different times—up to five days apart. This can create problems with the timing of registration and equity of access.

Mailing the brochure with a pay per piece method will assure that patrons receive the brochure at almost the same time. Organizations with members that accept registrations from both members and non-members usually mail a brochure to their members and then use different conduits for distributing additional brochures. Tracking the returns from various distribution locations is an important marketing effort and the agency should use some type of method for coding the brochures used in each distribution conduit so those that are most effective can be identified.

Timing of Registration

Ideally, registration should be possible when the patron receives the brochure. However, this can become a major issue if everyone does not receive the brochure at the same time. Thus many agencies indicate a starting date for accepting registrations. In addition, in many municipal operations and some YMCA's, residents or members are given a priority registration period. Clearly communicating the date at which each group, e.g. residents, nonresidents, members, or the general public may begin registering is important.

Fees

In registering for a program, patrons are making a commitment to participate, which is intensified when they are required to pay a fee at the time of registration. The policy in most agencies is that the patron is not registered until the fee is paid. The fee for each program should be specified and the form should make it easy for the patron to total his/her fees. However, because of the use of line-item accounting practices, some governmental agencies require a separate check for each program so that the fee for any class that is closed may be returned. Alternatives to this include accepting one check and informing the patron that any refunds could take up to 30-60 days or providing them with a voucher that can be used for a future enrollment. Any of these alternatives are less desirable for the patron than returning his/her money.

How differential pricing is handled is important. If club members or community residents receive a lower price than non-members or non-residents, this should be stated. How this is communicated can both enhance it as a benefit and reduce its adverse impact. For example, one community states the price for participating and then states the discounted price for residents. This method clearly presents the price difference as a benefit to residents and a penalty to no one.

Credit Cards

The problem of credit cards must also be dealt with during registration. It is assumed that credit card use will increase sales volume. However, allowing individuals to use credit cards costs the agency three to five percent of total sales, which must be paid to a credit card company for collecting fees. In many municipal government operations, there is resistance to using credit cards because most municipal fees are mandatory and it makes no sense to give away three to five percent of the fees. However, fees for recreation and leisure services are not mandatory, and most practitioners agree that using credit cards to pay for services will most likely increase sales volume.

Cancellations/Refunds

Most agencies have a minimum number of participants that must be reached before a program is operated. Make certain this operational procedure is part of the information provided in the advertising brochure. In addition, make certain patrons know the procedures you will follow in handling their registration for a class that does not reach minimum enrollments. Agencies should give full refunds for classes that are canceled.

Likewise, make certain participants know what will be done with their registration if the class is full when their registration arrives. Some agencies place them on a waiting list until the class begins. If this is the case, the patron needs to be notified about what is occurring. For example, if you have already told patrons they are registered unless they hear differently, they will need to be notified they are not registered, but instead have been placed on a waiting list. Clear, on-going communication needs to be implemented to maintain customer confidence and satisfaction.

The agency's policy regarding the cancellation of one's space in a non-fee program should also be made known. No-shows can be an especially difficult problem when spaces in a program are limited, demand is high, and no fee is charged for the program. Some restaurants keep lists of people who make reservations and then do not show up. After a certain number of no-show incidents, reservations are no longer accepted from offending individuals.

Another solution is to charge a refundable reservation fee at the time of registration and return the fee to those who attend. Forfeit fees in athletic leagues are a good example of this technique, which could be implemented more frequently in other programs to solve the problem of no-shows. In one case, a refundable one dollar fee was charged to those registering for a downhill slalom ski course. In a previous year, many individuals had registered and then did not run the course even though staff members were waiting in freezing temperatures at the end of the course. When the refundable fee policy was implemented, almost all who registered actually participated in the slalom run. With this technique, only those who do not participate actually pay. They are in essence charged a penalty for denying someone else the opportunity or for unreasonably putting a burden on the agency.

Transfers

Some agencies will allow those already registered to transfer their registration to another class with available space prior to the beginning of a program. When using this option, be certain to state the terms of the offer, e.g., this may be done up to one week prior to the start of the program.

Guarantees

Another feature being offered in some agencies is a guarantee of satisfaction with their programs. If a customer is dissatisfied, they may receive a voucher for another program or a full refund. Often, some activities such as golf fees or athletic league fees for teams are exempted from this policy.

Computerizing Registration

Should you computerize your registration? There are several software packages currently available to accomplish this. Dobmeyer (1986) suggests it is not cost effective to computerize unless the agency exceeds 5,000 registrations per year. However, as the software becomes less expensive and more sophisticated, this cost/benefit ratio can change. Systems that are currently available will produce registration lists, keep track of enrollment numbers, produce lists of under-enrolled classes, maintain waiting lists for classes, and track revenue, expenses, and net revenue. In addition, they will permit the generation of many analytical marketing reports allowing the tracking of up to twelve socio-demographic variables that can be cross-tabulated with each other to facilitate target marketing to specified groups. Thus registration data can support the agency's marketing effort with current registrants. Remember, however, that nonusers are not included in this data base. Eventually, most programs are likely to computerize their registration because the systems will enable any number of functions to be performed with a single data entry.

Operating Registration

How well a registration is operated sends messages to patrons about the quality of the agency and its programs. The brochure was the first contact with the patron: registration is usually the second, and also the first patron-initiated contact. Good customer service is also essential at this stage of the service encounter in order to keep the patron satisfied. Following are some additional suggestions for operating a well-organized registration.

Additional Considerations

- Provide enough staff to handle the anticipated number of registrants. Supervisory staff should keep track of how long it is taking individuals to register and make adjustments as needed so that registrations can be completed in a reasonable time.
- Schedule registration at a time consistent with local customs. Early morning, evenings, or other time slots when patrons are available should all be scheduled.
- Completely orient and train staff before registration:

  a. Emphasize the need to be courteous to patrons.
  b. Try to have established, objective methods for handling potential points of disagreement. For example, if registrants must show that they are residents of the community, determine in advance how this point is to be established. Must one have a driver's license with an appropriate address or a voter registration card? Do not leave it up to the registration staff to improvise methods for verifying age, height, weight, skill level, residency, and so forth.
  c. Fully inform registration personnel about program details, waiting lists, fee payment policies and methods, refund procedures, nonresident registration policies, and the like.
  d. Have details about each program available for the registration staff. Agencies often become too lax and do not require that contract leaders completely inform the agency about program details. Remember, in the eyes of the public this is the agency's program, and the public ex-

pects agency personnel to know the details of its operation.

- Establish well-defined and well-organized queues.
- Provide simple and clear registration forms. Try to arrange for individuals to have completed as much of the registration form as possible before receiving the attention of registration personnel.
- Carefully instruct cashiers how to accept payment and properly record and account for each type of program fee.
- Provide additional, well-oriented staff for agency telephones immediately before, during, and shortly after the registration period.
- Provide adequate pens and space for writing at the registration location.

Queuing Procedures

Queuing is simply standing in line waiting for a turn to be served. There is an old story about the British: when two or more British people get together, the first thing they must determine is how the queue will be organized. Often we do not think of managing a queue until it has gotten out of control. That queues can get out of control and become a major problem was made clear by the poorly conceived queuing system at a "Who" rock concert in Cincinnati, Ohio, on December 3, 1979. Only a limited number of reserved seats were sold by the Riverfront Coliseum management. Approximately 80 percent were unreserved "festival seating" (Stuart 1979).

Instead of taking care of the order in which to serve people at the point of sale, the management let the audience scramble for desirable seats the night of the concert. Because of the group's popularity, the audience began gathering for the 8:00 p.m. concert in mid-afternoon. It was the usual practice for the coliseum to open its doors two hours before a concert. On this evening, however, the "Who" were late in setting up their equipment, so the doors did not open until about 7:00 p.m. In addition, all of the doors around the coliseum did not open at the same time. The crowd at the end of the coliseum that was delayed in opening became unruly and charged the doors for admission. In the ensuing melee, eleven young people were trampled and killed (Thomas 1979). Poorly conceived queuing, then, can create major problems.

There is evidence that standing in a queue can be an anxiety-producing experience (Mann 1973). Traditionally, leisure programmers ignored queues and assumed that the program began when the patrons entered the facility itself or came into the program. Programmers did not worry about the queue.

Standing in a queue may be the participant's first self-initiated contact with a program. Successfully managing queues requires that the programmer adequately deal with the first two laws of service delivery (Maister 1985): satisfaction = perception minus expectations, and it is hard to play catch-up ball. The patrons' satisfaction will depend on both their level of expectation and their perception of actual performance. As long as their perception of performance equals or exceeds their expectations, they will be satisfied. However, if it does not, they will be dissatisfied and it will be difficult to ameliorate this dissatisfaction with your performance in the operation of the program. There is evidence that queues for concerts, movies, sporting events, and other leisure events are perceived as occasions for socializing (Mann 1973). So, participants usually arrive expecting to have a positive, satisfying experience. The key is to operate registrations in a satisfactory manner so you do not begin a program in a deficit condition of patron dissatisfaction.

To better manage queues, it helps to understand the sociological principles that underlie the behavior of people in queues. Mann (1973) points out that queues are governed by the "rule of distributive justice," which was first outlined by Homans (1961). According to Mann, the rule as applied to queuing suggests that, if a person is willing to invest large amounts of time and suffering in an activity—that is, standing in a line—there should be an appropriate reward—that is, preferential treatment. If individuals in a queue are to believe the queue is fair, they must perceive "a direct correspondence between inputs (time spent waiting) and outcome (preferential service)" (1973, p. 48). Violating this principle creates stress and anxiety.

Four sources of stress and anxiety are associated with being in queues. First, there is the problem of queue jumping. This practice is a breach of distributive justice and a threat to the social order of a queue. Second, individuals are responsible for guarding their own territory. People in the queue are expected to remain vigilant and protect the queue position directly in front of them from queue jumpers. Their stress level is elevated when someone does jump the queue directly in front of them. When this happens, the individual bears the responsibility of dealing with the queue jumper and protecting the position. Third, one must make sure of being in the right queue for the service desired. When there are several queues for different services, poorly identified queues are a source of anxiety and stress. Finally, there is the problem of how long one will have to wait before receiving service. Not knowing how long the wait will be is also stress producing.

If the stress and anxiety of queuing are reduced, queuing will be eliminated as a possible source of participant dissatisfaction with the event. Furthermore, a well-managed queue can contribute to the overall satisfaction with a leisure experience. Program implementation begins with the queue. The burden of managing it rests with the recreation staff. How the queue is to be operated, then, needs to be well planned.

Four Types of Queues

The first step in managing stress-free, enjoyable queues is to define them with barriers or other physical guides and to reduce the possibility of queue jumping. Four types of queues can be established (Mann 1973): (1) single line with single service, (2) multiple lines with multiple service, (3) single line with multiple service, and (4) station-to-station service. In the United States, the single line with single service and multiple line with multiple service queues seem to be the most popular. These two types work well if the service being provided to each patron is similar in the amount of time it will take to deliver. However, the multiple line with multiple service approach can be terribly stress producing. Because of the differential service needs of each patron, some lines move much more rapidly or slowly than others. The solution is the single line with multiple service approach. This approach seems to be gaining popularity in the United States partly because it better implements the rule of distributive justice. It is the method of choice for large registrations where patrons may be registering for one or more programs and for themselves, a whole family, or a group of people.

The station-to-station method of queuing is effective when a series of steps must be undertaken to complete a transaction. This method essentially links together various combinations of the first three methods. One must make certain that no unacceptable, stress-producing bottlenecks occur in this type of queue.

Several other procedures can also be implemented to ensure stress-free, enjoyable queues:

1. Register the order of arrival, using a recognized system. A take-a-number or similar system determines the order of service and eliminates the need for a physical queue and its associated problems.

2. Improve the speed of service. This can be done by having more service stations or reducing the burden of completing the transaction. For example, do patrons have to place their name, address, and phone number on a separate card for each program they enter? Must they write a check for each separate program? Eliminating repetitious actions will help speed service with no additional personnel.

3. Assure the certainty of service. If patrons know there is enough service to meet their needs, much of the stress will be alleviated. Guaranteeing this will not always be possible. However, if queue managers know that the service is adequate, they should let the patrons know that their waiting is not in vain. A corollary to this is to let queuers know as soon as possible that they cannot expect service so that they can stop investing their time.

4. Start service for the patron while they are in line. An in-process wait seems shorter than a pre-process wait (Maister 1985), so one should create the perception that service has started as soon as possible. For example, one could distribute registration forms, instructions about the event, instructions about the queue, brochures about other events, etc. Station-to-station queues often create this perception since individuals move through a series of encounters that provide some service at each step.

5. Post the time required in the queue. Keep queuers informed about how soon they can expect service. The Disney organization does an excellent job of informing patrons about the

waiting time before they can gain access to an attraction. For example, they post signs in many queues that state, "Approximate Waiting Time is 30 Minutes." A pizza restaurant in Champaign, Illinois, posts a sign in its queue, informing patrons that "From this point you will be eating pizza in approximately 10 minutes." Providing this information creates reasonable expectations for queuers about how long it takes in the queue before receiving service. This helps avoid unreasonable expectations, complaints, and unnecessary anxiety.

6.   Have the queue move forward toward the point of service. When designing the queue, make certain that queuers are actually moving toward the point of service or at least have the illusion of progressing toward it. This builds anticipation and relieves anxiety.

7. Make the queue fun. Standing in a queue can be incorporated into the leisure event itself. This is a desirable goal and can both decrease stress and make queuing part of the whole experience. For example, at Disneyland the queue area for each attraction is thematically developed as part of the attraction and is designed to build excitement for the forthcoming experience. When the author was a faculty member at the University of Illinois, the football team received a bid to play in the Liberty Bowl in Memphis, Tennessee. The local Liberty Bowl committee treated queuers waiting for tickets to hot coffee, donuts, and entertainment from a pep band. Their efforts certainly turned a boring queue into an enjoyable event that helped build excitement for the Liberty Bowl itself. Implementing similar activities can help make queues a positive component of the event.

Public agencies should not be a part of giveaways when service for all who desire it is inadequate, or if the event is not properly organized and operated. Sponsors who wish to participate in giveaways at public agency events should be required to provide enough service for all and to follow queuing guidelines developed by the agency to ensure an orderly and fair queue.

While employed in a public agency, the author was once involved with a group of puppeteers who performed in a park one Sunday afternoon. Their performance was excellent. Some 150 to 200 children were seated on the lawn in front of the stage watching the performance. Parents were standing in a semicircle behind the children. At the end of the performance, a cast member came onto the stage with a box of candy suckers and announced that the children in the audience would be treated to a sucker. All of the children immediately stood up and began pressing forward. Many were very small and were getting crushed against the stage. Children who already received a sucker could not leave the scene because they were trapped against the stage by the children still trying to press forward. The worst that happened is that some parents were anxious and upset, and some children were crying and frightened.

Two points need to be made. First, the puppet performance was excellent, and there was no need to add a sucker giveaway to the event. Secondly, the way the giveaway was handled damaged what was, up to that point, an excellent event. If giveaways are not handled properly, they can be a detriment to an event rather than a positive contribution. Giveaways that do not have sufficient service for all also create problems. People who are not served usually feel that the queue was unfair and are disappointed. An agency suffers too much adverse publicity when it allows incomplete or poorly managed giveaways to occur under its auspices.

Two final issues to be discussed are pre-queues and no queues. Despite well-developed agency plans for queues, patrons will often take matters into their own hands and begin pre-queues before the start of the official agency queue. One needs to anticipate this possibility and be prepared to deal with it. One must decide if the order established by the pre-queue will be recognized and how it will be recognized. No matter how well one plans, an uncomfortable interface always occurs when the time comes to make the transition between the pre-queue and the official queue. Some agencies have therefore stopped using a queue for determining the order of admission to events and now use a system of random drawing for admission positions. The N.C.A.A. has done this for "Final Four" public tickets.The demand is simply too great and queue management too much of a hassle to do otherwise. A number of college campuses have also implemented such a system for admission to rock concerts and other high-demand events.

Some people object to a random draw system because it totally eliminates the rule of distributive justice. All who enter the drawing have an equal chance of being admitted to the event.

Without a queue, those who strongly desire admission do not have the opportunity to invest their time in a queue and thus receive the appropriate reward (preferential treatment).

How the queue is managed sends messages to patrons about the quality of the program. It is usually the first face-to-face contact the agency has with the patron. Queuing needs to be considered a part of the program and should be dealt with during the implementation stage. It needs to be managed to maximize its positive contribution to participant satisfaction with a program.

Conclusion

Implementation includes efficiently registering participants at a location and time that is convenient for them. There are a variety of registration methods, each with its own advantages and disadvantages. Understanding queuing behavior is essential to properly managing queues. Queues that are fairly and efficiently managed at registration and at program locations contribute to patron satisfaction with services.

References, Chapter Thirteen

Dobmeyer, E. 1986. *Registration Techniques*. Manhattan, KS: Learning Resources Network.

Homans, G.C. 1961. *Social Behavior: Its Elementary Forms*. New York: Harcourt.

Maister, D. H. 1985. The Psychology of Waiting in Lines. In J.A. Czepiel, M. R. Solomon, and C. F. Surprenant (Eds.). *The Service Encounter* (176-183). Lexington, MA: Lexington Books. D.C. Heath & Co.

Mann, L. 1973. Learning to Live with Lines. In J. Helmer and N.A. Edginton (Eds.), *Urbanmen: The Psychology of Urban Survival* (42-61). New York: Macmillan.

Peterson, J. A. and B.B. Hronek. 1992. *Risk Management: For Park, Recreation, and Leisure Services* (2nd ed.). Champaign, IL: Sagamore Publishing.

Stuart, R. 1979, December 5. Cincinnati Officials Order Inquiry into Concert Crush That Killed 11. *New York Times*, 1, D21.

Thomas, R.M., Jr. 1979, December 4. 11 Killed and 8 Badly Hurt in Crush Before Rock Concert in Cincinnati. *New York Times*,1, 13.

Documents With Limited Circulation

Documents and brochures from the following agencies were cited in this chapter.

City of Kettering Parks, Recreation & Cultural Arts Department, 3600 Shroyer Rd. Kettering, OH   45429

Recreation & Community Services Department, 1 West Campbell Ave. #C31, Campbell, CA 95008

Santa Clara Parks and Recreation Department, 1500 Warburton Ave. Santa Clara, CA   95050

Sunnyvale Parks and Recreation Department, P.O. Box 3707, Sunnyvale, CA   94088-3707

Photo courtesy of Joliet Park District, Joliet, Illinois. Photo by Ann Miller.

14

Staffing and Supervising Program Operations

Staffing recreation services involves recruiting, selecting, orienting, training, deploying, supervising, appraising, compensating, and contracting staff. A detailed treatment of personnel management in leisure service organizations is offered by Culkin and Kirsh (1986). In this chapter, the essential elements of the process are outlined, and personnel management problems and techniques associated with supervising program operations are outlined.

Most recreation agencies have well-developed, written policies for the management of full-time personnel in the agency. Unfortunately, this is not always true for part-time and seasonal employees, even though leisure service agencies typically employ a large number of such people to operate their many recreation facilities and programs.

Programmers are usually the first-line, full-time employees in a recreation agency. According to Sterle and Duncan (1977), the two primary roles of program supervisors are program development and development of leadership personnel. In many agencies, face-to-face delivery of the recreation service is accomplished solely by the part-time and seasonal workers. This is the case in many commercial recreation operations such as water parks, tennis facilities, and amusement parks. This is also true in municipalities, not-for-profit organizations, church recreation, and other organizations that operate recreation services.

McKinney and Chandler (1991) suggest that this practice has become popular because it increases staffing flexibility and lowers labor costs. With part-time workers, programmers can match the number of staff to their needs on a seasonal basis. In addition, because the interest in many recreation activities is cyclical, programmers can also hire staff who can lead and teach the activities currently being demanded with no commitment to their future employment.

However, there are problems created by this practice. First, part-time staff are less loyal to the organization and its programs (McKinney and Chandler 1991) and thus may not promote the long-term interests of the organization by building customer loyalty. Patrons rarely know if an employee is part-time or full-time, so the organization is judged by the performance of part-time as well as full-time employees. Second, there is a higher rate of employee turnover among part-time and seasonal workers. The result of this is a need to frequently recruit and train new employees. Both of the preceding problems lead to a third problem—the need for close supervision of their work performance.

Programmers will not be able to personally deliver all of the recreation services under their direction. As a successful professional football coach once said, "It does not matter how much I know about how to play football. What matters is how much the players on the field know about playing football." He was implying that he had a tremendous role in teaching and preparing the players to play the game. The same is true for the delivery of recreation services. Recent research suggests that seasonal employees are more happy and motivated when supervisory practices create a work environment that is challenging and provides employees the skills needed to perform at the level desired (Henderson and Bialeschki 1993). Thus, operating successful programs will often depend on how well the programmer can recruit, train, deploy, and supervise a part-time and seasonal staff.

Position Analysis

Staffing begins with an understanding of the agency's goals and objectives. Staff members who can fulfill the agency's goals and objectives and deliver program services consistent with the agency's programming philosophy need to be hired. In most instances, organized recreation services are people-to-people services involving face-to-face interactions between patrons and staff members in a leadership, instructor, or customer service role. It is therefore essential that qualified and well-trained staff members be placed in these roles. The first step in acquiring an adequate staff is to complete a job analysis.

Mathis and Jackson (1982) define job analysis as "a systematic investigation of the tasks, duties, and responsibilities of a job, and the necessary knowledge, skills, and abilities someone needs to perform the job adequately" (p.143). A job analysis contains all of the information necessary to develop and administer the job, including a detailed statement of work behaviors and other information relevant to the job. A job description, orientation and training needs, and information for employee appraisal are derived from the data in a job analysis.

One outline of information to be contained in a job analysis is provided by the Position Analysis Questionnaire (PAQ), developed by McCormick, Shaw and De Nisi (1979). The PAQ identifies six job dimensions that characterize most jobs. In analyzing a job, one should use these six dimensions as a checklist for determining what is required to perform the job. The six dimensions and examples of work statements that might be characteristic of a recreation leader's job are contained in Exhibit 14-1 on page 294.

A job analysis is a thorough study of the principal components of a job, including the necessary knowledge, skills, and abilities plus other unusual facts about or requirements for doing the job. Each job in an agency requires different knowledge, skills, and abilities. *Knowledge* is a body of information one must possess that is directly applied to the performance of the job. For example, knowledge about water chemistry would be required for a pool operator. *Skill* is the possession of a demonstrable competence to perform a learned psychomotor act. Skill in water rescue techniques would be required for a lifeguard. An *ability* is a current competence to perform a behavior that can be observed or that results in an observable product. An ability to develop and write a weekly playground program plan would be required of a playground leader. Obviously, one must have a clear concept about the job and its functions before an accurate and thorough job analysis can be prepared.

Exhibit 14-1.
Recreation Leader Job Analysis

1. Information Input. Where and how does the worker get the information used in performing the job?
   Examples: Uses policy manuals.
                           Takes verbal direction.
                           Uses leadership instruction manuals.

2. Mental Process. What reasoning, decision-making, and information-processing activities are involved in performing the job?
   Examples: Makes decisions about safe playground practices.
                           Makes decisions while leading activities.
                           Maintains order and discipline on playground.

3. Work Output. What physical activities does the worker perform and what tools or devices does he or she use?
   Examples: Leads games and other recreation activities.
                           Must set-up and take-down recreation equipment.
                           Must be able to drive a van.

4. Relationships with Other Persons. What relationships with other people are required in performing the job?
   Examples: Instructs and leads activities.
                           Must relate to all playground users.
                           Needs to work cooperatively with other workers.

5. Job Context. In what physical or social context is the work performed?
   Examples: Works out-of-doors.
                           Works in a fun, social atmosphere.
                           Works in constant interaction with patrons.

6. Other Characteristics. What activities, conditions, or characteristics other than those already described are relevant to the job?
   Examples: Must work unusual hours.
                           Often works without constant, direct supervision.
                           Must be able to tactfully enforce rules.

(Adapted from McCormick 1979)

Although an agency may have a personnel department, preparing statements of the principal components of a position is often assigned to the program supervisor requesting the position. Programmers should therefore fully understand and be able to articulate the knowledge, skills, and abilities necessary to perform a job. Incumbents in a similar position in another agency are a good source of information about what is required to do a specific job.

Job Description

Job analysis data are used to write a job description, which is a summary of the duties and responsibilities of the job. The job description is not as detailed as the job analysis, but it must be representative of the principal components of the job and give an applicant a good indication of what the major responsibilities include and what qualifications one must possess. Exhibit 14-2 includes a general outline of a job description.

Exhibit 14-2.
General Outline of a Job Description

Function Statement
   A general statement of the responsibilities of the position.

Supervision
   A statement specifying to whom the employee is responsible.

Domains
   Statements outlining the major areas of responsibility of the employee.

Task Statements
   A list of work behaviors that distinguish the position.

Worker Traits
   A list of the knowledge, skills, and abilities that are essential for the position.

Desired Education Experience
   A statement of the education, training, and/or experience required and/or desired for the position.

Special Requirements
   A list of any special knowledge, certifications, or other specific requirements for the job.

Exhibit 14-3 is a sample job description for a playground leader; it was developed using the outline in Exhibit 14-2 on page 295. Notice that the job description outlines the nature of the position, the requirements for employment, the nature of the work to be performed, the type of supervision to be performed, and special requirements needed. The personnel department in an agency will usually have a specific outline for job descriptions that are to be used in the agency. However, any outline is likely to include components similar to those in this example. Exhibit 14-4 on page 297 is a sample job description for a front desk attendant in a health or racquet club. Compare these two descriptions to see how the jobs differ. After the two descriptions have been compared, complete Exercise 14-1 on page 298.

Exhibit 14-3.
Job Description: Playground Leader

Basic Function and Responsibility
    Under general supervision and direction, playground leaders plan and operate recreation programs at assigned locations. Leaders are also responsible for supervision, safety, and light maintenance of play areas.

Supervision
    Playground leaders are responsible to the recreation supervisor of their geographic region.
    Must be able to function independently with only periodic supervision.

Domains
    Plans and operates playground recreation program.
    Is responsible for the safe operation of playground and play area.

Task Statements
    Plans weekly recreation program.
    Promotes program to area patrons.
    Leads and operates programs.
    Supervises play apparatus area and general playground.
    Recognizes and removes safety hazards from playground.

Worker Traits
    Knowledge of recreation program activity planning.
    Knowledge of game rules.

(continued)

Knowledge of developmental abilities and activities.
Ability to deal tactfully and effectively with children and adults when enforcing rules and regulations in a recreation setting.
Ability to recognize safety hazards.

Desired Education and Experience
Completion of college-level courses in recreational leadership is required (or desired).
Previous experience in leading recreation activities and/or working with children is desirable.
Specialized knowledge of specific recreation activities is desirable.

Special Requirements
Must possess a valid vehicle operator's license.
Applicants with certification in first-aid will be given priority.

Exhibit 14-4.
Job Description: Front Desk Attendant

Basic Function and Responsibility
Under general supervison and direction, front desk attendants oversee the operation and smooth functioning of the club, including greeting patrons, explaining rules and policies, taking reservations, making sales, and other duties as assigned.

Supervision
Front desk attendants are supervised by the management personnel on duty.

Domains
Public relations.
Operate facility.
Sales.

Task Statements
Greets patrons by name and issues equipment.
Makes reservations for equipment and facilities.
Makes sales of equipment and club services.
Explains club rules and policies.
Checks in users and assigns court space or equipment.

Worker Traits
Knowledge of club policies and rules.

(continued)

Knowledge of game rules and techniques.
Knowledge of club equipment and facilities.
Skill in learning and remembering club members by name.
Ability to deal tactfully and effectively in enforcing club rules and policies.
Ability to explain and interpret club policies.
Ability to make sales.

Desired Education Experience
Completion of college-level courses in recreational leadership or appropriate physical education courses is required (or desired).
Previous experience in the operation of recreation facilities or hospitality facilities is desirable.
Specialized knowledge of specific club activities is desirable.

Special Requirements
Applicants with certification in first-aid will be given priority.

Exercise 14-1.
Developing a Recreation Worker Job Description

In class, use the outline of a job description in Exhibit 14-2 and develop a job description for a part-time or seasonal recreation worker's position. Critique each other's job descriptions by considering the following questions:

- **Is the job description specific enough?**
- **Does the job description make clear the actual duties and requirements of the position?**
- **Are the items included representative of the complete job?**

Recruitment

Recreation agencies recruit a large pool of part-time and seasonal employees to meet their needs throughout the year. When an agency employs a large number of part-time workers turnover is often heavy. Because of this, recruitment, orientation, and training are constantly going on in the agency.

Recruitment involves obtaining a pool of candidates who are qualified to assume the agency's positions. Ray and Grossman (1980) observe that "managers often fall into the trap of assuming that the right employees will come along as summer approaches" (p. 98). Recruitment should be done before the actual need for employees' services. The idea is to have a pool of qualified applicants who are ready to assume agency positions when they are needed. Agencies recruit from both within and outside their organization.

Internal recruitment

Internal recruitment is an important source of employees for an organization. If overused, it can lead to charges that employment practices in the agency are "closed" and "you need to know someone" in the organization to get a job there. If true, these practices can lead to legal problems for the agency. Even if they are not true, the belief that they are will eventually diminish the number of applicants, and the agency's ability to attract a sufficiently large pool of qualified applicants will be hampered.

Despite these problems, internal recruitment is still an important source of employees, and it is implemented in several different ways. The promotion or transfer of existing employees is one method of internal recruitment. Promotion and transfer to more desirable or higher paying jobs is a strong motivator for employees. It is also more cost effective for the agency to use employees who have been oriented and are already familiar with policies and operational procedures rather than to again train new employees. Internal promotion and transfer can be initiated by the supervisor or requested by part-time and seasonal employees to whom a list of currently available jobs has been distributed.

Agency recruitment is also accomplished by using current and former employees to recruit new employees (Mathis and Jackson 1982). This method can be used only in conjunction with a widely distributed, open announcement of available positions to the public at large. However, current and former employees are often part of a community network of individuals who have the requisite knowledge, skills, and abilities to be good recreation workers. The potential usefulness of this network should not be overlooked.

A final internal recruitment method is to examine previous applicants for positions currently available in the agency. Technically this is not an internal recruitment method, but it does make good use of resources invested previously in obtaining a pool of applicants. If the agency has a sufficiently large pool of good applicants, there will always be some on file when needed. A general practice of most programmers is to keep a file of such applicants indexed by their ability to lead or instruct specific recreation activities.

External recruitment

External recruitment involves an organized effort to attract employees from sources outside the organization. A mandatory part of external recruitment is announcing the availability of positions to the general public. This should be done through the local print and broadcast media and through issuing and posting job announcements. In addition, external recruitment involves an organized and focused effort to make the availability of positions known to individuals who are likely to be qualified, that is, the targeting of recruitment efforts. Recruiting in high schools for summer leaders is one example. Recruiting in junior college and senior college recreation, physical education, and hospitality curricula is another targeted recruitment source for seasonal and part-time employees. Still other sources might be church youth groups, recreation clubs or hobby groups, and other recreation agencies. External recruitment, then, involves announcements to the general public and a targeted recruitment effort focused on specific groups of individuals who are likely to possess the knowledge, skills, and abilities to be good employees.

Selection

Once a pool is assembled, the programmer must select the applicants who will actually be hired. Selection techniques usually involve either a test, an interview, or both. In any case, the criteria on which selection is made must be valid indicators of the qualifications actually needed to perform the job. The focus of legislation passed in recent years has been to make certain that job selection is made on bona fide occupational qualifications (BFOQs). Selection must be based on criteria that actually relate to the performance of the job. This same legislation has also identified a number of criteria that may not be used, including race, color, religion, sex, age, or national origin. Race and color are never exceptions, and age is an exception only if it can be demonstrated that it is a BFOQ.

Culkin and Kirsch (1986) recommend that employers "exercise caution in taking advantage of these permissible exceptions" (p.13). The burden for demonstrating the validity of any criterion used in selecting employees for a job clearly rests with the employer. Demonstrating validity is necessary even for part-time and seasonal employees.

Orientation

All new employees, including those who are part-time and seasonal, should receive an orientation to the agency. The goals of an orientation are to create an initial favorable impression of the agency for the employees, to help them adjust to the demands of their job, and to enhance their acceptance in the agency. For many of the young people hired to staff part-time and seasonal recreation jobs, the job will be their first work experience. They often need special help in adjusting to simply having a job, in addition to needing help with the specific responsibilities of the job itself.

The orientation should include three types of information (Mathis and Jackson 1982, p. 230). First, the nature of the organization should be outlined. The orientation should answer the following questions for new employees: Who are they working for? What is this organization trying to accomplish? What is their role in helping the organization accomplish its goals?

Second, the nature of a typical workday should be outlined. What can employees expect their workday to be like on this job? What is a typical order of events in a workday? What kinds of tasks will they do in a typical day? From the orientation, the employees should have a good idea of what to expect from a typical workday.

Finally, the work rules, policies, procedures, and special skills needed to perform their role in the agency should be covered. Often, work rules, personnel policies, and procedures that apply to all of the agency's employees will be covered at a general orientation session conducted by the personnel department.

However, the task of covering job-specific policies, procedures, and special skills needed to perform the job will be the responsibility of the programmer. How much training is needed before assigning a new employee to work is a matter of agency practice. For example, the Disney organization requires every employee to complete Traditions I, a one-day orientation session. Part-time and seasonal ticket takers must also complete an additional four days of training before an actual duty assignment (Pope 1987).

Although this level of preassignment training is desirable, most agencies simply cannot afford it. Part-time and seasonal employees often do not need to know every detail of agency operation, only the essential information to get started on the job and keep themselves and the agency from problems. For example, each new employee must receive an orientation regarding emergency procedures before an actual assignment. This is a must, and failure to do so could cause undue harm to patrons and place the agency in a litigious situation. Most part-time and seasonal employees are given an orientation and some training, and are then placed in a position where they are closely supervised and given on-the-job training.

New employees should not be subjected to information overload during the orientation. All of the information covered will be very familiar to the programmer and totally new to the employee! Because of this, an orientation program should also include, within one to two weeks of the original orientation, a time for the new employees to meet and ask questions about what they may not have thoroughly understood the first time.

Training

Training is the process whereby employees acquire the knowledge, skills, abilities, concepts, and attitudes they need to fulfill the responsibilities of their position in the agency. The amount and content of training depends on job responsibilities and how much of the required knowledge, skills, abilities, concepts, and attitudes employees possess when hired.

Part-time and seasonal employees often have fewer skills and need more training than full-time employees in order to fulfill their job responsibilities in the manner desired by the agency. The Disney organization is firmly committed to thoroughly training part-time and seasonal workers (Pope 1987).

They never allow workers to learn on the job, but make certain that they thoroughly know a job before a duty assignment. Part-time and seasonal employees often need instruction in how to operate specialized pieces of equipment and apparatus. Training in leadership skills, recreation planning, and game rules are also often needed as well.

Peters and Waterman (1982) point out in their book *In Search of Excellence* that a major difference between a production and a service organization is that in the latter, the product is manufactured and delivered simultaneously. A supervisor in a leisure service organization must therefore provide employees with excellent, thorough training, followed up with close, on-going supervision (McKinney and Chandler 1991).

One aspect of training is to make certain that staff members have the activity skills necessary for the specific program they have been hired to lead, direct, or supervise. In training part-time and seasonal recreation employees, it is especially important to convey the type of recreation service the agency desires to offer and how they should treat patrons in face-to-face interactions. The recreation experience a patron has is in large part dependent on interactions with recreation workers. However, training in the appropriate face-to-face demeanor and how to interact to obtain compliance with policies and rules are only part of the training that part-time and seasonal recreation workers usually need. Exhibit 14-5 on page 304 includes an outline of a training program for staff members who will be responsible for supervising a recreation area or building. The program instructs employees in what is expected of them and exactly what the supervision of an area or facility involves. It defines the role and function of the task and prepares individuals to fill the role.

Training and retraining are important and time consuming tasks for programmers. The types of training that are needed become obvious as programmers observe their staff operate programs and facilities. A general rule is that, if the programmer wants something accomplished a specific way, instructions for performing the procedure must be included in the training process. A well-trained staff is an essential ingredient to a successful program and well worth the time invested.

Exhibit 14-5.
Training Outline For Area Supervisors

As part of your ongoing duties you will be assigned the responsibility to supervise park areas and facilities. This is one of the most difficult assignments you will have. When you supervise an area, your responsibility is to protect the facility, to protect the programs in operation at the facility so that participants may have the experience they desired from participation, and finally to protect the drop-in patrons of the facility. Following are ten duties you must perform in order to fulfill the supervisor's role:

1. You must actively work at supervising. Supervising time is NOT your break—supervision cannot be accomplished from the employee lounge or office window.

2. You should circulate around the grounds or building and let your physical presence be known. Make certain all patrons know there is a supervisor on duty—someone who is in charge of the facility. Make certain to wear your uniform so that you are easily identified.

3. Supervisors should protect organized programs in operation at the facility from harassment by other users (especially drop-in users) of the facility.

4. Talk to patrons and encourage them to participate in organized programs. Know the answers to their questions. To do this, you must be familiar with all of the services available from the agency.

5. Give the job your own personal touch. Make your area of responsibility a place you would like your own children, brothers and sisters, or friends to attend.

6. Handle any trouble or problems that may erupt in the area. You must be aware of locations where trouble is likely to happen and become familiar with the patrons likely to cause trouble.

7. Get at problems likely to occur in the area aggressively. Try to anticipate problems and head them off.

8. Try to get "pick-up" activities started. Always have a few activities to suggest to patrons who seem to have run out of things to do.

9. Accept people as they are. Blacks and whites, long-hairs and baldies, young people and old people, etc., should all receive the same courteous treatment from you. Every user is a VIP and should be treated with courtesy and respect.

10. Use the magic mirror of your smile. Handle people with a smile and in a courteous manner.

Appraisal

Appraisal involves evaluating how well employees are performing their responsibilities. The information acquired in appraisal is used to determine compensation, placement of employees (transfer or promotion), and training needs (Mathis and Jackson 1982). Appraisal is most often used to determine eligibility for a raise, but one should not overlook using it to identify employees who are qualified to assume different responsibilities in the agency and to determine training needs.

There are two types of appraisal: informal and formal. Informal appraisal is conducted whenever the supervisor believes it is necessary. The day-to-day personal interactions of the supervisor with employees will give employees feedback about how well the supervisor believes they are performing.The supervisor's reactions and comments about an employee's work are communicated during site visits, over coffee, and in similar settings, thus providing informal evaluative feedback to the employee.

The agency should also have a formal appraisal system during which the supervisor's impressions and observations of the employee's performance become a matter of written record. Four decisions need to be made before implementing a formal appraisal system.

Who will conduct the appraisal?

Recreation programmers are almost always designated as the ones responsible for appraising the performance of the part-time and seasonal staff members under their supervision. However, a senior-level, seasonal staff member may be asked for input. For example, a public school teacher who is hired to direct a summer day camp may have significant input to the appraisal of younger, less experienced camp counselors. Although the programmer may have the final responsibility for appraising part-time and seasonal employees, it is important to obtain input from employees who are qualified to make such judgments and who are in a better position to have firsthand information about an employee's performance.

It is also common practice in recreation operations to obtain input from patrons about the performance of employees. Patron ratings are often obtained at facility operations and after program operations. These data should also play some role in the overall appraisal of the employee.

How will appraisal data be collected?

Several methods can be used to collect appraisal data (Culkin and Kirsh 1986; Mathis and Jackson 1982). Programmers in most instances will be required to use an employee appraisal instrument that already exists in the agency. They should examine the appraisal instrument before the appraisal period. This is necessary so that supervisors know what employee behaviors they should be observing and can take note of specific behaviors during their on-site observations. It is also important to explain the appraisal system and instrument to employees before they begin work. Employees should understand the criteria on which they will be evaluated, who will do the evaluation and how it will be used in determining raises and personnel actions.

A popular method of appraisal in organizations with many different positions is an all-purpose rating scale that uses the duties and responsibilities outlined in the job description as the evaluation criteria. An example of an all-purpose rating scale applied to the job description for a playground leader (Exhibit 14-3) is contained in Exhibit 14-6 on page 308. With this method, each position in the agency is rated in the same manner, but the appraisal criteria in each case are those required by the job. Now complete Exercise 14-2 on page 307.

It is also important for the programmer to record critical incidents of employee performance. Critical incidents are highly favorable and highly unfavorable actions in an employee's performance (Mathis and Jackson 1982, p.294). When a critical incident occurs, the programmer writes it down. These notes are the basis for comments recorded on the formal review instrument.

Exercise 14-2
Using an Employee Appraisal Instrument

In class, use the employee appraisal instrument included in Exhibit 14-6 to develop an appraisal instrument for the job described in the job description in Exhibit 14-4. When finished, discuss the following questions:

- Does the appraisal instrument include all of the major responsibilities?

- Will the employee and supervisor clearly understand the items that are to be observed and evaluated during the appraisal?

If the incident is unfavorable enough to cause an unsatisfactory performance rating, it is recommended that a consultation review with the employee be held within twenty-four hours of the incident. During this consultation, the written documentation should be shared and discussed with the employee. The employee should be asked to sign off on the incident report, acknowledging that he or she has been advised of the incident. The employee should also have the opportunity to make a written comment on the report. In this way, personnel incidents are thoroughly documented and become a part of the employee's record. This procedure is also recommended for exceptional performance. In either case, the procedure creates a written record that can be used to justify any personnel action required, including promotions, demotions, raises, denial of a raise, dismissal, transfer, or recommendation for training.

When will appraisal occur?

Frequent and timely feedback is essential if the employee appraisal system is to fulfill a redirecting function in the agency. With full-time employees, the normal practice is to conduct an appraisal midway through the probationary period and again at the end. At the end of the probationary period a decision is made to either place the employee on permanent status or dismiss him or her. Once an employee is on permanent status, then performance is usually appraised either semi-annually or annually.

Exhibit 14-6.
Employee Appraisal Instrument
Employee Performance Evaluation Report

Employee's Name: Appraisal Date:
Department: Job Title:
Employment Date:
Appraisal Period: From: To:
Reason for Review: ( ) Mid-Probation   ( ) Probation   ( ) Annual
                               ( ) Annual   ( ) End of Season

Factors Considered in Rating and Comments	% Weight value	1 Unsatis-factory	4 Satis-factory	7 Above average	10 Excep-tional	Factor total
1. Plans weekly recreation program.	_____	( )	( )	( )	( )	_____
2. Promotes program to area patrons.	_____	( )	( )	( )	( )	_____
3. Leads and operates programs.	_____	( )	( )	( )	( )	_____
4. Supervises play apparatus area and general playground.	_____	( )	( )	( )	( )	_____
5. Recognizes and removes safety hazards from playground.	_____	( )	( )	( )	( )	_____
6. Demonstrates knowledge of recreation program activity planning.	_____	( )	( )	( )	( )	_____
7. Demonstrates knowledge of game rules.	_____	( )	( )	( )	( )	_____
8. Demonstrates knowledge of developmental abilities of children.	_____	( )	( )	( )	( )	_____
9. Demonstrates skill in face-to-face leadership of games and activities.	_____	( )	( )	( )	( )	_____

(continued)

Exhibit 14-6.

Factors Considered in Rating and Comments	% Weight value	1 Unsatis- factory	4 Satis- factory	7 Above average	10 Excep- tional	Factor total
10. Demonstrates ability to deal tactfully and effectively in enforcing rules and regulations with children and adults in a recreation setting.	____	( )	( )	( )	( )	____
11. Demonstrates ability to recog- nize safety hazards.	____	( )	( )	( )	( )	____

100%   Adjective Rating
                                          (Total of all factors)

Additional Comments and Plan for Improvement:

Comments/Reactions of Employee Regarding Evaluation:

Reviewer's Comments:

Rater: _____ Date: _____ Reviewer: _____ Date:_____

Employee:_____ Date: _____ Dept. Head: _____ Date:_____

Note: Signature of employee does not mean agreement or disagreement with rating but indicates that the evaluation has been reviewed.

Adjective Rating Equivalents
1.00 - 2.99 = Unsatisfactory
3.00 - 5.99 = Satisfactory
6.00 - 8.99 = Above average
9.00 - 10.00 = Exceptional

Instructions
1. Prepare this rating carefully and with sound judgment.
2. Be sure to rate each criterion separately and do not apply a generalized view of the overall employee performance.
3. Comments are encouraged and are required for any factor rated exceptional or unsatisfactory.
4. Use additional sheets of paper if necessary to record coments or plan of action.

(Adapted from a form used in Plano, Texas)

In many organizations, part-time and seasonal employees are never given permanent status, although they are usually appraised when their responsibilities in the agency end. For example, the performance of all summer employees would be appraised at the end of the summer program. A performance appraisal usually determines whether they will be hired for the next operation of the program. In some agencies, part-time employees who work more than a specified number of hours per week (more than twenty hours, for example) are treated the same as full-time employees.

How should the performance appraisal interview be conducted?

The appraisal interview should be conducted immediately after each performance appraisal. These interviews provide an opportunity to communicate directly with employees about their strengths and weaknesses.

Employees usually approach an appraisal interview with a great deal of concern. It is useful for both the supervisor and the employee to remember that the worth of the employee as a human being is not judged here, but rather the worth of their job performance for a specified period of time. The appraisal interview is also an important opportunity to set an agenda with the employees for retraining or reorganizing how they will conduct their work. This is a primary time for counseling employees on how to do the work and to discover weaknesses that may need to be corrected through additional training.

Compensation

There are three types of employee compensation: pay, incentives, and benefits (Mathis and Jackson 1982). *Pay* includes the direct wage or salary that the employee receives. *Incentives* include commissions or bonuses for exceptional performance. These are rarely given in recreation positions except in some private health clubs where a commission may be paid on the volume of memberships or services and products sold by an employee. *Benefits* include medical insurance, retirement, workmen's compensation, and other benefits given by the agency. Most full-time recreation employees receive pay and benefits for their positions. Part-time and seasonal employees usually receive pay and minimal benefits. This latter group is the focus of this section.

Often, wages for part-time and seasonal employees are purposely kept low to keep agency operating costs low. As stated earlier, many recreation agencies operate with a large number of part-time and seasonal employees. A low wage structure for these employees enables many recreation businesses to remain profitable. Thus there is usually pressure in an agency to keep part-time and seasonal wages low.

Programmers usually bear the direct adverse effect of this strategy because they are forced to operate program services with low-wage, untrained employees whom they must train extensively and supervise closely. Even though wages are low, programmers are well advised to develop a merit-based compensation plan. It is important to have a sufficiently attractive incentive pay structure so that one can retain the employees already trained, thereby avoiding having to constantly retrain new employees.

The usual practice in incentive plans is to make all raises merit based and to require that employees spend a certain amount of time in a specific pay grade before being eligible for a raise. For example, an employee earning the minimum wage may have to complete 1,000 hours (about six months at 40 hours per week) before being eligible to be considered for a raise. The raise, however, is not automatic after 1,000 hours. The employee still must have a favorable or exceptional merit review and must spend the requisite time at the beginning pay rate. The performance appraisal will then determine how well the employee is performing the responsibilities of the position and his or her eligibility for a raise in pay.

Part-time wages paid by the agency must be competitive with prevailing rates for similar part-time work in the area. The availability of part-time workers will partly determine the prevailing rate. Agencies can control how selective they can be in hiring by where they position themselves in the local part-time wage market. Obviously, offering wages on the high end of what generally prevails in the community will assure the agency first choice of available workers.

Part-time and seasonal employees rarely receive any benefits other than those required by law. Employers are usually required to pay Social Security and workmen's compensation insurance on every employee. One benefit that part-time and seasonal workers in recreation operations often receive is the opportunity to use the employer's facilities free of charge. For example, employees at a water park may be admitted to the park on their day off. These types of benefits, which are low cost to the agency, should be used and promoted as part of the compensation package. Sometimes they also can provide a sufficient incremental advantage to enable the agency to attract better part-time and seasonal employees.

Contracting For Personal Services

It is becoming common practice for agencies to contract for the services of individuals rather than place them in the agency's employ. For example, athletic league officials are contracted for a per-game fee to officiate athletic contests. Or, a person may be contracted to teach a tennis class consisting of sixteen one-hour lessons. The instructor is given a flat rate or a percentage of the revenue and is not placed in the employ of the agency. As a result, these individuals do not receive any benefits from the agency. Contractors are supposed to pay their own Social Security, income tax, and workmen's compensation.

This practice is controversial. Using a contract arrangement definitely reduces direct costs for the agency because it does not have to pay benefits and the practice eliminates exposure to the requirements of a number of employment laws (Moiseichik, Hunt, and Macchiarelli 1992). However, maintaining control of the quality of contract services is sometimes difficult. The individual under contract is not an employee and thus not subject to direct supervision and control. Any irregularities in performance or delivery of service are contract violations rather than personnel matters. Compliance with a contract can be enforced, but it is a more cumbersome and less direct process.

The Internal Revenue Service has recently begun a crackdown on this practice since their studies have revealed that many employers ". . . are misclassifying employees as independent contractors to avoid paying employment taxes" (Moiseichik, Hunt, and Macchiarelli 1992, p. 63). The major group of employees who have been investigated thus far are athletic league officials and at least two city recreation departments were required to pay back taxes that would have been due if the workers were correctly classified as employees.

Making certain both the contract and the contractual relationship reflect the following features will increase the likelihood that a worker will be accepted as a contractor (adapted from Moiseichik, Hunt, and Macchiarelli 1992). The agency must not control the detail and manner of how work is performed by a contractor and they must not directly supervise their performance of the work. Contractors should not be subject to the agency's personnel policies and cannot be hired, fired, or disciplined under them. They are not paid through the agency's payroll system, there are no payroll deductions from their contract price, and they are paid a lump sum for the completed project or on the amount of items completed—for example the number of games officiated. Furthermore, they supply all of their own equipment and materials; they are free to provide their services to other agencies; they are obviously in business for themselves as evidenced by a letterhead, business address, and phone; there is a definite term to the contract period; and their work is not scheduled by the agency.

Because of the potential tax liability of these arrangements, it is important to have a well-written contractual arrangement with these individuals. Exhibit 14-7 on page 314 is a Contract For Individual Services used by the Mesa, Arizona Parks, Recreation, and Cultural Division. The terminology in this contract focuses on the service provided rather than the person since there are some questions about whether or not there can be a "contract employee." An agency can, however, contract for the services of an individual or a group.

Exhibit 14-7
Contract For Individual Services

Mesa Parks and Recreation
Contract For Individual Services

Date: _____

It is agreed by and between Mesa Parks and Recreation of Mesa, Arizona, hereinafter referred to as "City", and _____, hereinafter referred to as "Second Party", as follows:

That Second Party agrees to perform for the City the service or services described below, and the City agrees to pay the Second Party for such services as provided below.

(1). Person who will provide service:

Name:_____Soc.Sec. No._____
Address_____
City: _____Zip_____
Phone (Day)_____Phone (Evening)_____

(2) Services to be performed:

a._____

b._____

c._____

d._____

e._____

f._____

(continued)

g.————————————————————————

(3) Services to be conducted for the following period:

a. Beginning _____ and continuing through _____

b.Hours:_____Days/Frequency:_____

(4) Place or Places where services will be provided:

————————————————————————

————————————————————————

————————————————————————

(5) The City shall pay _____ per hour/activity (circle one) for services rendered and no deductions shall be subtracted therefrom. The Second Party does not participate in any fringe benefits of the City, nor does the City provide liability insurance for the Second Party.

(6) The Second Party is performing the above services and is acting as an independent contractor and is not an employee of the City of Mesa.

———————————————   ———————————————————

Second Party   Date

Approved and execution witnessed by:

———————————————   ———————————————————

Immediate Supervisor   City of Mesa

By: Parks and Recreation Director

———————————————

Section Supervisor

(Source: Mesa Parks, Recreation and Cultural Division, Mesa, Arizona. *No warranty is given regarding the legal appropriateness of this statement for the reader's use and the reader is cautioned to not copy this statement as any such statement should be developed and approved by the agency's legal counsel.*)

Supervising Operations

One of the unique requirements of operating a service industry is the need for close, on-going supervision. "The nature of leisure services is that once the service has been delivered it cannot be recalled" (Edginton and Edginton 1993, p. 42). Thus quality must be assured at the time of delivery and on-site observation and supervision of services is a key method for accomplishing this.

There are three objectives to accomplish during these visits. First, the programmer needs to verify that a program is actually being conducted. Usually, many details must be coordinated before a program can actually occur. If any one of these details is not completed, the program may not occur or it will occur with problems. If one is using a contract employee to deliver the service, on-site verification of operation is a necessary part of a performance audit to assure contract compliance.

A second objective of these visits is to observe program operations to make certain they are being delivered as intended by the agency and at the level of quality desired by the agency. During a visit one may face any of several operational problems including program cancellation, poor staff performance, unsafe conduct of a program, inadequate facility preparation, etc. Interactions that will occur with patrons at this time are what McCarville (1993) terms "key encounters." Failure to reconcile these irritations to the patron's satisfaction may result in the agency losing its patronage.

Berry and Parasuraman (1991) indicate that there are five general dimensions that influence a customer's assessment of service quality including reliability, tangibles, responsiveness, assurance, and empathy (p. 16). On-site visits provide an opportunity for demonstrating the agency's commitment to quality service. Exhibit 14-8 on page 317 contains specific activities to accomplish during these visits that address each of these dimensions.

Exhibit 14-8
On-Site Visit Quality Assurance Activities

Dimension	Activities
Reliability	Confirm scheduled service is being operated as advertised and intended by the agency. Make adjustments necessary to bring service up to quality standards if warranted.
Tangibles	Confirm cleanliness of facility and equipment. Check safety of equipment and operational practices. Confirm the neatness of the appearance of personnel.
Responsiveness	Initiate contact with patrons to confirm your willingness to help them and provide prompt service or to resolve their problems.
Assurance	Present a demeanor of confidence and courtesy. Make certain you and your on-site staff know the answers to questions and willingly provide them to patrons.
Empathy	Present a caring, empathetic demeanor. Make certain on-site personnel have sufficient authority to make reasonable exceptions to policies and rules so that service can be customized to meet patron needs.

In all cases the visiting programmer must exhibit these behaviors and confirm that on-site personnel are also exhibiting them.

(Adapted from Berry and Parasuraman 1991).

The third objective of the visits is to observe on-site leadership staff and to gather data to use in appraising staff performance. On-site visitations are important to staff members conducting programs because programmers can give verbal directions to staff to make any necessary corrections in operations. Programmers can also give immediate feedback about the quality of work being done. Observations of how well part-time staff members are functioning will also reveal any need for additional training. Remember, however, that contractors are not subject to this type of supervisory direction.

On-site supervision of recreation and leisure services can accomplish several important program management functions. It is time consuming and often occurs at odd hours, but it is an essential part of the programmer's job.

Conclusion

Staff members who actually operate program services are often part-time or seasonal employees. They must be recruited, oriented, trained, and supervised. Since recreation is very often a people-to-people service, a well-trained and well-supervised staff is essential to successful program delivery. Conducting on-site supervision of service delivery is a necessary quality control function that the programmer must perform.

References, Chapter Fourteen

Berry, L. L., and A. Parasuraman. 1991. *Marketing Services: Competing Through Quality.* New York: The Free Press.

Culkin, D.F., and S.L. Kirsch. 1986. *Managing Human Resources in Recreation Services.* New York: Macmillan.

Edginton, C.R., and S.R. Edginton. 1993. Total Quality Program Planning. *Journal of Physical Education, Recreation, and Dance,* 64 (8), 40-42, 47.

Henderson, K.A., and M.D. Bialeschki. 1993. Optimal Work Experiences as "Flow": Implications for Seasonal Staff. *Journal of Park and Recreation Administration,* 11 (1), 37-48.

Mathis, R.L., and J.H. Jackson. 1982. *Personnel: Contemporary Perspectives and Applications (3rd ed.)*. St. Paul, MN: West.

McCarville, R.E. 1993. Keys to Quality Leisure Programming. *Journal of Physical Education, Recreation, and Dance, 64* (8), 34-36, 46-47.

McCormick, E.J., J.D. Shaw, and A.S. DeNisi. 1979. Use of PAQ for Establishing the Job Component Validity of Tests. *Journal of Applied Psychology, 64* (1), 51-56.

McKinney, W.R. and C.L. Chandler. 1991. A Comparative Assessment of Duties Between Full-Time and Part-Time Recreation Leaders. *Journal of Park and Recreation Administration, 9* (1), 13-29.

Moiseichik, M., S. Hunt, and D. Macchiarelli. 1992. Recreation Sports Officials: Contractors or Employees? *Journal of Park and Recreation Administration, 10* (1), 62-70.

Peters, T.J., and R.H. Waterman, Jr. 1982. *In Search of Excellence: Lessons from America's Best Run Companies*. New York: Harper & Row.

Pope, N.W. 1987. Mickey Mouse Marketing. In J.L. Crompton (Ed.), *Doing More With Less in Parks and Recreation Services* (168-176). State College, PA: Venture Publishing.

Ray, M.B., and A.H. Grossman. 1980. Recruiting and Selecting Professional Personnel. In A.H. Grossman (Ed.), *Personnel Management in Recreation and Leisure Services* (89-1160). South Plainfield, NJ: Groupwork Today.

Sterle, D.E., and M.R. Duncan. 1977. *Supervision of Leisure Services*. San Diego, CA: Campanile Press.

Photo courtesy of Parks and Recreation Department, Aurora, Colorado.

15

Developing a Program Pricing Philosophy

Pricing is one of the four "p's" of marketing. A marketing approach to programming requires that programmers be concerned with the costs of services and how to generate the revenue to pay for them as well as designing and producing program services. Although commercial agencies have always had to charge prices appropriate to insure the survival of the agency, more recently public and not-for-profit agencies have also become concerned with pricing issues. Today at least one in three dollars in public recreation budgets is from fees and charges and this percentage is increasing in many communities as tax income fails to provide the financial base to provide the quantity or quality of programs desired (Brademas and Readnour 1989). Howard (1988) has stated that "The real issue facing recreation managers today is no longer the question of 'should we charge' but rather one of 'how much?'" (p. 1).

Although the issue of establishing a price seems, at first glance, a simple matter, the prices charged in commercial, public, or not-for-profit agencies have many implications. Charging for services can accomplish a variety of policy objectives for an agency. Howard and Crompton (1980) have identified six objectives of pricing including the efficient use of all financial resources, fairness or equitableness, providing maximal opportunity for participation, rationing, developing positive user attitudes, and commercial sector encouragement (p. 419). A key point is that the price set for services will determine who may or may not participate in an activity. Patrons who cannot afford the price charged are excluded from participation. Therefore the price established for services in any type of agency must be affordable by the intended target market or the program will not reach its intended audience.

Pricing also determines the amount of revenue an agency will receive and thus enables the agency to recover some or all of its costs of production. The financial goals of the agency will determine the contribution the price charged will make to overall agency revenue. For example, in a commercial agency, fees and charges are the sole source of revenue. Thus they must be set to recover all of the costs of production plus contribute to the agency's overhead costs and profit margin. In many not-for-profit and governmental agencies, the revenue from fees and charges represents a secondary funding source that is usually used to accomplish one of two ends—expanding the quantity of services offered or enhancing their quality.

To better manage program pricing practices, agencies need to implement a program management accounting system. In this chapter and in Chapters Sixteen and Seventeen, such a system is outlined. Management accounting is an accepted field of accounting that is distinctly different from financial accounting (Anthony and Welsch 1981). The purpose of financial accounting is to prepare information for reporting the financial performance of the organization to parties outside the organization. To ensure that each organization's report is comparable to the reports of other organizations, financial accounting reports are prepared according to strict, "generally accepted accounting principles and unified by the basic equation, Assets = Liabilities + Owner's equity" (Anthony and Welsch 1981, pp. 9-10).

In contrast to financial accounting, management accounting information is prepared for three different purposes, each of which is governed by a different set of principles. A management accounting system prepares information for internal use by managers (Horngren 1970). The information can be prepared for the following three purposes: (1) full cost accounting, which is used to determine the full cost of producing a good or service in an agency; (2) differential accounting, which is used to examine fiscal differences between alternate courses of managerial action; and (3) responsibility accounting, which is used to account for the financial performance of subunits in an organization. These subunits are called responsibility centers. They are areas of operational responsibility such as individual programs or work groups that produce programs whose financial performance is isolated so that the costs and revenues associated with them can be matched and observed. To implement the recommended program management accounting system, both full cost and responsibility accounting must be used.

Although a management accounting system requires preparing additional accounting data beyond those needed for the financial accounting system, the management accounting system uses financial accounting information as its data base. It is a reinterpretation of the same information so that programmers can use it in fulfilling their responsibility to manage the organization's resources to achieve the goals and objectives of the organization (Horngren 1970). The system also provides the data necessary to implement a procedure for systematically developing appropriate fees for programs and services.

Implementing and using a program management accounting system in an agency can be accomplished in six steps. Some agencies may already have completed some of these steps. It is important to realize that this system will have to be implemented in phases over a period of several years. The following steps need to be taken to implement the system:

1. The agency needs to develop a comprehensive policy to guide its pricing decisions (covered in Chapter Fifteen).
2. Operational units in the agency need to be identified as either line or service units (covered in Chapter Sixteen).
3. Line-item object-classification budgets that match revenues with expenses needed to operate a program should be prepared for each of the line units identified in step two (covered in Chapter Sixteen).
4. With appropriate methods of cost allocation, service unit costs need to be allocated to line units (covered in Chapter Sixteen).
5. An analysis of cost, volume, and profit is used to calculate the full cost of service production (covered in Chapter Seventeen).
6. A price for an individual service is established using the conjoint implications of two data sets—the principles from the agency's comprehensive pricing policy and the production cost data developed in the cost-volume-profit analysis. (covered in Chapter Seventeen).

In this chapter and in Chapters Sixteen and Seventeen, the way each of these steps can be accomplished is outlined. In most of the examples, a public recreation system is used as the model.

This type of agency was selected because it is the most complex type of agency in which prices need to be established. Even though a public system is used as the example, the general principles outlined can be used in any leisure service agency.

Developing a Comprehensive Guide to Pricing Decisions

Howard and Crompton (1980) suggest that there are two major pricing strategies—cost-based pricing and pricing not directly based on cost. The authors outline two methods of establishing a price that are not cost-based: going-rate pricing and demand-oriented pricing. In going-rate pricing, the agency bases the price for a service on the price other providers are charging for similar services. In demand-oriented pricing, the agency bases the price on "what the traffic will bear." With this latter method, the agency is trying to charge all it can get or whatever the patrons are most likely to pay for a service. The price established with both of these techniques is not based on how much it actually costs the agency to provide the service; the price can be above, below, or equal to agency costs. Although these two methods are widely used, they are not recommended because they lack precision in revealing where agency resources are being used to subsidize services. The program management accounting system assumes that knowing the full cost of service production is a prerequisite for establishing fair prices for agency services and for guiding the allocation of agency subsidies.

An agency's pricing philosophy is determined by its role in society, the funding available to fulfill this role, and the types of services offered by the agency. For example, the role of a commercial agency is to market goods and services in a manner that is socially responsible and that maximizes profits. Their only source of funding is through earned income that is generated from the sale of goods and services. To fulfill their role in society they must set prices that recover all production costs and contribute sufficient profit to give owners a fair return on their investment. In contrast to this, public and not-for-profit agencies generally have third-party funding in the form of tax or fund raising income that can be used in one of two ways. It may be used to pay for services in full, thus making them available at a zero price to the consumer or they may be used to partly pay the costs for many services and concurrently requiring the user to pay part of the costs thus providing subsidized services.

As a profession we believe that having access to ongoing opportunities for enjoyable, fun, or peak experiences enhances the quality of life. Each provider has specific responsibilities in creating access to these opportunities. Not-for-profit organizations usually have a specific group or program they are interested in promoting. Thus, their concern is more focused and less comprehensive. Economic efficiency and consumer demand generally establish the target markets for commercial recreation enterprises. The result is that they, too, usually have a narrow range of products and a small, carefully defined target market. The public system, however, is responsible for ensuring equal access to leisure opportunities (Wicks 1987) and thus has a more comprehensive responsibility and public funds for use in fulfilling this social welfare function. Although it is true that participation in leisure is beneficial to the individual and to society, it does not necessarily follow that each public leisure program is of immeasurable benefit (Ellerbrock 1982). Furthermore, the system cannot meet all demand from tax revenues. Sorting out who to charge and how much to charge them; and who to subsidize and how much to subsidize them are the major philosophical issues to be resolved in an agency's pricing policy.

Pricing Public Recreation: Current Issues

Local public park and recreation systems in the United States have frequently found themselves in a financial dilemma while implementing fees and charges for services. Ironically, public systems that have implemented fees have often done so in a piecemeal or rushed way and have alienated patrons because of a poorly conceptualized fee and charge system. Yet public systems that have not implemented fees and charges often lack adequate resources to operate comprehensive recreation services, and they too have alienated patrons because of incomplete services. The issue is not one of deciding whether or not to charge: to have a comprehensive community recreation system, fees and charges must be implemented to supplement tax-generated revenue. Rather, the issue is one of determining how to use fees fairly to recover the costs of providing service and how to use tax revenue to provide subsidized services. Wicks (1986) has demonstrated that citizens hold definite yet different views regarding the services and the clients who should have priority in receiving subsidized services. In the future, agencies with a heterogeneous population will very likely need to administer a differential pricing scheme for the same services for different population cohorts. When implementing a fee and charge system, then, agencies must remain sensitive to constituent views and desires regarding the distribution of tax dollars and the subsidization of various programs and client groups.

The egalitarian social philosophy that characterized the recreation movement through the first decade of this century was predicated on two assumptions that today seem rather naive or at least outdated. First was the assumption that recreation services were good for people and that providing more services led to accomplishing more good. Although this may be true, the political and economic resource base supporting ever-expanding services was eventually exhausted. Second was the assumption that all recreation programs were of equal value and in the public interest. Although public recreation officials may be able to do many useful things with other people's money, this does not mean they have the right to tax people to meet all identified recreation needs. The increasing diversification of program interests, the demand for program sophistication, and a diminishing willingness to pay with public dollars for services that seem to provide private benefit have led taxpayers to rebel against supporting public services, including public recreation.

Furthermore, public agencies have undertaken a diverse set of operations, which requires that they implement different pricing strategies. Soderberg (1988) points out that some agencies operate facilities that are intended to be revenue producing and must compete with other similar for-profit agencies in their service area. The operation of athletic stadiums, arenas, raceways, and other similar spectator event sites are examples of revenue-producing operations. The operation of regional tourist attractions that are most frequently attended by tourists from out of town as opposed to community residents is another example of an operation that needs a different pricing strategy.

Community dissatisfaction with public recreation, which has resulted in a withdrawal of political and financial support, has occurred not because the public questions the contribution that recreation can make to human existence, but because the public questions whether society as a whole should pay for providing recreation opportunities. The issue is: Who benefits and who pays? Although a significant number of agencies have instituted fees and charges, in many cases this revenue has only broadened the resource base for continuing to provide all things to all people. However, current financial management techniques used in agencies do not keep adequate track of financial activity to truly match revenue with expenses (Howard and Selin 1987). Consequently, managers are unable to achieve congruence between pricing practices and the agency's social welfare philosophy and policies. Correcting this problem begins with the development of a new philosophy concerning the role and function of recreation services, with particular focus on who benefits and who pays. There is also a need to develop policies to implement the philosophy and the financial management techniques that will enable agencies to achieve congruence between fiscal practice and agency policy.

A New Philosophy: The Service Category System

A new philosophy regarding fees and charges should provide a base for differentiating services on the basis of who benefits and who should pay for the service. Economists have differentiated goods in the economy in this manner and have designated three different types of goods: public, merit, and private (Howard and Crompton 1980). Programs offered by an agency can also be put into these three categories. Adopting a philosophy that acknowledges these three levels of good shifts the social welfare philosophy of the public recreation agency away from the notion that all services are of equal value and should be provided for everyone. This egalitarian philosophy is replaced with one that provides a basis for sorting out costs and benefits derived from various program services and provides a rationale for who should pay. In this conceptualization, each type of program has specific characteristics that imply who should pay for it. To develop a comprehensive fee and charge policy, agencies need to establish three categories for pricing programs that parallel these three types of economic good, that is, public, merit, and private programs. Each category has features that distinguish it from the other categories. These features are outlined below.

Public Programs

Public programs are the basic programs supported totally by tax dollars and are available to patrons free of charge. Theoretically, these programs are equally available to all. However, it is operationally not possible to make services equally available. For example, a park cannot be placed equidistant from all patrons. Operationally, a public program is beneficial to all, even though only some will actually use the program. Its provision is clearly in the "public interest" (Friedmann 1973). Since the public at large derives benefit from these programs, it is assumed that their cost will be paid through public financing. Public programs, then, are available with no fee to users—they are completely subsidized services.

Ideally, the public recreation movement would like all services to be in this category. However, the diverse demands for programs almost always exceed a community's ability to totally pay for them. It should be the goal of public agencies to use public tax dollars to provide a core set of free recreation programs for all citizens. Usually public programs include provision for park areas or facilities, low-organization events such as drop-in activities, special events, single-time block instructional workshops, and the like. Public programs usually do not require specialized leadership, the use of expensive equipment or facilities, or other high-cost components. What is to be included in this category varies from community to community, depending on the resources available and the community's willingness to support public recreation.

In not-for-profit organizations, the services that would be offered at no cost to the user are those that directly accomplish the stated social purpose of the agency. For example, scouting would not charge for the basic weekly meeting. Nor would a Boy's Club charge a daily admission fee to its after-school program in a low-income neighborhood. A corporate recreation program may not charge for use of the basic fitness facility since its purpose is to keep company health care costs low. A commercial facility may offer such a service as a "loss leader," i.e. an activity priced below cost to attract a specific target market to enhance profitability in some other way. Examples of this would be teaching introductory racquetball lessons at a loss to attract new customers or operating the nursery at such a facility at a loss to obtain customers during the usually low volume day time.

Merit Programs

Merit programs are partly subsidized with tax dollars, but also have user fees attached to help recover some of their production costs. In not-for-profit or commercial agencies, the source of these subsidy dollars is different but the basic concept is the same. In not-for-profit agencies it is third-party funding from fund raising or donations. In commercial agencies the source is profits from other activities that are used to subsidize the costs for other activities that are used as "loss leaders." In this case the price charged would recover part of the costs of production.

The benefits derived from merit programs can be partly attributed to the public interest and private individual gain. For example, one could argue that a summer recreation program directly benefits each child who participates and also to some extent the public at large. Partitioning out the proportion of individual and private benefits accrued from merit goods is obviously problematic. However, the key element of the "merit good" concept is that some benefit accrues to both public and private interests. Thus, it is assumed that these goods will be jointly paid for with both individual and public funds. There are widely differing philosophies about the appropriate groups to subsidize and to the percentage of subsidy they should receive. Operationally, merit programs are services that are partially subsidized for any reason.

Private Programs

Private programs are paid for entirely by the participants. It is assumed that the benefit from private goods or private programs is received exclusively by the individuals using the program—not by the general public. In a free society, people may use their own personal resources to purchase any goods or services they believe will benefit them, including recreation services. Since the decisions are private and the benefit derived is private, it is assumed that the individual will pay the full cost of acquiring these services. These programs are the principle type offered by commercial agencies.

Summary

Collectively, it is through the public and merit programs that the social purposes of governmental and not-for-profit agencies are fulfilled. Market positioning and targeting may be accomplished by commercial agencies using these types of pricing philosophies. Public programs are the basic free system—they are completely subsidized, free services directed to accomplish the mission of the agency. Merit programs are partly subsidized services.

In allocating resources to merit programs, the agency is further defining who it wants to subsidize with tax dollars and other nonuser-generated sources of revenue. It is important to recognize that, with limited resources, an agency probably cannot have all the public and merit programs for which demand can be documented. Decisions for allocating resources between these two types of services are policy-level decisions that should be made by a policy-level board.

Policy Implementation

Implementing the service category system in an agency is time consuming and involves iterations among the philosophical and policy concepts presented above, the accounting data base of the agency, the local political process, and the realities of local resources. If agencies fail to distinguish adequately among these three levels of service and continue to act as if everything provided by the agency is in the public interest, agencies will have a further erosion in the quality of services they offer. In implementing this system, one should first determine what the publicly provided programs in a community should and can be in view of the public resource limitations of the community. If all nonpublic sources of funding were cut, what could the community support and what would it choose to support?

Second, programs, services, and facilities that are truly private and self-sustaining need to be identified and the true costs of providing them recovered from the users. Continuing to subsidize programs in public recreation systems because of inadequate policies and poor accounting procedures cannot continue. Frequently, agencies have programs they designate as "self-sustaining." But often the accounting procedures in the agency are so inadequate that only direct costs can be identified and recovered (Howard and Selin 1987). Indirect or overhead costs cannot be identified and continue to be subsidized with public tax dollars. This practice makes self-sustaining programs merit rather than private programs and siphons away resources from program areas that the agency, from a social policy standpoint, may prefer to subsidize.

Finally, agencies will need to develop policy guidelines for how to subsidize the merit programs to be offered to constituents. Decisions about whom to subsidize can be made around many variables such as participant characteristics, program types, and geographic service areas. An agency may be required by law or charter to subsidize certain groups. Typically, communities choose to subsidize youth, teenagers, senior citizens, disabled citizens, and other vulnerable groups who do not have the personal resources to acquire needed services. Other communities choose to subsidize certain specific types of program services. For example, the U.S. Navy will not charge for any physical fitness activity because of the priority and importance of fitness activities to their mission—combat readiness. Subsidizing program costs with tax dollars should occur only in those program services that are wholly or partly in the public interest.

Before subsidization decisions can be made, the social welfare functions of a local recreation system must be well conceptualized. Many programs currently operated by public systems are truly merit goods that are presented as public or private goods. Agencies need to realize that subsidies are instruments through which the social welfare function of public recreation is carried out; therefore, comprehensive policies should be formulated to ensure that the subsidies are being used to achieve the results desired.

At the local level, developing policies to implement the proposed social welfare function of local recreation systems requires a serious review of the agency's facilities, services, and functions. The overall goal of policy development should be to preserve the public recreation system, first by identifying the goods offered. Those that are truly public should be funded totally through public financing. The second goal is to identify the private goods being offered and to make certain that they are not actually merit goods receiving inappropriate public subsidy. The final goal is to further develop the social welfare function of public recreation. This can be done by giving clearer direction to the subsidization of merit goods so that the community's social welfare desires are realized.

An example of how one community accomplished this is provided in Exhibit 15-1, page 333, the pricing policy adopted by the Elmhurst Park District Board of Commissioners, Elmhurst, Illinois. In this policy, an additional category has been created. The "basic public" category equates with the public category just discussed. The "extra public" category equates to the merit services previously discussed. The "enterprise" category equates with the public category and requires recovery of all operational and capital costs so there is no public subsidy. The "private" category requires recovery of all operational costs but does not require the recovery of capital costs. Based on the examples provided, this "enterprise" category includes activities requiring expensive, dedicated facilities, whereas the "private" category includes programs that typically utilize more general, multiple-use facilities. Although there is some difference in terminology from that used in the book, the basic principles outlined in this policy will need to be dealt with in any agency that is attempting to develop a pricing philosophy.

Implementing these policies in any agency will require an accounting methodology and budgeting procedure that pro-vides the data needed to allow congruence between fiscal prac-tice and policy. The program management accounting system outlined in the next two chapters is such a system.

Conclusion

Systematically determining prices for an agency's pro-grams is an important program management function. The price charged for a service often determines which patrons will have access to the service. Issues relevant to pricing decisions were

Exhibit 15-1.
Categories of Park District Service

	Basic Public	Extra Public	Private	Enterprise
Definition	services provided by the District available to all people	additional services provided by District; an embellishment of a basic service	private business offers this service within District boundaries	services that are designed to meet the ENDS policies and provide surplus funds
Who Pays?	all age levels in the District benefit either directly or indirectly	individual participant benefits most; all members of community benefit somewhat	some community benefit; users who participate benefit	some community benefit; users who participate benefit
Who Benefits?	the community pays through taxes; no user charges	partially subsidized by taxes; individual users pay all direct and some indirect costs.	no tax subsidy; users pay full OPERATIONAL costs, both direct and indirect.	no tax subsidy; users pay at least CAPITAL and OPERATIONAL cost (dir & indir)
Feasibility for Exclusion	not feasible to exclude or limit individuals from service or benefit	feasible and desirable to exclude or limit individuals	feasible and desirable to exclude or limit individuals	feasible and desirable to exclude or limit individuals
Examples	Celebration of the Arts, Winter Sports, Baseball Fields, Outdoor Tennis	Adult Softball, Summer Day Camps, Lighted Ball Fields, Lighted Tennis	Aerobics, Karate, Extended Day Care	Golf Course, Courts Plus, Pro Shops, Refreshment Stands

Notes:

1. Not-for-profit organizations are not considered private businesses.

2. Director is to use discretion in setting fees until 1994 to phase in appropriate fee increases for recreation programs in each category.

3. Indirect costs = all out-of-pocket costs associated with a program i.e. wages, FICA, retirement, contractual services, continuing education, program printing & postage, athletic field electric & maintenance, tournament fees internal and external

4. Indirect Costs = All out-of-pocket costs plus administrative & supervisory wages, office support staff, utilities, general postage, promotional and marketing, advertising and registration costs. All of these are expressed by applying a 15% factor to the total of direct costs.

5. Recreation programs or facilities can be offered even if a private entrepreneur already offers a similar service within the community provided the benefit appears to be great enough. Other services may thereby be subsidized and the tax burden relieved.

discussed. A pricing philosophy that sorts out costs and benefits and serves as a basis for a differential pricing scheme was outlined. In addition, a step-by-step procedure for implementing a program management accounting system was provided.

References, Chapter Fifteen

Anthony, R.N., and G.A.Welsch. 1981. *Fundamentals of Management Accounting*. Homewood, IL: R.D. Irwin.

Brademas, D.J., and J.K. Readnour. 1989. Status of Fees and Charges in Public Leisure Service Agencies. *Journal of Park and Recreation Administration, 7* (4), 42-55.

Ellerbrock, M. 1982, January. Some Straight Talk on User Fees. *Parks and Recreation 17*, 59-62.

Friedmann, J. 1973. The Public Interest and Community Participation; Toward a Reconstruction of Public Philosophy. *Journal of the American Institute of Planners 39* (1), 2-12.

Horngren, C.T. 1970. *Accounting for Management Control: An Introduction* (2nd ed.). New York: Prentice-Hall.

Howard, D. 1988. Pricing Public Parks and Recreation. In G.G. Lamke and D.L. Dustin (Eds.), *User Fees for Public Recreation? A Question of Equity* (1-9). San Diego, CA: Institute for Leisure Behavior, San Diego State University.

Howard, D.R., and S.W. Selin. 1987. A Method for Establishing Consumer Price Tolerance Levels for Public Recreation Services. *Journal of Park and Recreation Administration, 5* (3), 48-64.

Howard D.R., and J.L. Crompton. 1980. *Financing, Managing, and Marketing Recreation and Park Resources*. Dubuque, IA: W.C. Brown.

Soderberg, P. 1988. Implementing a Fee Program. In G.G. Lamke and D.L. Dustin (Eds.), *User Fees for Public Recreation? A Question of Equity* (1-9). San Diego, CA: Institute for Leisure Behavior, San Diego State University.

Wicks, B.E. 1987. The Allocation of Recreation and Park Resources: The Court's Intervention. *Journal of Park and Recreation Administration, 5*(3), 1-9.

Wicks, B.E. 1986, October. The Equitable Allocation of Publicly Provided Recreation and Park Services: Citizens' Perceptions of Equity. Paper presented at the 1986 Leisure Research Symposium, Anaheim, CA.

Additional Readings

Crompton, J.L. 1982. Psychological Dimensions of Pricing Leisure Services. *Recreation Research Review* 9(3), 12-20.

Crompton, J. L. 1984. How to Establish a Price for Park and Recreation Services. *Trends* 21(4), 12-21.

Manning, R., and S. Barker. 1981, September. Discrimination Through User Fees: Fact or Fiction? *Parks & Recreation,16* 70-79.

Photo courtesy of Parks and Recreation Department, Aurora, Colorado.

16

Determining Program Costs

An important part of implementing the program management accounting system is determining the cost of program production. In this chapter, three additional steps necessary for implementing the system will be discussed.

Establishing Line and Service Units

The second step in implementing a program management accounting system is to classify all subunits as performing either line or service functions. Managers have a good deal of discretion in defining what constitutes a unit. In any case, a unit should be headed by a manager who is responsible for its output. In most cases, the output will serve either a line or a staff purpose. However, the classification of units for cost purposes does not always dovetail neatly with the arrangement of units and personnel as defined by the organizational chart. Because of this, some activities of a unit may indeed be line functions and others may be service functions. Although it is possible to separate line from service costs in an individual unit, it is best to separate the line and service functions into their own units for cost analysis.

Line units are those units that are directly involved in the production and delivery of the organization's services and products. For example, recreation center staff members are directly involved in producing and supervising recreation services. Their work group and its costs of operation would therefore be classified as a line unit.

Service units provide services to other units and to the organization as a whole. They are not involved in producing the primary product or service of the organization. In a recreation and park department, the finance office would not be involved in directly producing recreation services and would therefore be classified as a service unit. Office clerical staff would also be classified as service personnel because they are not involved in the direct production and delivery of recreation services.

How an operational unit should be classified is less clear in some instances. One difficult unit in a park and recreation agency is the park department. Some of its activities involve providing service to other units, for example, cleaning recreation centers and lining ball diamonds. Other activities of a park department clearly result in the direct delivery of recreation services. Having well maintained and beautiful parks for passive recreation is clearly a direct service.

Understanding what is to eventually be done with these data is the best guideline in making these classifications. This whole procedure is predicated on the notion that the agency exists to deliver or produce some product. (Product here is used in the generic sense to include programs, parks, facilities, and other services produced by a park and recreation agency.) The reason for the agency's existence is outlined in its mission statement and in its long-range and short-range goals and objectives. In the current example, a park and recreation agency exists to deliver recreation and leisure services.

It is further assumed that all of the agency's resources are used to accomplish its mission. The final goal of the program management accounting system is to account for all of the agency's expenditures through its line units, since these units are directly engaged in accomplishing the agency's mission and in delivering its services. It is assumed that service units exist to serve line units. From the viewpoint of the organization as a whole, there is no need to have service units except to enable line units to accomplish their missions. When the missions of all individual line units are summed, collectively they are the mission of the organization as a whole. Therefore, in classifying units as line or service units, the manager must make certain that all of the legitimate service outputs of the agency are in line units so that the expenses of all output can be determined.

If providing parks for informal recreational enjoyment is a legitimate service output of the agency, then a portion of the park department's expenditures should be classified as a line unit output that provides the informal recreation program. The final objective in implementing this process is to determine as accurately as possible the full cost of producing each unit of agency output, that is each program, park, facility or other amenity. A classification decision that provides more accurate information regarding the full cost of each agency output is correct and desirable.

Classifying operational units as line or service units is an important step in this whole process. Since the manager will eventually be forced to write off all service unit costs to the line units they serve, it is foolish to try to bury costs and hide the true cost of production. The process is designed to reveal the true cost of production so that accurate decisions about pricing and subsidization can be made. Classification decisions that cause inaccuracies in the true cost of any one product will appear elsewhere and drive up the cost of some other product. All costs incurred by the agency will eventually need to be accounted for.

Preparing Line-Item Budgets

The third step in this process is to prepare line-item object-classification budgets for all units, both line and service, identified in the second step. This step is not as formidable as it might seem. Most agencies already have a line-item object-classification budget. If the agency uses a program budgeting procedure (Deppe 1981), which assembles the budget from the lowest administrative level to the top, these budgets already exist. They are the source of revenue and expenditure information from which agency budgets have been prepared.

It is not the purpose of this section to demonstrate how to develop a line-item object-classification budget. Readers interested in this topic should see Deppe (1983), Edginton and Williams (1978), or Rodney and Toalson (1981) for a complete explanation of this process. The purpose of this section is to make clear the need for matching revenues with expenses in budget preparation and to explain why service unit budgets do not have a revenue side.

Although general budgeting convention is to display revenues before expenses, in actual budget preparation one usually calculates expenses first, then identifies the amount and source of revenues that will support the activity. Using this principle of matching all expenses with the revenue requires all staff members to be concerned with the source of revenues for supporting their activities. This technique forces one to consider the number of dollars it will take to support an activity. It also forces one to identify the source of revenue for supporting each activity. In this latter instance, one begins at the time of budget preparation to observe where the revenue support for an activity is originating.

Line units will have both an expenditure and a revenue side to their budgets. However, service units will have only an expenditure side. Since service units exist only to support line units, service unit budgets do not have a revenue side. Their only source of revenue is from providing services to line units. Only line unit budgets, then, actually have a revenue side. The costs of service units must be allocated to line units.

Allocating Costs in the Agency

The fourth step in implementing the program management accounting system is to allocate all service unit costs to line unit budgets. The technique for accomplishing this is cost allocation. Before cost allocation is discussed, however, it is necessary to define and differentiate terms.

Cost

One must first distinguish between cost and price. "Cost is a measurement, in monetary terms, of the amount of resources used for some purpose" (Anthony and Welsch 1981, p. 10). Full cost is the total cost, that is, all of the resources used by the agency in developing a specific program. Cost includes all dollars the agency uses in producing a program, regardless of the source of those dollars. Dollars acquired through taxation, fees, donations and the like all represent a cost to a specific program when they are used to produce the program. The agency's costs for developing and offering a program are all of the resources used to produce the program. If an agency's resources were not used to produce program A then those same resources could be used to produce program B or program C. Any program represents a cost to the agency, whether or not the agency recovers any of its costs through fees or third-party payments.

Price

Price is the dollar amount the agency charges patrons to participate in a specific program. The price that patrons must pay is a cost to the patrons; that is, it is a resource they must give up to participate in the agency's program. In some cases such as a fully subsidized public program, there is zero cost to the patron. The price the agency charges to participate should be established through the conjoint implications of the full cost of production and the agency's fee and charge policy. Pricing is discussed in more detail in the discussions accompanying steps five and six of the program management accounting system included in Chapter Seventeen.

Cost Objective

A cost objective is any activity for which a separate measurement of cost is desired. The functions performed by line and service units are cost objectives. In the program management accounting system, service unit costs are handled as cost objectives in order to identify the full costs of their operations. Through one or more of the methods outlined in this section, the costs of these units are then allocated to line units so that the full costs of line unit operations can be identified.

The goal in implementing cost allocation is to determine as accurately as possible the cost of providing a program or group of programs, in other words the full cost of the cost objective. One must understand two types of costs in order to accurately classify and allocate them to cost objectives. All costs may be classified as direct or indirect costs.

Direct costs

Direct costs are those that can be traced to a specific cost objective. They can therefore be assigned as direct costs to a specific cost objective. For example, a direct cost of providing a swimming pool is the cost of chlorine. Chlorine is purchased only because the agency operates a swimming pool; this is the only use for chlorine in the agency. If the agency would no longer operate a swimming pool, it would no longer need chlorine. Chlorine, then, is a direct cost to the operation of a swimming pool. The cost of the chlorine would be assigned as a direct cost to the swimming pool operation in determining the full cost of its operation.

Indirect costs

Indirect costs are those that the agency incurs regardless of whether or not it operates a specific program. They are created by two or more cost objectives and are therefore not traceable to a single cost objective. For example, the cost of an office typewriter is an indirect cost to all program services and facilities. The agency will have a typewriter regardless of whether or not it operates any one specific program. Even so, this cost must be absorbed by all programs and services. The agency must give up resources to acquire the typewriter, and these foregone resources must be accounted for within the budgets of all the services provided. Indirect costs are often called "burden" or "overhead" costs.

According to Anthony and Welsch (1981), "The full cost of a cost objective is the sum of (1) its direct costs, plus (2) a fair share of its indirect costs" (p. 51). Through the accumulation of these costs, it is possible to determine the full cost of a specific cost objective. Exhibit 16-1 illustrates the structure of the cost of any single cost objective. The full cost of any cost objective, then, is made up of its direct and indirect or overhead costs.

Exhibit 16-1.
Cost Structure of a Program

Direct Costs
$325
+
Indirect Costs
$259
_____

Total Cost $584

Cost Allocation

Cost allocation is the process of identifying and assigning costs to various cost objectives. In the current case, the indirect costs of service units will be assigned to the direct costs of line units. Other indirect costs may need to be allocated to various cost objectives. The principles that follow will apply to either case. In implementing cost allocation, the programmer is faced with a number of decisions regarding how costs can or should be allocated. Three principles should be used to guide these decisions:

1.   Implementing cost allocation is an attempt to assign indirect costs to line cost objectives in a fair and equitable manner. The goal is to reflect the full costs of service production.
2.   The method of cost allocation selected should accurately reflect how much of an indirect cost a specific cost objective actually uses or consumes. Again, try to reflect reality.

Both of these principles affect the eventual accuracy and usefulness of the data to be developed. Because many cost allocation decisions need to be made and because management has a good deal of discretion in making them, management can do so in a manner that will influence the full cost of various programs. However, since all costs must eventually be accounted for in line operations, decisions initially favorable to the costs of one specific unit are almost always detrimental to those of some other unit. Pursuing accuracy as the guiding principle is not only the best policy, but it often must be resorted to in order to make everything reconcile properly.

3.   In any cost allocation method there is a trade-off between accuracy and cost. For example, it may be possible to achieve perfect accuracy of actual costs, but only at a very high cost of time and effort. Each of the methods outlined below provides various combinations of ease of implementation and degrees of accuracy. One needs to try to achieve as much accuracy as possible within the limits of reasonable effort. Remaining consistent over a period of time in how costs are allocated is as important as perfect accuracy

because consistency ensures reliability of data from one reporting period to another. One can begin with easily obtainable but less accurate cost allocation data in the initial stages of implementing a program management accounting system. These figures can then be replaced at a later time with more accurate cost data as they are researched and developed.

Cost Allocation Methods

Equal share of indirect expenses

In this method, each functional line unit receives an equal share of indirect expenses. For example, the salary of the Director of Parks and Recreation may be shared equally by the parks and the recreation divisions. Since there are two divisions, each is assigned one half of the director's salary. Obviously, if there were three line units, each would assume one third of the salary. With this method, each unit assumes an equal share of the indirect expense to be allocated. This is the easiest method to implement, but it may also be the least accurate.

With this method, no effort is made to base the indirect costs to be assumed by a unit on actual costs used by the unit. This method may often be appropriate, however. One could argue that the director's main responsibility is to maintain the organization's external relationships and provide overall direction to the agency. From this perspective, the time the director may spend with any one unit in a given time period is irrelevant to assigning the director's salary cost. The director's functional accomplishments are equally essential to both the parks and the recreation units, so they must share equally in the cost of having a director on staff. There can be many of these exceptions in organizations. It is often not practical to try to assign costs on a more sophisticated basis. Spending time and resources to achieve increased accuracy of cost allocation in these instances is nonproductive.

Percentage of budget

With this method, each line unit is assigned a percentage of indirect costs that equals its percentage of some overall budget figure. Again, let us use the director's salary of $60,000 as an example of an indirect cost to be allocated to the parks and the recreation units. Exhibit 16-2 displays the percentage of the overall budget assigned to each of these two line units.

Exhibit 16-2.
Budget Percentage Method of Cost Allocation

Parks Budget	$150,000	33%
Recreation Budget	$300,000	67%
Total	$450,000	100%

In this case, $20,000, or 33 percent, of the director's salary cost would be allocated to the parks department budget; the remaining $40,000, or 67 percent, would be allocated to the recreation department budget.

In allocating costs with the percentage of budget method, one is assuming that the actual use of the cost to be allocated is accurately characterized by the percentage of the overall budget each of the individual line units currently consumes. Although this method is easy to implement, the accuracy of the data generated is contingent on the validity of the assumption outlined above. In the case of the director's salary, one could argue that the director's time is spent in proportion to the size of each line unit's relative size in the organization. Allocating the director's salary with a method based on the relative size of each line unit is justifiable in this type of situation. Whether these assumptions for allocation are valid is usually best determined by on-site managers who are close enough to the situation to know how time is spent.

Time budget study

Determining how individuals or units actually spend their work time through a time budget study provides the most accurate data on which to allocate costs. With this method, the time a service unit spends on each cost objective is studied. The percentage of time is then used as the database for allocating the indirect costs of the service unit to line units. The actual allocation of costs is similar to the percentage of budget method, except that more accurate data are being used to develop the percentage figures for allocating the costs.

This is a very accurate method. However, conducting the study is itself a costly and time-consuming process. Because of this, one must make certain that the data to be developed are important enough to warrant the research effort. Once time budget figures are developed, agencies usually continue to use the percentages generated in the inital study unless drastic alterations in work assignments or practices warrant altering the percentages. Time budget figures should be periodically verified on a three- to five-year staggered rotation schedule. In this way, agencies do not have to conduct these time-consuming and costly studies each budget period. The percentages are of course altered if there is any apparent change in operational practices.

Cost-tracking system

With this method, the actual use of an item by a cost objective is tracked, and the actual cost of the item is charged back to the unit using it. This method is needed particularly where materials in addition to time are being used to complete a job. Tracking only time, which is the case in a time budget study, will often fail to give an accurate enough cost estimate of the true costs to be allocated from a service unit to a line unit. In park operations, for example, time (labor) and materials are often needed to complete a job, so cost tracking the materials is also necessary.

Cost tracking is often used to account for costs in an individual budget year. That is, the actual costs used are assigned to the various units who used them. These cost-tracking data accumulated over time can be used during the budget preparation process to estimate the percentage of costs that will be allocated from various service units to line units.

Space or measurement studies

This method of cost allocation is used in instances where one can determine the appropriate proportion of cost to allocate to a specific cost objective by measuring the relative proportion of overall costs that are being used by each cost objective. For example, the building shown in Exhibit 16-3, page 347, contains

10,000 square feet of space. This space is divided into four rooms: room A with 1,000 square feet, room B with 3,000 square feet, room C with 2,000 square feet, and room D with 4,000 square feet. In implementing this method of cost allocation, one calculates the respective proportion of the overall space each room accounts for. Thus, room A contains 10 percent of the total building space, Room B 30 percent, and so on.

In allocating building operating expenses such as electricity, water and sewer charges, gas or heating bills, and maintenance expenses, one can simply allocate a percentage of total costs to each room in proportion to the percentage of overall building space that each room actually represents. Thus, room A would be allocated 10 percent of these charges, room B 30 percent, and so on.

Although the building diagrammed in Exhibit 16-3 does not include any common areas such as hallways, a foyer, or rest rooms, most buildings do contain this type of space. Usually expenses of the common areas are allocated to the space represented by the usable rooms in a building. In the current example, then, the proportion of costs allocated to each room would not change, because the amount of usable space in the building would still be 10,000 square feet.

Exhibit 16-3.
Measurement Study Method of Cost Allocation

Room A 1,000 sq. ft.	Room B 3,000 sq. ft.
Room D 4,000 sq. ft.	Room C 2,000 sq. ft.

This method is useful in situations where one can accurately determine the proportion of costs to be allocated. Allocating costs for a fertilizing program in parks, maintenance in a building, and other similar instances are best handled in this manner.

In step four of the program management accounting system, then, the cost allocation decisions that are made enable one to allocate the indirect cost from service units to line operations. This procedure is necessary in order to allocate the indirect or overhead costs of service units to the direct costs of the line operating units that actually deliver services and thereby produce the agency's service output.

Conclusion

To determine program costs, three additional steps of the program management accounting system must be implemented. All operational units must be designated as either line or service units. Line-item object-classification budgets must be prepared for each operational unit. Indirect costs must be allocated to their cost objectives. Several methods of cost allocation appropriate for use in leisure service agencies were discussed. The program management accounting system recognizes program services as the line output of the agency and requires that all costs be reported in relation to their contribution to the development of program services.

References, Chapter Sixteen

Anthony, R.N., and G.A. Welsch. 1981. *Fundamentals of Management Accounting*. Homewood, IL: R.D. Irwin.

Deppe, T.R. 1983. *Management Strategies in Financing Parks and Recreation*. New York: Wiley.

Edginton, C.R., and J.G. Williams 1978. *Productive Management of Leisure Service Organizations*. New York: Wiley.

Rodney, L.S., and R.F. Toalson. 1981. *Administration of Recreation, Parks and Leisure Services*. New York: Wiley.

Photo courtesy of the City of Phoenix Parks, Recreation and Library Department, Phoenix, Arizona.

Pricing Program Services

The fifth step in implementing the program management accounting system is to isolate specific programs and to calculate the actual costs of providing an individual service. This is accomplished with cost-volume-profit analysis, which is also called break-even analysis or contribution margin theory. The same technique has various names because of different emphases in using the technique. The implications of this will become apparent later in this section.

Cost-Volume-Profit Analysis

Cost-volume-profit analysis of a specific activity or segment of an enterprise permits a complete financial analysis of the expected financial results of an activity. This analysis enables the programmer to match the revenue and expenses for an activity and to simultaneously account for changes in volume (participation level) and changes in production costs. The data generated by using cost-volume-profit analysis inform the manager about the actual costs of providing specific services. With this information, it is possible to then make cost-based decisions regarding the price to be charged for specific services.

Classifying Costs

To implement cost-volume-profit analysis, the programmer begins by examining the expenses or costs associated with a specific activity. To use this analysis, costs of a program must be classified as variable, fixed, or changing fixed.

Variable costs

Variable costs are those that change directly and proportionately with changes in volume. A variable cost is one that changes the same amount of money with the addition of each new participant or some other unit of volume (see Endnote 1). The cost of an instruction book to be used in a class is an example of a variable cost. The agency would need to purchase a book for each participant and would need as many books as there are participants in the class. If the book costs $5, $5 in variable costs would be added to the program for each participant who enrolls. Some programs will have several variable costs. Let us assume that the book is to be purchased for a ceramics instruction class. Glazes and a five-pound block of clay also need to be purchased for each participant. These three items sum to $22 in variable costs for the ceramics program; so for each participant added to this program, the agency would incur $22 in variable costs.

Fixed costs

Fixed costs are those that do not change with changes in volume, that is, the number of participants. These costs are fixed because they remain the same for the duration of a program, regardless of the number of participants. There are both direct and indirect fixed costs. In the previous section direct and indirect costs were defined. It is important to remember that the direct-indirect classification deals with the relationship of a cost to a cost objective, and the fixed-variable classification deals with the behavior of a cost in relation to changes in volume. It is therefore possible to have costs that are classified as direct fixed costs or indirect fixed costs.

An example of a direct fixed cost would be the cost of renting a ceramics lab for the program discussed above. This cost would be directly related to this specific cost objective, the ceramics program. It would also remain the same regardless of the number of participants in a program. Whether one or 30 people participate, the rental fee would remain the same. It is therefore a fixed cost. It is probably apparent that the notion of a fixed cost has limitations. That is, the notion of a cost remaining the same is only true within certain parameters. The ceramics lab does have a limited seating capacity and can therefore accommodate only a limited number of participants, for example, 30.

These parameters are known as the *relevant range*. All fixed costs, then, are fixed only within a specified relevant range.

An example of an indirect fixed cost is a proportion of some overhead cost that may be allocated to a specific cost objective or program. The ceramics program may be required to absorb some overhead increment of allocated cost, such as a share of office and administrative expenses, utilities, and advertising or marketing costs. The agency must incur these costs, but they are not directly traceable to a specific cost objective or program. They are fixed because they do not increase with each new participant added to a program.

Changing fixed costs

Changing fixed costs are those that change in the same direction, but not proportionately with changes in volume or the number of participants. These costs do not change the same amount for each participant added. Most often they are costs that change after certain numbers of participants are added. In the ceramics class, an instructor would be hired to teach the class of 30. The instructor's salary would be a direct fixed cost to this program. This instructor would need one teacher's aide when the program enrollment exceeded 20 participants. It would therefore be necessary to hire a teacher's aide when the 21st participant entered the class. From the 21st through the 30th participant, the agency would have the additional cost of one teacher's aide. The cost of the teacher's aide is therefore a changing fixed cost.

Since the cost of the teacher's aide does not go up with each participant added, it is not a variable cost. Since it is not a cost that is fixed over the relevant range of this program, that is, 30 participants (which is determined in this case by the capacity of the room), it is not a fixed cost. It is therefore a changing fixed cost. It changes in the relevant range of the program, but remains fixed from the 21st through the 30th participant.

Presenting Cost Data

Cost-volume-profit analysis can provide descriptive program management information in two ways: by tabling the data or by placing them in a graph. Each of these methods has unique ways of revealing important information regarding cost behavior.

Tabling cost data

To illustrate this technique, the ceramics program cited earlier will be developed further. Following are a set of facts regarding the program:

1.   Fowler Community Arts Center has a ceramics lab, which can be rented for $25 per hour. The lab can accommodate 30 people, and the rental fee includes the use of a kiln as needed.

2.   The instructor to be hired makes $10 per contact hour and can teach 30 students. The instructor needs an aide to assist with any class exceeding 20 students. The aide makes $5 per hour.

3.   Each participant will use an instructional book costing $5, clay costing $11, and glazes costing $6.

4.   Each program operated in the arts division must absorb $100 in overhead expenses for administrative and supervisory wages, advertising and marketing of the arts programs, and office expenses for handling registration.

5.   The arts supervisor estimates that she will spend eight hours of her time on this ceramics program for hiring, training, and supervising the staff. The arts supervisor makes $15 per hour.

6.   The program will operate for ten weeks, two nights per week, two hours per evening.

The first step in analyzing these data is to classify each cost and determine any additional facts needed to solve the problem. The only fact needed is that there will be 40 hours of instruction time (two hours per night x two nights per week x ten weeks = 40 hours). The data from these facts are displayed in Table 17-1 on page 355.

Table 17-1.
Ceramics Instruction Cost Data

Cost items	Actual cost
Fixed Costs	
Direct fixed costs:	
Instructor	
40 Hours x $10/Hr =	$400
Rent	
40 Hours x $25/Hr =	1,000
Indirect fixed costs:	
Overhead	100
Supervisor	
8 hours x $15/Hr =	120
Changing fixed costs:	
Aide (from 21st through 30th participant)	
40 Hours x $5.00/Hr =	200
Total fixed costs	$1,820
Variable Costs	
Books	$5
Clay	11
Glazes	6
Total variable costs/person	$22

The reasons for classifying most of the costs as they are classified in Table 17-1 have already been explained. The classification of the art supervisor's salary has not yet been explained, however. The supervisor's time has been classified as an indirect fixed expense because this salary continues whether or not the supervisor works on this specific program. Although the supervisor is a line unit employee, this cost is an indirect but fixed cost to this program. When the supervisor spends time on this program, it must be charged with the dollar value of the supervisor's time in order to account for all of the actual cost of producing the program.

These data can then be placed in a cost-volume-profit table, Table 17-2. This table shows various volumes of participation as column headings. Choosing the levels of participation to include in such a table is somewhat arbitrary. In this case, 30 was included as the largest level of volume because it is the maximum capacity of the program. Twenty and 21 were included because they represent a breaking point at which the changing fixed cost of a teaching aide is introduced. Ten and 15 participants were also included as volume levels. An agency's operational policies and the programmer's previous experience with volume levels will dictate choices of volume levels to include. For example, the agency may not operate an adult program with fewer than ten participants. In this case, ten represents the lowest level of activity that would be used in a table and also the lower limit of the relevant range. Rows in the table show various cost items and different cost summaries.

Table 17-2.
Ceramics Class
Cost-Volume-Profit Table

Cost items	Number of Participants					
	5	10	15	20	21	30
Direct Fixed Costs						
Instructor	400	400	400	400	400	400
Rent	1,000	1,000	1,000	1,000	1,000	1,000
Indirect Fixed Costs						
Overhead	100	100	100	100	100	100
Supervision	120	120	120	120	120	120
Changing Fixed Costs						
Teaching aide					200	200
Total fixed costs	1,620	1,620	1,620	1,620	1,820	1,820
Variable Costs						
$22/participant	110	220	330	440	462	660
Total Costs	1,730	1,840	1,950	2,060	2,282	2,480
Cost/Participant	346	184	130	103	109	83

The cost per participant, which is the final row in Table 17-2, is also known as the break-even point. At each volume specified, the cost-per-participant dollar amount represents the price that each participant must be charged if the agency is to recover all of its costs associated with producing the program. With these data, it is possible to determine how much it costs the agency to produce a specific service. How this break-even point is used in setting a price for a specific service is discussed in step six.

Graphing cost data

These data can also be placed in a graph, which makes it possible to visually observe the behavior of each cost component. The data from the ceramics program in Table 17-2 are graphed in Exhibit 17-1, page 358.

Graphed data enable the programmer to clearly observe the behavior of each cost component. Direct and indirect fixed costs remain constant through the relevant range and are therefore represented by a line that is parallel to the volume line—fixed costs do not increase with increases in volume. Changing fixed costs are represented by a line that is also parallel to the volume line, but is entered on the graph in a stepped-up fashion to represent the incremental increase in fixed costs that are characteristic of changing fixed costs. Variable costs are represented by a sloped line, the steepness of which will vary depending on the amount of variable costs per person. A large amount of variable costs per person will result in a steep line, while a small amount of variable costs per person will result in a less steep line.

The total cost line summarizes the fixed, changing fixed, and variable costs. This line often coincides with the variable cost line on the finished graph, but only because the variable cost component is added above the fixed cost line, which was already drawn. The variable cost component of total costs can be graphed separately, as is done in Exhibit 17-2. The total cost line, then, coincides with the variable cost line on a total cost graph only because fixed and variable costs have been summarized on the graph.

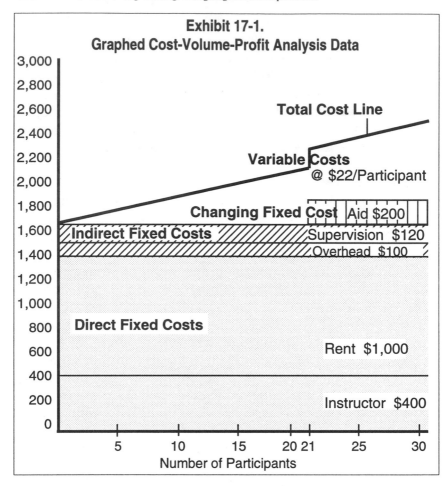

Exhibit 17-1.
Graphed Cost-Volume-Profit Analysis Data

Total Cost Line

Variable Costs @ $22/Participant

Changing Fixed Cost   Aid $200

Indirect Fixed Costs   Supervision $120

Overhead $100

Direct Fixed Costs

Rent $1,000

Instructor $400

Number of Participants

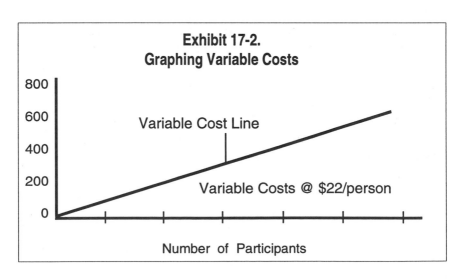

Exhibit 17-2.
Graphing Variable Costs

Variable Cost Line

Variable Costs @ $22/person

Number of Participants

Graphing the break-even point

Once the variable costs have been added to the fixed costs and graphed, the break-even point at each level of participation can be determined from the graph as well as from the tabled data. As demonstrated in Exhibit 17-3, the break-even point is determined by drawing the vertical line A-B directly above any participation level. In this example, line A-B has been drawn above ten participants, but lines can be drawn at any participation level. The break-even point is the point at which similarly drawn lines intersect the total cost line. In Exhibit 17-3, the break-even point for ten participants is $1,840. In this case one would need to charge each participant $184 ($1,840 divided by ten participants) to break even. The advantage of the graph over the tabled data is that the programmer can observe the steepness of the total cost line and can quickly see the break-even point at any level of participation.

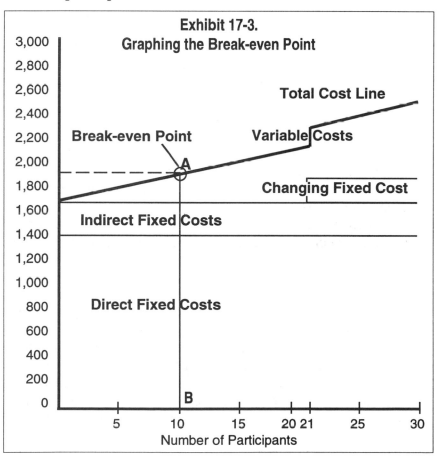

Exhibit 17-3.
Graphing the Break-even Point

Applying the revenue line

Once the total cost graph is completed, one can draw revenue lines that represent various levels of revenue. Exhibit 17-4 on page 361 is a total cost graph of the ceramics class with the revenue line A-B added to it. Line A-B illustrates the behavior of revenue at $150 per person. It is possible and advisable to draw additional revenue lines that estimate the behavior of different pricing levels within the parameters of the current cost structure. The point at which line A-B crosses the total cost line is also a break-even point, that is, the point at which revenue equals the cost of producing the program. With this method, we can observe the effect of various prices on the minimum participation level needed to break even. With the previous method, we can observe the effect of various participation levels on the price we will need to charge to break even. Once the total cost graph is completed, either approach can be used to determine a minimum price or minimum participation level. When one is determined, the other is also determined. However, the one to take precedence in determining price and participation level is a matter of circumstances.

In Exhibit 17-4, the break-even point occurs somewhere between the 12th and 13th participant. With 12 participants, revenue is $1,800 ($150 x 12) and costs are $1,884 ($1,620 in fixed costs + 12 x $22 per person in variable costs). With 12 participants, costs still exceed revenue. With 13 participants, revenue is $1,950 ($150 x 13) and costs are $1,906 ($1,620 in fixed costs + 13 x $22 per person in variable costs). With 13 participants, revenue exceeds costs by $46.

When revenue estimates are used to determine participation levels, the break-even point will seldom occur with a whole unit of participation. Since it is not possible to have part of a person in a program, the break-even point is established at the next highest volume level. This practice also ensures that the agency does not incur a loss. In this case, the break-even point with a revenue of $150 per person is 13 participants.

In Exhibit 17-4, the area above the break-even point shaded with vertical lines represents profit for the agency. The area below the break-even point shaded with dots represents a loss to the agency. Volume above the break-even point on the graph will result in a profit or retained income for the agency, that is, income in excess of production costs. Volume levels below the break-even point will result in a loss, which will need to be compensated for with increased fees, through subsidization with tax dollars, with third-party donations, or with profits from other activities.

Exhibit 17-4.
Plotting the Revenue Line

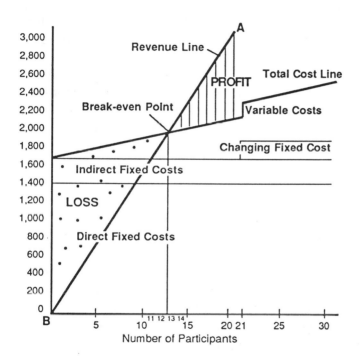

This latter situation often occurs in a commercial recreation operation where one activity is used as a "loss leader" to draw customers into a facility or program. For example, the nursery in a court facility may operate at a loss, which is subsidized by profits from increased court usage because the nursery is available.

In actual practice, once accurate costs for program production have been determined, the programmer usually determines a price, estimates a reasonable volume level expected, and estimates total revenue to be earned. If the estimated total revenue is not sufficient to cover costs, then the programmer must subsidize the cost of the program, try to reduce costs to match revenues, increase prices, or not operate the program. If the program is operated and revenue from participants does not cover the production costs, then the program is being subsidized by the agency. There has been a tendency in public recreation to simply hide these costs. The program management accounting system will not allow this to happen. Managers using this system are required to identify all costs and to match them with revenues.

Cost-volume-profit analysis enables the programmer to isolate specific activities to match costs with revenues generated. With this technique, it is possible to accurately determine the full cost of producing services and then to use this information in determining a price.

Establishing a Price

The sixth and final step in implementing the program management accounting system is to determine the price that the agency will charge for a service. This determination should be made by using the data developed in the cost-volume-profit analysis, the implications of the agency's pricing policy developed in the first step, and some consideration of other factors that may mitigate the price to be established.

Cost-volume-profit analysis provides data that enable a programmer to estimate the financial performance of a specific program. A program's financial performance can be classified into one of the following three cases: (1) the program's revenue may be less than its production costs (representing a loss to the agency); (2) the program's revenue may equal the cost of production—the break-even point at which the agency recovers all of its costs of production; or (3) the program's revenue may exceed production costs, which provides the agency with revenue in excess of its production costs. This excess revenue is known as a contribution margin, that is, a margin of revenue over actual production costs that may be applied to agency profits or retained income.

In addition to the actual cost data developed through cost-volume-profit analysis, the manager also needs to ascertain from the service category system whether a program is a merit, a private, or a public service. A public service is offered at no cost to the public. A merit service is offered at a price that is less than what would be required for full cost recovery; the price enables the agency to recover some of its production costs. Often, the price charged for a merit program is based on recovering only the direct costs of a program, and no attempt is made to recover any indirect costs. A private service is offered at a price that will enable the agency to fully recover its production costs.

Additional Considerations

Before establishing the price, one must also anticipate possible consumer resistance to a price. Howard and Selin (1987) have established that there is a price tolerance zone within which a price may be established. Furthermore, this zone varies from activity to activity, which suggests that across-the-board price increases are a poor pricing strategy. A price must be set for each activity.

The price established must also consider the attitude of the target market toward pricing. Kerr and Manfredo (1991) documented that intention to pay is most significantly influenced by past use and past fee paying. That is, individuals who are used to paying a fee for a given service and are frequent consumers of it will have the least resistance to price increases. Reiling, Criner, and Oltmanns (1988) have suggested that the two most persuasive arguments to present to influence attitudes about paying are to compare the price proposed with commercial rates for the same service and to provide data about the cost of provision (data from the cost-volume-profit analysis outlined in this chapter).

An additional point to understand is price elasticity, i.e. the relationship of the activity being charged for to the overall price for participation. For example, when the agency operates tourist attractions, the prices at these are somewhat inelastic because the price of admission to the museum is a very small part of the cost of travel. Admissions to amenities constitute about 10 percent of the travel dollar. Thus, the $2.00 admission charge to a museum could probably be doubled without adversely affecting demand, because it would have such a small impact on the overall cost of a trip to a museum for a tourist. This is price elasticity, and the specific example provided is an example of an inelastic price. With information from these basic sources, the programmer determines the price to charge for a program. Exhibit 17-5 includes a work sheet that brings together the data necessary for determining the price of a program. A programmer faces many possible circumstances in establishing program fees. But remember, although quantitative data about the costs of production can be developed, the final price established must also take into consideration the agency's pricing policy and the target market's attitude toward pricing. Below are outlined some of these typical circumstances.

Exhibit 17-5.
Program Cost Pricing Work Sheet

Programming Unit _____   Activity/Program Title _____

Fixed Costs	Changing Fixed Costs	Variable Costs (per unit)
Personnel (Total) $ _____	Personnel (Total) $ _____	Personnel (Total) $ _____
Services Contractual (Total) $ _____	Services Contractual (Total) $ _____	Services Contractual (Total) $ _____
Commodities (Total) $ _____	Commodities (Total) $ _____	Commodities (Total) $ _____
Materials (Total) $ _____	Materials (Total) $ _____	Materials (Total) $ _____
Other Expenses (Total) $ _____	Other Expenses (Total) $ _____	Other Expenses (Total) $ _____
Capital Outlay (Total) $ _____	Capital Outlay (Total) $ _____	Capital Outlay (Total) $ _____

(continued)

Exhibit 17-5.

Fixed Cost Total $ _____
Add_____ $ for overhead rate*

Total adjusted   Total Changing Fixed   Total Variable Costs
  Fixed Costs $ _____   Costs $ _____ $ _____

*Optional–added to recover overhead or burden costs based on cost allocation studies and agency policy.

Establishing a Price

1. Total adjusted fixed costs $ _____
2. Total changing fixed costs $ _____
3. Total variable costs per unit ($_____) x
    Expected number of participants (no.   ) = ____ $ _____
4. Subtotal (add lines 1 + 2 + 3) $ _____
5. Divide subtotal (line 4) by
    expected number of participants (no.   ) =____ $ _____
6. Multiply result on line 5 by
    _____% of desired cost recovery = $ _____

The last figure (the result on line 6) represents the price it is necessary to charge each participant in the program in order to achieve the desired level of cost recovery. "Percent of cost recovery" represents the contribution the agency wants an individual participant to pay towards the cost of providing a program. Percentage of cost recovery can range from 0% to an excess of 100%. The meaning of various levels of percentage of cost recovery are outlined below.

0 % A Public Good, totally subsidized service--the user contributes nothing to the cost of providing the service.

1 % to 99 % A Merit Good, users contribute a percentage of the cost of providing a service–tax dollars are used to fund the remaining percentage of costs in excess of user fee contributions.

100 % A Private Good, users contribute the full cost of providing the service–no tax dollars are used.

100 % + A Private Good, users contribute in excess of actual costs for providing the program–excess income is used to subsidize other programs.

(Source: Dr. Jerry Burnam, College of Applied Life Studies, University of Illinois at Urbana-Champaign)

Public Services

Public services are offered by the agency at no charge to the user. The agency does not recover any of its costs of production from a public service. Cost-volume-profit information for public services simply informs the programmer about the costs of producing the various services provided at no charge to the public. The data are useful for determining the comparative cost of the various public programs that the agency is offering free of charge. When the cost structure of public programs is examined, some savings and areas for cost reduction will often become apparent. Using cost-volume-profit analysis, then, is useful for documenting where the agency's resources are being spent, for identifying which groups are receiving subsidized services, and for determining the cost of each program service provided.

Private Services

Private services are offered at a price that will enable the agency to recover all of its direct and indirect costs of producing the program. The use of cost-volume-profit analysis provides the programmer with an accurate statement of the actual costs of production. These figures can be used as data for determining and justifying the price to be charged for a program. In a public or not-for-profit agency, obtaining full cost recovery for these types of services is important so that funds intended to subsidize public and merit services are not used to subsidize services that are supposed to be self-sustaining.

In a commercial recreation operation, knowing the full cost of production is equally important. If the agency is to make a profit and stay in business, it must make a margin of profit beyond actual production costs. It is normal practice to use cost-volume-profit analysis to determine actual production cost at an estimated level of volume and then to add on a margin of profit to actual production costs. In these cases, each program is expected to contribute a margin of profit to the overall profits of the agency. This increment is known as the contribution margin. For example, all programs may be offered at cost plus a 15 percent contribution margin to agency profit.

Public and not-for-profit agencies also use the contribution margin concept. Although these types of agencies are not profit making, they often develop retained income from some program services. This retained income is frequently used to help subsidize merit and public services or to make up for losses incurred in the operation of less successful private services.

Merit Services

Merit services are offered by the agency at a price that will permit a partial recovery of agency costs. Merit services can be thought of in two ways—either as programs that receive a partial subsidy or as programs that partly recover their costs of production. In reality, they actually do both. However, which component the agency chooses to emphasize can influence how these programs are thought about and treated in the agency. Using cost-volume-profit analysis to examine the actual costs of producing merit programs establishes a base from which a price can be determined. *Knowing the cost of producing a program does not necessarily mean the agency will charge a price that permits a full recovery of its production costs.* Merit services are one case in which production costs are simply the starting point in determining a price for participation.

The price actually charged for a merit service will be determined by production costs, the dollars available from other sources (primarily donations and tax dollars, depending on the type of agency) to subsidize the program, and the agency's policies regarding the type of program under consideration. Determining a price for merit services is clearly more complicated than simply using cost-volume-profit analysis to determine actual production costs and adding on a contribution margin. The process is somewhat the opposite of adding a contribution margin for profit and in this case involves subtracting a "subsidy margin" that reduces the actual price to the user. Through the subsidies allocated to merit services, the social welfare function of the agency is implemented, so allocation of these subsidies should occur with accurate cost data. Cost-volume-profit analysis provides the programmer with accurate data so that the actual dollar amount of a subsidy can be determined. In this way, the programmer and the agency know how much and for what programs their subsidy dollars are being used. Now complete Exercise 17-1 on page 368.

Exercise 17-1.
Cost-volume-profit analysis

Complete the following problem outside of class, then discuss your solution in class. See Endnote 2 before discussing the problem.

Problem Situation:

You are an athletic league manager of the Prairie Softball Center. You must determine the costs, set the fees, and market each league you intend to operate. The center is divided into five separate divisions. You are responsible for the operation of one division. The center manager requires that each division share equally in the $80,000 of administrative costs incurred by the center.

Each league that you operate must share equally in your $26,000 salary (including fringes), and they must share equally in the administrative costs assigned to your division. You operate 20 leagues annually. One of the leagues you intend to operate is a co-ed, slow-pitch, 12-inch softball league. Your next step is to collect the balance of the costs that would be incurred by the operation of this program. You gather the following data:

1. You can handle a minimum of ten teams and a maximum of 20.
2. You plan to play a double round-robin schedule in the league.
3. You have five well-maintained and well-lighted diamonds available to you at the center.
4. All necessary equipment will be purchased from the center's working cash fund in bulk lots to minimize costs.
5. You decide that each team in the league must have a minimum of 12 and a maximum of 18 players on the team roster. There must be a balance of the sexes and always at least 50 percent females on each team.
6. To maximize control and minimize complaints, you plan to assign two umpires per game at a cost of $12 per game per umpire.
7. The center will supply you with bats, which were purchased in bulk at $8 each. Each team will receive four bats.
8. The center has purchased softballs in bulk at a cost of $3 per ball. You will provide a new ball for each game played and consider the balls as expendable equipment.
9. Each team is expected to maintain its own score books. You will supply two books per team at a cost of $1.50 each.
10. Each diamond will be supplied with a set of catcher's equipment which the center purchased at $180 per set. Each league is charged for the full cost of the catcher's equipment.
11. You plan to operate the league on Monday, Wednesday, and Friday evenings by using all five diamonds. You can operate a maximum of two games per evening on each diamond with the allotted time of two hours per game. The second game on each diamond must use the field lights, which cost $10 per hour to operate.

(continued)

12. The maintenance unit will drag and prepare each diamond by setting the bases, lining the diamond, and lightly watering and raking between each game. You are charged $20 per diamond per evening for this service.
13. You plan to award trophies to the first-place team. The trophies will cost $100.

Assignment:
1. Prepare a break-even analysis table for this problem.
2. What is the difference in cost between ten and 20 teams? Explain what makes up these cost differences.
3. What are the overhead or indirect costs of this program?
4. What are the variable costs of this program?
5. Show a break-even analysis table for a single round-robin tournament with 20 teams.
6. What is the difference in cost per team for a single compared with a double round-robin tournament with 20 teams?

Conclusion

How to analyze the relationship of cost to volume was discussed. The program management accounting system requires that each program service be isolated and its costs of production and the revenues associated with the program be matched so that its financial performance can be observed. Implementing the system will give the programmer factual cost data about each program service so that cost-based pricing decisions can be made. It will also enable accurate decisions regarding the subsidization of programs.

References, Chapter Seventeen

Kerr, G.N., and M.J. Manfredo. 1991. An Attitudinal-Based Model of Pricing for Recreation Services. *Journal of Leisure Research*, 23. 37-50.

Reiling, S.D., G.K. Criner, and S.E. Oltmanns. 1988. The Influence of Information on Users' Attitudes Toward Campground User Fees. *Journal of Leisure Research, 20.* 208-217.

Suggested Readings

Becker, R.H., D. Berrier, and G.D. Barker. 1985. Entrance Fees and Visitation Levels. *Journal of Park and Recreation Administration* 3, 28-32.

Crompton, J.L. 1981, March. How to Find the Price That's Right. *Parks & Recreation*, 32-40.

Ellis, T., and R.L. Norton. 1988. *Commercial Recreation.* St. Louis, MO: Times Mirror/Mosby College Publishing.

Manning, R., E. Calliman, H. Echelberger, E. Koenemann, and D. McEvan. 1984. Differential Fees: Raising Revenue, Distributing Demand. *Journal of Park and Recreation Administration* 2, 2-38.

Endnotes

1. Variable costs are costs that increase an equal amount with each additional unit of volume. In most leisure services, the volume unit is the individual participant. However, this is not always the case. For example, in a band contest, variable costs may be dependent on the number of bands entered—not the number of band members. The same is often true for calculating the costs of athletic leagues and tournaments.

2. If you followed instructions and are reading this before discussing the cost-volume-profit exercise in class, you are indeed fortunate. The solution to the exercise is given in the addendum to this chapter! Please try to solve the exercise yourself before reading the solution.

Chapter 17 Addendum
Solution to Exercise 17.1.

The first task in solving this problem is to organize the data. Below are the facts and constraints relevant to solving this exercise.

Facts and Constraints

Item #	Data
1	10 to 20 teams
2	double round-robin league
3	5 lighted diamonds
4	2 games per diamond per evening
4	play 3 evenings per week
4	1/2 of games under lights

The next task is to classify costs as fixed, changing fixed, or variable.

Fixed Costs

Fixed costs are classified as either indirect or direct costs.

Item #	Cost Data	
P.S.	Indirect agency: $80,000/5 = 16,000/20 =$	$800
P.S.	Indirect unit: $26,000/20 =$	1,300
10	Direct: catcher's equipment:	
	$180 \times 5 = 900$	900
13	Direct: trophies	100
	Total Fixed Costs (10 through 20 teams)	$3,100

Changing Fixed Costs

In this problem, it is most convenient to handle the following costs as changing fixed costs. Because of the nature of a round-robin tournament, the number of games to be played is not solely a function of adding another team (which would make it a variable cost). The number of games to be played is also dependent on the number of teams already included. The formula for calculating the number of games to be played in a double round-robin tournament is: $(n) \times (n - 1)$ with n = the number of teams to play in the tournament.

Item	Cost Data (per game)	
6	Umpires: 12 x 2 =	$24
8	Balls: 3 x 1 =	3
11	Lights: 10 x 2 = 20/2 =	10
12	Diamond maintenance: 20/2 =	10
		$47 / game

Variable Costs

Variable costs in this problem are costs that are the same for each team added to the league. Bats and score books are the only true variable costs.

Item #	Cost Data (per team)	
7	Bats: 8 x 4 =	$32
9	Score books: 1.50 x 2 =	3
		$35/team

Cost-Volume-Profit Table for
Double Round-Robin Softball League

Costs	Number of Teams (volume level)		
	10	15	20
Fixed Costs			
Center	$800	$800	$800
Division	1,300	1,300	1,300
Catcher's Equipment	900	900	900
Trophies	100	100	100
Total FixedCosts	3,100	3,100	3,100
Changing Fixed Costs			
47/Game	$(90)^a 4,230$	$(210)^a 9,870$	$(380)^a 17,860$

Cost-Volume-Profit Table for Double Round-Robin Softball League (cont.)

Variable Costs

35/Team	350	525	700
Total Costs	$7,680	$13,495	$21,660
Fee per team to break even	$768	$899.76	$1,083

[a] Number of games required to complete the tournament.

$10 = (10)\ (10 - 1) = (10)\ (9) = 90$
$15 = (10)\ (10 - 1) = (15)\ (14) = 210$
$20 = (20)\ (20 - 1) = (20)\ (19) = 380$

Answers to Questions

1. Total Costs for 20 teams are $21,660. (See column 3 in Table for details).

2. Difference in Costs between 20 and 10 teams is: $21,660 - $7,680 = $13,980. (This difference is made up of the increasing number of games that must be played with the addition of each new team to a round-robin league).

3. Overhead costs for the league include $800 in center administrative overhead plus $1,300 in unit overhead costs = $2,100.

4. Variable costs of the program include the costs incurred by team; that is, $32/team for bats plus $3/team for score books = $35/team.

5. Break-even table for a 20-team single round robin tournament.

Formula for calculating the number of games needed for a 20-team single round robin is (n) (n-1) /2. Therefore (20) (20 - 1)/2 = (20) (19) / 2 = 380/2 = 190 games.

Fixed costs for 20 teams	
Center	$ 800
Division	1,300
Trophies	100
Catchers equipment	900

Changing Fixed Costs	
$47 / game x 190 games	8,930

Variable costs	
$35 / team x 20 teams	700

Total Costs	$12,730

$12,730/20 teams = $636.50/team

7. $1,083.00/team   Double round robin
    -636.50/team   Single round robin

    $ -446.50/team   Difference

Note: The difference in cost between the 20-team double round-robin league versus the 20-team single round robin is $446.50 per team or $8,930 [20 x 446.50 = $8,930]. This is exactly the cost of playing 190 games [$47/ game in changing fixed costs x 190 games = $8,930]. The point here is that a round-robin programming format adds costs very rapidly because of each team needing to play every other team in each round.

In fact it would be much cheaper to play two 10-team double round-robin leagues than it is to play one 20-team double round-robin league. If you want to impress your instructor, calculate these costs and demonstrate why this is so!

(Source: Dr. Jerry Burnam, College of Applied Life Studies, University of Illinois, Urbana-Champaign)

Part V: Follow-up Analysis

In Part V, Follow-Up Analysis, a program is evaluated and a decision made about the disposition of the program. Programmers need to establish the worth of program services with systematically collected evaluation evidence. This evidence should be used to document program worth and to review program operations so that decisions can be made to properly manage program services.

This section includes three chapters. In Chapter Eighteen, program evaluation techniques are explained, and a general plan for developing program evaluations is outlined. Chapter Nineteen contains five program evaluation models. How to make decisions about program services is discussed in Chapter Twenty.

Photo courtesy of Joliet Park District, Joliet, Illinois. Photo by Ann Miller.

18

Program Evaluation Techniques

Evaluation is an elastic concept that is used to describe many activities. Evaluating program services is the eighth step in the Program Development Cycle. It is the start of the follow-up analysis stage of the cycle and the antecedent to making a decision about the disposition of a program. Through the use of program evaluation data, the programmer makes a decision based on an analysis of evidence about the future of a program.

Evaluation Defined

Suchman (1967) stated that "an evaluation is basically a judgment of worth—an appraisal of value" (p.11). Suchman's central theme is that evaluation involves making judgments of worth. This definition of evaluation was further developed by Worthen and Sanders (1973), who state that "evaluation is the determination of the worth of a thing" (p.19). They also indicate that the determination of merit or worth is the touchstone of evaluation. This latter point is very important. Evaluation has not taken place until a judgment of worth or value has occurred. Evaluation is not simply collecting data; it also requires that a judgment of worth within the context of some value system be made with the data collected.

Most evaluation scholars distinguish between everyday evaluation based on casual perceptions and more systematic evaluation. The former does not require the use of systematic procedures or the presentation of objective evidence. The latter requires both and uses the scientific process to control the intrinsic subjectivity of everyday evaluation.

Many programmers evaluate their program services informally. An objective of this chapter is to help programmers move from informal to more formal evaluation procedures. The definition of evaluation to be used, then, is that *evaluation is judging the worth of program services on the basis of an analysis of systematically collected evidence.*

Purposes of Evaluation

Evaluation is often imposed on programmers by a board, a third-party funding agency, or a higher level administrator. As a result, evaluation is often viewed as an add-on responsibility imposed on the programmer or as a procedure undertaken with some trepidation, since it may result in an adverse view of the programmer's efforts. The viewpoint used in this book is that evaluation is part of the programmer's ongoing responsibility in operating and managing program services—it is not an add-on responsibility. Making judgments of worth about program services can serve the programmer and the organization in three ways: in program development, in organizational management, and in establishing accountability.

Program Development

Evaluation data can be used in program development. With the data gathered in an evaluation, the programmer can help improve and refine programs by determining what works, what does not work, and why things work the way they do. Evaluation data can help analyze the value of the contribution of each part of a program and thus facilitate program revision. Evaluation data can also boost staff morale. Although the results of an evaluation will sometimes indicate that a program is performing poorly, the majority of the services being operated are probably doing well and will receive a favorable evaluation. Staff morale is enhanced by favorable evaluation reports, and programmers should recognize their positive effects.

Evaluation, as it is currently conducted, will also result in new needs being discovered, even though this is not the purpose of evaluation. Needs identification is part of the needs assessment step of the Program Development Cycle. However, clients often identify new needs on evaluation instruments, leading to the discovery of new needs.

Organizational Management

Evaluation can help improve organizational management by using the information that evaluation generates. This information helps the programmer make informed decisions about how to modify programs, what services to drop, and which to continue. All of these alternatives can be made with systematically collected and analyzed evaluation data, rather than with individual perceptions or other less systematic methods.

In addition, evaluation data will help the manager answer the ultimate evaluation question: Is this the best use of these resources in this organization at this time? The answer to this question is an important one for improving management of the organization and helping it move toward meeting its goals. It is an especially difficult question in a leisure service organization because leisure services often attract a committed core group of participants (Howard and Crompton 1980, p. 380). If one continues all programs that have a constituency, there will be few programs to cancel, even long after they cease to be useful to the organization. Leisure service organizations that have the benefit of annual resource increases can often ignore these issues and simply add new services with the additional resources received. In a retrenchment situation, however, decisions to eliminate programs must be made. Evaluation data can provide the information and rationale necessary for determining which services to drop.

Another difficulty may occur if programs are continued each year without sufficient review and revision. When the organization's mission changes, these programs may no longer be included within the organization's current mission, even though they have a constituency. Evaluation data can provide the manager with the information and justification needed to terminate such programs.

Ultimately, the evaluation for each program operated must examine the question of whether the resources needed for the current program can be put to better use.

Establishing Accountability

Evaluation data can help the organization establish accountability by documenting program outputs. With these data, what is being accomplished in the agency's programs is documented with systematically collected evidence. This information can also provide evidence that the organization's goals are being met. The programmer can then effectively communicate these accomplishments to funding agencies and other publics, thereby justifying the expenditures necessary to continue services.

These three purposes of evaluation cumulatively result in providing evidence that the programmer is an effective manager. The use of evaluation data in the management of the leisure service agency helps establish that the manager is involved in the ongoing review of program services based on an analysis of evidence. It also helps establish that the manager takes action on the basis of program reviews to make certain that organizational goals are being accomplished. Evaluation, then, contributes significantly to the management of program services and the management of leisure service agencies. Now complete Exercise 18-1.

Exercise 18-1.
Comparing Purposes of Evaluation

In class, analyze and compare the three purposes of evaluation. Consider the following points:

- How do these three purposes differ?
- How are these three purposes similar?
- How do these three purposes complement each other in a comprehensive evaluation system?

Planning an Evaluation

Evaluation is not a single activity or procedure. Most leisure service organizations will not have any one evaluation procedure that can meet all of the organization's evaluation needs. An agency will most likely have several procedures operating simultaneously to meet the diverse evaluation needs of the agency. Because of this diversity, programmers should understand how to plan an evaluation to meet a specific evaluation problem and the issues inherent in implementing an evaluation. Grotelueschen, et al. (1974) provide an outline for planning an evaluation. A modified form of this outline, which is included in Exhibit 18-1, is used to organize the material that follows in this chapter. When an evaluation is planned, each of the steps outlined should be followed in the order presented.

Exhibit 18-1.
Evaluation Planner

1. Purpose: Why evaluate?
2. Audience: Who is the evaluation for? What questions do they want answered? What will they do with the information?
3. Process: How will the evaluation be conducted?
4. Issues: What questions should the evaluation address?
5. Resources: What resources are needed to conduct the evaluation?
6. Evidence: What evidence should be collected?
7. Data-gathering: How is the evidence to be collected?
8. Analysis: How can the evidence be analyzed?
9. Reporting: How can evaluation findings be reported?

Purpose: Why Evaluate?

The first question to answer in planning an evaluation is to determine why the evaluation is being conducted. Three purposes for conducting an evaluation were outlined in the previous section. Although programmers may be able to meet more than one of these purposes with a single evaluation, often they cannot do so. The point here is that in identifying a single purpose, the programmer is setting priorities to provide focus to the evaluation effort. Often a single evaluation will meet only a single purpose. When the programmer attempts to meet several purposes, the focus necessary to actually answer the evaluation question may never be achieved. The reason for specifying a purpose is to provide the necessary focus. In this way, the specific evaluation need identified as the reason for conducting the evaluation in the first place can actually be met. Rather than conducting one evaluation with broad, poorly focused purposes, programmers are best advised to conduct several well-focused evaluations specifically designed to fulfill a well-defined purpose.

The first step, then, is to determine whether the evaluation is being conducted to help in program development, organizational management, or organizational accountability. As precisely as possible, make a statement about the purpose for the evaluation. Following are three examples of such statements:

1.   This evaluation is being conducted to determine participant-reported outcomes with program services.
2.   This evaluation is being conducted to help make decisions about the disposition of program services.
3.   This evaluation is being conducted to judge the worth of our agency's distribution of program services.

Audience: Who Is the Evaluation For?

Evaluation data are not generated and used in a void. Patton (1978) has indicated that "people, not organizations use evaluation information" (p.63). He goes on to document that the two most important factors contributing to the use of evaluation information are political considerations and the personal factor, which "refers to the presence of an identifiable individual or group of people who personally cared about the evaluation and the information it generated" (p. 64). Data generated by an evaluation are used by someone in an organization to make a judgment of worth and subsequently to make a decision based on this judgment. People use the results of evaluation, and unless it addresses their concerns, it will go unused. Identifying who will actually use the evaluation data and what they expect to do with the information is an important step in planning an evaluation.

House (1977) has suggested that evaluation is a persuasive argument rather than scientific proof that must respond to a specific rather than a universal audience. As House says, "Thus the situation the evaluator faces is almost always an appeal to particular audiences that he can define with some precision. If he cannot define his audiences, the evaluation is indeterminate" (p.9). When compared with the epistemological rules, methods, and justifications acceptable in social science, the rules that evaluation audiences will accept are less well codified and not as universal. They are, in fact, situationally specific. Part of any evaluation therefore includes uncovering the rules of acceptance that will establish the ultimate rationale for the asserted values of a program beyond which there is no need for further elaboration. To accomplish this, the programmer must define with some precision the evaluation audience who will actually use the information and must determine what questions it is important and relevant to answer.

One's position in the scheme of a social program determines the types of information deemed relevant and therefore desired for evaluation (Weiss 1973). For example, top administrators and boards generally are interested in a summary of broad issues and the impact of program services to facilitate their decision to drop, modify, or continue a program. They are also interested in the data that establish accountability for the funds being used in providing services. Program directors and middle managers are most interested in strategies that are effective in achieving desired ends. Direct service personnel are usually most concerned with the effects of various face-to-face intervention techniques. Other possible users of information include external funding agencies, the public, clients, national associations, other providers of similar services, and so on. People's position in an organization, then, determines to some degree the evaluation questions they will be interested in having answered. Although it may be desirable to meet the evaluation needs of the entire organization with one evaluation, this often may not be possible.

Determining the evaluation audience and consequently the evaluation data they desire is the second step in planning an evaluation. Identifying a specific audience is a necessary part of any evaluation in order to focus information needs, to guide the selection of an appropriate process for conducting the evaluation, to identify salient values, and to guide interpretation of objective data that will be gathered.

While planning a custom-designed evaluation, one must develop a priority of information needs from the evaluation audiences identified and address as many needs as possible within the budget and other constraints. It will probably be impossible to meet all identified needs. Therefore, it is important to have established the priorities that emerge from identifying the primary audience and the primary purpose for conducting the evaluation.

The answers to these first two questions about purpose and audience provide a framework for developing the remainder of the evaluation. Any process developed must fulfill the identified purpose of an evaluation and meet the information needs of a well defined evaluation audience. Now complete Exercise 18-2.

Exercise 18-2.
Specifying the Evaluation Purpose and Audience

In class, discuss the importance of first identifying the purpose of the evaluation and the evaluation audience. Consider the following questions :

- How does specifying the purpose and audience of an evaluation help focus the evaluation?
- Why not accomplish several purposes with one evaluation?
- Why does an evaluation have to be tailored to meet the needs of a specific audience?

Process: How Will the Evaluation Be Conducted?

What specific technique will be used to conduct the evaluation? Howe (1980) has identified six general techniques: professional judgment, measurement, discrepancy, decision oriented, goal free, and transaction-observation. The technique one selects determines how the evaluation will be conducted. Each technique uses different methods and is best suited for a specific type of evaluation.

All techniques are either process models or preordinate models. Each type of model includes different preordained decisions and leaves the evaluator with different choices and responsibilities.

Process models identify a procedure for conducting the evaluation, but do not identify the criteria on which judgments of worth will be made. An example of a process model is the use of goals and objectives. Goal and objective technology explains very precisely a technique for writing goals and objectives, but the technology does not provide the original goals. Embodied in any set of goals and objectives is a point of view about what is important to accomplish and what may be ignored because it is less important. When using goals and objectives in evaluation, programmers must provide the original goals, and in doing so they provide a value structure for the evaluation. In choosing a process model, then, evaluators will need to provide the criteria on which judgments of worth will be made.

Preordinate models provide both the techniques for accomplishing the evaluation and the criteria on which judgments of worth will be made. An example of this type of evaluation process is the use of standards. An evaluation procedure that uses standards gives the programmer specific steps for collecting data and a set of criteria (the standards) on which the worth of program services will be judged. Programmers are often tempted to use preordinate models because the entire technique is explicated; the programmer therefore has little to do except implement the already established technique. A caution programmers must exercise in using preordinate evaluation models is to make certain that the value system embodied in the preordinate model is consistent with the already identified purpose of evaluation and that the data developed from the evaluation meet the identified needs of the evaluation audience.

The evaluation planning steps that follow can be used in two ways. First, they can be used to analyze a preordinate model to make certain that the programmer understands how it deals with each of the planning steps. Second, they can be used as a planning agenda for determining how a process model or a custom-designed model will be implemented.

Issues: What Questions Should the Evaluation Address?

Determining the questions to be addressed in an evaluation is a critical step. In selecting the questions, the programmer must be concerned with validity and values. To be valid the questions must be true indicators of the values asserted for the program. For example, programmers often use attendance figures as an indicator of a program's worth. Attendance is a valid indicator of program impact; that is, how many and who were served. It is not a valid indicator of program quality, nor can it document program outputs (what actually happened to the individuals in the program).

Programs can be judged by a variety of indicators. However, some will be more valid and therefore more important than others. The programmer will probably be unable to include everything everyone thinks is important to have answered in an evaluation. Therefore, what is included in the evaluation must be determined with some care.

Exhibit 18-2, page 387 outlines the five components of all program services: program inputs, processes, products, outputs, and outcomes. Program inputs include all of the resources a programmer may place into a program. Program processes include all of the various components that guide and direct the interactions in a program. Products refers to the program itself, which is produced by combining the resources and processes. The product can include various activity types offered in a variety of delivery formats. As illustrated in Exhibit 18-2, these first three components are under the direct control of the programmer. If recommended procedures have been followed, the programs emerging from this process will have been developed in response to identified needs.

Program outputs are the direct, immediate consequences of program participation. These consequences have been identified in the literature as user satisfaction, fun, flow, arousal, pleasure, self-expression, and achievement. They are the direct and immediate consequences of participation. Program outcomes are the cumulative, long-term consequences of ongoing opportunities to experience the immediate outputs of participation. They are the long-term social benefits of having a leisure

Exhibit 18-2.
Program Components

Direct Control

Indirect Control

Inputs

    Staff

    Facilities

    Materials

    Goals

    Etc.

Processes

    Leadership style

    Rules

    Instruction method

    Schedule

    Etc.

Products

    Activity type

    Programmed experiences

    Delivery format

Outputs (immediate)

    User satisfaction
    Participant achievement

Outcomes (long-term)

    Better community
    Increased life satisfaction

service system that provides ongoing opportunities for leisure participation. They are the social goals our profession professes to meet.

Although programmers have direct control of inputs, processes, and the resultant products, they have less control over outputs and outcomes because of the nature of social interaction. Once the program is actually implemented, interacting individuals come into the program and differentially interact with the program created. Each participant therefore has his or her own experience in the program. Because of this, control of program outputs and outcomes is more problematic than the control of inputs, processes, and the program services that are to be delivered.

A single evaluation may focus on one or more of these components. However, because inputs, processes, and programs are under the direct control of programmers, they often focus on evaluation questions about these three components to the exclusion of questions about items over which they have only indirect control. Therefore, questions about program outputs and outcomes—What happened to the participant in the program?—are often excluded. Securing answers to these latter two program components is critical in documenting program accomplishments and in developing a database from which the agency can establish accountability.

One assumption of this text is that the goal of a program evaluation is to focus on the first four components. The fifth component, long-term outcomes, is the focus of larger community surveys and social science investigations into the consequences of leisure participation. Some work in this area has already been done through life satisfaction studies in which leisure does seem to play a minor role in contributing to overall life satisfaction.

An item pool of possible evaluation questions that inquire about all four of the components that are of concern in program evaluation is contained in an addendum to Chapter Nineteen. This pool is intended to provide samples of questions that could be developed in conducting an evaluation.

Resources: What Resources Are Available
For Evaluation?

Every program manager must understand that evaluation costs money. At the very least, it will cost staff time that could have been spent in other activities. Other expenses are also associated with evaluating: expenses for printing evaluation forms, collecting and analyzing data, and preparing and distributing the evaluation report.

One resource that may currently exist in the agency is data that are already routinely collected. At least part of the evaluation data needed may be obtained by reanalyzing or reinterpreting data that have already been collected in the organization. Evaluation does not always require the collection of new data. Other evaluation resources the agency may have access to are colleagues, universities, cooperative extension agencies, and consultants. All of these are potential resources for helping the agency conduct evaluations.

Evaluation does consume resources. Once the decision to evaluate is made, the questions and issues to examine can quickly grow to a very large and unmanageable number. Each piece of information obtained adds incrementally to the cost of the evaluation. Because of this, it is important to focus the evaluation with the procedures outlined in this section to avoid the expense of answering unimportant or irrelevant questions. It is also important to do some cost/benefit analysis of the answers to be obtained. To determine the potential benefit of possible questions, consider the following:

- If this question is answered, what could be done with the information?
- Is there some management implication in obtaining an answer to this question?
- Is this information worth the cost of obtaining it?

Although there are many questions it would be nice to have answered, program evaluation should remain focused on those questions that enable the manager to improve program development and program management or to establish accountability in a meaningful way.

Evidence: What Evidence Should Be Collected?

Evidence is any information that may be used in making judgments of worth about the issues raised in the evaluation. The evaluation effort is usually focused on the issues identified earlier in this process. Once these issues are identified, the search for evidence begins.

Many types of evidence may be gathered, such as descriptions of personnel, participants, operational procedures, and processes; goals and objectives; costs; and program outcomes. Participant judgments about various components of a program may also be collected on open-ended or scaled questionnaires. What type of evidence is most appropriate will depend on the issues being investigated and the specific requirements of the evaluation audience.

A major consideration in this step of planning an evaluation is to determine the sources and quality of the evidence. Although much evidence may be collected, the evaluator should be sure to collect the most relevant and valid evidence.

A concern in gathering evidence is to make certain that the evidence collected presents a balanced and comprehensive view of the program and its impact. There is a tendency to give undue attention to forcefully or articulately presented, positive or negative, extreme views about a program. The evaluator should make certain that the final evaluation report is balanced and represents the typical or average view about the program. There is also a tendency to focus evaluation data on specific components of a program that may be positive or negative rather than on judging the worth of the overall program and its components.

The programmer should also be concerned about the validity and reliability of the evidence collected. Evidence should be logically accepted as a measure or indicator of the issues being addressed in the evaluation. The validity of the evidence in evaluation studies is often not well thought out. Validity basically asks the question: Is the evidence being collected a true indicator of the issue being addressed? For example, if one issue of the evaluation of a swimming program is to document participant achievement, then a piece of evidence would be some measure of the participants' swimming skills.

Reliability of the evidence must also be assured. To be reliable, the evidence must be accurate and consistent. Reliable instruments allow one to obtain consistent results each time the instrument is used. For example, a rubber yardstick would not yield consistent measurement of distance and would therefore be unreliable because it would not allow consistent results.

At some point, the programmer is going to try to demonstrate that participation in a program led to certain outcomes. Establishing cause and effect is one of the most difficult social science problems. It requires that three propositions be dealt with simultaneously—time-order, covariation, and control of rival causal factors (Denzin 1979). To establish cause and effect, one must establish that the cause came before the effect, that is, time-order. In evaluating program services this is usually accomplished because the program occurs before the observation or measurement of effect. One must also establish covariation between the presumed cause and effect: for every change in the cause, there is corresponding change in the effect. If the presumed cause leads to little or no change in the effect, one cannot assert a cause-and-effect relationship. The final proposition is controlling for rival causal factors. One must be able to demonstrate that participation in the program–not some other possible explanation–is what led to the observed change in the effect.

These three propositions are best controlled through the use of good research design. Although it is not intended that this be a research text, some elementary knowledge of research design can enable the evaluator to develop better evaluations. A frequently used research design is schematically represented in Exhibit 18-3 on page 392. The X represents the treatment or program and the letter O represents observation or measurement. This research design is known as a one-shot case study (Campbell and Stanley 1963). With this design, a program occurs, and then measurement occurs after the program. This is the typical scenario in many leisure service agencies in which program evaluations are completed at the end of a program.

Although this design does control for time-order—the treatment occurs before measurement of the presumed effect— it does not control for covariation or rival causal factors. Since there is no measurement before the program, there is no baseline data with which to compare the postprogram measurement. It is therefore difficult to demonstrate that participation led to the observations obtained in the postprogram measurements. In addition, without a preprogram test, it is difficult to assert that participation led to the obtained postprogram measurements, because one does not know if participation led to the changes or if some other rival causal factor led to the observed change. For example, the postprogram scores could have been a result of the participants' previously obtained skill and have nothing to do with their participation in the current program.

Exhibit 18-3.
One-Shot Case Study Research Design

X   O

Some of the problems with a one-shot case study design can be addressed with a one-group pretest-posttest design (Campbell and Stanley 1963), diagrammed in Exhibit 18-4. In this design, a pretest is introduced, and the programmer now has some baseline data with which to compare postprogram results. This design enables programmers to better demonstrate the effect of the program because they can now document the change, using measurements taken before and after participation. In this case, covariation is easier to demonstrate. The problem of possible rival causal factors accounting for the change rather than the program itself still remains, however.

Exhibit 18-4.
Pretest-Posttest Research Design

O   X   O

Many of the problems associated with the previous research designs can be dealt with in the classical pretest-posttest control group design (Campbell and Stanley 1963), illustrated in Exhibit 18-5 on page 384. This design features the addition of a control group (the group not receiving the treatment) to the previous design. It also features randomized assignment (R) of subjects either to the experimental group (the group receiving the treatment or participating in the program) or to the control group. With this design, it is possible to control for time-order, to demonstrate covariation between the experimental treatment and the assumed result, to document the possible effects of rival causal factors. For example, if the control group shows changes in the pretest and posttest scores similar to the experimental group one would begin to question whether the experimental treatment was having any effect on the changes observed or whether these changes were being caused by other factors.

Exhibit 18-5.
Classical Experimental Research Design

R	O	X	O
R	O		O

One problem with this design is that treatment or participation in a program is withheld from the control group. This is obviously a difficult set of circumstances to deal with in leisure service agencies. Patrons register for programs to receive services, not to have them withheld! One can deal with this problem in the following manner. First, the research design diagrammed in Exhibit 18-6 can be used instead of the design diagrammed in Exhibit 18-5. The design in Exhibit 18-6 includes all of the features of the design in Exhibit 18-5, but treatment for the control group is added after the experiment. In this way, all who initially registered eventually receive the program. To administer such a scheme would require informing participants at the time of registration that they were participating in an experiment and that they would be randomly assigned to different groups who will receive the program at different times.

Exhibit 18-6.
Modified Classical Experimental Research Design

R	O	X	O		
R	O		O	X	O

Programmers often get the impression that pretest-posttest social science studies must be conducted on each program operated in order to evaluate services. This is not the case. The effects of a program service should be documented initially, but, once it is established that a specific program service leads to predictable outcomes, it is unnecessary to document these outcomes each time. After cause and effect have been established, one may return to using the first design outlined (Exhibit 18-3, page 392) and simply document that participants have had the predicted outcomes. In this way, program outcomes are continually monitored and documented.

A final concern regarding the collection of evidence is establishing the credibility of the programmer as an evaluator. When people evaluate programs they are responsible for developing, there are inherent conflicts of interest. The credibility of the programmer as an evaluator will be compromised if there is no ongoing critical review and analysis of program services. If only glowing successes are reported in evaluation reports, the programmer's credibility as an evaluator will be in question.

Data-Gathering: How Is Evidence to Be Collected?

In this section we will discuss how the evidence is to be obtained, how to actually collect the data, when to collect the data, how much to obtain, and from whom.

Techniques for Data Collection

There are many ways of collecting data for evaluation studies. Techniques that could be used include questionnaires, interviews, conversations, observation schedules, participant observation, anecdotal data, standardized tests, checklists, and rating scales. Programmers most frequently collect data by using questionnaires they have designed, talking to patrons to obtain feedback about program services, and through on-site observation of programs. These three strategies produce a good assortment of data to use in judging program worth.

However, typical data collection practices have several flaws. First, the questionnaires are usually not validated instruments for data collection. The validity and reliability of the instrument is usually not established in any meaningful way. Second, discussions with patrons and observations of ongoing programs are usually not guided by an interview or observation schedule. Often, each program supervisor in an agency conducts different interviews and looks for different items when observing programs in operation. Evaluation practice in agencies could be greatly improved by using validated instruments and by increasing the reliability of the interview and observation methods.

Instrument validation is a technical matter beyond the scope of this book. However, validity begins with a conceptual linkage between the issues being investigated and the questions asked on an instrument. When developing instruments, one should constantly review the rationale for including each question and how it logically links to and is a measure of the issues being examined.

Interviews and observations are less formal methods of gathering data. Most programmers handle on-site visitations to programs as public relations exercises in which they deal with any observed problems or emergencies and chat with patrons— listening to any comments, good or bad, that the patron cares to make about the program. Often, each programmer in an agency tends to look for different items for judging how well the program is actually going. To be useful for evaluation, observations and interviews need to be handled more systematically.

When observing, the programmer may function in any one of the following modes: passive, covert observer; an active, participant-observer; or an overt, full participant (Howe 1993). Each of these modes provides a variety of depths of involvement and access to the actual experience of participants. In any case the primary techniques are careful observation of peoples' activities and recording them, i.e. taking field notes.

Interviewing individuals during these visits is not simply a time to chat with patrons. They should be considered a guided conversation (Howe 1993) that is driven by a structured or unstructured interview schedule. The use of a conversationalist demeanor is a conscious effort to establish a rapport that elicits the information needed. Both of these naturalistic evaluation methods can be made more systematic and reliable by using the following techniques.

•Identify specific observation tasks or interview items.

All programmers who will be involved in interviewing or observing programs should jointly develop the necessary interview forms and observation schedules. The result of this will be the development of comprehensive schedules that incorporate the collective wisdom of all program supervisors. Furthermore, everyone who conducts an interview or observation will be examining the same items. This increases the reliability of the process. Variation will no longer be the result of who actually conducts the interview or makes the observation.

•Have detailed instructions about how to make observations.

Getting uniformity of practice in conducting the interview or observation also contributes to reliability. With good instructions, it should not matter who actually conducts the interview or makes the observation—the results should be similar.

•Train and prepare staff for making observations and conducting interviews.

Have staff members make independent observations of the same event, using a jointly developed schedule, and then collaborate in comparing how and why they scored the event the way they did. The objective is to get consistency of results or inter-rater reliability.

•Require immediate and detailed reports.

Recording observations immediately after making them is necessary in order to have accurate reports. Recalled observations are often less accurate than those recorded immediately.

•Validate the observations.

Information obtained through interviews or observations should always be validated. This is accomplished by seeking out additional verification of the information from other independent sources. Interviewers should try to discover if other patrons hold the same view or try to find additional incidents of what has been observed. In either case, one is attempting to determine whether the reported or observed characteristic is typical of the program or is a single occurrence.

Data-gathering practices currently used in agencies are not unacceptable, but the techniques can be improved. Improving them will result in more reliable and valid data on which to make judgments of worth.

Drawing a Sample

Gathering data almost always involves drawing a sample. There is a belief among program practitioners that drawing a sample means handing out questionnaires to whoever can be easily reached or whoever wants to complete them. Practitioners have little understanding of how to implement a random sampling procedure and even less confidence that doing so is necessary in the first place. Random sampling improves data in a number of ways. One of the most important is that it is the surest way to obtain a sample that is representative of the patron group you wish to characterize.

Given the question—How can one characterize the views of a whole population by simply getting information from a few members of the population—the answer is random sampling. Understanding random sampling is not complicated, and once the rationale for drawing a random sample is understood, programmers will accept no substitute!

Population is a technical term for a cohort of individuals who are defined with some precision. For example, the members of a programming class could be defined as a population. In this case, since the class probably includes twenty to thirty individuals, one would probably not draw a sample but would conduct a census to obtain data from the entire population. A population could also be defined as all freshmen at a university, all undergraduates at a university, or everyone registered at a university. At some point, as the population increases in size, conducting a census becomes increasingly difficult and expensive.

The sampling problem then becomes one of trying to find out the information that would have been obtained in a census, but by gathering data from a sample instead of from the entire population. When a sample is collected, one can never be sure of obtaining the true value that would have been obtained through a census. Actually, one obtains an estimate of what the population value might be. There are many ways of determining who might be included in a sample from the entire population.

A sample could include only those whose names begin with A. It could include only those whose social security number begins with an odd number. It could include the first 500 patrons to come to a swimming pool on a Sunday. One can always devise a method for obtaining a sufficient number of individuals to make up a sample. The question is: Are they representative of the entire population?

Using random selection procedures increases the probability that the sample selected will be representative of the population from which it is drawn. This occurs because random selection is not a helter-skelter method as is popularly believed. It is a precise method of selection in which every individual in the defined population has an equal and independent chance of being selected for the sample. Because of this, samples selected through random selection procedures have the highest probability of being representative of the population from which they are drawn. Three methods for drawing a random sample will be discussed: simple random sampling, systematic sampling with a random start, and matrix sampling.

Simple random sampling

Drawing a simple random sample involves several steps. First, it is necessary to have a consecutively numbered sample frame (a list) of the entire population. In leisure program evaluation studies this is frequently possible because the programmer is often gathering data from individuals who have registered for a program. A list of registered participants can be used as the sample frame.

The second step is to determine how large a sample to draw. There is no simple answer to this question. However, as the size of the population decreases, the proportion of individuals to be included in the sample must increase. For example, to make certain there is good representation of a group of fifteen individuals, it would be necessary to sample approximately 50 percent of the population of fifteen. Yet polling organizations will often use a sample of 2,000 to represent the entire population of the United States. A general rule of thumb is that for populations under 500 a sample of 50 percent of the population should be drawn; from 500 to 1,500, approximately 30 percent; from 1,500 to 2,500, 25 percent; and over 2,500, 400 individuals should be sufficient. The reader is cautioned that these figures are very gross recommendations and that developing a sampling plan is a technical matter that depends on a number of factors. The help of a qualified statistician should be sought for recommendations on a specific data collection problem.

The third step is to randomly select individuals from the sample frame to be included in the sample. This is done by first identifying the range of digits needed in sample numbers. For example, a sample of 20 from a population of 100 would need 20 three-digit numbers from 001 to 100. Twenty randomly selected numbers from these 100 would identify the individuals to be included in the sample. To sample from a population of 1,000, one would need four-digit numbers ranging from 0001 to 1,000. And so on for any size population.

A table of random digits is used to randomly select the sample (a table of random digits can be found in any statistics book). Determine in advance the direction in which to move through the table after selecting the first number, close your eyes, point to a number in the table, and then open your eyes. This is the first number, but it may not be usable if it does not include a number within the desired range. For example, if the first three-digit number selected was 301, it could not be used to select a sample of 20 from a population of 100. One must then systematically move through the table of random digits until the desired number of usable numbers is identified. Any duplicate numbers are simply ignored.

With this procedure, each person in the population has an equal and independent chance of being included in the sample. If one assumes that all information desired is randomly distributed throughout the entire population, then a random sample thus drawn is the best method of assuring that data being gathered will also be randomly distributed throughout the sample.

This method works fine for small samples, but it becomes cumbersome with samples larger than 100. There are computer programs that can do this procedure. However, many times the sampling technique presented below will be used instead.

Systematic sampling with a random start

Systematic sampling with a random start is used to select a sample from a sample frame with many individuals. With this procedure, one actually selects only one random number and then every Kth individual from the sample frame. The Kth individual is determined by the sample interval, which is identified before the sampling procedure begins.

This method is useful in many situations encountered in evaluating recreation programs. For example, how might a sample be selected from a softball league with 1,200 participants? The league consists of 100 teams with 12 individuals on each team roster.

The first step is to determine the size of the sample to be drawn. With a population of 1,200, the sample should be at least 30 percent of the population, or 360 individuals ($.30 \times 1,200 = 360$). The next step is to determine the sample interval or the number between each player selected for inclusion in the sample. To determine the sample interval, divide the population by the desired sample size, thus $1,200 - 360 = 3.33$. This means that every 3.33rd individual would be selected. Since this is not possible, go to the nearest whole number, which in this case is every third individual. Generally, one would select the interval that would yield the larger sample, since one would not want a sample smaller than was originally determined.

The next step is to consecutively number individuals on team rosters. For example, each of the 100 team rosters would probably be numbered from 1 through 12. If all of the rosters were arranged in order, the individuals could be numbered from 0001 through 1,200. Arranging the rosters in this manner and consecutively numbering the team members develops a sample frame.

Then, a table of random digits should be used to select the first number to be included in the sample in the same manner as described for collecting a simple random sample. Once the first number is identified, then every Kth individual is selected for inclusion in the sample. In this case, every third number from the first number is selected. If the first usable number identified from a table of random digits is 1,195, then this individual is included in the sample. One then proceeds and includes every third individual from this individual, including the 1,198, 0001, 0004, 0007, 0010, and so on until the entire sample is drawn.

Although this technique technically violates the assumption of a random sample, that is, that every individual has an equal and independent chance of selection, it is frequently used. With this technique, there is actually only one randomly selected individual. This technique is frequently used because it is an expedient method for selecting a sample. However, because of inherent problems with the method, one must be cautious. It is especially important to understand how the lists being used to draw the sample are arranged. For example, if the first person on the rosters discussed above is the team captain and if the first number randomly selected and the interval being used cause the first person on the roster to continuously be included in the sample, it may be advisable to select a new starting point. If it does not matter that team captains are heavily represented in the sample, then the problem can be ignored. The point is that this method can create problems, and the programmer must be on guard against biasing results with the sampling method.

This technique is also useful for creating a sample from a population of unknown individuals. To do this, there must be a system for numbering individuals. For example, this method could be used to randomly draw a sample from all who were going to attend a garden show. The first step would be to estimate the total number of individuals who might attend the show, let us assume approximately 5,000. In this case, it would be necessary to draw a sample of 400 from the estimated 5,000 attendees. Assuming that entry to the garden show would involve purchasing a ticket at a controlled access point, one could consecutively number every individual who purchased a ticket, or sell consecutively numbered tickets in the first place. These tickets, numbered from 0001 through 5,000, are the sample frame.

Next, determine a sample interval: $5,000 - 400 = 12.5$. Thus every twelfth ticket purchaser will be sampled. One then proceeds as described above to identify the numbers of individuals who will be interviewed by randomly selecting the first individual and then identifying all remaining individuals by successively taking every Kth individual (in this case every twelfth individual). This technique can be applied in many situations that recreation programmers face and will result in data superior to other less systematic methods.

Matrix sampling

Matrix sampling is also useful in many situations, especially for sampling from populations who use drop-in facilities with no controlled access point or ticket sales. For example, how does one randomly sample users of a park that is open from 6:00 a.m. to 10:00 p.m. daily? To do so, a sample frame must be established by creating a matrix of time blocks x days of the week and consecutively numbering the time blocks. Exhibit 18-7 illustrates such a matrix. In this matrix, there are 112 possible times (16 hours x 7 days = 112) to collect data in this facility. One then decides what percentage of the total time blocks will be sampled. At this point, time slots during which individuals will be contacted are being discussed. Since people are the actual units of analysis, the numbers cited above can be used only as a rough guide for determining the sample size. Unless there are accurate data about when and how many people use the area, it will be necessary to initially sample rather heavily to make certain the sample obtained is truly representative of the typical users of the area.

Exhibit 18-7.
Sampling Matrix for Park Area

Days of the Week

Time	M	T	W	TH	F	SA	SU
6:00	1	2	3	4	5	6	7
7:00	8	9	10	11	12	13	14
8:00	15	16	17	18	19	20	21
9:00	22	23	24	25	26	27	28
10:00	29	30	31	32	33	34	35
11:00	36	37	38	39	40	41	42
12:00	43	44	45	46	47	48	49
1:00	50	51	52	53	54	55	56
2:00	57	58	59	60	61	62	63
3:00	64	65	66	67	68	69	70
4:00	71	72	73	74	75	76	77
5:00	78	79	80	81	82	83	84
6:00	85	86	87	88	89	90	91
7:00	92	93	94	95	96	97	98
8:00	99	100	101	102	103	104	105
9:00	106	107	108	109	110	111	112

In this case, it would be reasonable to begin with a sample of 40 percent of the time slots. This would result in 45 of the 112 possible time slots being selected for sampling (112 x .40 = 44.8). Once this is determined, it is a matter of using the method outlined in the section on a simple random sample to randomly select 45 time slots from the population of 001 to 112 time slots for inclusion in the sample.

Implementing randomization sampling methods will greatly improve the quality of data collected in program evaluations. Random sampling is the best method for assuring that the sample is representative of the whole population. Now complete Exercise 18-3.

Exercise 18-3.
Drawing a Sample

Outline how a sample would be obtained to evaluate the following two programs:

- A Spring Fling one-day special event to be held at a fair grounds with a controlled access point. Approximately 3,000 patrons are expected to purchase tickets.
- A public swimming pool operation. The pool is in operation for a public swim from 1:00 p.m. through 9:00 p.m. daily for 90 days during the summer season. Normally, the pool has 30,000 daily users during a season.

In class, discuss the following questions in analyzing your sampling outline:

- Does your sampling plan use a randomized method for selecting the sample?
- Have you planned to obtain a sufficiently large sample?
- How will you avoid sampling individuals twice in the public swimming program?

Data Sources

When sources of data are being identified, information should be obtained from people who are in a position to have the information desired. Many may have an opinion about the quality of a program, and it is important to obtain a variety of viewpoints. However, some individuals are better situated than are others to know what actually happened in a program. For example, the program participants, the program leader, and the program supervisor who made occasional visits while the program was in operation are all in a position to have firsthand information about what actually occurred. The evaluator should therefore identify the sources where the most knowledge may be obtained and make certain that evidence is systematically collected from these sources. Additional information collected from other sources can then be used to provide further insight and to validate the data obtained from the primary information sources.

Other Considerations in Data Collection

A final consideration in data collection is to decide when the data will be collected and how intrusive the collections will be. Programmers could collect pretest data at the time of registration, through a mail-out before the start of a program, at the beginning of a program, or at some other time. One can collect postprogram data at the final program session, or through a mail-out shortly after a program has ended.

There are many possibilities for timing data collection. Different results will probably be obtained, depending on when the data are collected. Standard practice is to obtain preprogram data at the time of registration and postprogram data at the final program session. There is some question about this technique, for those individuals who have dropped out of the program are not included in its evaluation. They may have some valuable insight into the program, however. A mail-out to all who originally registered for the program is a costly but more inclusive procedure.

Programmers must also be concerned with how intrusive the evaluation procedure will be. Patrons register for programs to participate in them—not to complete evaluation forms. This is another reason that the evaluation instrument must be well focused in the first place. Patrons will not answer all of the questions the programmer can develop. A general guideline here is that, if the instrument cannot be completed in fewer than ten minutes, it is probably too long and needs to be further revised and focused. There is also an ethical problem: if programmers believe an individual's leisure is important, they will not want to intrude unnecessarily.

Analysis: How Can the Evidence be Analyzed?

After the data are collected, they must be analyzed to determine what they indicate about the program. In this step, the data are placed into a meaningful pattern that gives insight into the worth of the program being evaluated. There are many ways to conduct an analysis. The method chosen should provide insight into the concerns of the evaluation audience and should be appropriate for the type of evidence collected. In addition, the audience should be able to understand the analytical technique. For example, it is not useful to use statistical regression if the evaluation audience has no understanding of this statistical technique.

Because the data to be analyzed will be either quantitative or qualitative, the analysis should be appropriate for the type of evidence gathered. Statistical analysis is one method of placing quantitative data into a meaningful pattern. It should include reporting the distribution of scores (score tallies or percentages of responses in each category), measures of central tendency (mean, mode, and median), measures of dispersion (variance and standard deviation), and measures of association (correlations). Evaluation data analysis is seldom conducted to make predictions about future programs, but is focused instead on reporting current program outcomes, and interpreting the meaning of the documented outcomes.

Quantitative data analysis is useful in analyzing evaluation data, but much of evaluation data is qualitative, naturalistic evidence that must be pieced together into a coherent whole with rhetorical comment. When writing this material, the programmer should remember that its primary purpose is to share the participant's leisure experience with the evaluation audience (Howe 1993). The meaningfulness of qualitative data can often be made apparent by comparing evaluation results with some other known entity. Following are a number of possible comparisons that could make the data more meaningful:

- Time series data: compare program results over time.
- Discrepancy comparisons: compare intended versus actual program inputs, processes, products, outputs, and outcomes.
- Need reduction: compare results obtained with the amount of need in the community. How much need was met (reduced) with the operation of this program?
- Standards: compare program results with established standards, legal mandates, or administrative directives.
- Inter- or intra-agency comparisons: Compare program results with other programs in an agency, or compare the program with similar programs in other agencies.

Techniques that can be used in making these comparisons include critical review, journalistic accounts, historical review, and content analysis. In all data analysis, the primary objective is to develop results in a manner that can give the evaluation audience meaningful insight into the issues of the evaluation so that the worth of the program is made apparent.

Reporting: How Can Evaluation Findings Be Reported?

Communicating the results of an evaluation can take many forms. During the early, formative stages of a program, oral reports and short written reports can be used effectively. Other reporting formats that have been used to give the evaluation audience insights into the program are testimony from participants, movies, still photographs, videotapes, slide shows, and actual participation in the program by the evaluation audience. All of these formats can be used effectively in various situations.

Even though there are many possible reporting formats, the use of a written, summative report with the familiar spiral binding seems to be the most common. This practice is likely to continue because of its universal understandability, its documentary value, and its ease of access. In preparing such a report, the practitioner is faced with many decisions about what to include and how to organize it. Following is a guide for organizing an evaluation report, along with an outline of the recommended content of sections that could be included in the body of such a report.

Recommended Organization

The typical evaluation report should contain the following sections and be organized in the sequence outlined below:

1. Title page
2. Author or authors and their affiliation
3. Evaluation audience—who is to receive the report
4. Executive summary—a one-page summary of the procedures and results
5. Table of contents
6. Lists of tables, figures, and photographs
7. Body of the report
8. Appendices: all items not likely to be available elsewhere, such as survey instruments, data tables, letters of testimony, and newspaper articles
9. References

The Body of the Report

Item number seven, the body of the evaluation report, can contain many different sections. It is not recommended that all sections described in the following paragraphs be included in every report. What will be included should be determined by the purpose of the evaluation, the audience who will receive the report, and the specific process used in the evaluation.

Purpose of the evaluation

Why the evaluation was conducted should be specified in all reports to conceptually outline the framework for the evaluation. Purposes can include program improvement, documenting accountability, improving planning, aiding policy analysis, assessing program impact, aiding managerial monitoring, and justifying continued funding.

Evaluation questions

This section is the next logical extension of the "purpose" section. Here, the reader of the report should be told the major questions asked in the evaluation study and the criteria used to make evaluative judgments of worth.

Description of the program

The history of the program (if it has one) and the setting, including the location, the persons using the service, and the activities of the program, should be outlined. The person writing the report should attempt to portray to the evaluation audience the five Ws and the H of a journalistic story: the who, what, when, where, why and how of the program.

Evaluator's background

This section should be used to establish the credibility of the program's evaluator. Information presented should include the evaluator's affiliation, academic and professional background, a bibliography of other evaluation work or academic work, and an exploration of the evaluator's values and biases. Who the evaluator is and how he or she views the evaluation process should be exposed.

Summary of regulations

A summary—and possibly an interpretation—of federal, state, local, professional, or administrative regulations and directives affecting or mandating the evaluation of the program should be included. Many evaluations undertaken today are mandated because of participation in some externally funded program. A brief explanation of such an arrangement would be in order.

Data-gathering and analytical methods

Regardless of the data-gathering technique used, an accurate and complete description of how the data were collected should be included. Procedures for analyzing the data should also be reported. If social science techniques have been used, the conventions normally applicable to reporting them should be observed. However, depending on who the evaluation audience is, some additional interpretation beyond what is normally required in the academic press may be in order. It is the responsibility of the evaluator to present the evaluation audience with a report that is comprehensible to them.

Findings

Reporting the summarized data and interpreting their meaning should be included in this section. Helping the evaluation audience understand the findings should be paramount in reporting them. It is very important that findings be conceptually integrated into the report. Organizing them around some of the key evaluation issues or questions identified earlier in the report is one very useful method. Others that have been used include organizing results along geographic areas, age groups, and program areas. Again, the only principle to follow is to use the method that leads to the clearest understanding of the findings.

Use of the report

One problem interfering with the use of evaluations has been the lack of action based on evaluation reports. Evaluators can attempt to remedy this situation by making suggestions to the evaluation audience about how the results and the report can be used. Some possible uses would include the following: (1) use the report as a beginning and collect the same evaluation information over time so that time-series data can be developed; (2) release the whole report or sections of it to the press for a public relations program; and (3) use the report as a catalyst for public action on an item of public concern that may have come out of the report. Evaluation takes scarce resources from agencies. The more potential payoffs there are from these expended resources, the more likely an agency is to engage in evaluation.

Contract

Any evaluation done by a consultant from outside an agency should be conducted with an appropriate contract. A copy of this document and a brief review of how the contract has been fulfilled is usually included in the final report.

Conclusions

This is the section where value judgment questions are answered. What was the worth of the program? Evaluation has not occurred until these judgments are made—one has only gathered and reported data up to this point. No matter how scientific the data-gathering phase may have been, evaluation does not occur until the information is integrated with a value system and a judgment made about the program's worth.

In developing this section, stick to the original purpose of the evaluation and the data that have been generated. However, the unintended outcomes often have more impact than the intended ones. Do not hesitate to cite additional findings beyond those mandated by some type of preordinate evaluation design. The report is strengthened if additional audiences that concur with the conclusions can be cited. Letters from participant observers and comments from the staff, the press, and other parties of interest should be used.

Minority reports

Evaluation is not value free. Although one may start with objective data, during the process of evaluation those data are interpreted and the final judgment of worth made with subjective values. Often a significant divergence of opinion can evolve from such studies—issues can be simultaneously good and bad from different perspectives. These differing views may come from a minority of the evaluation team, the program participants, project staff, special interest groups and so forth. Significant dissent should be accommodated in the final report.

Any evaluation study should include the evaluation purpose, questions, methodology, results, findings, and the rationale and logic of the conclusions. As does the scientist, the evaluator exposes the findings, and the logic for alternate interpretation and challenge. Programs supported with public money in a free society should be open to this kind of scrutiny.

Recommendations

What kind of future action should be taken with the program? No firm guidelines about the appropriateness of having evaluators make recommendations has emerged. Usually only three alternatives exist: continue the program as is, continue the program with modifications (at either a higher or lower level than at present), or drop the program. During the investigation, if evaluators discover modifications they believe will strengthen a program, they should be identified in the report. Whether or not to recommend termination or continuation of a program will vary with each situation, and the evaluator will have to make the best decision possible, depending upon prevailing circumstances. Either course of action should be accompanied by a rationale anchored in the purpose and findings of the evaluation.

Additional Considerations

By selecting appropriate sections from the above list, an evaluator should be able to assemble a logical and thorough report. Other points that may help in preparing evaluation reports include:

1. Know when decisions are to be made and submit all reports on a timely basis.
2. Issue formal and informal reports as work progresses.
3. Make informal reporting sessions a time for problem solving.
4. Make the report descriptive so that those unfamiliar with the program can gain insights into its activities.
5. Prepare different reports for different evaluation audiences.
6. Expand on your work by examining collected data to see if they could be reanalyzed and reinterpreted to answer other evaluation questions.

The evaluator, either in house or out of house, must accept the responsibility for presenting the evaluation audience with a final report that is understandable in their terms and frame of reference. The foregoing discussion will give evaluation report writers a coherent framework that can be used in organizing an evaluation report.

The preceding outline for planning an evaluation is a useful guide for developing an evaluation. It is also useful for analyzing the suitability of an existing evaluation model for a specific evaluation project. There are many things to consider in planning an evaluation. The preceding discussion will help the programmer organize and focus the evaluation effort.

Conclusion

Evaluations of program services are conducted by programmers to aid in program development, to help better manage the programming organization, and to provide accountability for program services. A nine-step procedure for planning an evaluation was outlined. These steps may be used for planning an evaluation or analyzing an existing evaluation model.

All evaluations can be improved by using better research designs, randomized methods of obtaining a sample, and schedules for obtaining observation and interview data. How to improve each of these techniques was discussed in the chapter.

References, Chapter Eighteen

Campbell, D. T., and J. C. Stanley. 1963. *Experimental and Quasi-Experimental Designs for Research.* Chicago: Rand McNally.

Denzin, N.K. 1979. *The Research Act.* (2nd ed.). New York: McGraw-Hill.

Grotelueschen, A.D., D.D. Gooler, A.B. Knox, S. Kemmis, I. Dowdy, and K. Brophy. 1974. *An Evaluation Planner.* Urbana: Office for the Study of Continuing Professional Education, College of Education, University of Illinois at Urbana-Champaign.

House, E.R. 1977. *The Logic of Evaluative Argument* (N.7) Los Angeles, CA: Center for the Study of Evaluation, University of California.

Howard, D.R., and J.L. Crompton. 1980. *Financing, Managing and Marketing Recreation and Park Resources.* Dubuque, IA: Wm. C. Brown.

Howe, C.Z. 1980. Models for Evaluating Public Recreation Programs: What the Literature Shows. *Journal of Physical Education and Recreation* 51(8):36-38.

Howe, C.Z. 1993. The Evaluation of Leisure Programs: Applying Qualitative Methods. *Journal of Physical Education, Recreation, and Dance,* 64 (8), 43-47.

Patton, M.Q. 1978. *Utilization-Focused Evaluation.* Beverly Hills, CA: Sage.

Suchman, E.A. 1967. *Evaluative Research.* New York: Russell Sage Foundation.

Weiss, C.H. 1973. *Evaluation Research.* Englewood Cliffs, NJ: Prentice-Hall.

Worthen, B.R., and J.R. Sanders. 1973. *Educational Evaluation: Theory and Practice.* Belmont, CA:Wadsworth.

Photo courtesy of School-Community Recreation, Madison Metropolitan School District, Madison, Wisconsin.

19

Five Program Evaluation Models

In this chapter, five models for conducting recreation program evaluations are outlined. The five models were chosen because they provide examples of a variety of approaches to leisure service evaluation. Many other evaluation models are in use, but these five provide the reader with a good background about how recreation program evaluation may be approached. Each model is accompanied by the evaluation outline explicated in the previous chapter to explain the logic and technique of each model.

Importance-Performance Evaluation

Importance-performance analysis was reported by Martilla and James (1977) as a useful technique for examining the desirability of product attributes. The technique is based on research findings demonstrating that participant satisfaction is a function of both patron expectations about attributes of a program they consider important and patron judgments about their experience of agency performance on these attributes. In importance-performance evaluation, patrons are administered a test before their participation in a program to determine which program attributes are most important to them. Patrons are also administered a postprogram test with the same items included on the preprogram test. The purpose of the postprogram measurement is to determine how well the agency performed in delivering the identified program attributes.

One of the most useful features of the technique is the method used for reporting results. Results of the pre- and post-measurements are plotted on a two-dimensional matrix, as illustrated in Figure 19-1, page 416. Importance data are plotted on the vertical axis of the matrix. The resulting quadrants are named (in clockwise order from the upper left-hand quadrant) "concentrate here," "keep up the good work," "possible overkill," and "low priority."

Figure 19-1.
Importance-Performance Scoring Matrix

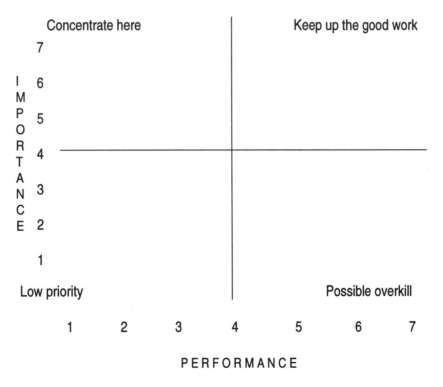

Importance-Performance Scoring Matrix

Where each piece of data is plotted is a function of both its importance to the patrons and their judgment about how well the agency performed on delivering the attribute. Data reported in the "concentrate here" quadrant represents attributes that were important to patrons but were not, in the patrons' judgment, delivered well by the agency. Data reported in the "keep up the good work" quadrant were important to the patrons, and in their judgment were delivered well by the agency. Similarly, the logic of the remainder of the matrix can be ascertained.

Importance-Performance Evaluation Plan

The evaluation plan for importance-performance evaluation follows.

1. Purpose: The purpose is to judge the worth of agency performance in providing program services based on patron perceptions about the importance of program attributes and performance of the agency on selected attributes. This technique is particularly useful for formative evaluation of new, developing program services or the evaluation of existing services whose attendance may have dwindled.

2. Audience: Program supervisors and administrators are the most likely audience for this evaluation technique. Importance-performance evaluation is very useful for program development and for monitoring how well the agency is meeting patron expectations. It is not especially useful for establishing agency accountability, nor does it produce a good comprehensive, summative evaluation.

3. Process: The first step is to develop a list of key program attributes to examine. There are three recommended sources for obtaining these attributes: a review of the literature for the program being evaluated, knowledgeable staff, and focus group interviews with patrons. Developing a list of pertinent program attributes on which to judge the worth of program services is a very important step in this evaluation model and one that should be given sufficient attention. The second step is to develop an instrument to measure how important these attributes are to potential patrons and to collect the importance data. The third step is to develop an instrument to collect performance data from patrons and then to actually collect the data. The items included on the performance instrument are the same items included on the importance instrument, but with some modification for verb tense and other grammatical adjustments to make the instrument read properly. See Exhibit 19-1 on page 418 for an example of importance-performance items. The final step is to plot the data onto the matrix and interpret them.

Exhibit 19-1.
Importance-Performance Items

Importance

How important to you are the following features of our swimming pool program?

		Very important			Important		Not important	
1.	Low admission for public swimming.	7	6	5	4	3	2	1
2.	Opportunity to take swimming lessons to improve your swimming.	7	6	5	4	3	2	1
3.	Cleanliness of pool.	7	6	5	4	3	2	1
4.	Opportunity to meet new people.	7	6	5	4	3	2	1

Performance

How well were you satisfied with the agency's performance on the following items?

OR

Below are various features of our public swimming program. How well did the agency perform on these items?

		Very satisfied			Satisfied		Not satisfied	
1.	Keeping the cost of admission for public swimming low.	7	6	5	4	3	2	1
2.	Providing lessons for improving your swimming.	7	6	5	4	3	2	1
3.	Providing a clean pool.	7	6	5	4	3	2	1
4.	Providing opportunities to meet new people.	7	6	5	4	3	2	1

4. Issues: The issues examined in importance-performance evaluation are patron judgments about how important key program attributes are to their participation in and satisfaction with a specific program. The second issue is patron judgments about how well the agency performed in delivering the key program attributes.

One problem with importance-performance evaluation is the assumption that what is important to patrons in a program is static. Elsewhere in the text it has been established that a program is a dynamic, emergent production. Because of this, patrons may initially be attracted to a program with a set of perceptions about what they consider important. During the course of experiencing a program, however, what is important to patrons may change. Evaluators using this technique should remain cognizant of this possibility.

5. Evidence: The evidence collected is patron perceptions of importance and performance on key program attributes.

6. Data Gathering: Data are gathered with the instruments developed before and after a program. Guadagnolo (1983) reported that the instruments can easily be administered on site and need not be mailed to patrons. He also indicated that the questionnaire seems to be easily understood and is therefore easy to complete, which leads to high return rates.

7. Analysis: Data are analyzed on a matrix, with the vertical axis representing importance and the horizontal axis representing performance. See Figure 19-2 on page 420 for an example of importance-performance analysis.

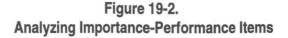

Figure 19-2.
Analyzing Importance-Performance Items

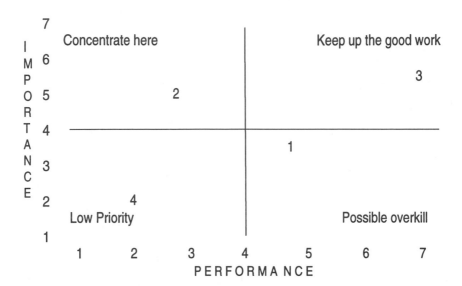

8. Resources: The resources needed to conduct this evaluation include instrument printing, time for instrument development, data collection, analysis, and reporting.

9. Reporting: From the analysis illustrated in Figure 19-2, one can interpret and report results of an importance-performance evaluation. In this case, it is evident that item #1 (a low admission price for swimming) is not an important issue to patrons, but they believe the agency did a good job in keeping the price low. The agency may be doing an overkill on this item. Item #2 (providing lessons to help patrons improve their swimming skills) was an important issue to patrons, but they did not believe the agency did a good job in its instructional program. This is an item on which the agency needs to concentrate. Item #3 (providing a clean pool) was important to patrons, and they believed the agency did a good job. The agency needs to continue performing at its current level on this item. Item #4 (providing opportunities to meet new people) was not important to patrons, and they did

not believe the agency did a good job in helping them meet new people. Since this is not an important issue to the patrons, the agency seems to be performing at an appropriate level, and no change in effort would be warranted.

Similarly, all items included in an importance-performance evaluation are analyzed and reported. The results are easy to interpret and they provide the agency with clear managerial direction. Now complete Exercise 19-1.

Exercise 19-1.
Applying Importance-Performance Evaluation

In class, identify a program to evaluate with the importance-performance evaluation method. Pick a program that is familiar to a significant number of class members. Be sure to jointly consider the following points:

- Is importance-performance evaluation the appropriate evaluation method for the program selected? Why or why not?
- Where were the items to be included in the evaluation obtained? Were patron views about what is important in a program solicited?
- How would a programmer use the information likely to be generated with this evaluation?

Service Hour Evaluation

The service hour approach to program evaluation was developed to expand on the traditional "head count" attendance statistic. This expansion was accomplished by including the amount of time spent in a program, in addition to the actual number of participants. Because of the varying length of time programs are offered, the addition of the time variable enables the final statistic to more accurately reflect the amount of service delivered. For example, a service hour (SH) is one participant (P) in a program for one hour (H). The formula then is:

$$P \quad \times \quad H \quad = \quad SH$$

With this approach, a program with 30 children that lasts for one hour would be credited with delivering 30 service hours. A program with only15 children that lasts for two hours would also get credit for delivering30 service hours. With a "head count" system, the former program would be credited with 30 participants and the latter program with 15 participants. Failure to include the time variable can dramatically alter measurement of the quantity of the agency's service output.

In the service hour approach to program evaluation, both the number of participants and the amount of time they are served are collected. A service hour is the basic unit of output from the leisure delivery system and the unit of analysis used in the service hour evaluation approach.

A classical issue of concern for publicly financed leisure service providers has been the distribution of services along designated variables. The public recreation literature is full of statements about the recommended distribution of services; for example, the program should serve all age groups; a variety of program areas should be offered; and programs should serve both sexes. As part of their statement of purpose, many agencies include statements about providing a variety of leisure opportunities to all ages, income ranges, genders, races, and so forth in the community. However, few systems for recording and analyzing how program services are distributed have been developed. Most agencies therefore have no system for evaluating how well their program distribution policy is being implemented.

Once service hour data are collected, the distribution of the service hours delivered can be analyzed along many variables. Analysis of this distribution makes it possible to evaluate the distribution of agency services. Below are 12 variables that could be tracked in such a system. The first six are classical areas of concern that consistently appear in recreation programming literature as items that must be considered in designing a comprehensive program of services. Their inclusion in the system should be mandatory.

1. Age groups
2. Program areas
3. Program formats
4. Sex of participants

5. Geographic locations
6. Activity
7. Operating division
8. Ethnic background
9. Fee versus service programs
10. Special populations
11. Rank (military rank for use in military recreation)
12. Status, for example, active duty military, family of active duty military, or retirees

Service Hour Evaluation Plan

The evaluation plan for the service hour approach to evaluation follows.

1. Purpose: The purpose is to provide information about the distribution of program services to help improve organizational management and document compliance with agency policy.

2. Audience: Service hour data may be used in different ways by programmers, administrators, and policy makers.

3. Process: Service hour data are collected as a measure of recreation service output and analyzed along selected dimensions of organizational concern.

4. Issues: The issue being examined is the distribution of program services along any dimension selected for analysis. The major issue is the equity of distribution of program services along dimensions identified by the agency.

5. Resources: To operate the evaluation system requires instruments for collection, time to accomplish data collection, time and equipment to analyze data, and materials and time to report and interpret the information collected.

6. Evidence: The evidence collected is the service hour. The service hour is used as the unit of analysis in this evaluation technique.

7. Data Gathering: Data are recorded by program leaders and collected and analyzed by program supervisors or administrators.

8. Analysis: The distribution of program services along selected variables is documented. A variety of analyses that will provide insight into the distribution of services may be completed. In addition, service hour data accumulated over several years provides a database for additional analyses as needed.

9. Reporting: A written report summarized in various ways is used to document the distribution of services in a specific time period along a variety of dimensions. Reports that document changes over time may also be developed.

Implementation

Two forms are used in the system. One is the program activity report (Exhibit 19-2, page 425) and the other is the special event report (Exhibit 19-3, page 426). The special event report is used on all activities such as special events, rentals, and club meetings that do not meet on a regularly scheduled basis as a class would meet. The program activity report is to be used on all programs that require a registration (paid or unpaid) and meet on a regular basis.

Exhibit 19-2.
Service Hour Evaluation Program Activity Report Form

1. Age Group

    01. Preschool (under 5)
    02. Elementary school (5-12)
    03. Junior high (13 and 14)
    04. Senior high (15-17)
    05. Young adult (18-20)
    06. Middle-aged adult (21-40)
    07. Older adult (41-60)
    08. Senior citizen (60-up)
    09. Mixed age group

2. Program Areas
    01. Arts and crafts
    02. Athletics
    03. Dance
    04. Drama
    05. Hobbies and clubs
    06. Language arts
    07. Music
    08. Science and nature
    09. Social recreation
    10. Volunteer services
    11. Special populations
    12. Other

3. Program Formats

    01. Open house
    02. Special event
    03. Skill development
    04. Competition
    05. Clubs and groups
    06. Self-directed, noncompetitive

4. Gender

    01. Males
    02. Females
    03. Coed

5. Geographic Locations

    01. Ace Recreation Center
    02. Banter Recreation Center
    03. Center Recreation Center
    04. Stevenson Recreation Center
    05. Fifth Street School
    06. King School
    07. Veterans Park
    08. Austin Gardens
    09. Maple Park
    10. Trip

6. Operating Division

    01. Athletics
    02. Cultural arts
    03. Maintenance
    04. Neighborhood recreation centers
    05. Senior citizen
    06. Special activities

7. Activity Number

Activity
Dates of operation
Leader
Reporting date

8. Number of leaders
9. Number of individuals enrolled
10. Number of hours of operation
11. Attendance at each session

Session	1	2	3	4	5	6
	7	8	9	10	11	12
	13	14	15	16	17	18

Exhibit 19-3.
Service Hour Evaluation Special Event Report Form

1. Age Group

    01. Preschool (under 5)
    02. Elementary school (5-12)
    03. Junior high (13 and 14)
    04. Senior high (15-17)
    05. Young adult (18-20)
    06. Middle-aged adult (21-40)
    07. Older adult (41-60)
    08. Senior citizen (60-up)
    09. Mixed age group

2. Program Areas

    01. Arts and crafts
    02. Athletics
    03. Dance
    04. Drama
    05. Hobbies and clubs
    06. Language arts
    07. Music
    08. Science and nature
    09. Social recreation
    10. Volunteer services
    11. Special populations
    12. Other

3. Program Formats

    01. Open house
    02. Special event
    03. Skill development
    04. Competition
    05. Clubs and groups
    06. Self-directed, noncompetitive

4. Gender

    01. Males
    02. Females
    03. Coed

5. Geographic Locations

    01. Ace Recreation Center
    02. Banter Recreation Center
    03. Center Recreation Center
    04. Stevenson Recreation Center
    05. Fifth Street School
    06. King School
    07. Veterans Park
    08. Austin Gardens
    09. Maple Park
    10. Trip

6. Operating Division

    01. Athletics
    02. Cultural arts
    03. Maintenance
    03. Neighborhood recreation centers
    05. Senior citizen
    06. Special activities

7. Activity Number

Activity
Dates of operation
Leader
Reporting date

8. Number of leaders
9. Number of individuals enrolled
10. Number of hours of operation
11. Attendance

Each form contains 11 sections of information that must be reported accurately. The variables on which data are to be collected can be chosen by the agency. The variables included in these example forms are for illustration purposes only, although they are considered by most administrators to be very important.

Number 1: Age Group

The agency can nominally define the age group categories it wishes to track. Once service hour data are collected with this tracking information, a report about the number and percentage of service hours delivered to each defined age group can be generated. In a similar way, reports about each additional variable included in the system can be developed.

Number 2: Program Areas

The program activity areas offered by the agency can also be tracked. There are many ways of nominally defining program activity areas, so the agency must select a method that results in a meaningful analysis for its operation.

Number 3: Program Formats

How a program is organized varies from program to program. By tracking this dimension, the agency can ensure that it offers programs in a variety of formats.

Number 4: Gender

By tracking the gender of participants, the agency can determine whether it is providing an equal amount of service for males and females.

Number 5: Geographic Location

Examining the geographic distribution of program services is made possible by tracking the location of services. In this example, specific program sites are identified. If the agency operates so many sites that the list would become too long, some other type of service area designation could be used.

Number 6: Operating Division

In this section, the relative output of various organizational divisions within the agency can be tracked and analyzed.

Number 7: Activity Number

All activities in an agency should be assigned a code number to be reported here. With this information, a report for a specific program could be developed if necessary.

Number 8: Staff

In this section, the number of staff members normally used for operating the program is reported. For most programs this will be one or two. However, for special events it could be a larger number.

Number 9: Enrollment

In this section, the number of individuals enrolled in the program (paid or unpaid) should be recorded. For programs that meet regularly, the number reported here should be the number of people who officially enrolled minus the number who officially withdrew. For special event programs, this section may or may not be applicable.

Number 10: Hours of Operation

This section is used to report the normal length of a session.

Number 11: Attendance

In this section, the count of the actual number of participants attending is reported. For programs that meet on a regular basis, the attendance at each session should be reported. For programs that meet only once, there is just one line for reporting the number of participants.

Reporting Format

Information developed from the service hour evaluation system for programs that meet regularly is reported as illustrated in Exhibit 19-4 on page 429. Information developed for special events is reported as illustrated in Exhibit 19-5, also on page 429.

Exhibit 19-4.
Program Attendance Report Format

Activity (name)   Geographic location (name)
Age group (name)   Program format (name)
Program area (name)   Operating division (name)

A.   Enrollment
B.   Sessions (number of sessions)
C.   Total attendance
D.   Average session attendance
E.   Percentage of attendance
F.   Service hours
G.   Staff hours
H.   Efficiency ratio

Explanation:

A.   Enrollment (given)
B.   Sessions (given)
C.   Total attendance (add attendance at all sessions)
D.   Average session attendance (divide total attendance by the number of sessions)
E.   Percentage of attendance (divide total attendance by potential attendance)
F.   Service hours (normal session length x total attendance)
G.   Staff hours (normal session length x number of staff x number of sessions)
H.   Efficiency ratio (service hours - staff hours)

Exhibit 19-5.
Special Event Report Format

(If enrollment was required for the program, the report will be identical to the Program Activity Report Format. If enrollment was not required the report will be shorter.)

Activity (name)   Geographic location (name)
Age group (name)   Program format (name)
Program area (name)   Operating division (name)

A. Attendance
B. Service hours
C. Staff hours
D. Efficiency ratio

(continued)

Exhibit 19-5.

Explanation:

A. Attendance(given)
B. Service hours (attendance x hours of operation)
C. Staff hours (number of staff x hours of operation)
D. Efficiency ratio (service hours - staff hours)

Application of the Service Hour Approach

Once the foregoing information is collected, an agency's services can be analyzed in many ways. Local needs would be the primary determinant of what reports would be developed. Below are examples of possible uses of the system.

Individual program report

It is possible to develop a report on an individual program, as is illustrated in Exhibit 19-6. This type of a report is valuable in its own right. It can also be compared with reports of previous operations of the same program and with reports of the operation of similar programs within a community recreation system.

Exhibit 19-6.
Service Hour Report on an Individual Program

Recreation Center Girls Softball Tournament

Girls softball	Barrie Recreation Center
Elementary school	Tournament or leagues
Athletics	Athletics division
Females	

A.	Enrollment	21	E.	Percentage of attendance	76%
B.	Sessions	12	F.	Service hours	288
C.	Total attendance	192	G.	Staff hours	18
D.	Average session attendance	16	H.	Efficiency ratio	16

Activity summary

It is possible to summarize all girls' softball tournaments and develop a report as illustrated in Exhibit 19-7. This technique could be used for any activity tracked.

Other summaries

It is possible to summarize your entire operation along any of the variables used for tracking. For example, the programmer could tell how many service hours were offered on an annual, monthly, or weekly basis to each age group or to which gender and at what locations. Through these comparisons over time and with each other, one can begin to see overloads and deficiencies in the distribution of program services. The major problem is to focus the reports that will actually be developed so that the agency is not overloaded with information.

Exhibit 19-7.
Service Hour Activity Summary Report

Girls Softball Tournaments Summary

Girls softball (summary)   All locations
Elementary school   Tournament or leagues
Athletics   Athletics division
Females

A.	Enrollment	145	E.	Percentage of attendance	77%
B.	Sessions	12	F.	Service hours	2,016
C.	Total attendance	1,344	G.	Staff hours	126
D.	Average session attendance	16	H.	Efficiency ratio	16

Attention-directing uses

The percentage of attendance statistic and the efficiency ratio are both designed as attention-directing devices. These devices will alert the programmer to areas that may need further investigation. The percentage of attendance is calculated by dividing potential attendance (the number who enrolled in a class and should be attending) into actual attendance.

The second attention-directing device deals with staff efficiency. It identifies how many staff hours it took to produce the service hours delivered. The smaller the ratio number, the more staff time it takes to produce one hour of service. A ratio of 1 would indicate that it takes one hour of staff time to produce one service hour.

It is assumed that a community would, over time, identify an acceptable level of percentage of attendance and staff efficiency ratio. Any programs below a specified level would be examined further to try to ascertain the problem. Both of these attention-directing devices achieve meaning only on a comparative basis within an individual agency.

The service hour approach to evaluation assumes that it is important to track the distribution of program service output along a number of different variables. The worth of an agency's distribution of service can be judged with the data developed using this system. The system does not address program quality, and this is one of the weaknesses of the method. It does, however, provide a quantitative measure of service output that can be analyzed to provide information to help improve the management of the agency. It can also provide data to use in helping the agency remain accountable.

Satisfaction-Based Evaluation

Satisfaction-based program evaluation provides data about participant satisfaction with program services. These data can be used to judge the worth of program services. The assumption of the technique is that the worth of programs can best be determined by identifying the degree to which programs have provided leisure experiences for participants. Participant-reported satisfaction with leisure engagement is a well-accepted measure of leisure outcome (Beard and Ragheb 1979; Christensen and Yoesting 1977; Driver and Brown 1975; Driver 1977; Hawes 1978; Tinsley, Barrett, and Kass 1977; Tinsley and Kass 1978). Thus participant-reported satisfaction with leisure programs is used in this evaluation technique as a theoretically valid evaluation criterion on which the worth of leisure programs can be judged.

The evaluation plan for satisfaction-based evaluation follows.

1.   Purpose: The purpose of satisfaction-based evaluation is to provide theoretically valid measures of the outcome of leisure engagement. These data can be used to help develop program services and to help the agency account for the outcomes resulting from participation in its program services.

2.   Audience: Program managers, program supervisors, and administrators are the primary audiences this evaluation technique will serve.

3.   Process: The technique requires the collection and analysis of participant-reported satisfaction with programs.

4.   Issues: The major issue investigated by the technique is whether programs are providing leisure experiences. This is determined by investigating the number and types of satisfaction being met by a program.

5.   Resources: The resources needed to conduct the evaluation are a valid and reliable instrument for data collection and the time needed to analyze the data collected.

6.   Evidence: The evidence collected is participant-reported satisfaction with participation in a program.

7.   Data Gathering: Data are gathered by having participants complete an instrument at the end of a program, thereby self-reporting their satisfaction with the program.

8.   Analysis: Satisfaction domains are calculated and the resulting data are analyzed by time-series or program-by-program comparisons.

9.   Reporting: Data can be reported on a program-by-program basis, in a summary report of a programming season, or in an annual report.

Satisfaction Items and Domains

There are currently ten domains with 25 items. They are contained in Exhibit 19-8. Some or all of the domains may be included in an individual evaluation.

Exhibit 19-8.
Satisfaction Domains and Items

Achievement

I learned more about the activity.
It was a new and different experience.
I became better at it.
My skills and ability developed.

Physical Fitness

I enjoyed the physical exercise.
It keeps me physically fit.

Social Enjoyment

I enjoyed the companionship.
Enjoying it with my friends.

Family Escape

Escaping from my family for awhile.
I was able to be away from family.

Environment

The area was physically attractive.
The freshness and cleanliness of the area.
I liked the open space.
The pleasing design of the facility.

Risk

I liked the high risk involved.
I liked the chance for danger.

Family Togetherness

Our family could do this together.
It brought our family together more.

Relaxation

It gave my mind a rest.
I experienced tranquility.
I got to relax physically.

Fun

I had fun.

Autonomy

I had control over things.
I was in control of what happened.
It gave me a chance to be on my own.

The instrument used in the satisfaction-based evaluation technique is contained in Exhibit 19-9 on page 435. The instrument is scored with a seven-point Likert scale. A "not applicable" choice is included in the instrument. This choice allows respondents an alternative when they believe the satisfaction items are inappropriate or not applicable to the specific program they are in. An item investigating the importance of the program to the individual is included to investigate the importance of a program in relation to all of the participant's other leisure pursuits.

Exhibit 19-9.
Leisure Program Evaluation Form

Listed below are statements that may reflect your satisfaction with this program. Please indicate by circling the appropriate number on each scale the degree to which each statement contributed to your satisfaction with this program. Statements that you believe do not apply to this program should be marked by circling the 0 in the Not Applicable column.

	Very satisfying		Satisfying		Contributes no satisfaction		Not applicable
1. I learned more about the activity	7	6	5	4	3	2	1	0
2. I had control over things	7	6	5	4	3	2	1	0
3. The cleanliness of the area	7	6	5	4	3	2	1	0
4. I enjoyed the physical exercise	7	6	5	4	3	2	1	0
5. I enjoyed companionship	7	6	5	4	3	2	1	0
6. I liked the high risks involved	7	6	5	4	3	2	1	0
7. I had fun	7	6	5	4	3	2	1	0
8. It gave my mind a rest	7	6	5	4	3	2	1	0
9. Our family could do this together	7	6	5	4	3	2	1	0
10. Enjoying it with my friends	7	6	5	4	3	2	1	0
11. I experienced tranquility	7	6	5	4	3	2	1	0
12. Escaping from family for awhile	7	6	5	4	3	2	1	0
13. It was a new/different experience	7	6	5	4	3	2	1	0
14. I liked the open space	7	6	5	4	3	2	1	0
15. I liked the chance for danger	7	6	5	4	3	2	1	0
16. The area was physically attractive	7	6	5	4	3	2	1	0
17. I became better at it	7	6	5	4	3	2	1	0
18. It keeps me physically fit	7	6	5	4	3	2	1	0
19. It brought our family together more	7	6	5	4	3	2	1	0
20. I got to relax physically	7	6	5	4	3	2	1	0
21. I was in control of what happened	7	6	5	4	3	2	1	0
22. My skills and ability developed	7	6	5	4	3	2	1	0

(continued)

Exhibit 19-9.

23. I was away from family awhile 7   6   5   4   3   2   1   0
24. It gave me a chance to be on my own 7   6   5   4   3   2   1   0
25. The pleasing design of the facility............7   6   5   4   3   2   1   0

Below are two statements about participating in this program. Please circle a number on each scale that best reflects your view.

1.   Please compare this program with all of your other leisure pursuits. Compared with your other leisure, what priority would you assign this program?

One I would least like to give up						One I would give up first
7	6	5	4	3	2	1

2. Which of the following statements reflects your overall satisfaction with this program?

Delighted	Pleased	Mostly satisfied	Mixed	Mostly dissatisfied	Unhappy	Terrible
7	6	5	4	3	2	1

It is assumed that as a matter of public policy it is preferable to cancel programs that are less important rather than those that are very important to patrons compared with all of their other leisure pursuits. An overall satisfaction item is also included to investigate patrons' overall summative judgment about their satisfaction with a program. Previous use of this form has established that neither gender nor age biases responses to the items.

Scoring the Leisure Program Evaluation Form

A list of individual items and the domains in which they are included appear in Exhibit 19-8, page 434. Domain scores are calculated by simply averaging the items scored in each domain for each respondent. For example, the scores for two subjects on the relaxation domain are illustrated in Exhibit 19-10 on page 437. In this case, subject 1 responded to all three items in the domain. Therefore, the number 3 was used as the divisor in calculating the domain score for subject 1. Subject 2 responded to only two items in the domain, so the number 2 was used as the divisor in calculating the domain score for subject 2.

Exhibit 19-10.
Calculating Satisfaction Domain Scores

Relaxation Domain	Subject 1	Subject 2
8. It gave my mind a rest.	7	4
11. I experienced tranquility.	5	7
20. I got to relax physically.	6	No score
	18	11
	18/3 = 6	11/2 = 5.5

To calculate a domain score across all participants in a single program, an average of all of the scores across all participants is calculated.

Data from the satisfaction-based program evaluation can be used in several different ways. First, the data can document participant-reported program outcomes. With a postprogram administration of the instrument, data about what actually happened to participants in the program can be gathered. Programmers can use the data to document what is actually happening to participants in their programs and to establish accountability with their funding source. The technique provides systematically collected participant-reported outcome data resulting from participation in leisure services. With these data, the programmer does not need to assert the value of a program based on hearsay. Instead, systematically collected data from the participants themselves can be used.

Second, satisfaction data can be analyzed to determine if programmatic goals are being achieved. For example, in one administration of the instrument, the highest rated satisfactions on a Fall Foliage Tour were "fun," "environment," "social enjoyment," and "relaxation" (Rossman 1983). Similar analyses of participant-reported satisfactions with different program services can aid the programmer in investigating whether program services are providing appropriate satisfactions. This use of the technique aids in program development.

Third, satisfaction data from various programs can be compared to investigate the differences in satisfactions provided by different program services. For example, the summarized reported satisfactions for all athletic programs could be compared with similar data for all cultural arts programs. In this way, differences in the type of satisfaction provided by different types of services can be documented. This analysis will help the programmer in organizational management by helping determine appropriate program directions for the agency.

Satisfaction-based program evaluation can be used in several different ways for various purposes. The data collected are participant-reported satisfactions with participation in agency program services. With this technique, judgments about the worth of program services are made using data collected directly from participants in the program. Now complete Exercise 19-2.

Exercise 19-2.
Using Satisfaction-Based Program Evaluation Data

In class, choose a program to evaluate with satisfaction-based program evaluation. Consider the following points:

- Is satisfaction-based program evaluation the most appropriate evaluation method to use for this program?
- How will the worth of a program be documented with satisfaction-based evaluation data?
- Which purpose of evaluation will be used to focus the evaluation?

Goal and Objective Evaluation

Using goals and objectives to evaluate program services is a process evaluation model that is a logical extension of the use of goals and objectives for program management and design purposes covered previously in Chapters Four, Seven, and Nine. The procedures recommended are based on the discrepancy evaluation method explicated by Stake (1967) and Provus (1979) and applied to the evaluation of therapeutic recreation programs by Peterson and Gunn (1984). Because it is a process model, the content of the goals and objectives are not specified. What follows, then, is a framework for the process.

There are three features to the model that make it a distinct method.

1. Goals and objectives are developed hierarchically ending with precisely specified expected outcomes for participants thus enabling a comparison of expected with actual outcomes (Peterson and Gunn 1984). The programmer thereby states what is to be accomplished through the program.
2. The actual operation of a program is compared with its design (Stake 1967). This specific feature requires one to examine not only outcomes but also program inputs and processes. This expands the inquiry into the possible causes of discrepancies.
3. The program standards that form the basis of comparison should be derived from the program staff and the client population served (Provus 1971). The evaluation audience and their value system are thereby incorporated in the evaluation.

Thus, implementation of a discrepancy evaluation model requires well written and valid goals and objectives that may be used to determine the worth of a program. Furthermore, the technique admonishes us to take an expansive view of a program including its inputs, processes, and outcomes rather than a focal, microscopic one focusing on a single feature of the program. When implemented correctly, value inputs from the evaluation audience are incorporated into the overall evaluation plan.

Goal and Objective Evaluation Plan

1. Purpose: The purpose is to judge the worth of program services by examining the discrepancies between the program design and its actual operation.
2. Audience: This method is amenable to most every party of interest provided that the goals and objectives are written to reflect their value perspective. The process is very adaptable but is application sensitive, i.e. it must be implemented correctly to provide the results desired.
3. Process: There are three steps to the discrepancy evaluation method —"... 1) defining program standards; 2) determining whether a discrepancy exists between some aspect of program performance and the standards governing that

aspect of the program; and 3) using discrepancy information either to change performance or to change program
standards" (Provus 1971, p. 183).

4.   Issues: goals and objectives can be developed to measure
inputs, processes, or outcomes. Whether all of these should
be developed depends on the specific program being evaluated.

5.   Evidence: The specific content of the conforming evidence
depends on the type of statement being examined. In each
case, the terminal objective, the final one, in the hierarchy
should be written so the evidence needed to confirm its
accomplishment is evident to the staff and clients associated with the program.

6.   Data Gathering: The techniques used are varied, again
depending on the specific content of the terminal objectives. Techniques typically used are observations of participant behavior, evaluation surveys, attendance or other
types of statistical data, interviews, etc.

7.   Analysis: The primary analytical framework is one of comparing intentions with actual results and noting any discrepancies. How well this can be accomplished is dependent on how clear, specific and measurable the standards
statements are and the thoroughness of the observations
and data collections.

8.   Resources: Two principle resources needed are staff time
and expertise in implementing the method.

9.   Reporting: The typical report is a written document presenting each objective and the data gathered about it. This
should include an analytical statement about whether or
not the standard is met with a notation of any discrepancy
observed and how it is to be reconciled.

Implementation

The use of goals and objective evaluation is predicated on
well-written objectives that are used to determine if actual implementation is congruent with the intentions stated or if there is a
discrepancy. An example is provided in Box D of Figure 9-3 on
page 180. Included there are three program design outcomes for
a guitar class with an example of the terminal performance
objectives that will be used to measure the accomplishment of

design goal #3—At the end of the program, 90% of the students will be able to correctly identify the parts of the guitar.

The procedure then is to conduct the class, determine the percentage of students who can correctly identify the six parts of the guitar and compare the observed level of performance with our stated objective. If 90% or more of the students can correctly identify the six parts of the guitar, there is congruence. If fewer than 90% can identify them, there is a discrepancy.

Determining congruence between intentions and actual performance and noting any discrepancies is the basic method of goal and objective evaluation. However, to thoroughly use the discrepancy approach requires one to not only state behavioral outcomes but to also state program inputs and process goals. Figure 19-3 on page 442 outlines the basic analytical framework for discrepancy evaluation. One can observe in this figure that design goals with measurement objectives are developed for program inputs, processes, and outcomes.

Furthermore, there is an assumed relationship between the inputs to a program, the animation plan, and the outcomes desired. To conduct an evaluation using goals and objectives, then, one determines the congruence between intended versus actual observations of inputs, processes, and outcomes and makes note of any discrepancies for further analysis. In addition, the assumed relationships between inputs, processes, and outcomes are examined to investigate their logic and validity. Any discrepancies are also noted for further analysis.

Discrepancies may be reconciled by changing the intended measure to be more realistic. For example, in the current case, one may modify the design goal so the desired result is that 80% rather than 90% of the students correctly identify the six parts of the guitar. However, omissions in inputs or animation processes may also account for failures in outcomes. For example, one intended input may have been a videotape for each student to take home that explained and showed the parts of the guitar. However, this feature may have been dropped due to budget constraints or to the late arrival of the tapes. Thus, the discrepancy in failing to reach the goal of 90% of the students being able to correctly identify the six parts of the guitar may be explained by an omission in the designed inputs of the program.

A similar analysis may also be demonstrated in how a program was animated. The amount of time in the program

Figure 19-3.
Analytical Framework for Discrepancy Evaluation

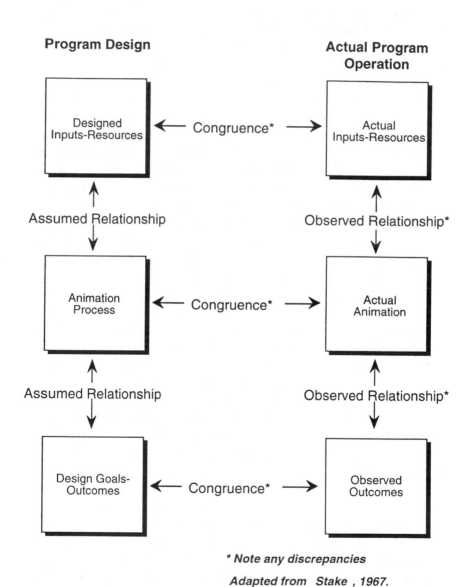

Program Design

Actual Program Operation

Designed Inputs-Resources ← Congruence* → Actual Inputs-Resources

Assumed Relationship   Observed Relationship*

Animation Process ← Congruence* → Actual Animation

Assumed Relationship   Observed Relationship*

Design Goals-Outcomes ← Congruence* → Observed Outcomes

* Note any discrepancies

Adapted from Stake , 1967.

devoted to identifying the parts of the guitar may have been too short, or this labeling activity may not have been reinforced in subsequent lessons. Each of these could account for the failure of 90% or more of the students being able to correctly identify the six parts of the guitar.

Thus, the use of goals and objectives for evaluation is a very flexible technique that can be applied in many situations. It requires well-written goals and objectives that are developed within the framework outlined in order to facilitate making the judgments required to evaluate.

Triangulated Evaluation

Judging the worth of leisure services is a value-laden enterprise. A single program may be viewed as both good and bad at the same time from different perspectives. In addition, many evaluations use a single methodology to gather the data to be reported for evaluation purposes. The technique used in social science to deal with multiple perspectives and realities is triangulation (Denzin 1978; Bullock and Coffey 1980).

The triangulated approach to evaluation assumes that the data need to be gathered from multiple perspectives and with multiple methods. Fuszek (1987) has adopted this strategy in conducting program evaluations in the parks and recreation department in Austin, Texas. Discussing the methodology used in Austin, he states that the "primary emphasis (is) placed upon pragmatic or qualitative assessment—i.e. how do all the parts/ players fit (or not fit) together to achieve program goals—as opposed to relying solely on quantitative measurement or efficiency studies?" (Fuszek 1987). He then outlines seven methods to obtain data for use in judging the worth of program services. When this multiple-perspective, multiple-method approach is undertaken, it will more likely capture the true picture and worth of a program. The technique that follows is but one example of how the concept of triangulation may be applied to the evaluation of leisure services.

This example shows a triangulation of research methods and data sources. The research methods were developed from a series of consulting interviews that the author conducted with programmers in five agencies over the past decade. In these interviews, it was revealed that the two major methods used by programmers in evaluating their programs were observation during on-site inspection of program services and interviews with participants. Both of these methods of data gathering are legitimate, but neither is usually implemented in an appropriate fashion.

Often, different programmers in the same agency look for different items when they make on-site visits. Therefore, there was no reliability of observations. The first step in improving this method of data gathering is to have program supervisors jointly develop a single observation schedule of what needs to be examined when observing program operations. Training program supervisors in observation data-gathering methods, as discussed in Chapter Eighteen, is also necessary to improve this technique.

The second technique used by programmers was to talk to patrons. Often these contacts were very informal, public relations exercises rather than data-gathering sessions. Again, there were often as many different interview agendas as there were supervisors. In many cases, program supervisors simply chatted about whatever the patrons wanted to discuss. To improve this method of data gathering, an interview schedule should be developed. Admittedly it is somewhat intrusive to have program supervisors with clipboards interviewing patrons in program services. At the very least, supervisors should have a few focused questions they want answered in these discussions. In addition to being viewed as public relations exercises, these discussions should be considered opportunities to gather data about the quality of program services from a primary data source—the patron.

Program supervisors should be prepared to validate unanticipated information they may gather in these interviews. Information is validated by pursuing and verifying or refuting information from additional sources—usually other patrons. Material gathered with this technique will be a combination of information the programmer was seeking and information that patrons have on their minds. In either case, the information should be validated by being verified from multiple sources.

The third method of gathering data is through a questionnaire. Two instruments are recommended, one administered to participants and the other to face-to-face leaders. Gathering data with instruments either through a census or a survey is the third method of data collection in the triangulated evaluation approach.

In addition to triangulating methods, it is recommended that data sources also be triangulated. In selecting sources of information, one needs to identify individuals who are the most knowledgeable about what actually occurred in a program. Some experienced programmers believe they can assess the worth of a program service by their own observation and analysis. A triangulated approach assumes that, in order to get a more complete picture about the worth of a program, one must obtain data from multiple perspectives. Furthermore, the approach assumes that some sources of information are better situated than others to have primary knowledge about what actually occurred in a program and are therefore better sources of information. Part of triangulated evaluation, then, is identifying primary data sources and designing instruments and techniques for aggressively and systematically gathering information from these sources.

In the current example, the three most knowledgeable sources are assumed to be the face-to-face program leader, who has direct, first-line contact with a program; the program supervisor, who makes frequent supervisory contact with a program; and patrons, who are actually experiencing the service. They are therefore the three sources to be systematically pursued. Instruments and techniques for gathering data from these sources have been developed and are illustrated and discussed below.

Triangulated Evaluation Plan

The plan for the triangulated evaluation procedure is outlined below.

1. Purpose: The purpose of the triangulated approach to evaluation is to help program supervisors in making disposition decisions about program services. The data gathered in this approach provide the programmer with information for determining whether to drop, modify, or continue without change a program service. The technique helps

with program development and organizational management.

2. Audience: Program supervisors and program administrators are the primary audiences for this evaluation technique.

3. Process: The process involves the collection of evaluation data from three sources with three data collection techniques and the summary analysis of this information.

4. Issues: Program leader, program supervisor, and patron views about program outcomes, inputs, and processes are examined.

5. Resources: Instruments for data gathering, training in how to use the instruments, and time for data collection and analysis are all necessary.

6. Evidence: Leader observations, supervisor observations and interview data, and patron-reported satisfactions with outcomes and arrangements as selected by the program supervisor are all collected.

7. Data Gathering: Three instruments are provided, including the recreation leader/instructor evaluation form (Exhibit 19-11, page 447), the recreation program observation schedule (Exhibit 19-12, page 450), and the recreation participant evaluation form (Exhibit 19-13, page 452).

8. Analysis: The data are analyzed on the program evaluation summary format (Exhibit 19-14, page 453).

9. Reporting: The final report is written according to the format outlined in Exhibit 19-14.

Instruments

Three instruments are used in the triangulated evaluation procedure. The first is the recreation leader/instructor evaluation form, presented in Exhibit 19-11. This form is completed by the agency employee with direct contact in a program. The items on the instrument are examples of what might be asked of this type of employee. Questions are included that inquire about the adequacy of the program schedule, equipment and supplies, the facility, supervisory support, and program operation.

Exhibit 19-11.
Leader/Instructor Evaluation Form

Program   Date

Leader/Instructor

Season

A second instrument is the recreation program observation schedule, presented in Exhibit 19-12, page 450. This is used to record observations of on-site visitations and inspections of program services by supervisors. The items observed can be

Please help us evaluate and improve our services by answering the questions below. Your feedback is important to our operation. All information is confidential. Please place an (X) on each line to indicate your opinion about the quality of service.

	Rating				
	Poor			Excellent	
	(1)	(2)	(3)	(4)	(5)
Program Schedule					
1. Length of individual program meetings	( )	( )	( )	( )	( )
2. Time program met	( )	( )	( )	( )	( )
3. Day of week program was held	( )	( )	( )	( )	( )
Equipment and Supplies					
4. Material provided for program operation	( )	( )	( )	( )	( )
5. Equipment provided for program operation	( )	( )	( )	( )	( )

(continued)

Exhibit 19-11.

Facility	Rating				
	Poor			Excellent	
	(1)	(2)	(3)	(4)	(5)
6. Appropriateness of facility for program	( )	( )	( )	( )	( )
7. Safety of facility and equipment	( )	( )	( )	( )	( )
8. Cleanliness of facility	( )	( )	( )	( )	( )
9. Facility access and preparedness— was facility open on time and ready to go?	( )	( )	( )	( )	( )

Supervisor Support

	(1)	(2)	(3)	(4)	(5)
10. Supervisor provided adequate orientation training	( )	( )	( )	( )	( )
11. Supervisor provided ongoing cooperation and direction	( )	( )	( )	( )	( )
12. In the absence of your immediate supervisor were other Bureau personnel helpful in solving your problems?	( )	( )	( )	( )	( )

Program Operation

	(1)	(2)	(3)	(4)	(5)
13. For this program, were the number of people enrolled appropriate?	( )	( )	( )	( )	( )
14. How well were the Bureau's goals for this program achieved?	( )	( )	( )	( )	( )
15. My performance in this program was . . .	( )	( )	( )	( )	( )

16. Do you believe there is sufficient demand
    to offer this program again?   Yes _____   No _____

Additional Feedback

Please give us additional suggestions or comments you believe will help improve our services or help you do a better job serving our constituents.

altered to meet the needs of a specific agency. Note the rating scale included on the instrument. Each rating number is defined to try to improve reliability. Any item rated 1 should be taken care of immediately while the supervisor is on site and the action taken noted in the section provided. Items rated 2 should be taken care of before the next session of the program and any action taken noted in the space provided. Items rated 3 should be taken care of as time permits and as alternative arrangements become available. Items rated 4 need no further action.

A designated area on the instrument is provided for recording additional data bits—unsolicited information gathered in the process of inspecting programs. In this section, specific interview questions that program supervisors may want patrons to answer can also be added. Some examples are provided.

The third instrument used is the participant evaluation form, presented in Exhibit 19-13, page 452. What is presented is a format for the instrument. To use this instrument, the programmer selects items for inclusion on the form from the item pool presented in the addendum to Chapter Nineteen.

To achieve some uniformity of evaluation data across all programs, it is recommended that the agency establish a list of five to eight questions to include on the evaluation instruments for all programs. An example of such a list is included in Exhibit 19-13. An individual program supervisor could then select an additional eight to ten questions from the item pool that would specifically apply to the program being evaluated. In this way, some data are unique to a specific program. The reader will notice that the questions included in the item pool deal with program inputs, processes, and outputs. Any instrument should include an assortment of each type of question.

The final instrument used in the triangulated approach to program evaluation is the program evaluation summary format, presented in Exhibit 19-14, page 453.This instrument includes various pieces of information that are necessary to comprehensively evaluate a program.The reader will notice that the outline includes a number of pieces of information that derive from evaluation techniques explained in previous sections of this chapter.

In Section II program goals are assessed. Specifically, the programmer is asked to answer why the agency is conducting the

Exhibit 19-12.
Program Observation Schedule

Program _____   Location_____
Date Observed _____   Activities Observed _____
Time Observed From_____ : _____   To _____ : _____

Observation Checklist

Rating Scale

4	3	2	1
Excellent	*Good*	*Poor*	*Inadequate*
No modification is warranted.	But could be improved if alternatives available.	Alternative arrangements must be made before next program offering.	Immediate action must be taken to correct the situation.

Facility
1. Is the facility adequate for this program?   _____
2. Is the equipment adequate for this program?   _____

Staff
3. Are there a sufficient number of staff on duty to handle this program?   _____
4. Are the staff available to participants?   _____
5. Are staff tactful and courteous to participants?   _____
6. Are staff in control of the program, i.e., no horseplay or loitering observed?   _____

Program
7. Are adequate safety precautions being practiced?   _____
8. Is the program being conducted consistent with the Bureau's advertised description?   _____
9. Are the activities appropriate for the goals and objectives of the program?   _____

(continued)

Exhibit 19-12.

Problems noted (list all 1s and 2s) Action taken (date)

Data Bits (Describe instances of behavior that either refute or confirm a program's accomplishments or note any positive or negative comments from participants–get name and phone if possible.)

Get feedback on the following:

How important is this program to you in view of your other leisure pursuits?

Does this volleyball league provide you with an appropriate level of competition?

Signature

_____

Exhibit 19-13.
Participant Evaluation Form

Please help us to evaluate our programs by answering the questions below. Your feedback is needed to help us serve you better. Please indicate how strongly you agree or disagree with each statement by circling the response that most closely reflects your belief. All individual responses will remain anonymous and will only be used in a summarized form.

Recommended Questions

[Responses for all the items below are to be a five-point Likert scale format with the following response categories:]

1	2	3	4	5
Strongly disagree	Disagree	Neutral	Agree	Strongly agree

[It is recommended that the following eight items be included on all instruments. Program supervisors will select other items from the Item Pool provided in the Chapter Nineteen Addendum to complete the instrument.]

1. I had fun in this program.
2. I enjoyed this program because my skills and abilities developed.
3. I liked this program because of the chance for physical exercise it provided.
4. I liked this program because of the opportunities for social contact it provided, i.e., making new friends or enjoying being with people.
5. I enjoyed this program because of the facility or setting in which it was held.
6. Overall, I am highly satisfied with this program.
7. My personal reasons for participating in this program were fulfilled.
8. In relation to all my other leisure activities, this program is very important to me.

Please feel free to comment further about this program on the back of this form. Please return the form to the program leader or mail to the Agency of Recreation and Parks. Thank you for your help!

In Section I, the statistical summary, five pieces of statistical data are reported. These include data about participation impact, staffing requirements, program costs, program revenue, and a cost analysis of the program.

Exhibit 19-14.
Program Evaluation Summary Format

Program————————————————   Location ————————————

Dates of Operation ————————————————————————————————

I. Statistical Summary
  A.   Participation Impact

   Number of Sessions (NOS)_____ Number of Enrollments (NOE) _____
   Potential Attendance (PA) = (NOS) X (NOE) ————————————————
   Actual Total Attendance (ATA) ————————————————————————
   Average Attendance (AVA) = (ATA) / (NOE) ——————————————
   Percentage of Attendance = (ATA) / (PA) ——————————————

  B.   Staff

   Number of Staff (NBS)———— Number of Staff Hours ————
   Staff/Participant Ratio = (AVA) / (NBS) ——————————————

  C.   Costs

   Salaries   ————————————————————————
   Equipment   ————————————————————————
   Supplies   ————————————————————————
   Facilities ————————————————————————

   Total (TOTC) ————————————————————

  D.   Revenue

   Agency Funds or Appropriated Funds   ————————————————
   User Fees or Nonappropriated Funds   ————————————————

   Total (TOTR) ——————————————————

(continued)

Exhibit 19-14.

E. Cost Analysis

Net Cost (TOTC) _____
Average Cost per Participant (TOTC / NOE) _____
Average Cost per Participation (TOTC / ATA)_____
Percent Self-supporting (User Fees / TOTC) _____

II. Goals: Why was this program conducted? How does it fit in with the overall goals of the [agency name]? What were the specific goals of this program?

III. Procedures: Briefly describe what is involved in operating this program.

IV. Evaluation Data:

A. Program Observations: Summarize reports from ongoing on-site supervision of the program. Number of visits and a general report of conditions found.
B. Leader/Instructor Report: Summarize the leader's or instructor's reports about program operations.
C. Participant Feedback: Report participant feedback about the program, including oral testimony, tabulated evaluation items, phone calls, etc.
D. Other Data Bits: Information from other data sources.

V. Supervisor's Analysis of Evaluation:

What is this program accomplishing?
Who is the program serving?
Is this program the best allocation of these resources?
How does this program compare with other similar programs in the agency?
Does this program fit into the Bureau's mission?

VI. Program Disposition: This program should be:

Continued as currently operated.
Dropped (identify possible impacts below).
Modified as noted below.

Signature _____ Date _____

program and how its fits in with the overall mission of the agency. In this way, each program must be justified with data each time it is evaluated. In Section III, procedures, a brief explanation of what is involved in operating the program is included in the report. One should not write the complete program plan in this section, but a much shorter explanation about what it takes to operate the program.

Section IV contains the summated evaluation data collected with the instruments recommended in the triangulated approach. In Section V, the evaluator is required to analyze the program by formulating responses to the questions asked using the evaluation data reported in the previous section. By using this outline, the programmer is required to analyze the program on the basis of evaluation evidence rather than on hearsay or other less reliable information. The analysis must be supported by the data. In a similar fashion, after completing the analysis, the programmer must make a program disposition decision, based on the results of the evaluation data, to either continue the program as currently operated, to drop it, or to modify it. If either of the latter two decisions is made, the programmer must provide the following information. For a program that is to be dropped, the programmer must speculate about possible effects that dropping it might have on the agency. For a program that is to be modified, the programmer must specify the modifications to be made.

The organization of the summary format requires that the report of the evaluation be developed in a logical manner and that the decisions be based on logical conclusions drawn from systematically collected data. Evaluation is thereby based on an analysis of evidence systematically collected from agency patrons and programs. Now complete Exercise 19-3 on page 456.

Exercise 19-3.
The Evaluation Report

Examine the outline for the evaluation summary report and discuss the following questions:

- What does each section of the outline add to judging the worth of a program service?
- What additional questions may be added?
- Which items may be eliminated? How would the usefulness of the report be altered if they were eliminated?

The triangulated approach to program evaluation is a concept suggesting that multiple methods should be used to collect data from multiple sources. An example of how this technique may be used was presented, along with a rationale for why each method and data source was selected for inclusion.

Comprehensive Evaluation

Throughout Chapters Eighteen and Nineteen it has been emphasized that no single technique will adequately address all evaluation questions. Comprehensive evaluation in an agency calls for the use of several different techniques. To implement a comprehensive program evaluation in an agency, several things must happen. First, the agency must allocate resources, including staff time, training, and the materials and other resources needed to conduct the evaluation.

Second, agency management needs to create an open evaluation atmosphere. When an agency conducts evaluations, some will reveal inadequate programs. It is the responsibility of management to create a sanction-free atmosphere so that problem programs can be identified and dealt with. If program managers want only good evaluation reports, they can get them by severely sanctioning the first programmer to deliver a report about a bad program. But if the agency hopes to identify programs performing inadequately, an atmosphere needs to be created in which programmers can report these programs without adverse sanction.

Third, the agency needs to assess how it is currently evaluating. Every agency makes judgments of worth about program services and makes disposition decisions with this evidence. Once the current system is identified, it needs to be made more formal and systematic. Incorporating ideas developed in this chapter and Chapter Eighteen into the system will help achieve this end.

Finally, the agency needs to consciously develop a comprehensive evaluation system. To be comprehensive, the system should be made up of the following five components: formative evaluation, summative evaluation, ongoing in-depth evaluation, an evaluation database, and strategic evaluation strategies. Each of these components fulfills a unique role in providing a comprehensive evaluation program for an agency.

Formative evaluation occurs while a program is being implemented; its purpose is to enhance new programs. The data produced must be readily available to facilitate the adjustments needed during the trial-and-error period of program development.

Summative evaluation occurs at the end of a program to provide the data needed to make a final, summative judgment about the worth of a program and to assist with its future operation. Because a programmer may be responsible for evaluating many programs, summative evaluation procedures cannot be as cumbersome as the evaluation techniques used for in-depth analysis.

Ongoing in-depth analysis of program services involves using evaluation techniques to thoroughly investigate and judge the worth of an individual program. In some cases, however, this component may be so time consuming that only a portion of the agency's programs could be evaluated in this manner in any one year. In this case, it is recommended that all programs be evaluated on a rotating, scheduled basis—for example, every three years. The triangulated evaluation procedure is useful for accomplishing this analysis. An evaluation review committee can also be appointed to conduct an in-depth evaluation of a specific program, using evaluation techniques appropriate to the program. Evaluation committees can be made up of only staff, staff and board members, community advisory committee members, patrons, or any combination of individuals who would be qualified to judge the worth of a program service.

An evaluation system must also provide the agency with an evaluation database. This database is a pool of systematically collected information about the worth of agency programs. Finally, the database is used in preparing strategic evaluation reports. The agency may be required to develop these reports to answer unanticipated questions from a board, the public, or any other source. Too often agencies cannot answer unanticipated questions because they have no database to analyze.

How the evaluation techniques discussed in this chapter fulfill these five components is outlined in Exhibit 19-15.

Exhibit 19-15.
Components of a Comprehensive Evaluation System

Formative Evaluation
  Program Observation Schedule (TRI)
  Patron Interviews (TRI)
  Other Data Bits (TRI)

Summative Evaluation
  Program Observation Schedule (TRI)
  Leader/Instructor Evaluation Forms (SAT and TRI)
  Participation Statistics (SH and TRI)
  Fiscal and Budget Data (TRI)
  Importance - Performance Data (I - P)
  Discrepancy Analysis (G and O)

Ongoing In-depth Analysis
  Program Evaluation Summaries (TRI)
  Program Review Committees (Selected Techniques)
  Discrepancy Analysis (G and O)

Evaluation Database
  Service Hour Summative Statistics (SH)
  Program Evaluation Summaries (TRI)
  Participant Outcome Reports (I - P and SAT)

Strategic Evaluation
  Analysis of Service Hour Data (SH)
  Analysis of Program Evaluation Summaries (TRI and SAT)
  Analysis of Participant Reported Outcomes (TRI and SAT)

Key
I - P   Importance - Performance Evaluation
SAT   Satisfaction-Based Program Evaluation
SH   Service Hour Evaluation
TRI   Triangulated Evaluation Approach
GO   Goal and Objective Evaluation

Conclusion

Five models for use in leisure service evaluations have been presented. The theory behind each model and its assumptions were outlined. Each model was analyzed using the nine evaluation planning steps as an analytical framework. Before using the models presented or any other evaluation model, programmers must make certain that the model meets their evaluation needs.

Comprehensive evaluation in an agency should have five components. No single method can accomplish all five components. How each of the evaluation models included in this chapter would contribute to the components of a comprehensive evaluation was outlined.

References, Chapter Nineteen

Beard, J.G., and M.G. Ragheb. 1979, October. *Measuring Leisure Satisfaction.* Paper presented at the Leisure Research Symposium, New Orleans.

Bullock, C.C., and F. Coffey. 1980. Triangulation as Applied to the Evaluative Process. *Journal of Physical Education and Recreation 51(8)*, 50-52.

Christensen, J.E., and D.R. Yoesting. 1977. The Substitutability Concept: A Need For Further Development. *Journal of Leisure Research 9*, 188-207.

Denzin, N.K. 1978. *The Research Act* (2nd ed.). New York: McGraw-Hill.

Driver, B.L. 1977. *Item Pool for Scales Designed to Quantify the Psychological Outcomes Desired and Expected From Recreation Participation.* Fort Collins, CO: Rocky Mountain Forest and Range Experiment Station.

Driver, B.L., and P.J. Brown. 1975. A Socio-psychological Definition of Recreation Demand, With Implications for Recreation Resource Planning. In *Assessing the Demand for Outdoor Recreation*. Washington, D.C.: U.S. Government Printing Office.

Fuszek, R. 1987, October. *Program Evaluation in Municipal Parks and Recreation.* Paper presented at the National Recreation and Park Association Annual Congress, New Orleans.

Guadagnolo, F.B. 1983, October. *Application of the Importance-Performance Scale in Program Evaluation.* Paper presented at the Leisure Research Symposium, Kansas City, MO.

Hawes, D.K. 1978. Satisfactions Derived From Leisure-Time Pursuits: An Exploratory Nationwide Survey. *Journal of Leisure Research* 10, 247-264.

Martilla, J.A., and J.C. James. 1979. Importance-Performance Analysis. *Journal of Marketing* 41(1) 77-79.

Peterson, C.A., and S.L. Gunn. 1984. *Therapeutic Recreation Program Design: Principles and Procedures* (2nd ed.). Englewood Cliffs, NJ: Prentice-Hall, Inc.

Provus, M. 1971. *Discrepancy Evaluation: for Educational Program Improvement and Assessment.* Berkeley, CA: McCutchen Publishing Corporation.

Rossman, J.R. 1983. Participant Satisfaction with Employee Recreation. *Journal of Physical Education Recreation and Dance* 54(8), 60-62.

Stake, R.E. 1967. The Countenance of Educational Evaluation. *Teachers College Record, 68.* 523-540.

Tinsley, H.E.A., T.C. Barrett, and R.A. Kass. 1977. Leisure Activities and Need Satisfaction. *Journal of Leisure Research* 9, 110-120.

Tinsley, H.E.A., and R.A. Kass. 1978. Leisure Activities and Need Satisfaction: A Replication Extension. *Journal of Leisure Research* 10, 191- 202.

Addendum: Leisure Program Evaluation Item Pool

The following items have been arranged by categories. Programmers are to select items most pertinent to their operation or specific program.

Staffing
1.   The leader (instructor, coach, etc.) was on time for the program.
2.   The leader was well prepared.
3.   The leader was knowledgeable about the subject matter.
4.   The leader was excellent.
5.   The leader made the class interesting.
6.   The leader was dynamic.

7. The leader motivated me to get better at the activity.
8. The leader was boring.
9. The leader attempted to cover too much.

Price
10. This program was too expensive.
11. The fee for this program was reasonable.
12. I would have paid more for a program of this quality.

Scheduling
13. The length of individual class meetings was too long.
14. The length of class meetings was just right.
15. Class meetings were too short.
16. This program was scheduled at a bad time for me.
17. This program was scheduled at a good time for me.
18. The day of the week the program was scheduled was good (bad) for me.
19. I would have preferred that the program be held on a different day of the week.
20. The facility the program was held in was too small.
21. This facility was very enjoyable.
22. This facility was inadequate.
23. I had trouble getting to this facility.
24. I would prefer a different location for this program.
25. The facility was clean.
26. The facility was dirty.

Program Structure
27. The progression of this program was logical.
28. This program was creatively planned.
29. The level of this program was too difficult for me.
30. Instructional materials for this class were excellent.
31. This program went further into the activity than I desired.

Equipment
32. There was not enough equipment available for this program.
33. The equipment used in the program never worked properly.
34. There was plenty of equipment to conduct this program.

35.   I had access to all of the supplies and equipment I needed for this program.

Club Organization
36.   I am an active member of this club.
37.   I seldom attend club functions.
38.   This club does not meet my needs.
39.   Club officers are doing an excellent job of running the club.
40.   The (agency) provides excellent support services to this club.
41.   This club's activities are one of my most important leisure pursuits.
42.   Club officers do not represent the desires of most club members.

League Organization
43.   This league involved too many games.
44.   League awards are overemphasized.
45.   League awards are important to me.
46.   League games were too long.
47.   The minimum number of players allowed on the roster was too small.
48.   The maximum number of players allowed on the roster was too large.
49.   Roster size for the league was adequate.
50.   The league entry fee was appropriate.
51.   Teams in the league were well matched according to ability.
52.   Game officials maintained good control of games.
53.   Game officials were knowledgeable about the rules.
54.   Game officials started play on time.
55.   Playing facilities were generally available at the scheduled starting time.
56.   Playing facilities were usually in excellent shape.
57.   This league was too competitive.
58.   Our team was not competitive in this league.
59.   (Agency) personnel were helpful.
60.   (Agency) personnel were available when needed.
61.   The league management system was adequate.

Future Intents
62.   I intend to continue in this program next session.
63.   I would attend a more advanced session of this program.

Program Outcomes—General
64.   This program was one of the best I've participated in.
65.   As a result of this program, I will participate in this activity more frequently.
66.   This program made me more aware of my own interests and talents.
67.   I looked forward to attending this program.
68.   During the week, I often remembered my pleasant experience in this program.

Program Outcomes—Specific
69.   In this program, my skills and ability developed.
70.   This program introduced me to a new skill.
71.   Participation in this program increased my feelings of self-worth.
72.   This program gave me an opportunity to demonstrate my competence to others.

Physical Fitness
73.   This program keeps me physically fit.
74.   I enjoyed the physical exercise I got in this program.

Social Enjoyment
75.   I enjoyed this program because it enabled me to be with others who have interests similar to mine.
76.   I enjoyed this program because I participated with my friends.
77.   I enjoyed the companionship with others in the program.
78.   I liked meeting new people in this program.

Exploration
79.   I enjoyed discovering new things in this program.
80.   I liked seeing new sights.

Autonomy
81.   I felt I had control over things in this program.

82.   This program gave me a chance to be on my own.

83.   This program helped me to get away from it all for a while.

Risks
84.   I liked the high risks involved.

85.   I liked the chance for danger in this program.

Family Orientation
86.   I liked participating in this program with my family.

87.   I enjoyed this program because it enabled me to be away from my family for a while.

Relaxation
88.   In this program, I enjoyed experiencing tranquility.

89.   The most satisfying aspect of this program was that it gave my mind a rest.

90.   This program pleased me because it relaxed me physically.

Photo courtesy of St. Louis County, Missouri, Parks and Recreation. Photo by Gretta Kraft.

20

Making Decisions About
Program Services

The final step in the Program Development Cycle is to decide what will be done with a program—that is, what will be its disposition. The final disposition of a program should be made on evidence gathered during the evaluation phase. Only three choices can be made: to operate the program again with no changes, modify it, or terminate it. Although this may seem like only three alternatives, one must remember that modification includes a broad range of alternatives. In addition, many scenarios for dropping a program must be considered.

It is somewhat of a misnomer to include in the Program Development Cycle a single stage called the decision-making stage. Program development involves a series of decisions. Ronkainen (1985) agrees with this view: "Product development is a sequential process involving not one decision point, but rather a series of go/no decisions" (p. 97). The programmer is faced with a series of decisions in developing programs; at each step in the cycle a decision must be made about whether to proceed with the program concept or to abort it. Completing each step in the cycle also requires that the programmer make numerous decisions about the details of program development.

Furthermore, program development involves strategic decision making. Ronkainen (1985) points out that the central element in strategic decision making is the "incomplete state of knowledge concerning the nature of the problem or the components which must be included in a successful solution" (p.98). Decision making in program development is difficult partly because of the nonroutine nature of strategic decision making.

Program Life Cycle

Determining the disposition of a program will be influenced by the current position of a program in the program life cycle. The program life cycle is a concept that draws an analogy between a program and the biological life cycle of animals (Crompton and Lamb 1986). It assumes that programs go through a transition analogous to birth, life, and death.

Figure 20-1 presents a diagrammatic representation of the program life cycle, which includes five stages: introduction, growth, maturation, saturation, and decline. Every program in an agency's program inventory will be located at a different stage in the cycle. Each stage has unique characteristics.

Figure 20-1.
Program Life Cycle

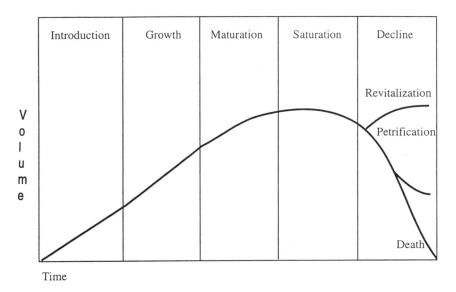

Introduction

The introduction stage is characterized by the considerable amount of the programmer's effort to introduce and successfully launch a new program. Grgen-Ellson (1986) reports that three factors lead to the successful introduction of new services—thorough market research, a well-planned implementation, and continual monitoring and ongoing support of the new service. Even with thorough preparations, however, the agency's cost per participant will probably be high during this stage because of the relatively small number of program patrons.

During actual implementation, programmers must monitor the operation of a new service very closely to make certain it is being delivered as intended by the program designer. Two marketing problems must be dealt with during the introduction stage—getting the target market to try the program for the first time and getting the target market to continue using the service once they try it (Kotler and Andreasen 1987).

Rodgers and Shoemaker (1971) have identified a four-step process that individuals go through in adopting a new behavior pattern. The first step includes acquiring knowledge about the new service and becoming convinced it has some usefulness to them. In the second step, the prospective client must be persuaded to participate, that is, be moved from having an interest to being motivated to take action. In the third step, a person makes a decision to accept the new program and participate in it or to reject participation. Often, the decision process is accompanied by either a vicarious experiencing or by an actual trial of the service. The final step is confirmation, during which an individual decides to become an ongoing participant or to stop participating in the service.

This latter step is often influenced by people's experience with a program during the third step when they may have actually tried the program. This is why it is very important to monitor the introduction of a new service.

Growth

During the growth stage, the number of patrons in a program increases most rapidly. There is heavy demand and tremendous growth. The major task programmers face during this stage is to make certain that sufficient service is available to meet the demand.

How to deal with excess demand for a program service is somewhat problematic. In a public agency, there is always considerable political pressure on a programmer to meet all the demand for a service. In a commercial agency there is also considerable economic pressure to meet all the demand for profitable services. In any agency, an inability to meet demand has the potential for eroding the credibility of the agency in the eyes of its consumer public. The agency must therefore anticipate potential demand and be prepared to meet it.

Maturation

During the maturation stage, program growth slows, as does the rate of increase in new patrons (Howard and Crompton 1980). Usually this is the longest stage for most programs. Thus, most of your programs will be in this stage, and most of your marketing efforts will deal with mature programs (Kotler and Armstrong 1993). It is important to continue to manage mature programs by altering their market mix, seeking new markets through further segmentation, and/or modifying the program as indicated from your analysis of the evaluation data.

Saturation

When a program's growth slows and the number of patrons enrolled levels off, the program is in the saturation stage. During this stage, enrollments are made up of almost all repeat business. The management task in this stage is one of servicing an existing clientele. Additionally, since several other suppliers may be offering the same program service, the programmer is often competing for market share, that is, a portion of the total market.

There are four strategies the programmer may adopt during the saturation phase to help maintain a program's enrollments (Kotler and Andreasen 1987):

•Market leadership: Take the leadership in program innovation. Try to maintain the agency's position as the best provider of this service.

•Market challenge: Take the offensive and challenge the market leader through any number of strategies, including price discounting, program innovation, improved service, and better distribution.

•Market follower: Try to maintain the current market share by duplicating the market leader. The market follower must know how to maintain its current customers by keeping its prices low and its quality high. It must also remain aware of market trends and be prepared to enter new markets as they open.

•Market targeting: Try to identify a unique segment of the market that can be serviced without threatening the larger suppliers. By finding a unique, profitable market niche, the agency can maintain a patron group for its services.

During the saturation stage, then, the programmer has an opportunity to make adjustments to the marketing mix of a program in order to maintain enrollments. Making adjustments during this stage may avoid having a program enter the decline stage.

Decline

The decline stage is characterized by falling enrollments. Decline can be rapid or slow. For example, specific types of craft activities can be popular in a given year, but the following year no one may be interested. Once a program begins the decline stage, the programmer will need to decide whether to try to revitalize the program, allow it to die, or allow the program to petrify. A program has petrified when there are a "relatively small number of enthusiastic participants remaining in the program, which may then run itself, providing no social or economic grounds for abolishing it" (Howard and Crompton 1980). Continuing a weak program, however, can be very costly to an agency in both economic inefficiency and staff time. Weak programs often take an inordinate amount of staff time. For these reasons, eliminating programs in the decline stage should be seriously considered.

The Life Cycle Audit

To manage a program, programmers should be able to estimate its current position in the life cycle. Exhibit 20-1 on page 472 illustrates a life cycle audit form that may be used to determine the current position of a program in the life cycle. Where a program is placed in the cycle should reveal typical program management problems that must be dealt with.

Exhibit 20-1.
Program Life Cycle Audit

Program ――――――― Program Manager ――――――― Date ―――――――

Program Impact Data

	Actual			Estimated	
	92	93	94	95	96
Enrollment	――	――	――	――	――
Attendance	――	――	――	――	――
Service hours	――	――	――	――	――
Annual growth rate	――	――	――	――	――
Staff hours	――	――	――	――	――
Staff/participant ratio	――	――	――	――	――
Average cost per participant	――	――	――	――	――
Revenue	――	――	――	――	――

Life Cycle

Place an "x" where you believe the program is currently located on the life cycle. Use the stage indicators below to help you place the program.

(continued)

Exhibit 20-1
Program Life Cycle Stage Indicators

Introduction Stage
1. Staffing costs are high–staff hours needed to operate the program are high and the staff/participant ratio is high.
2. Attendance and service hours are low.
3. Program enrollment is at one-half or below its capacity.
4. Average cost per participant is high.

Growth Stage
1. The number of staff hours needed for program operation goes down. Staff/participant ratio goes down.
2. Enrollment, service hours, and attendance increase substantially.
3. Average cost per participant goes down.
4. Revenue goes up.
5. Enrollment is at 75 percent or greater of capacity.

Maturation Stage
1. Rate of revenue increase slows. Average cost per participant goes down.
2. Staff hours and staff/participant ratio decrease.
3. Enrollments are still at 75 percent of capacity but have fallen.

Saturation Stage
1. Revenue levels begin to decline. Average cost per participant begins to go up.
2. Enrollments and attendance have stabilized–there are no new patrons entering the program. Growth rate has stabilized.
3. Service hours level off and begin to decline.
4. Staff/participant ratio begins to increase.

Decline Stage
1. Staff hours increase. Staff/participant ratio increases.
2. Revenue declines significantly.
3. Average cost per participant increases.
4. Enrollment is below 25 percent of program capacity. Attendance has dropped significantly.

(Adapted from a form used by the Anaheim Parks, Recreation and Community Services Department as reported by Crompton and Lamb, 1986, pp.226 - 227)

Altering the Marketing Mix

Conventional marketing wisdom suggests that each stage of the program life cycle requires a unique market mix At each stage, different components of the marketing mix. (product, price, promotion, and place) will need to be changed so that they can help to continue the life of a program. Explore this idea by completing Exercise 20-1.

Exercise 20-1.
Altering the Market Mix

In class, select a program service and discuss how the market mix may need to be different at each stage of the program life cycle. Use the matrix below to guide your discussion.

Market mix
Components   Life Cycle Stages

	Introduction	Growth	Maturation	Saturation	Decline
Product					
Price					
Promotion					
Place					

After completing your discussion, consider the following questions:

- **In which stages can price seem to play the largest role?**
- **Does the usefulness of promotion ever wane as a strategy for obtaining additional patrons?**
- **When is it most likely that the programmer would alter the product in order to influence the life cycle of a program?**
- **In which stage(s) is place or distribution most likely to be used to alter the life cycle of a program?**

Program Modification

One of the most difficult programming decisions is to know how and when to modify a program. Although a program may need to be modified at any time, the later part of the saturation stage and the early part of the decline stage are almost always critical times.

An understanding of leisure theory provides the best guidance about how to modify a program (Little 1993). The leisure theory discussed earlier in the book suggests that, for a program to provide a leisure experience to constituents, it must continue to be a novel experience. Programmers must modify a program to keep it novel and enticing. One way to monitor this is to closely watch patrons' reported outcomes from participation.

Remember that a service can be altered by changing any one of the six elements of a program. As outlined in Chapter Three, it is not necessary to alter the entire program, only one or more components of it. Often, then, at the end of the saturation stage or during the decline stage, the programmer must modify a program. Patron feedback is the best source of data about any modifications that may be necessary.

Implementing Program Modifications

Almost all programs will have a core group of participants who like things "just the way they are." Thus, programmers must understand the situations they are facing in recommending modifications to a program. How difficult it will be for the programmer to implement change in a program will depend on two variables: the degree of change and the amount and type of information available about the advisability of change. The degree of change can range from small, incremental change, to large, major change in the program. The information the programmer may have about the advisability of change or to justify the change recommended can range from a large amount of pertinent, detailed, quantitative information to a very small amount of intuitive, qualitative, judgmental information derived from experience or casual observation. The quality and quantity of information will vary greatly and will affect how easily the programmer will be able to implement change.

Figure 20-2 is a graphic representation of four decision situations created by various combinations of information availability and the degree of change contemplated. Included in the matrix is the mode of change to be recommended, which implies the degree of change that will result, and the basis or rationale for making change.

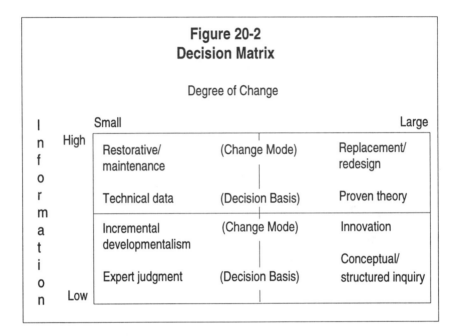

Figure 20-2
Decision Matrix

Degree of Change

		Small		Large
I n f o r m a t i o n	High	Restorative/ maintenance	(Change Mode)	Replacement/ redesign
		Technical data	(Decision Basis)	Proven theory
		Incremental developmentalism	(Change Mode)	Innovation
		Expert judgment	(Decision Basis)	Conceptual/ structured inquiry
	Low			

In the first decision mode, restorative/maintenance, a small degree of change is proposed. The basis for recommending this change is technical information about the program. Restoration decisions are characterized by the use of technical information to implement the small, incremental changes needed to restore a program to its original design. Because the change recommended is small and the information available is great, this is usually an easy change to implement. An example of this would be increasing the number of staff at a day care operation to comply with a new child care law. This change would continue the program as designed and keep it within the minimal requirements of the law.

In the second mode, a program is completely replaced with a new service or a completely redesigned service. The rationale for this is a proven theory or method. Although the change implemented is great, the information base for the change is also substantial, and thus the change is usually easy to implement. The only block may be a lack of understanding of the rationale for the change by the patrons who will be affected. This situation will require that the programmer communicate the basis for the change to the patrons. An example of this would be replacing a traditional summer playground program with specialty camps such as sports or arts camps scheduled so they may also serve as day care. The information base for such a change could be declining enrollments in the playground program, the success of similar camp programs in other communities, the expressed need in the community for summer day care, and an expressed desire for program services with a more defined focus.

The third mode is incremental developmentalism, which involves small changes based on a small amount of information. The basic rationale for these changes is the experience and expert judgment of staff. Usually these changes are so small that the experienced practitioner is allowed the leeway to make them based on their expertise. Because the changes recommended are small, they are relatively easy to implement. This type of a decision is typical of the modifications made in many recreation programs that are developed through trial and error, with only small adjustments at each decision point.

Little (1993) provides several examples of modifying programs with this type of decision strategy. For example, in observing the operation of a summer day camp, she noted that varying levels of the campers' abilities led to the need to alter certain activities so all of the children could feel competent. With a similar technique, she determined that a drama skit activity included in a weekend program operated for incarcerated mothers and their children could be retained if its implementation was changed from requiring the mothers to create the skits to simply acting out canned skits. Both of these were small, incremental changes that could be made because of her understanding of leisure behavior and how it constrained participation in the current programs. It is important to point out here that although the changes were small and the information used to justify the changes seemed minimal, the knowledge base and analysis required to identify them were not. Previous experience with programs and a knowledge of leisure behavior that was directly applicable to the current programs were both necessary to successfully modify these programs. Changes of this type are easier to implement if the programmer's credibility has built up over time with a record of successful changes.

The final decision mode is innovation, which is characterized by a low level of information being used to recommend a substantial change. Creative thinking and innovative design techniques discussed in Chapters Nine and Ten are the typical methods used to develop the data needed for this type of recommended change. These techniques produce a low information level because these data are often considered "soft" since they are not derived from quantitative analysis. This is one of the most difficult changes to have accepted. A successful track record of implementing innovative programs will help the programmer have this type of a change accepted. An example of this type of change would be the recommendation to begin a major new special event or program service never tried in a community.

Modifying programs is an essential part of program management. The programmer must develop the skills necessary to analyze programs, to note their deficiencies, and to be able to recommend and have accepted the modifications that will keep them viable. Understanding the resistance one is likely to face in implementing modifications is important to successfully accomplishing them.

The Birth and Death of Programs

An important implication of the life cycle concept is that in a healthy organization, some new programs will be introduced and some existing programs terminated each year. Introducing and terminating programs is a normal event in managing the program inventory of a leisure service organization. In addition, eliminating programs will be an economic necessity in a retrenchment situation. With static economic resources, the programmer can obtain the resources necessary to introduce new programs only by eliminating some of the old ones.

It is therefore critical that a leisure service programming operation have a formal procedure both for identifying new program services to launch and for eliminating program services that have outlived their usefulness to the organization. The first two stages of the Program Development Cycle (in Chapter Five) provide a formal procedure for developing and launching programs. A formal elimination strategy will be discussed below.

Program Elimination

Programmers tend to add programs—not eliminate them. Only adding programs to an organization's inventory will lead to a deterioration of service quality. Eventually, the professional staff will simply be spread too thin to do a thorough job on each program. Even the best programmers have a limit on the number of programs they can successfully manage.

In most leisure service organizations, three primary forces work against eliminating programs—staff, patrons, and organizational political forces. First, staff members too often develop an "ownership" of programs they have created. They are therefore reluctant to eliminate a program because they consider its elimination a personal or professional failure. Programs have life cycles, and the useful life of almost all good programs will eventually end. Often this termination has nothing to do with the competence of the professional staff—it is a predictable consequence of beginning a program. The only question is when it will occur.

Professional staff members, then, need to realize that eliminating some programs each year is a normal and necessary part of program management. All viable organizations must constantly search for new products and services to bring to the marketplace.

Not-for-profit organizations, municipal leisure service agencies, church recreation operations, and other similar leisure service organizations with a third-party funder encounter two additional forces that make it difficult to eliminate programs. Patrons who make up a core group of participants will lobby against eliminating a program. These groups are very committed to the continuation of a specific activity. Although these groups often are very small, the intensity of their commitment is great, and they will attempt to ensure continuation of "their" activity, regardless of its economic efficiency.

The second force is board members and higher-ranking administrative personnel, who will often respond to the efforts of groups lobbying for the continuation of a program recommended for elimination by the professional staff. Since leisure services in these types of organizations are often subsidized, it is therefore possible to continue economically inefficient services.

These latter two cases can best be dealt with by having program criteria established and accepted by the various parties before actually making disposition decisions. Making decisions from an economic profitability model is much more objective and easily determined. Because of this, commercial recreation operations have clearer decision criteria, and the elimination of unprofitable services is required.

Once the decision is made to eliminate a service, the programmer must determine an elimination strategy. How will the service be eliminated? Following are three possible strategies for eliminating a program service:

•Retrenchment: A program can be continued with reduced expenses. Often, because the retrenched service is not the same service originally provided with a higher level of funding, enrollments decline.

•Staged: A reduction of a program service can be staged. Such a strategy can be phased in over a period of time so that current participants can find alternate services to meet their needs.

•Sudden: A service can simply be eliminated immediately. This is often possible with services that have outlived their useful life.

Conclusion

The final step in the Program Development Cycle is to make a decision about the disposition of a program. It is important that decisions be warranted by the evaluation data collected about the program. The current place of the program on the program life cycle will partly determine the disposition of a program. The programmer must decide whether to modify, eliminate, or continue a program. All healthy programming organizations should be adding some new programs and eliminating existing ones each year.

References, Chapter Twenty

Crompton, J.L., and C.W. Lamb, Jr. 1986. *Marketing Government and Social Services.* New York: Wiley.

Grgen-Ellson, N. 1986. Increasing the Probability of New Product Success. *Journal of Retail Banking 8,* 25-28.

Howard, D.R., and J.L. Crompton. 1980. Financing, Managing and Marketing. *Recreation & Park Resources.* Dubuque, IA: Wm. C. Brown.

Kotler, P., and A.R. Andreasen. 1987. *Strategic Marketing for Nonprofit Organizations.* Englewood Cliffs, NJ: Prentice-Hall.

Kotler, P., and G. Armstrong. 1993. *Marketing: An Introduction* (3rd ed.). Englewood Cliffs, NJ: Prentice-Hall.

Little, S.L. 1993. Leisure Program Design and Evaluation. The *Journal of Physical Education, Recreation and Dance,* 64(8), 26-29, 33.

Rogers, E.M., with F.F. Shoemaker. 1971. *Communication of Innovations.* New York: Free Press.

Ronkainen, I.A. 1985. Using Decision-Systems Analysis to Formalize Product Development Processes. *Journal of Business Research 13,* 97-106.

Index